What people are saying

"Here at Citibank we use the Quick Course® computer training book series for 'just-in-time' job aids—the books are great for users who are too busy for tutorials and training. Quick Course® books provide very clear instruction and easy reference."

Bill Moreno, Development Manager
Citibank
San Francisco, CA

"At Geometric Results, much of our work is PC related and we need training tools that can quickly and effectively improve the PC skills of our people. Early this year we began using your materials in our internal PC training curriculum and the results have been outstanding. Both participants and instructors like the books and the measured learning outcomes have been very favorable."

Roger Hill, Instructional Systems Designer
Geometric Results Incorporated
Southfield, MI

"The concise and well-organized text features numbered instructions, screen shots, useful quick reference pointers, and tips...[This] affordable text is very helpful for educators who wish to build proficiency."

Computer Literacy column
Curriculum Administrator Magazine
Stamford, CT

"I have purchased five other books on this subject that I've probably paid more than $60 for, and your [Quick Course®] book taught me more than those five books combined!"

Emory Majors
Searcy, AR

"I would like you to know how much I enjoy the Quick Course® books I have received from you. The directions are clear and easy to follow with attention paid to every detail of the particular lesson."

Betty Weinkauf, Retired Senior
Mission, TX

QUICK COURSE®

in

MICROSOFT®

OFFICE 2000

ONLINE PRESS INC.

Microsoft®*Press*

PUBLISHED BY
Microsoft Press
A Division of Microsoft Corporation
One Microsoft Way
Redmond, Washington 98052-6399

Library of Congress Cataloging-in-Publication Data
Quick Course in Microsoft Office 2000 / Online Press Inc.
      p.cm.
     Includes index.
     ISBN 0-7356-1083-5
     (Original ISBN 1-57231-981-X)
     1. Microsoft Office. 2. Microsoft Word. 3. Microsoft Excel for Windows. 4. Microsoft
PowerPoint (Computer file). 5. Microsoft Access. 6. Microsoft Outlook. 7. Microsoft
Publisher. 8. Microsoft FrontPage. 9. Business - - Computer programs. 10. Word processing.
11. Electronic spreadsheets. 12. Business presentations - - Graphic methods - - Computer
programs. 13. Time management - - Computer programs. 14. Personal information
management - - Computer programs. 15. Web sites - - Design. 16. Web publishing.
I. Online Press Inc.
HF5548.4.M525Q53 1999
005.369 - - dc21   98-31912

Printed and bound in the United States of America.

14   QWT   7 6 5

Distributed in Canada by H.B. Fenn and Company Ltd.

A CIP catalogue record for this book is available from the British Library.

Microsoft Press books are available through booksellers and distributors worldwide. For further information about international editions, contact your local Microsoft Corporation office or contact Microsoft Press International directly at fax (425) 936-7329. Visit our Web site at www.microsoft.com/mspress. Send comments to *mspinput@microsoft.com*.

AutoSum, FrontPage, Microsoft, Microsoft Press, the Microsoft Press logo, NetMeeting, Outlook, PhotoDraw, PowerPoint, Windows, the Windows logo, Windows NT, the Windows Start logo, and Wingdings are either registered trademarks or trademarks of Microsoft Corporation in the United States and/or other countries. Fast-Track Training, Online Press, and Quick Course are registered trademarks of Online Press Inc. Other product and company names mentioned herein may be the trademarks of their respective owners.

Unless otherwise noted, the example companies, organizations, products, people, and events depicted herein are fictitious. No association with any real company, organization, product, person, or event is intended or should be inferred.

A Quick Course® Education/Training Edition for this title is published by Online Training Solutions, Inc. (OTSI). For information about supplementary workbooks, contact OTSI at 15442 Bel-Red Road, Redmond, WA 98052, USA, 1-800-854-3344. E-mail: quickcourse@otsiweb.com.

Authors: Joyce Cox, Polly Urban, and Christina Dudley
Acquisitions Editor: Susanne M. Forderer
Project Editor: Anne Taussig
Body Part No. X08-0007703

From the publisher

Quick Course®... The name says it all.

In today's busy world, everyone seems to be looking for easier methods, faster solutions, and shortcuts to success. That's why we decided to publish the Quick Course® series.

Why Choose A Quick Course®?

When all the computer books claim to be fast, easy, and complete, how can you be sure you're getting exactly the one that will do the job for you? You can depend on Quick Course® books because they give you:

- Everything you need to do useful work, in two easy-to-tackle parts: "Learning the Basics" (for beginning users) and "Building Proficiency" (for intermediate users).

- Easy-to-follow numbered instructions and thorough explanations.

- To-the-point directions for creating professional-looking documents that can be recycled and customized with your own data.

- Numerous screen shots to help you follow along when you're not at the computer.

- Handy pointers to key terms and tasks for quick lookup and review.

- Consistent quality—the same team of people creates them all. If you like one, you'll like the others!

We at Microsoft Press are proud of our reputation for producing quality products that meet the needs of our readers. We are confident that this Quick Course® book will live up to your expectations.

Jim Brown,
Publisher

Content overview

1 Microsoft Office Basics   1

After an overview of Microsoft Office 2000, you write a letter in Word while learning the techniques used in all the applications for creating and saving files, giving instructions, applying formatting, editing text, printing, and getting help.

2 Word Basics   30

You learn how to simplify typing by using AutoText and AutoCorrect. You also learn Word-specific editing techniques and how to organize documents in outline view. Then you search for and replace text and check your document's spelling.

3 More About Word   52

You explore Word's built-in templates for creating common business documents, and then you combine two documents to demonstrate some of Word's formatting capabilities, including styles. Finally, you create and format a table.

4 Excel Basics   76

You build a simple worksheet as you learn how to enter, edit, and format information. Then you enter formulas that perform simple calculations, set up a calculation area, and experiment with more complex formulas. Finally, you print the worksheet.

5 More About Excel   104

You work with multiple workbooks and explore more advanced features such as IF functions and consolidating data. You also set up a worksheet with links to data on a different worksheet. Then you create, format, and print a graph.

6 PowerPoint Basics   126

You use the AutoContent Wizard to create a presentation and investigate ways of refining the text the wizard provides. Next you use a design template to create another presentation. Finally, you combine your two presentations.

7 More About PowerPoint   146

You add clip art to your presentation and learn how to import graphics from other sources. Then you create a couple of graphs. You also see how to add special effects to an electronic slide show and how to run it.

8 Access Basics   168

We show you how to create a database and enter records in a table in both table and form views. Then you learn how to change the table's structure by setting its field properties, and how to find, move, and sort records.

9 More About Access 188

You create tables and establish relationships between them. Next you design a form to enter data and construct queries to extract information. Then you share your data by creating printed reports and by creating data access pages for Web viewing.

10 Communicating with Outlook 218

We show you how to use the Inbox to send and receive e-mail, and we discuss how to organize your messages. Then you learn how to use Contacts to manage information about people in your life, and to streamline your communications work.

11 Managing Your Time with Outlook 240

We show you how to use Outlook's Calendar and Tasks components to manage your time more effectively. You learn how to track appointments and meetings, send meeting requests to colleagues, keep a to-do list, and delegate tasks.

12 Publisher Basics 268

You use one of Publisher's wizards to get started, and then we show you how to move around a publication and work with text. Next you learn about frames, and finally, you take a look at some of Publisher's formatting capabilities.

13 More About Publisher 298

We show you ways to spruce up a publication by adding visual elements. You create a logo, a couple of tables, and a WordArt title. Then you insert graphics from the Clip Gallery and use the drawing tools to create a graphic of your own.

14 FrontPage Basics 322

We introduce you to FrontPage, Microsoft's Web authoring program. First you use a wizard to create a simple site. Then you learn how to organize and link pages, add and edit text, and insert and manipulate graphics.

15 More About FrontPage 346

We take a look at some of the more complex elements you can add to a web by showing you how to create hyperlinks and bookmarks. We show you how to prepare your web for publication and how to publish it on a server.

16 More Office Techniques 366

We discuss Office's language options and then introduce the Office shortcut bar. Next you recycle documents from one application to another, and finally, you take a look at Office's Web publishing capabilities.

Index 389

Content details

1 Microsoft Office Basics   1

Getting Started 4
Entering Text..6
Selecting Text 7
Giving Instructions..9
    Using Menu Bar Commands 9
        Choosing Shortcut Menu Commands....................12
        Using the Toolbars 13
Saving Files..16
More Ways to Create New Files 17
Opening Existing Documents 18
Manipulating Windows 19
Simple Editing..20
    Deleting and Replacing Text......................................20
    Moving and Copying Text 20
    Undoing and Redoing Commands 21
Simple Formatting...22
Printing Files 24
    Previewing Files 24
    Changing Page Layout 25
    Straightforward Printing...26
Getting Help 27
Quitting 29

2 Word Basics   30

Using AutoText..33
Using AutoCorrect 36
Word Editing Techniques 37
    Deleting and Replacing Text......................................37
    Moving and Copying Text 39
    Organizing Documents...40
Finding and Replacing 44
    Finding Text 44
    Replacing Text 46
Checking Spelling and Grammar 48

3 More About Word   52

Using Word's Templates 54
More About Formatting 58
    Making Titles Stand Out 59
    Adding Borders and Shading 60
    Setting Up Multiple Columns 62
    Creating Lists 63
    Adding Headers and Footers 64
Formatting with Styles 68
    Using Word's Predefined Styles 68
    Creating Custom Styles..69
Creating Tables 72

4 Excel Basics 76

An Overview of Workbooks 79
Entering Data 80
    Entering Dates and Times 83
Selecting Ranges 84
Editing Entries...84
    Copying and Moving Entries 85
    Dragging and Dropping Entries
        Between Worksheets 86
    Clearing Cells...87
    Inserting and Deleting Columns...88
Formatting Entries...89
    Changing the Display of Numbers 89
    Changing Column Widths 90
Simple Calculations 91
    Doing Arithmetic...91
    Totaling Columns of Values 93
        Using the AutoSum Button 93
        Using the SUM Function 93
    Referencing Formula Cells in Other Formulas 94
Naming Cells and Ranges 95
Efficient Data Display..97
More Calculations 99
    Averaging Values..99
    Calculating with Names 101
Printing Worksheets...102

5 More About Excel 104

Working with Workbooks..106
    Copying Entries Between Workbooks 107
    Moving Sheets Between Workbooks 107
    Deleting Sheets...108
Formulas That Make Decisions 109
    Using Nested IF Functions...110
    Copying Formulas 111
Consolidating Data...113
Linking Worksheets..115
    Testing Links...117
Creating Graphs 117
    Sizing and Moving Graphs..120
    Updating Graphs 121
    Changing the Type 121
    Using Custom Graph Types 123
Previewing and Printing Graphs 124

6 PowerPoint Basics   **126**

Using the AutoContent Wizard 128
Editing Slides in Slide View 131
    Adding Subordinate Points...134
    Deleting Slides in Slide View 135
Organizing Slides in Outline View 136
    Deleting Slides in Outline View..138
Using a Design Template 138
    Adding Slides 140
    Moving Text Between Slides 141
Merging Presentations in Slide Sorter View...142
    Reordering Slides in Slide Sorter View 144
Applying Templates..144

7 More About PowerPoint   **146**

Adding Clip Art to Slides...148
    Sizing and Positioning Clip Art 150
    Cropping Clip Art..151
    Adding Clip Art to the Background 152
Adding Graphs 153
    Using a Graph AutoLayout 153
        Changing the Graph Type 156
        Adding a Title 157
        Repositioning the Legend..158
        Adding a Border 159
        Moving and Sizing Graphs 160
    Using the Insert Chart Button...161
        Separating Slices 162
Adding Special Effects..163
Running an Electronic Slide Show 166

8 Access Basics   **168**

Setting Up a Database 170
Creating a Table 172
Entering and Deleting Records 174
    Entering Records in a Table 174
    Entering Records in a Form 176
    Deleting Records 178
Changing a Table's Structure 178
    Setting the Field Size..179
    Setting the Format 180
    Specifying an Input Mask 181
    Assigning a Caption 182
    Setting a Default Value 183
    Requiring Entries..183
    Other Properties..183
    Testing the Changes 184
Working with Records 185
    Finding Specific Records 185
    Moving Fields 186
    Sorting Records 187

9 More About Access   188

Creating One Table Based on Another 190
Creating Forms...191
Establishing Table Relationships 196
   Viewing Hierarchical Data 201
Using Queries to Extract Information 202
   Selecting Specific Fields 202
   Selecting Specific Records...204
   Editing Data in Query Datasheets 205
   Using Logical Operators 206
   Updating Records 208
   Moving Records 209
Sharing Your Information 211
   Using Reports to Print Information..211
   Creating Data Access Pages 215

10 Communicating with Outlook   218

Using the Inbox...222
   Composing Messages..222
      Attaching Files to Messages...224
   Sending and Receiving Messages 224
      Replying to Messages...226
      Forwarding Messages...227
   Managing Messages 228
      Deleting Messages 228
      Creating New Folders...229
Managing Contacts 231
   Creating Address Cards...231
   Editing and Adding Information 234
   Deleting Contacts 235
   Organizing Contacts...235
      Creating New Categories..236
      Switching Views..237
   Using Your Contact List with E-mail 238
   Tracking Contacts 239

11 Managing Your Time with Outlook   240

Using the Calendar..242
   Scheduling Your Time 243
      Entering Appointments..243
      Entering Recurring Appointments...245
      Scheduling Events 247
      Editing Appointments...249
      Editing Recurring Appointments...250
      Canceling Appointments 251
      Finding Appointments 252
   Planning a Meeting...253
      Sending Meeting Requests 253
      Responding to Meeting Requests 256

Keeping a To-Do List 257
    Adding Tasks...257
    Adding Recurring Tasks..259
    Editing Tasks...260
        Designating Tasks as Complete..261
        Deleting Tasks 262
    Managing Tasks 262
    Delegating Tasks 265
        Dealing with a Task Request 267

12 Publisher Basics   268

Using a Wizard to Create a Publication 271
Moving Around a Publication...275
    Zooming In and Out 276
Working with Text..277
Using a Wizard to Make Design Changes 279
    Changing the Basic Design 279
    Changing the Color Scheme..281
Using a Design Set to Create a Publication 282
    Changing Personal Information 284
    Reusing Text from Another Publication 284
Working with Frames..285
    Sizing Frames...286
    Moving Frames 287
    Adding Frames 289
Changing the Look of Words and Paragraphs 291
    Formatting Headings 291
    Adding Lines and Shading 292
    Changing Text Colors 294
    Setting Up Multiple Columns 294
    Working with Lists..296

13 More About Publisher   298

Adding Visual Text Elements 303
    Creating a Logo..303
    Using WordArt for Fancy Type Effects 305
    Working with Tables...308
Adding Graphics to a Publication 311
    Sizing and Positioning Graphics 313
    Adding Borders 315
    Changing Graphic Colors..315
Drawing Your Own Graphics 316
    Grouping Objects 318
    Rotating Objects...319

14 FrontPage Basics   322

Web Site Concepts 324
Creating a Web...324
    Deciding What Information You Need 324
    Using a Wizard...325

Reorganizing a Web 329
   Deleting Pages 331
   Adding Pages 332
Working in Page View 334
   Adding and Editing Text 335
   Using the Page Tabs 336
   Formatting Text 338
      Changing the Paragraph Alignment 338
      Changing Paragraph Spacing 339
      Creating Numbered and Bulleted Lists 339
   Adding Clip Art and Graphics 340
Enhancing Your Web 343
   Modifying a Theme 343

15 More About FrontPage   346

Adding Hyperlinks 348
   Linking to a New Page 348
   Linking to an Existing Page 351
   Adding E-mail Hyperlinks 351
   Adding Links to Other Web Sites 352
Adding Bookmarks 354
Working with Navigation Bars 356
Preparing Your Web For Publishing 358
   Checking Hyperlinks 358
      Checking in Hyperlinks View 359
      Checking in Reports View 360
      Editing Hyperlinks 361
   Previewing a Web 362
Publishing a Web 364
   Finding a Web Presence Provider 364
   Sending the Web to a Server 365

16 More Office Techniques   366

Using More Than One Language 368
Using the Office Shortcut Bar 371
   Customizing the Office Shortcut Bar 373
      Displaying and Hiding Toolbars 374
      Displaying and Hiding Buttons 374
Recycling Office Information 376
   Importing and Exporting Information 376
   Copying and Pasting Information 379
   Linking and Embedding Information 379
Office Web Publishing 384

1

Microsoft Office Basics

After a brief overview of the components of Microsoft Office 2000, you write a letter in Word while learning the techniques used in all the applications for creating and saving files, giving instructions, applying formatting, editing text, printing, and getting help.

The sample document for this chapter is a simple letter written in a straightforward style with classic formatting. You can easily adapt this letter to meet a variety of business and personal needs.

Document created and concepts covered:

*Produce simple
documents like this
letter right away*

*Adjust the top margin to
make the document sit
lower on the page*

*Vary the alignment
to add interest and
to balance the page*

*Use bold and
underlining for
emphasis*

July 1, 1999

Emma Shakes, President
Tip Top Roofing, Inc.
4239 East Lake Avenue
Lakewood, WA 98403

RE: 1998/99 CARSON AWARDS

Dear Ms. Shakes:

I am pleased to be the bearer of good news! Yesterday, the Carson Committee voted unanimously to present one of its 1999 awards to your company, **Tip Top Roofing**. Your efforts during the past year to forge the industry alliances needed for a successful asphalt-shingle recycling program are an impressive demonstration of Tip Top Roofing's ongoing commitment to the environment.

As you know, the prestigious Carson Awards recognize companies who work to ensure that their business practices are environmentally sensitive. This year's awards will be presented at the Carson Gala Dinner on Friday, July 23, 1999. I will contact you next week with further details.

Again, congratulations!

Ted Lee

*Justify paragraphs
to give the letter
a formal look*

A s you probably know, Microsoft Office 2000 is a *suite* of applications. However, Microsoft Office is much more powerful than the sum of its component parts because it "glues" the applications together in such a way that you no longer have to think in terms of applications per se. You can instead focus on the documents (files) you need to work with to accomplish specific tasks. Of course, you still need to know enough about the Office applications to be able to create and manipulate your documents, so let's take a quick look at what's included in the Office suite.

Microsoft Office comes in several editions that include various combinations of primary and secondary applications. Here's a list of the primary applications:

Word processor

- **Microsoft Word.** This full-featured word processor lets you write, edit, and print text documents. You can control the look of the text by changing the font, style, and size of its characters and by setting such elements as indents, line spacing, tabs, and margins. And you can check the accuracy of your words using the built-in spelling and grammar checkers.

Spreadsheet program

- **Microsoft Excel.** This spreadsheet program lets you use efficient, built-in functions as shortcuts for performing mathematical, financial, and statistical calculations. These calculations can be as simple as totaling a column or row of values or as complex as figuring the rate of return on an investment under varying circumstances.

Presentation program

- **Microsoft PowerPoint.** This presentation program lets you put together sophisticated slide shows or electronic presentations with professional-looking graphic effects. You can format the slide text in a variety of eye-catching ways and add charts, tables, and pictures for even greater impact.

Database program

- **Microsoft Access.** This database program lets you store and organize information in sets of tables. After creating a database, you can look at the information as a list (in columns and rows), or you can look at each item of information in a form, as though it were on an index card. You can also sort the information, perform calculations, compute statistics such as totals and averages, and create reports.

- **Microsoft Outlook.** This desktop information management program provides one location for handling your e-mail, calendar, contacts, and task lists.

  Information manager

- **Microsoft Publisher.** This desktop-publishing program gives you the tools necessary to create professional-looking publications such as newsletters, flyers, and business cards with very little effort.

  Desktop publishing program

- **Microsoft FrontPage.** This Web authoring program lets you easily create impressive Web sites with little or no knowledge of the underlying HTML (HyperText Markup Language) coding system.

  Web authoring program

In addition, your edition of Office may come with some or all of the following applications:

- **Microsoft PhotoDraw,** which you use to create and manipulate graphics for both printed and Web documents.

- **Microsoft Graph,** which you use to turn tabular data into graphs and charts.

- **Microsoft Clip Gallery,** which is a collection of ready-made graphics that you can import into the primary applications.

- **Microsoft Organization Chart,** which provides the tools for creating diagrams such as organization charts.

- **Microsoft WordArt,** which you use to mold text into various shapes for logos and headlines.

- **Microsoft Map,** which quickly converts appropriate data, such as a worksheet showing Sales By State, to a map format.

Your edition of Office may also include Microsoft's Web browser, Internet Explorer, which allows you to view information on the World Wide Web or on your organization's intranet. You also use Internet Explorer to preview documents you create for use in Web environments.

This book is a fast-paced introduction to Microsoft Office 2000. We start by covering some of the basic skills used in all the applications. Then we devote two chapters each to the

Office enhancements

Occasionally, Microsoft releases other small applications designed to enhance Office. These are often available for free downloading from the Internet. (Check Microsoft's Web site at http://www. microsoft.com.) Microsoft may also include them in future releases of Office. Although these applications are not covered in this book, the techniques you will learn here will allow you to explore them on your own.

seven primary tools. Finally, one chapter shows how to recycle information from one application to another for maximum efficiency, and how to publish and preview documents for Web environments. In 400 pages, we can't hope to cover all the ins and outs of Office and we don't try to. But we don't just skim the surface, sticking with the easy stuff. We focus on the most useful features—the ones people will use frequently and the ones more people would use if they knew how. By the time you finish this Quick Course, you'll have a firm understanding of the important features of Word, Excel, Power-Point, Access, Outlook, Publisher, and FrontPage, and you'll know enough about Office to experiment on your own with the features we don't cover in detail. What's more, you'll have created real documents that will serve as models for those you'll need to generate on the job, at school, or for personal use.

Common commands and
techniques

Because of its many components, you might think that Office would be difficult to master. Not so. An important aspect of this integrated suite is that you use the same techniques and commands in all the applications to carry out common tasks. Though each application has a particular focus, the techniques for tasks such as editing, formatting, saving, and printing are similar, and the experience you acquire with one application can be applied to another. For the rest of this chapter, you work with Word to create a letter. In the process, you learn basic techniques for working with all the Office applications.

Getting Started

We assume that you've installed Office on your computer and that you allowed the Office Setup program to stash everything in the default locations on your C: drive. (If Office was installed on your computer by a network administrator, be sure to read the adjacent tip.) We also assume that you've worked with Windows before. If you are new to Windows, we recommend that you take a look at the *Quick Course® in Microsoft Windows* book that is appropriate for your operating system so that you can quickly come up to speed.

Well, without any more preamble, let's start one of the Office programs and take a look around:

Different configurations

We wrote this Office book using a computer running Windows 98. If you are using a different version of Windows, you might notice slight differences in the appearance of your screens. We are also using a Typical installation of Microsoft Office 2000. If a network administrator installed Office on your computer, your setup may be different from ours. Don't be alarmed. Your network administrator may have installed some programs and not others, depending on what your job or class requires. You should still be able to follow along with this book, or you can simply skip the sections that don't apply to you.

1. Click the Start button at the left end of the Windows taskbar and then choose New Office Document from the top of the Start menu to display this dialog box:

Starting a new document

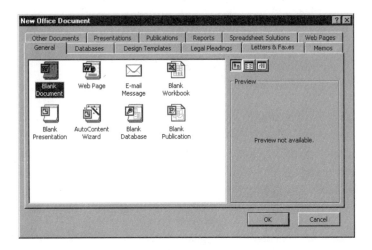

2. Double-click the Blank Document icon. Microsoft Word 2000 starts and opens a new, blank document.

3. If necessary, click the Office Assistant's Start Using Microsoft Word option. (We discuss the Office Assistant on page 27; you can ignore it for now.)Your screen now looks something like this:

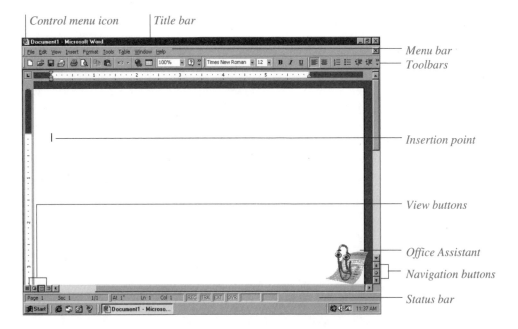

Before you get going, let's display more of the document window by turning off the Windows taskbar:

Turning off the taskbar →

1. Click the Start button, click Settings, and then click Taskbar & Start Menu (Windows 98) or Taskbar (Windows 95 and NT 4).

2. In the Taskbar Properties dialog box, click the Auto Hide check box to select it, click OK, and then click a blank area of the Word window to make sure that the window is active. The taskbar disappears, and the Word window expands to fill up the newly available space.

Temporarily redisplaying the taskbar →

3. Point to the bottom of the screen to make the taskbar temporarily reappear, and then move the pointer away from the bottom of the screen to hide the taskbar again.

Entering Text

Let's start by writing a paragraph. Follow these steps:

Insertion point →

1. The blinking *insertion point* indicates where the next character you type will appear on the screen. Type the following:

I am pleased to be the bearer of good news! Yesterday, the Carson Committee voted unanimously to present one of its 1999 awards to your company, Tip Top Roofing. Your efforts during the past year to forge the industry alliances needed for a successful asphalt-shingle recycling program are an impressive demonstration of Tip Top Roofing's ongoing commitment to the environment.

As each line of text reaches the right edge of the window, the next word you type moves to a new line. This is called *word wrapping*. When entering text in Word, PowerPoint, Publisher, and FrontPage, you don't have to worry about pressing the Enter key to end one line and start another. The applications take care of that chore for you, filling each line with as many words as will fit. (As you follow our examples, don't worry if your word wrapping isn't identical to ours. Word wrapping can vary, depending on the printer you are using.)

2. Press Enter to end the paragraph. Your screen looks like the one shown at the top of the facing page.

Correcting mistakes

The Office applications correct some simple typos, such as *teh* (the) and *adn* (and)—we explain how this works on page 38. If you spell a less common word incorrectly, Word, PowerPoint, Publisher, and FrontPage flag the mistake with a red, wavy underline. We show you some simple editing techniques on page 20, but in the meantime, if you make a spelling mistake and want to correct it, simply press the Backspace key until you've deleted the error and then retype the text.

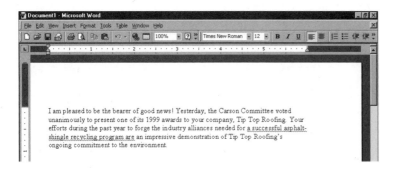

Word may flag words and phrases it suspects have grammatical problems with a green, wavy underline. (We discuss Word's grammar feature in more detail on page 48.) Now that you have some text on the screen, let's see what you can do with it.

Selecting Text

Before you start to work on this paragraph, we need to discuss how to select text. In all the Office applications, knowing how to select text efficiently saves time because you can then edit or format all the selected text at once, instead of one letter or word at a time. The simplest way to learn how to select text is to do it, so follow these steps to select some text blocks:

1. Move the pointer to the word *unanimously* and notice that the pointer is shaped like an I-beam when it is over text.

2. Double-click the word. It changes to white on black (called *highlighting*) to indicate that it is selected, as shown here:

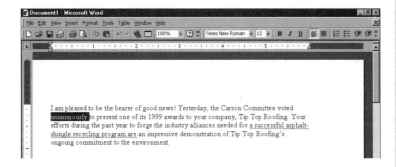

3. Point to the left of *Tip* and click the left mouse button to position the insertion point at the beginning of the word. Then point to the right of *Roofing*, hold down the Shift key, and click the left

Whole word selection

By default, Word selects whole words. For example, if you start a selection in the middle of a word and drag beyond the last character, the entire word is selected. If you drag to the first character of the next word, that entire word is also selected, and so on. To tell Word to select only the characters you drag across, choose Options from the Tools menu, click the Edit tab, deselect the When Selecting, Automatically Select Entire Word check box, and click OK.

Shift-clicking

mouse button. (This action is sometimes referred to as *Shift-clicking*.) Word highlights the words between the two clicks:

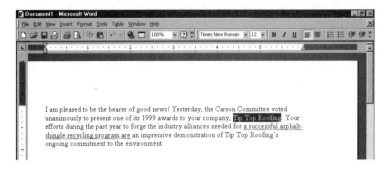

4. Point to the left of the word *recycling*. Hold down the left mouse button, drag to the right until *recycling program* is selected, and release the mouse button. Using this technique, you can highlight exactly as much or as little text as you need.

Extending a selection with the Shift key

5. Click an insertion point to the left of the *Y* in *Yesterday*. Hold down the Shift key, press the Right Arrow key until the entire word is highlighted, and release the Shift key.

6. Without moving the selection, hold down the Shift key, press the Down Arrow key, and then press the Right Arrow key until the entire sentence is highlighted, like this:

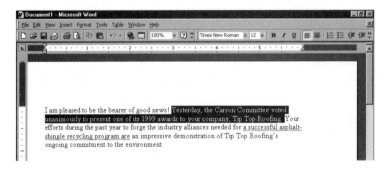

7. Next try pressing different Arrow keys while holding down the Shift key. As long as you hold down Shift, Word extends the selection in the direction of the key's arrow.

8. Release the Shift key and press Home. Word moves the insertion point to the beginning of the line where the selection starts and also removes any highlighting.

With slight variations, the techniques we've covered so far can be used in all the Office applications. The next selection technique, however, applies only to Word and PowerPoint. Let's run through the steps here:

1. Move the mouse pointer to the far left side of the window. When the pointer changes to a right-pointing arrow, it is in an invisible vertical strip called the *selection bar*.

The selection bar

2. Position the arrow pointer in the selection bar adjacent to the line that contains the words *Tip Top Roofing* and click the left mouse button once. Word highlights the line like this:

Selecting lines

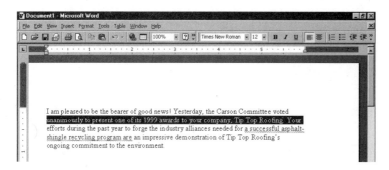

3. Now highlight the entire paragraph by double-clicking in the selection bar next to the paragraph. (You can also drag the pointer in the selection bar to select multiple lines or paragraphs, or triple-click to select the entire document.)

Selecting paragraphs

Giving Instructions

Now that you know how to select text, let's look at how you tell the Office applications what to do with the selection. You usually give instructions by choosing menu commands, or by clicking buttons and boxes on toolbars.

Using Menu Bar Commands

As with other Windows applications, all the commands you use in the Office applications are arranged on menus, which are in turn arranged on the menu bar that sits below the title bar of each program window. The menus are designed so that once you become familiar with the location of the commands in one Office application, you know where to find the same or similar commands in any other Office application.

Because the procedure for choosing menu bar commands is the same for all Windows applications, we assume that you are familiar with it. If you are a new Windows user, we suggest that you spend a little time becoming familiar with the mechanics of menus, commands, and dialog boxes before proceeding. Here, we'll run through the steps for choosing a command and do some useful exploring at the same time:

Expanding menus

1. Click View on the menu bar to pull down that menu, and continue pointing to the word *View* until Word expands the menu to display all its commands, as shown here:

As you have just seen, Word determines which commands you are most likely to use and initially displays only those commands on each menu to reduce clutter. However, you can easily display hidden commands, either as you did here or by clicking the two arrows at the bottom of the short menu.

In all the Office applications, the View menu provides commands for customizing the screen display, but the actual commands vary from application to application. Notice that the icon next to the Print Layout command (see the adjacent tip) appears pressed, indicating that print layout is the page view currently in effect. Choosing the Normal, Web Layout or Outline command puts that view into effect and deactivates print layout.

Corresponding buttons

For some menu commands, an icon appears to the left of the command name. The icon indicates that a corresponding button for this command exists or can be added to a toolbar on one of the application's toolbars. In the case of the view buttons, the icons appear at the left end of the status bar at the bottom of your screen rather than on a toolbar.

2. Turn off the ruler by clicking the Ruler command on the View menu. Word hides the ruler located above and to the left of the document window. (If your ruler was already turned off, choosing Ruler turns it on. Choose the command a second time to turn it back off.)

3. Click the View menu again and notice that the Ruler command is now visible on the short menu and no longer has a pressed check mark next to its name, indicating that the command is turned off. Commands that can be turned on and off are called *toggle commands*. Choosing a checked toggle command turns off that particular command without affecting the status of any other commands.

 Turning off the ruler

Toggle commands

4. Choose the Ruler command to turn on the ruler.

5. Click the View menu again and point to the Toolbars command, which has an arrowhead to the right of its name, to display this *submenu*:

Submenus

When a command is followed by an ellipsis, you have to supply more information by setting options in a *dialog box* before an Office application can carry out the command.

Dialog boxes

6. Choose Customize to display its dialog box. This dialog box is multilayered, with each layer designated at the top by a tab like a file folder tab. The Options tab is currently displayed.

7. If necessary, click No in the Office Assistant's message box to decline the offer of help with this feature. Then click the Toolbars tab at the top of the dialog box to display the options shown on the next page.

Re-appearing ruler

When the ruler is turned off, you can temporarily display it by pointing to the gray bar below the toolbars. The ruler drops down and remains visible while the pointer is over it. When you move the pointer, it disappears.

Turning toolbars on/off

8. Click the Clipboard, Control Toolbox, Database, and Drawing check boxes to turn on those toolbars. Then click Close. Your screen now looks something like this one:

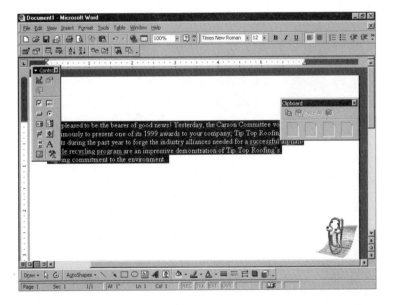

Notice that toolbars can appear across the top or bottom of the window, down the sides, or floating over the workspace. (We'll talk more about toolbars in just a minute.)

Choosing Shortcut Menu Commands

For efficiency, the commands that you are likely to use with a particular object, such as a block of text, are combined on special menus, called *shortcut menus*. Shortcut menus are also available for window elements, such as the toolbars. You access a shortcut menu by right-clicking the object. Follow these steps:

1. Point to one of the toolbars, right-click to display the toolbar shortcut menu, and choose Database from the menu to turn off the Database toolbar.

2. Right-click a toolbar to display the shortcut menu again. You don't want to repeat step 1 to turn off the toolbars one at a time, so choose Customize from the bottom of the menu to display the dialog box you saw earlier, deselect all the check boxes except Standard, Formatting, Clipboard, and Menu Bar, and then click Close.

3. Right-click the Office Assistant and choose Hide from the shortcut menu to temporarily turn off the Office Assistant.

Hiding the Office Assistant

Using the Toolbars

Another way to give an instruction to an Office application is by clicking a button on a toolbar. This is the equivalent of choosing the corresponding command from a menu, and if necessary, clicking OK to accept all the default settings in the command's dialog box. The Office applications all come with several built-in toolbars, each of which is equipped with buttons that provide a simple way of quickly carrying out common commands. You will use some of the toolbars frequently, and others you may never use. Throughout this book, we use buttons whenever possible because they are usually the fastest way to access commands.

By default, Word displays its two most useful toolbars—the Standard and Formatting toolbars—on a single toolbar row below the menu bar. It overlaps the toolbars and, as with menus, initially displays only the most frequently used buttons on each bar. As shown on the next page, each toolbar has a *move handle* at its left end and a *More Buttons button* at its right end, both of which allow you to display the toolbar's hidden buttons.

Buttons vs. commands

How do you decide whether to use a button or a command? You can always use a command to carry out a particular task, but you can't always use a corresponding button. Clicking the button usually carries out its associated command with its predefined, or default, settings without any further input from you. When a command is not represented by a toolbar button, or when you want to use a command with something other than its default settings, you need to choose the command from a menu.

Once you are familiar with the buttons on these toolbars, you'll recognize many of them on the toolbars of the other applications. As you have seen, more specialized buttons are gathered together on the other toolbars. For example, the buttons you use to work with the Office Clipboard (see the tip on page 21) are gathered on the Clipboard toolbar. You can display and hide any toolbar at any time. You can also move and resize the toolbars. Let's experiment:

(see the tip on page 21)

1. Familiarize yourself with the buttons and boxes on the toolbars by moving the pointer slowly over each one until the button's name appears in a box below the pointer. You can use this helpful feature, which is called *ScreenTips*, to identify buttons on toolbars in all the Office applications.

2. Double-click the title bar of the floating Clipboard toolbar to "dock" it above the document, as shown here:

Notice that when a toolbar is docked along one of the edges of the window, it loses its title bar and acquires a move handle.

3. Point to the Clipboard toolbar's move handle and drag the toolbar into the toolbar row so that it joins the overlapped Standard and Formatting toolbars.

4. Drag the Clipboard toolbar from the toolbar row over the document, where it becomes a floating toolbar once again.

5. Drag the floating toolbar all the way to the right side of the window. Just when you think it is going to disappear from the screen, the toolbar changes shape and docks itself along the right edge.

Personalized menus and toolbars

As you have seen, Office's menus and toolbars adjust themselves to the way you work, making more commands and buttons available as you use them. Commands and buttons you don't use are hidden so that they don't get in the way. As a result, your menus and toolbars may not look exactly like ours, and occasionally, we may tell you to choose a command or click a button that is not visible. When this happens, don't panic. Simply pull down the menu and wait for all its commands to be displayed, or click the toolbar's More Buttons button to display its hidden buttons. If you ever want to restore your menus and toolbars to their original settings, choose Toolbars and then Customize from the View menu and on the Options tab, click Reset My Usage Data and then click Close. (You can also assign the toolbars to separate rows by deselecting the options in the Personalized Menus And Toolbars section of this tab.)

6. Experiment some more with moving the Clipboard toolbar to various positions, and docking and undocking it. (Notice that double-clicking the floating toolbar's title bar docks the toolbar wherever it was last docked.)

7. Finally, either click the Close button at the right end of the toolbar's title bar or right-click it and choose Clipboard from the shortcut menu to hide it.

Let's see how you can display more buttons on the Standard toolbar by displaying fewer buttons on the Formatting toolbar:

1. Point to the Formatting toolbar's move handle, and when the pointer changes to a four-headed arrow, drag it to the right until only the Font box, Font Size box, and Bold button are visible, like this:

Displaying more/fewer buttons

2. Press Home to remove any highlighting, then use any of the methods discussed on page 7 to select the first occurrence of *Tip Top Roofing*.

3. On the Formatting toolbar, click the Bold button.

The Bold button

4. For good measure, you want to underline the selected words as well. To display the Underline button, click the Formatting toolbar's More Buttons button to see this palette of the hidden buttons on that toolbar:

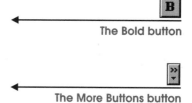

The More Buttons button

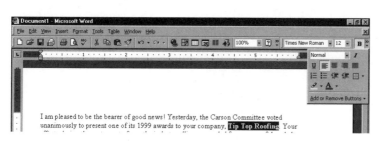

5. Click the Underline button. Word applies the format to the selected words and adds the Underline button to the displayed buttons on the Formatting toolbar. (You could also add italic formatting by clicking the Italic button.)

The Underline and Italic buttons

Saving Files

Until you save a document as a file on a disk, it exists only in the computer's memory and disappears if the computer is intentionally or unintentionally turned off. To save a document for the first time, you click the Save button or choose Save As from the File menu to display a dialog box in which you specify a name for the file. Thereafter, clicking the Save button or choosing the Save command saves the file without displaying the dialog box because the file already has a name. Follow these steps:

The Save button

1. Click the Save button on the Standard toolbar to display this dialog box:

Picking up on the first few words in the document, Word suggests a name.

Saving in another folder

Files will be saved in the folder designated in the Save In box. If you want to store a file in a different folder, click the arrow to the right of the Save In box, and then use the drop-down list to navigate to the folder in which you want the file to be saved. Next double-click that folder to display its name in the Save In box, and then click Save to save the file. You can also use the icons on the shortcut bar along the left side of the Save As dialog box to quickly navigate to common folders and recent files. (The shortcut bar also appears in the Open dialog box.) If the folder you want doesn't exist, you can create it by simply clicking the Create New Folder button (the fifth button to the right of the Save In box) before you save the file.

2. With the suggestion highlighted, type *Award Letter* in the File Name edit box. (The Office applications can handle long filenames, meaning that the filenames can include up to 255 characters, and they can contain spaces. They cannot contain the : * | \ < > " ? and / characters.)

3. Click Save to save the file in the My Documents folder on your hard drive. (Unless you specify otherwise, Word assumes you want to save the file in the My Documents folder. See the adjacent tip for information about saving in a different folder.)

From now on, you can click the Save button any time you want to save changes to this file. Because the application knows the name of the file, it simply saves the file by overwriting the old version with the new version.

More Ways to Create New Files

Part of the magic of a computer is that you can use the same information for different purposes without retyping the information each time. When you have already created one file and you want to adapt it for a different purpose, you can save the file with a new name to create a new file without destroying the old one. Try this:

1. Choose Save As from the File menu.

2. When the Save As dialog box appears, replace the name in the File Name edit box by typing *Tip Top Letter*, and click Save. Word closes Award Letter, and the filename in the title bar changes to Tip Top Letter.

You can create a totally new file at any time without closing any open files. Follow these steps:

1. Click the New button on the Standard toolbar. Word displays a new file called Document2, completely obscuring Tip Top Letter, which is still open.

The New button

2. Now type the following paragraph, misspelling the two occurrences of *Carson* as *Carsen* (Word, PowerPoint, Publisher and FrontPage underline any possible misspellings with a red, wavy line):

   As you no doubt know, the prestigious Carsen Awards recognize companies who work to ensure that their business practices are sensitive environmentally. This year's awards will be presented at the Carsen Gala Dinner on Friday, July 23, 1999. I will contact you next week with more details.

3. Press Enter at the end of the paragraph, and then save the document with the name *Carson Dinner*.

Opening Existing Documents

You now have a couple of open documents in separate, stacked windows. For good measure, open an existing document by following these steps:

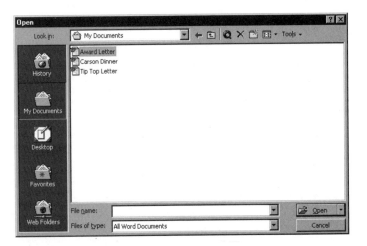

The Open button

1. Click the Open button on the Standard toolbar to display this dialog box:

2. With Award Letter selected, click Open.

File management

You can manage your files from within an Office application instead of using Windows Explorer or My Computer. From the Open or Save As dialog box, you can delete, rename, or move files. For example, if you right-click a filename in the Open dialog box, you can choose from several shortcut menu commands that let you print the file, send a copy of the file to a floppy disk, delete the file, or rename it.

Finding files

You can easily search for and locate files from the Open dialog box. Suppose you can't remember exactly what you called the Award Letter document or where you stored it. Simply click the Tools button and click Find. Next enter the appropriate drive in the Look In box, click the Search Subfolders check box to look in all subfolders of the selected drive, and check that File Name is selected in the Property edit box. Select the appropriate option in the Condition edit box and then enter *award* in the Value edit box. To begin the search, click Add To List to add your criteria to the criteria list, and then click Find Now. Office searches the specified drive and its subfolders for any documents with the word *award* in the filename and displays the one(s) it finds. Then select the document you want and click the Open button. If you have many files with similar names, you can refine the search by specifying other properties, such as text included in the document or its date of modification. You can save searches by clicking the Save Search button, naming the search, and clicking OK.

Manipulating Windows

We'll pause here to review some window basics. Follow these steps to move from one window to another:

1. Point to the bottom of the screen to show the Windows taskbar, and then click the Tip Top Letter document button. That document's window comes to the top of the stack and is displayed on your screen.

2. Choose Arrange All from the expanded Window menu. The three open documents arrange themselves so that they each occupy a third of the screen, as you can see here:

Arranging windows

Notice that the title bar of the active window is a different color than those of the inactive windows. Any entries you make and most commands you choose will affect only the document in the active window.

3. Click anywhere in the Carson Dinner window to activate it, and then click the Carson Dinner window's Maximize button (the middle of the three buttons at the right end of the window's title bar). The window expands to fill the screen, completely obscuring Tip Top Letter and Award Letter.

Maximizing windows

Simple Editing

When creating documents, typically you will start by typing roughly what you want the document to contain, and then you'll go back and do some editing until you are satisfied with the contents. In this section, we'll cover the editing techniques you can use in all the Office applications. (Because you are working in Word, you'll be dealing with text, but these techniques can be used with any type of entry.) Other techniques are covered in the chapters about specific applications.

Deleting and Replacing Text

First let's make a few small changes. Follow these steps:

1. Click an insertion point to the left of the *e* in the first occurrence of *Carsen*, press the Delete (Del) key to delete the character to the right, and without moving the insertion point, type *o*. The red, wavy underline that flags the typo disappears.

2. Click an insertion point to the right of the *e* in the second occurrence of *Carsen*, press the Backspace key to delete the character to the left, and again type *o*.

3. Select the words *no doubt* in the first line and press either Delete or Backspace to delete the words.

4. Double-click the word *more* in the last line and with the word highlighted, type *further* as its replacement.

5. Click the Save button to save Carson Dinner.

Moving and Copying Text

You can move or copy any amount of text within the same file or to a different file. Move operations can be carried out in all Office applications using the Cut and Paste buttons on the Standard toolbar. Similarly, copy operations can be carried out using the Copy and Paste buttons. Let's experiment:

The Cut button

1. In Carson Dinner, select the word *sensitive* and click the Cut button. Word removes the text from the document and stores it on the Clipboard, a temporary storage place in your computer's memory.

2. Click an insertion point to the right of the *y* in *environmentally,* and click the Paste button. Word inserts the cut text, preceding it with a space.

The Paste button

Now let's try copying text to a different file:

1. Choose Select All from the Edit menu to select all the text in Carson Dinner and then click the Copy button.

The Copy button

2. Choose Tip Top Letter from the Window menu or click its button on the taskbar to activate that document. Then maximize the window.

3. Press Ctrl+End to move to the end of the letter, press Enter to add a blank line, then click the Paste button to insert the selected paragraph.

Moving to the end of a document

Undoing and Redoing Commands

When you make an editing mistake, the Office applications provide a safety net: the Undo command. Try these steps:

1. You're not sure you need the paragraph you copied into the letter, so click the Undo button to reverse the paste operation from the previous steps.

The Undo button

The Redo button

2. Change your mind again and click the Redo button on the Standard toolbar to paste the paragraph back into the letter.

The Office Clipboard

Unlike the Windows Clipboard, which stores only your most recent cut or copied item, the Office Clipboard stores up to 12 items. So if you want to cut or copy several different items from one document and paste them into another, you can do so easily. After selecting one item and clicking the Cut or Copy button, cutting or copying another item displays the Clipboard toolbar (shown on page 14), where each item is represented by the icon of the program in which it was created. (The Office Clipboard stores copied items from any Windows application.) Point to an icon to have ScreenTips display its contents. To paste an item, click an insertion point and click the icon that represents the item you want to paste. To paste all of the items at once, click the Paste All button on the Clipboard toolbar. When you want to clear the items from the Clipboard, click the Clear Clipboard button. To turn off the Clipboard toolbar, click its Close button.

Undoing multiple actions

In Word, Excel, PowerPoint, and FrontPage, you can undo and redo several actions at a time. Click the arrow to the right of the appropriate button to display a list of actions with the latest at the top. Drag through the actions in the list that you want to undo or redo. You cannot undo or redo a single action other than the last one. For example, to undo the third action in the list, you must also undo the first and second.

Simple Formatting

Earlier you used the Bold and Underline buttons to make a few words stand out in the text. Now let's experiment with the document's font and font size:

Times New Roman ▼

The Font box

1. Select the entire document again and click the arrow to the right of the Font box to drop down a list of the available fonts.

2. Use the scroll bar on the right side to bring the top of the list into view. Then click Arial. The font of the text changes, and the setting in the Font box now reflects the new font.

12 ▼

The Font Size box

3. With the paragraphs still selected, click the arrow to the right of the Font Size box, and then click 11 in the drop-down list. Word changes the text and the setting in the Font Size box.

4. Now press End so that you can see these results:

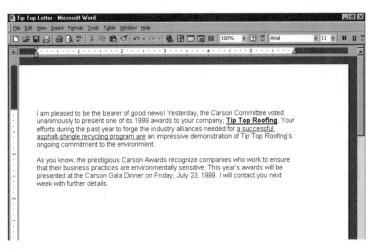

Using keyboard shortcuts

If your hands are already on the keyboard, using keyboard shortcuts to access commands can be more efficient. For example, you can press Ctrl+A to select an entire document instead of choosing Select All from the Edit menu. For more information about keyboard shortcuts, use Word's Help feature. (See page 27.)

You have just used toolbar buttons and boxes to apply common character formats to a text selection. *Character formats* affect the appearance of individual characters. They can be applied to any number of characters, from one to every one in a document. In Word, Excel, PowerPoint, and Publisher, you can also use toolbar buttons to change *paragraph formats* that affect the appearance of an entire paragraph. Let's see how changing a paragraph's alignment affects the way it looks:

1. Press Ctrl+Home to move to the beginning of the document, and then type the following, pressing Enter to end paragraphs and create blank lines where indicated:

July 1, 1999 (Press Enter)

(Press Enter)

Emma Shakes, President (Press Enter)

Tip Top Roofing, Inc. (Press Enter)

4239 East Lake Avenue (Press Enter)

Lakewood, WA 98403 (Press Enter)

(Press Enter)

RE: 1998/99 CARSON AWARDS (Press Enter)

(Press Enter)

Dear Ms. Shakes: (Press Enter twice)

Moving to the beginning of
a document

2. If necessary, tell the Office Assistant you want to write this letter without help. Then press Crtl+Home, and click the Align Right button on the Formatting toolbar's More Buttons palette to right-align the date. Then click the Align Left button on the More Buttons palette to restore the original alignment.

The Align Right and
Align Left buttons

3. Select the subject line (RE: 1998/99 CARSON AWARDS), click the Bold button, and then click the Underline button to make the line bold and underlined. Then click the Center button on the More Buttons palette.

The Center button

4. Now select the two main paragraphs, and click the Justify button on the More Buttons palette. Word justifies the paragraphs so that their lines are even with both the left and right margins:

The Justify button

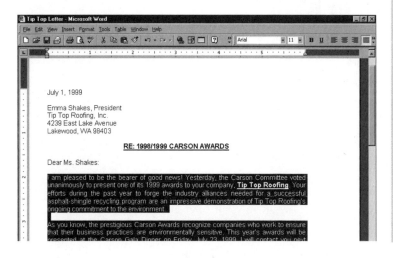

Click-and-type

You can enter text with a particular alignment. For example, to add a right-aligned date, point to where you want the date to appear, check that the pointer displays a right-alignment indicator, double-click, and type the date. If this feature doesn't work, check that you are in the print layout or web layout view. Then choose Options from the Tools menu and verify that the Enable Click-And-Type is selected.

5. Press Ctrl+End to move the insertion point to the end of the letter, type *Again, congratulations!*, press Enter four times, type *Ted Lee*, and press Enter again.

6. Choose Select All from the Edit menu, change the font to Times New Roman, and change the font size to 10.

7. Press Home and save the letter.

Printing Files

Whether you are writing a letter, generating a budget, producing a slide show, extracting information from a database, or creating a brochure, the end product of many of your Office sessions will be a printout. If you can print from any other Windows application, you should have no trouble printing from the Office applications.

Previewing Files

The letter you have written is only one page long and it has no header or footer. However, it is worth checking even a file this small in print preview to see how it looks on the page. Try this:

The Print Preview button

1. Click the Print Preview button on the Standard toolbar to display the whole page like this:

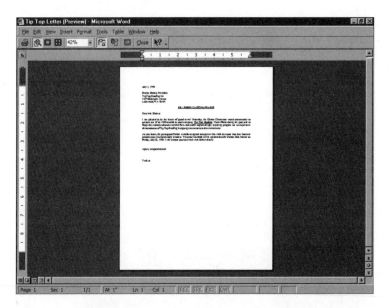

2. Move the mouse pointer over the letter, and when the pointer changes to a magnifying glass, click the left mouse button to zoom in. Click the mouse button again to zoom out.

← Magnifying part of the page

3. Close print preview by clicking the Close button on the Print Preview toolbar.

Changing Page Layout

For aesthetic appeal, suppose you want the letter to sit lower and take up more of the page. To modify the page layout by widening the top and side margins, follow these steps:

1. Choose Page Setup from the File menu to display the dialog box shown here:

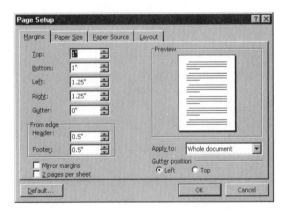

2. With the Top setting highlighted on the Margins tab, type *1.5* and press the Tab key twice to skip over the Bottom setting and highlight the Left setting.

3. Type *1.5* as the new Left setting, press Tab, type *1.5* as the new Right setting, and press Tab again.

4. Notice the effects of your changes in the Preview box on the right and then click OK to return to the letter.

5. Click the Print Preview button to see how the letter looks, and then click Close to close print preview and return to print layout view.

Editing in print preview

Suppose you zoom in on a section of a document and notice something you need to change. To edit a document in print preview, click the Magnifier button on the Print Preview toolbar to change the magnifying glass to an I-beam. Make your changes and then click the Magnifier button again. Then click the document to zoom out.

The Print button

Straightforward Printing

You can print directly from print preview by clicking the Print button located on the Print Preview toolbar. To print a file from print layout view, click the Print button on the Standard toolbar. Either way, Word prints the active document with the default settings: one copy of the entire document.

To print multiple copies or selected pages of a document, you must use the Print command on the File menu instead of the Print button on the toolbar. Follow these steps:

1. Choose Print from the File menu to display this dialog box:

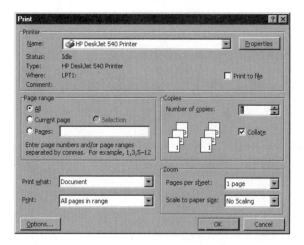

The Print dialog box tells you which printer Word will use. (See the adjacent tip if you need to switch printers.)

2. In the Copies section, type *2* in the Number Of Copies edit box to replace the default setting of 1.

3. Click the Pages option in the Page Range section and type *1-3* in the edit box to tell Word to print pages 1 through 3 only.

4. You aren't actually going to print using these specifications, so click Cancel to close the Print dialog box.

Rather than explain the other printing options in detail here, let's move on to the next section, where we show you how to get information about these options and other features of the Office applications.

Setting up for printing

When Windows was installed on your computer, a driver (control program) for the printer you use was also installed. If you have access to other printers, you can install their drivers by using the Add Printer Wizard in the Printers folder. (Choose Settings and then Printers from the Start menu.) The installed printers can all be accessed by your Office applications, but only one at a time. To switch printers, choose Print from the File menu, click the arrow to the right of the Name box in the Printer section of the Print dialog box, and then select the printer you want to use. When you click OK, your document is printed on the specified printer.

Getting Help

Are you worried that you might not remember everything we've covered so far? Don't be. If you forget how to carry out a particular task, help is never far away. You've already seen how the ScreenTips feature can jog your memory about the functions of the toolbar buttons. And you may have noticed that dialog boxes have a Help button (the question mark in the top right corner), which you can click to get information about their options. Here, we'll look at ways you can get information using the Office Assistant. Follow these steps:

The Microsoft Word Help button

1. Click the Microsoft Word Help button on the Standard toolbar to display the Office Assistant, which offers several options on how to proceed, as shown below:

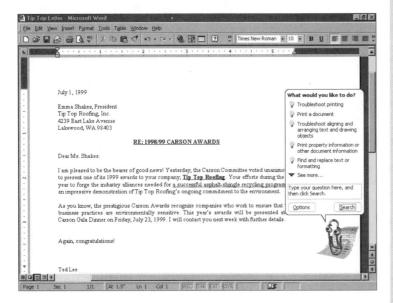

Because printing was the last procedure you completed, the Office Assistant's options are currently based on the topic of printing. (If you don't find any of the current options helpful, you can type a question in the Search box and then click the Search button to have the Office Assistant search for topics that most closely match your question.)

2. Click the Print A Document option. As shown on the next page, Word opens the Help window on the right side of the screen.

More about the Office Assistant

To make the Office Assistant temporarily disappear or reappear, choose Hide/Show The Office Assistant from the Help menu. To turn off the Office Assistant, click it and then click its Options button to open the Office Assistant dialog box. Deselect the Use The Office Assistant check box and click OK. You can also choose options that control when the Office Assistant appears, what tips it displays and whether it makes sounds. On the Gallery tab, click the Back or Next buttons to see other available options for the assistant (the default is the paper clip). Click OK to change the assistant. (You may need to insert your Office CD-ROM to complete the switch.) If the Office Assistant is turned on, it may display a light bulb above its icon, indicating that it has a tip for you. Click the light bulb to see the tip. To display the search box, click the Office Assistant. To move the Office Assistant, simply drag it.

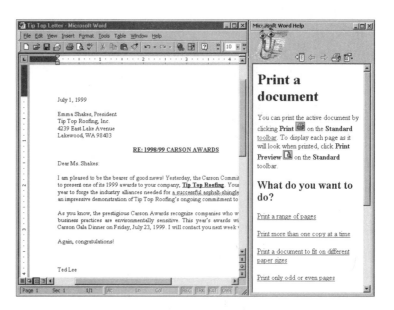

3. Read through the information and click the Print A Range Of Pages topic to display instructions on how to complete that task. Next click the Back button to return to the Print A Document topic, and then explore other options.

The Back button

To search for specific information in the Help window, try this:

1. Click the Show button to expand the Help window. Then click the Index tab to display these options:

The Show button

Accessing Help

If you have not turned off the Office Assistant, choosing Microsoft Word Help from the Help menu displays the Office Assistant. You then click a topic to open the Help window and click the Show button to display the Contents, Answer Wizard, and Index tabs. But if you have turned off the Office Assistant, choosing Microsoft Word Help opens the Help window directly, with the three tabs displayed. (See the tip on the previous page for information about how to turn off the Office Assistant.)

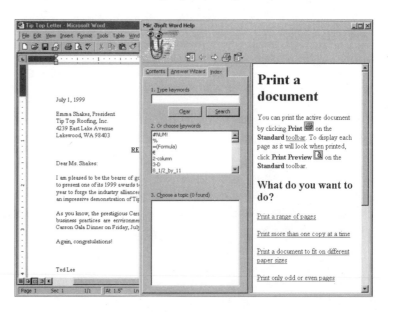

2. In the Type Keywords edit box, type *print*. The list below scrolls to display common keywords beginning with the letters you type.

3. Click the Search button to display a list of topics that contain the word *print*.

4. In the Choose A Topic list, click the Print A Range Of Pages option. In the right pane, Help displays the information for that topic.

5. Click the Help window's Close button.

We'll leave you to explore other Help topics on your own.

Quitting

Well, that's it for the basic Office tour. We'll finish up by showing you how to first close a document and then quit an application. Follow the steps below:

1. Display the Windows taskbar, right-click the Award Letter document button, and choose Close from the shortcut menu to close Award Letter.

2. To close the Tip Top Letter window, choose Close from the File menu. Click Yes if the Office Assistant asks whether you want to save the changes you have made to the document.

3. To close Carson Dinner, press Alt, press F (for *File*), and then press C (for *Close*). Save your changes if prompted.

4. To quit Word, simply click the Close button at the right end of the title bar. After Word closes, the Office Assistant leaves the screen.

Here are some other ways to quit an application:

- Choose Exit from the File menu.

- Press Alt, press F, and then press X (for *Exit*).

- Double-click the Control menu icon—in this case, the W—at the left end of the application window's title bar.

Other Help options

The Answer Wizard tab of the Help window provides a way to type questions without the Office Assistant interface. Type a question in the edit box and click Search. You then see a list of topics that most closely fit your question. You can double-click one of the topics to display its contents in the right pane. If you have a modem and are connected to the Internet, you can quickly access the Microsoft Office Update Web site, as well as other Microsoft Web sites where you can get help or technical support. Choose Office On The Web from the Help menu to start your Web browser, connect to the Internet, and display the Microsoft Office Update Web site.

2

Word Basics

We show you how to simplify typing by using AutoText and AutoCorrect. Then you learn Word-specific editing techniques and how to organize documents in outline view. Finally, you search for and replace text and check your document's spelling and grammar.

The document you create in this chapter describes a non-profit organization. However, you can adapt the document to fill a wide range of needs, such as describing a business, student club, or community group.

Document created and concepts covered:

Assign heading levels and reorganize your documents in outline view

Redmond Business Environmental Action Team

What is Redmond BEAT?

Redmond BEAT (Business Environmental Action Team) is a local chapter of USA BEAT, a network of companies who are actively working to ensure that their business operations are based on sound environmental practices.

How does it work?

Member companies agree to participate in two ongoing efforts: 1. They pledge to scrutinize their operations and wherever possible, implement procedures that will minimize any adverse effects on the environment. 2. They agree to field-test new "environmentally kind" products and services to evaluate their potential impact on both company costs and the environment.

When was it started?

Redmond BEAT was founded in 1989. USA BEAT, which currently has 210 local chapters, was founded in 1987.

Why was it started?

The chartering of Redmond BEAT was spearheaded by long-time Redmond resident Art Synkrafts, President of Creative GlassWorks. Struck by the incongruity between his family's efforts to recycle household waste and the fact that his company was sending several dumpsters of garbage to the Redmond landfill every month, Synkrafts began looking for other ways to dispose of the packaging in which his company received raw materials. His questions caused one of his suppliers, Jordan Manufacturing, to explore alternative packaging methods. The result was less garbage in the Creative GlassWorks dumpsters at no additional cost and negligible other effects for either company. In the meantime, Synkrafts learned about USA BEAT, and a few months of persuasive campaigning later, Redmond BEAT became the newest chapter of a rapidly growing national association.

Who can join?

Membership in Redmond BEAT is open to all companies licensed to do business in the city of Redmond.

Why should my company join?

Current members cite two main reasons for joining. Many companies are managed by people who were attracted to this area by its natural beauty and who want to be part of the effort to preserve it. Other companies stress the potential advantages in today's competitive markets of being perceived as a "green" company by consumers who are increasingly environmentally aware.

How can I find out more?

Come to a meeting. Redmond BEAT meets at 8:00 AM on the last Tuesday of every month at Towne Center. For more information, contact Ted Lee at 555-6789.

Find and replace text to maintain consistency

Use AutoText and AutoCorrect for often-used text

Check spelling to avoid embarrassing typos

Delete, move, and copy text until it reads exactly right

I n this chapter, you build on what you learned in Chapter 1 about Microsoft Office and Microsoft Word. If you are new to Word and haven't read Chapter 1, you should read that chapter before proceeding with this one.

With Word, you can apply fancy formats and add graphics and special effects to increase the impact of a document. But all the frills in the world won't compensate for bad phrasing, poor organization, or errors. That's why this chapter focuses on the Word tools that help you develop and refine the content of your documents. As the example for this chapter, you will create a *frequently asked questions page*, or *FAQ*, for an association called Redmond Business Environmental Action Team (BEAT). FAQs are often distributed in information packages about a company and are usually included as part of commercial Web sites on the Internet.

First let's enter a few headings to establish the basic structure of the document:

1. Start Word by choosing Programs and then Microsoft Word from the Start menu.

2. If necessary, turn off the ruler by choosing Ruler from the View menu. That way, you'll have a bit more room to work.

3. If you want to turn off the Office Assistant, read the tip on page 27. If you find the Office Assistant helpful, you might want to leave it turned on.

The Show/Hide ¶ button

4. Click the More Buttons button on the Standard toolbar and then click the Show/Hide ¶ button, which displays nonprinting characters such as paragraph marks and spaces.

5. Type *What is Redmond BEAT?* and press Enter. Word enters the heading, inserts a paragraph mark, and moves the insertion point to the next line.

6. Type *Why was it started?* and press Enter.

7. Continue entering the headings as shown on the facing page. (We've magnified the document to make it easier to read.)

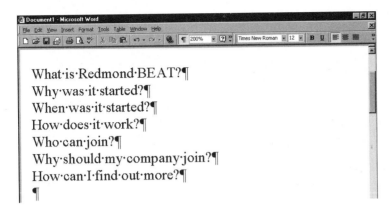

8. Now save the document by clicking the Save button, specifying *Frequently Asked Questions* as the name of the file, and clicking Save.

Now let's add some text under a couple of the headings:

1. Click an insertion point between the question mark and the paragraph mark at the end of the *What is Redmond BEAT?* heading, press Enter, and type the following:

   Redmond BEAT (Business Environmental Action Team) is a local chapter of National BEAT, a network of companies who are actively working to ensure that their business operations are based on sound environmental practices.

2. Click an insertion point between the question mark and the paragraph mark at the end of the *Why was it started?* heading, press Enter, and type the following:

   The chartering of Redmond

   There's *Redmond* again; that's the third time you've had to type it. Let's look at a couple of ways you can save keystrokes and ensure that the words and phrases you use repeatedly are always entered correctly.

Using AutoText

You use Word's AutoText feature to store text or a graphic so that you can later retrieve it by typing a shortcut name and pressing the F3 key. For this example, you'll turn a word you have already typed into an AutoText entry. Follow the steps on the next page to simplify the typing of *Redmond*.

Creating Web pages

As we mentioned, FAQ pages are often used in Web sites. If you plan to publish documents for use on the World Wide Web or on an intranet, Word can help make this process much easier. To turn an existing document into a Web page, choose Save As Web Page from the File menu. Word then saves the file with HTML (HyperText Markup Language) coding, which formats your document so that it appears in a Web browser similarly to the way it appears in Word. (For more information, see page 324.)

1. Right-click one of the toolbars and choose AutoText to display the AutoText toolbar.

2. Select *Redmond*, the word you just typed, and click New on the AutoText toolbar to display this dialog box:

3. Type *red* in the Please Name Your AutoText Entry edit box and click OK.

Now let's use the entry you've just created as you write a few more paragraphs for the FAQ:

1. In the paragraph that begins *The chartering of Redmond*, click an insertion point after *Redmond*, type a space, and then type the following (don't press the Spacebar after *red*):

   BEAT was spearheaded by long-time red

2. Press the F3 key. Word replaces *red* with the *Redmond* entry. (It also flags the text with a green, wavy underline.)

3. Continue typing the following paragraph, using the *red-F3* sequence to insert *Redmond* where indicated. Be sure to type the error marked in bold exactly as you see it so that you will have a mistake to correct later in the chapter. (Word will flag this and any other errors with a red, wavy underline.) Also include the **** characters, which are placeholders for information you'll add later.

resident Art Synkrafts, President of Creative GlassWorks. Struck by the incongruity between his family's efforts to recycle household waste and the fact that his company was sending several dumpsters of garbage to the red-F3 *landfill every month, Synkrafts began looking for other ways to dispose of the packaging in which his company received raw materials. His questions caused one of his suppliers, ****, to explore alternative packaging methods. The result was less garbage in the Creative GlassWorks dumpsters at*

Using AutoText to write a letter

You can use the All Entries button on the AutoText toolbar to help you with parts of a letter. When you click All Entries, Word displays several categories that are components of many business letters, such as a salutation. When you select one of the categories, Word displays options (for example, To Whom It May Concern:). When you select one of the options, Word automatically adds the text to your document. This feature can save you time and offer you choices for sections of your letters that you may not have previously considered.

*no additional cost and negligible other effects for either company. In the meantime, Synkrafts learned about National BEAT, and a few months of persuasive **campaining** later,* red-F3 *BEAT became the newest chapter of a rapidly growing national association.*

Suppose you forget the code for an AutoText entry. Does that mean you can't use the entry anymore? Not at all. Try this:

1. Click an insertion point at the end of the *How can I find out more?* heading, press Enter, and type *Come to a meeting* followed by a period and a space.

2. Click the AutoText button on the AutoText toolbar to display the AutoText tab of the AutoCorrect dialog box:

The AutoText button

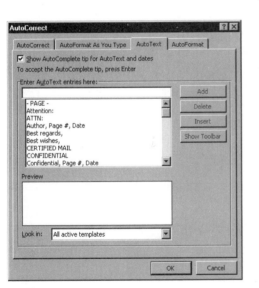

3. Scroll through the list, select *red*, and check the Preview box to see what the entry represents.

4. You could click the Insert button to insert the selected entry; instead, click Cancel to close the dialog box, and we'll show you another way to insert the entry.

5. Click the All Entries button on the AutoText toolbar to display a drop-down list of categories, most of which represent parts of a letter (see the tip on the facing page). Select Normal (the category to which the entries you create are assigned) and

AutoComplete

Some of the entries in the list on the AutoText tab of the Auto-Correct dialog box are entries for AutoComplete. All these "autos" may seem a bit confusing; put simply, after you type the first few characters of an AutoComplete entry, the entire entry appears. If it is correct, press Enter or F3 to insert the completed entry. If it is not correct, just ignore it and keep typing. Auto-Complete finishes the date, days of the week, months, and your name, in addition to the AutoText entries in the list.

then click *red*. Word inserts the *Redmond* entry at the insertion point.

6. Finish the paragraph by adding the text below:

   BEAT meets at 8:00 AM on the last Tuesday of every month at Towne Center.

7. Turn off the AutoText toolbar by right-clicking it and selecting AutoText from the shortcut menu.

   Now that you've simplified the typing of the word *Redmond*, you've probably noticed some other words that could benefit from the same treatment. How about *National BEAT* and *Redmond BEAT*? To simplify the typing of these entries, you'll use AutoCorrect.

Using AutoCorrect

You use the AutoCorrect feature when you want Word to automatically replace a name with its entry. AutoCorrect names should be unique sequences of characters that you are not likely to use normally in a document. Try this:

1. In the FAQ's first heading, select *Redmond BEAT*.

2. Choose AutoCorrect from the Tools menu to display the AutoCorrect tab of the AutoCorrect dialog box, shown below:

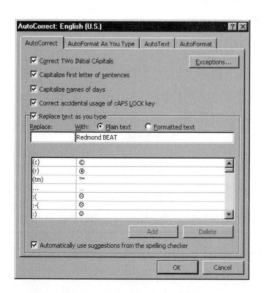

AutoText vs. AutoCorrect

How do you decide when to use AutoText and when to use Auto-Correct? Suppose you own a landscaping business. You know that you'd save a lot of time and effort if you could type *aspen* instead of having to type and italicize *Populus tremuloides* (the aspen tree's botanical name) every time you include this tree in a materials list for your wholesaler. When you communicate with your clients, however, you want to be able to refer to the aspen tree by its common name rather than its botanical name. This entry is a prime candidate for Auto-Text because you can control when Word replaces the name *aspen* with the entry *Populus tremuloides* and when it stays plain old *aspen*. If you use Auto-Correct instead, Word will always change the name *aspen* to *Populus tremuloides*.

Word is waiting for you to enter the name you want it to re-place with the selected text, which appears in the With edit box. Below is a ready-made list of words and symbols that Word replaces each time you type them.

3. In the Replace edit box, type *rb* as the name of the entry and click Add. Word adds the name and its replacement to the list.

4. Type *nb* in the Replace edit box, double-click *Redmond* in the With edit box to select it, and type *National*. The entry in the With edit box is now *National BEAT*. Click Add and then click OK to close the dialog box.

Now let's use these AutoCorrect entries so that you can get a feel for what time-savers they can be:

1. Click an insertion point at the end of the *When was it started?* heading, press Enter, and type this:

   nb, *which currently has **** local chapters, was founded in 1987.* rb *was founded in 1990.*

2. Next click an insertion point at the end of the *Who can join?* heading, press Enter, and type the following (be sure to mis-spell *the* as *teh*):

   Membership in rb *is open to all companies licensed to do business in* teh *city of* red-F3. *For more information, contact Ted Lee at 555-6789.*

Word Editing Techniques

In Chapter 1, we covered editing techniques that are common to all the Office applications, and you may have already done some simple editing in this chapter if you typed any words incorrectly. In this section, we briefly cover some more ways of revising documents. You'll make a few changes to the FAQ to get a feel for what's involved.

Deleting and Replacing Text

Word provides a few techniques for deleting and replacing text in addition to those covered in Chapter 1. You'll learn these Word-specific techniques as you add a new paragraph to the FAQ. Follow the steps on the next page.

AutoCorrect options

In the AutoCorrect dialog box are several options that take care of common typing "errors." Word can correct two initial capital letters in a word, correct sentences that don't begin with a capital letter, capitalize the names of the days of the week, and correct accidental usage of the Caps Lock key. You can turn any of these options on or off by clicking the corresponding check box. Word does not capitalize the next word following an abbreviation (such as *apt.* for *apartment*); click the Exceptions button to see or add to the list of abbreviations. You can also tell Word not to correct two consecutive initial capital letters in certain instances or not to make any other general corrections. At the bottom of the dialog box, you can deselect the option that tells Word to automatically correct your spelling if there is no question about what the correct spelling is (see page 48).

1. Click an insertion point at the end of the *Why should my company join?* heading and press Enter.

2. Type the following (including the non-italicized errors, which will be corrected by AutoCorrect, and the misspelling in bold):

   Current members cite two main reasons for joining. Many companies are managed by people who were first attracted to this area by its natural beauty adn *who therefore want to be part of* teh *effort to preserve it. Other companies stress* teh *potential advantages in today's competitive markets of being perceived as a "green"* comapny *by consumers who are increasingly **environmently** aware.*

Deleting a word to the left → 3. Click an insertion point to the right of the last *e* in *therefore* and press Ctrl+Backspace to delete the word to the left of the insertion point.

Deleting a word to the right → 4. Click an insertion point to the left of the *f* in *first* and press Ctrl+Delete to delete the word to the right of the insertion point.

Insert mode → As you have seen, Word is by default in *Insert mode*, meaning that when you click an insertion point and begin typing, the characters you enter are inserted to the left of the insertion point, pushing any existing text to the right. Word can also **Overtype mode** → operate in *Overtype mode*, meaning that when you click an insertion point and begin typing, each character you enter replaces an existing character.

Let's experiment a bit with overtyping. Suppose Redmond BEAT was actually founded in 1989, not 1990. Here's how to make this simple correction:

1. Click an insertion point to the right of the first 9 of 1990 under the *When was it started?* heading.

Turning on overtype → 2. In the status bar, double-click the overtype box (the fourth box, containing the letters *OVR*). The letters *OVR* are highlighted to indicate that you are now in Overtype mode.

3. Type *8*, which overtypes the second 9, and then type *9*, which overtypes the 0, so that the entry now correctly reads *1989*.

4. Double-click the overtype box to turn off Overtype mode. This step is important; you might overtype valuable information if you forget this step.

Turning off overtype

Moving and Copying Text

You can move any amount of text within the same document or to a different document. Move operations can be carried out either using the Cut and Paste buttons as discussed in Chapter 1 or using a mouse technique called *drag-and-drop editing*. Generally, you use drag-and-drop editing when moving text short distances, that is, when the text you're moving and the place you're moving it to can be viewed simultaneously. Try this:

Drag-and-drop editing

1. Under the *When was it started?* heading, select the sentence that begins *National BEAT*, including the space after the period.

2. Point to the highlighted text, hold down the left mouse button, drag the shadow insertion point to the right of the period following 1989, and release the mouse button. The selected text moves to the specified location. You have, in effect, transposed the two sentences in this paragraph.

Moving text with drag-and-drop editing

3. Now select the *When was it started?* heading and the paragraph below it. Point to the highlighted text and drag the shadow insertion point to the left of the *Why was it started?* heading. (If necessary, scroll the document so that you can see both headings before you drag.) The selection now appears above *Why was it started?*

The procedure for copying text is similar to that for moving text. Try copying some text with the drag-and-drop technique:

1. Use the vertical scroll bar to position the FAQ on the screen so that both the *Who can join?* and *How can I find out more?* sections are visible at the same time.

2. Under the *Who can join?* heading, click an insertion point to the left of the sentence that reads *For more information*.

3. Select the sentence by holding down Ctrl and Shift simultaneously and then pressing the Right Arrow key until you have highlighted the entire sentence.

Extend-selection mode

The extend-selection mode is yet another way to select text. Click an insertion point where you want the selection to start. Then turn on the extend-selection mode by pressing F8 or double-clicking the letters EXT in the status bar. You can then click where you want the selection to end, and Word immediately highlights all the text between the insertion point and the spot where you last clicked. To turn off extend-selection mode, simply double-click the letters EXT in the status bar or click elsewhere in the document.

Copying text with
drag-and-drop editing →

4. Point to the selected text, hold down the left mouse button, hold down the Ctrl key, and drag the shadow insertion point to the right of the last period in the document (after *Towne Center*). While you hold down the mouse button and the Ctrl key, a small plus sign appears next to the mouse pointer.

5. Release first the mouse button and then the Ctrl key. Immediately, a copy of the selected sentence appears in the location designated by the shadow insertion point, as shown here:

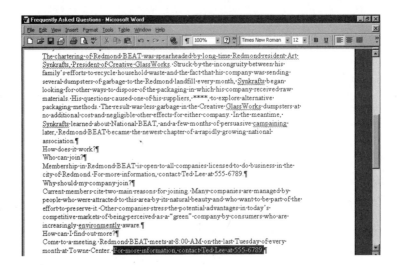

6. Now select the first instance of the *For more information* sentence and press Delete.

Organizing Documents

You have seen how to move text around in a document using cut-and-paste and drag-and-drop editing, but when a document has headings as well as ordinary text, it's often simpler to use Word's Outlining feature to move things around. Most people are accustomed to thinking of outlining as the process that precedes the writing of lengthy documents. With Word, however, outlining is not a separate process but simply another way of looking at a document. Once you use Word's Outlining feature with a particular document, you can switch to outline view at any time to get an overview of your work. In this section, you'll set up the outline for the FAQ and then use the outline to reorganize the document. Follow the steps on the facing page to get started.

Smart editing

When you cut or copy and paste text, Word guesses where spaces are needed for the text to make sense. For example, it removes spaces before and adds spaces after punctuation marks. You can tell Word to leave these kinds of adjustments to you by choosing Options from the Tools menu, clicking the Edit tab, clicking the Use Smart Cut And Paste check box in order to deselect it, and then clicking OK.

1. Choose Outline from the expanded View menu. Word displays the Outlining toolbar, which allows you to organize your document by assigning levels to the information on the screen. Because Word considers all the headings and paragraphs of the FAQ to be ordinary body text, they are each identified by a small hollow square in the selection area to the left.

Switching to outline view

2. Move the pointer over the Outlining toolbar, using ScreenTips to get an idea of what each button does. Then move to the end of the document by pressing Ctrl+End.

3. On a new line, type *Redmond Business Environmental Action Team* and then click the Promote button on the Outlining toolbar. Word moves the heading to the left and makes it bigger to reflect its new status. Notice the large minus icon next to the heading; it indicates that the heading has no subheadings or text.

The Promote button

4. Click the Formatting toolbar's More Buttons button and notice that Heading 1, the style that Word has applied to the heading, appears in the Style box. (See page 68 for more information about styles.) You can create up to nine heading levels, appropriately called Heading 1 through Heading 9.

Heading styles

5. Click an insertion point in the *How can I find out more?* heading and click the Promote button. Repeat this step for each of the other six headings to change them all to the Heading 1 style.

6. Press Ctrl+Home and click the Show Heading 1 button. Word collapses the outline, and only the level 1 headings are visible:

1

The Show Heading 1 button

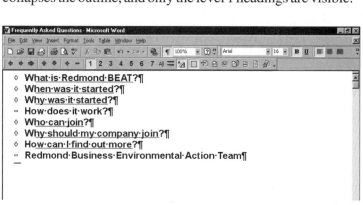

Deleting headings

To delete a heading from an outline, select the heading and press Delete. If you want to also delete the heading's subordinate headings and text, you can collapse the outline before you make your selection. Otherwise, it's best to leave the outline expanded so that you can see exactly which paragraphs will be affected when you press the Delete key.

Outline symbols

As already mentioned, a minus icon indicates that the heading doesn't have subordinate headings or text; a plus icon indicates that it does. In addition, Word puts a gray underscore below headings whose subordinate information is hidden. Now let's do a little reorganizing:

The Move Up button

1. Click an insertion point in the *Redmond Business Environmental Action Team* heading and then click the Move Up button repeatedly until the heading is at the top of the document.

The Move Down button

2. Select both the *When was it started?* and *Why was it started?* headings and then click the Move Down button once to move both headings below the *How does it work?* heading.

The Expand button

3. Click the Expand button to display the body text below the two selected headings. As you can see here, the paragraphs moved with their headings:

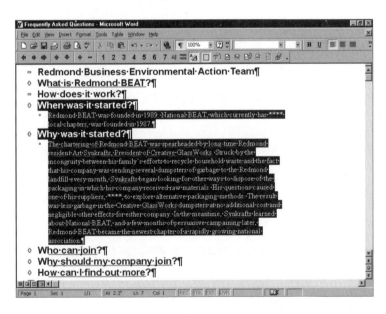

The Collapse button

4. Click the Collapse button to hide the text again.

What happens if you want to add information to the document while you are in outline view? Simple! Follow these steps:

1. Click an insertion point at the end of the *How does it work?* heading and press Enter. Word assumes you want to type another level 1 heading.

2. Click the Demote To Body Text button on the Outlining toolbar and type the following, including the errors in bold:

The Demote To Body Text
button

*Member companies agree to participate in two ongoing efforts: 1. They pledge to scrutinize their operations and wherever possible, implement procedures that will minimize any adverse **affects** on the environment. 2. They agree to field-test new "**environmently** kind" products and services to evaluate their potential impact on both company costs and the environment.*

3. Click the Show Heading 1 button to display only the headings.

   Notice that all the headings except the first should really be level 2. You have used the Promote button to bump headings up one level. Here's how to bump them down:

1. Select all the headings except the first and click the Demote button on the Outlining toolbar. Word both moves the selected headings to the right so that their relationship to the level 1 heading above is readily apparent, and changes their formatting. The minus icon to the left of the first heading changes to a plus icon, indicating that it now has subordinate headings and text.

The Demote button

2. Click the Show All Headings button to see these results:

The Show All Headings
button

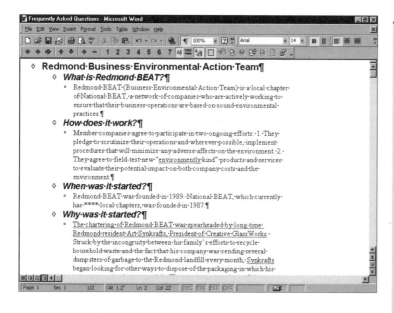

Subdocuments

In outline view, you can create a master document with separate but related subdocuments. Display the document in outline view, click an insertion point in a heading, and click the Create Subdocument button on the Outlining toolbar. Repeat this step for any other headings you want converted to subdocuments. Then save the file. Word saves each subdocument as a separate file with the heading as the filename. To access the file, you can click its hyperlink in the master document. For more information, see Word's Help feature.

Word's views

Well, after that brief introduction to Word's Outlining feature, let's switch to normal view so that you can move on with the rest of the chapter. By default, Word is in print layout view, which displays your document as it will look on a printed page and shows headers and footers as well as other page elements. Normal view displays all of the text while simplifying the page layout to make typing and editing easier. Here's how to make the switch:

The Normal View and Outline View buttons

1. Click the Normal View button at the left end of the horizontal scroll bar. Having set up the document's outline, you can return to outline view at any time by simply clicking the Outline View button at the left end of the horizontal scroll bar.

2. Click the Save button to save your work.

Finding and Replacing

With Word, you can search a document for specific characters. You can also specify replacement characters. As you'll see as you follow along with the next example, finding and replacing a series of characters is easy.

Finding Text

Editing during a search or replace

You can edit your document in the middle of a search or replace operation without closing the Find And Replace dialog box. Simply click the document window to activate it, make your changes, and then click anywhere in the Find And Replace dialog box to continue your search or replace. You can also click the Cancel button to close the Find And Replace dialog box and instead use the Next Find/GoTo and Previous Find/GoTo buttons at the bottom of the vertical scroll bar to complete your search without the dialog box in your way.

Recall that while typing the Redmond BEAT FAQ, you left the characters **** as placeholders for information that needed to be added later. Suppose you now need to locate the placeholders so that you can substitute the correct information. In a document as short as the FAQ, you would have no difficulty locating ****. But if your document were several pages long and numerous placeholders were involved, you would probably want to use the Find command to locate them. Follow these steps:

1. Press Ctrl+Home to move the insertion point to the top of the document.

2. Choose Find from the Edit menu. Word displays the dialog box shown on the facing page.

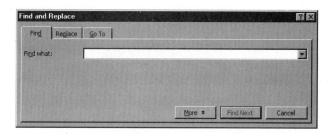

3. Enter **** in the Find What edit box and click Find Next. Word searches the document, stopping when it locates the first occurrence of ****.

4. Click Cancel to close the dialog box and then type *210* to replace the highlighted placeholder.

5. Click the Next Find/GoTo button at the bottom of the vertical scroll bar to repeat the Find command with the same Find What entry as the previous search. Word locates the second ****. (You can click the Previous Find/GoTo button to go back to the previous instance of the Find What text.)

The Next Find/GoTo and Previous Find/GoTo buttons

6. Replace the selection with *Jordan Manufacturing*.

Most of your searches will be as simple as this one was, but you can also refine your searches by clicking the More button in the Find And Replace dialog box to display additional options. You can then either use the options provided, or enter special characters to customize your search (see the tips on the next two pages). For example, suppose you regularly confuse the two words *affect* and *effect*. You can check your use of these words in the FAQ, as follows:

1. Press Ctrl+Home to move to the top of the document. Then click the Select Browse Object button at the bottom of the vertical scroll bar to display this palette of options:

The Select Browse Object button

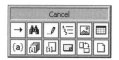

The Select Browse Object palette allows you to look through your document by heading, graphic, table, and so on.

The Find button

2. Click the Find button to display the Find And Replace dialog box again.

3. Click the More button to expand the Find And Replace dialog box, as shown here:

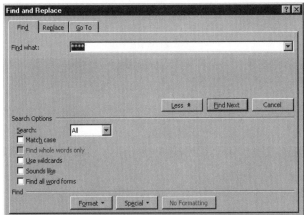

Finding and replacing formats

To search for text to which you have assigned a particular format, choose Find from the Edit menu, click the More button to expand the Find And Replace dialog box, click the Format button, and then click Font for character formats or Paragraph for paragraph formats. In the Find Font or Find Paragraph dialog box, specify the format you want to find, click OK to return to the Find And Replace dialog box, and click Find Next. Word highlights the next text entry formatted with that format. You can use the Replace command to change a particular format. For example, to change all bold text to bold italic, choose Replace from the Edit menu, click Format and then Font, click Bold in the Font Style list, and click OK. Next click the Replace With edit box, click Format and then Font, select Bold Italic in the Font Style list, and click OK. Back in the Find And Replace dialog box, simply click either Find Next and Replace or Replace All, depending on whether you want to confirm the replacement of each case of the specified format.

4. Enter *?ffect* in the Find What edit box. The ? is a *wildcard* character that stands for any single character.

5. Check that All is selected as the Search option. Then click Use Wildcards to tell Word to look for a string of characters that matches the Find What text, and click Find Next to start the search. Word stops at the word *affects* in the second paragraph. (You may need to move the dialog box by dragging its title bar so that you can see the text.)

6. This use of *affects* is incorrect, so click Cancel to close the dialog box and then change the *a* to *e*.

7. Click the Next Find/GoTo button to repeat the search. Word stops at the word *effects*, which is correct.

8. Click the Next Find/GoTo button again. The document contains no other instances of the Find What text, so click No when asked whether you want to continue the search.

Replacing Text

Often, you will search a document for a series of characters with the intention of replacing them. When you need to make the same replacement more than a couple of times, using the Replace command automates the process. Let's find all occurrences of *National BEAT* and change them to *USA BEAT*:

1. Press Ctrl+Home to move to the beginning of the document, and click the Select Browse Object button. Click Find, and click the Replace tab. (You can also use the Replace command on the Edit menu.) Word displays this dialog box:

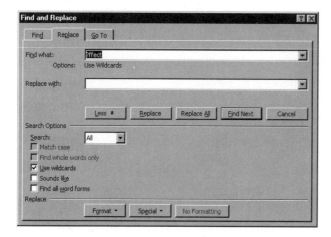

Notice the settings from the Find tab have been carried over to the Replace tab.

2. Replace the Find What text by typing *National BEAT*.

3. In the Replace With edit box, type *USA BEAT*. Click the Less button to decrease the size of the dialog box, and press Enter. Word highlights the first occurrence of the Find What text.

4. Click Replace. Word then highlights the second occurrence.

5. Next click Replace All to replace any remaining occurrences, and then click OK when Word tells you that two replacements have been made.

6. Click Close to close the Find And Replace dialog box.

   As with the Find command, you can use the Match Case, Find Whole Words Only, Use Wildcards, Sounds Like, and Find All Word Forms options to refine the replace procedure. (See the adjacent tip for more information.)

Refining your searches

By using the options available in the Find And Replace dialog box, you can complete more complicated searches in your Word documents. Use the drop-down list of Search options to search forward to the end of the document (Down) or backward to the beginning of the document (Up) from the insertion point, or to search the entire document (All). Click the Match Case option to find only those occurrences of the Find What text with the exact capitalization specified. For example, find the initials *USA* and not the characters *usa* in *usability*. Click the Find Whole Words Only option to find only wholeword occurrences of the Find What text. For example, find the word *men* and not the characters *men* in *mention* and *fundamental*. Click the Sounds Like option to find occurrences of the Find What text that sound the same but are spelled differently. Finally, click the Find All Word Forms option to find occurrences of a particular word in any form. For example, if the Find What text is the word *hide*, Word will also find *hid* and *hidden*. In addition to using the Use Wildcards option for wildcard characters (see page 46), you can also find special characters, such as tabs (enter ^t in the Find What edit box) and paragraph marks (enter ^p). For example, find every paragraph that begins with the word *Remember* by entering ^pRemember as the Find What text.

Checking Spelling and Grammar

Nothing detracts from a document like a typo. In the past, your readers might have overlooked the occasional misspelling. These days, running your word processor's spelling checker is so easy that readers tend to be less forgiving. For example, résumés and job-application letters with typos will more often than not end up in the recycling bin. The moral: Get in the habit of spell-checking all your documents, especially before distributing printed copies.

As we created the FAQ in this chapter, we deliberately included a few errors. Because Word flags any potential mistakes with wavy underlines, you can simply correct any spelling or grammar errors as you create your documents. Try fixing one of the misspelled words now by following these steps:

Automatic spell-checking and grammar-checking

1. Point to the word *campaining* in the *Why was it started?* paragraph and right-click it. Word displays this shortcut menu:

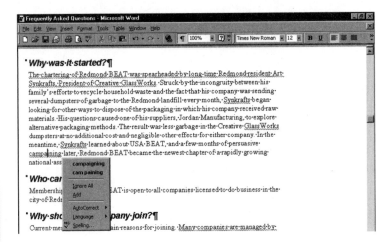

The Thesaurus

You can use Word's Thesaurus to look up synonyms for a selected word by choosing Language and then Thesaurus from the Tools menu. Word displays the Thesaurus dialog box and suggests alternatives for the selected word. To replace the word with an alternative, select the alternative in the Meanings list and click Replace. You can also select an alternative and then click Look Up to display a list of alternatives for the alternative. Click Cancel to close the Thesaurus dialog box without making any changes.

Word displays any words found in its dictionary that come close to the misspelled word. It also gives you the option to ignore the misspelling, add the entry to Word's dictionary, create an AutoCorrect entry for the word, change the language used, or take you to the Spelling & Grammar dialog box for more options.

2. Click *campaigning* to change the word to its correct spelling.

   To check the spelling of a document all at once, you can use Word's spell-checking capabilities in another way. Try this:

1. Press Ctrl+Home to move the insertion point to the top of the FAQ, and click the Spelling And Grammar button on the Standard toolbar. Starting with the word containing the insertion point, Word begins checking each word of the document against its built-in dictionary. When Word finds a word that is not in its dictionary, it displays this Spelling And Grammar dialog box:

The Spelling and Grammar button

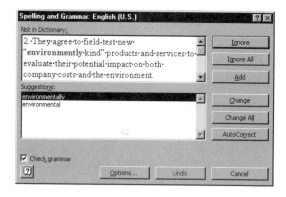

2. As you can see, Word stopped at the word *environmently*. Since this spelling is incorrect, click the Change All button to tell Word that you want to change this and any other occurrences of this misspelling to the suggested spelling.

3. Word next stops at *Synkrafts*. Click Ignore All to leave all occurrences of this last name as they are.

4. Word stops at *GlassWorks*. A possible substitute appears in the Suggestions list. You have spelled this name correctly and use it often. You don't want Word to flag it as a misspelling every time, so add it to Word's supplemental dictionary, which is called Custom.dic, by clicking the Add button. (You cannot add words to the main dictionary.)

Adding words to the dictionary

5. Word may flag the sentence that begins *The chartering of* because of its passive voice and in the Suggestions box offer

an alternative sentence in active voice. You want the sentence worded as it is, so click Ignore. (If you want Word to ignore every instance of passive voice in the document, you can click Ignore Rule.)

6. When Word reaches the end of the document, it closes the Spelling And Grammar dialog box and displays a message that the spelling and grammar check is complete. Click OK to return to your document.

7. Save and close Frequently Asked Questions and then close Word by clicking its Close button.

As you create documents and spell-check them, you will start to see that the words you use fall into several categories:

The main dictionary

- Common words that are included in Word's main dictionary. The majority of words fall into this category.

Document "dictionaries"

- Uncommon words that you use rarely. You will want to tell Word to ignore these particular words when spell-checking a document. Word will then attach those words to the document in which they are used as a sort of document-specific dictionary and will not flag them as misspellings if you spell-check the document in the future.

The supplementary dictionary

- Uncommon words that you use often in different kinds of documents. You will want to add these words to Custom.dic so that they are not flagged as misspellings.

Smart spelling checks

If your document contains duplicate words, such as *the the*, Word stops at the words and displays them in the Spelling And Grammar dialog box during a spelling check. To remove the duplicate word, click Delete. Word also stops at strange combinations of uppercase and lowercase letters. For example, Word would stumble over *nAtional* and would suggest *national* as an appropriate substitute. (This feature doesn't work if you have Correct Accidental Usage Of CAPS LOCK Key selected in the AutoCorrect dialog box.) To speed up the checking process, Word's suggestions generally have the same case as a misspelled word. For example, if the misspelling occurs at the beginning of a sentence and therefore starts with a capital letter, Word's suggestions also start with capital letters.

- Uncommon words that you use with a specific type of document. Instead of adding these words to Custom.dic, you might want to create a custom dictionary for use only with that type of document. To create a custom dictionary, choose Options from the Tools menu, click the Spelling & Grammar tab, click the Dictionaries button, and then click the New button in the Custom Dictionaries dialog box. Type a name for the dictionary, click Save, and then click OK. Before you can use the custom dictionary, you must open it by selecting it from the Custom Dictionary drop-down list in the Options dialog box and clicking OK. (You can also create and open custom dictionaries on the Spelling & Grammar tab that appears when you click Options in the Spelling And Grammar dialog box.) Then when you check a document's spelling, you can click the Add button in the Spelling And Grammar dialog box to add words to the custom dictionary. (Note that before starting a spelling check, it is a good idea to click the Options button and check which custom dictionary is in effect.)

← Custom dictionaries

You can't rely on Word's spelling and grammar checker to identify every error in your documents. Errors of syntax or improper word usage may slip by undetected in a spelling and grammar check. So be warned: you should always read through your documents and check thoroughly for any errors that Word might have missed.

Spelling and grammar options

Clicking the Options button in the Spelling And Grammar dialog box displays the Spelling & Grammar tab of the Options dialog box. You can tell Word whether to automatically spell- and grammar-check the current document or hide errors in the document. You can also tell Word to suggest alternatives for the misspellings it finds and to ignore words in capital letters or that contain numbers. In addition, you can create, edit, add, and delete custom dictionaries by clicking the Dictionaries button. To spell-check your documents without using Word's grammar checker, deselect the Check Grammar As You Type and Check Grammar With Spelling check boxes at the bottom of the dialog box. To change the grammar checker's options, click the Settings button to display the Grammar Settings dialog box. Here you can select and deselect various options for grammar and style. If you want to change the writing style for the grammar checker, click the arrow to the right of the Writing Style edit box and select another style, such as Casual or Technical.

3 More About Word

First you explore Word's built-in templates for creating common business documents, and then you combine two documents to demonstrate some of Word's formatting capabilities, including styles. Finally, you create and format a table.

Although you design a flyer for a specific organization in this chapter, you can use the techniques you learn to customize a flyer for your own purposes, including business, community, or campus announcements.

Documents created and concepts covered:

Create headers to carry page numbers and identifying information

Click a button to create a table

Combine two documents to create a new one

Set first-line indents and the space above and below paragraphs

Dress up headings with borders

Turn formatting combinations into styles

Click a button to create numbered and bulleted lists

Use multi-column formats to vary document designs

AIR POLLUTANT SOURCES
In Millions of Metric Tons

Contributor	Sulfur Dioxide	Carbon Monoxide	Nitrogen Oxides
Transportation	0.9	41.2	8.1
Industrial Emissions	3.4	4.7	0.6
Fuel Combustion	16.4	7.6	10.8
Solid-Waste Burning	--	1.7	0.1
Miscellaneous	--	6.0	0.2
TOTAL	20.7	61.2	19.8

Tip Top Roofing Wins Carson Award for Recycling Program

Yesterday, the Carson Committee voted unanimously to present one of its 1999 awards to **Tip Top Roofing**. The company's efforts during the past year to forge the industry alliances needed for a successful asphalt-shingle recycling program are an impressive demonstration of Tip Top Roofing's ongoing commitment to the environment.

The prestigious Carson Awards recognize companies who work to ensure that their business practices are environmentally sensitive. This year's awards will be presented at the Carson Gala Dinner on Friday, July 23, 1999.

REDMOND BUSINESS ENVIRONMENTAL ACTION TEAM

What is Redmond BEAT?

Redmond BEAT (Business Environmental Action Team) is a local chapter of USA BEAT, a network of companies who are actively working to ensure that their business operations are based on sound environmental practices.

How does it work?

Member companies agree to participate in two ongoing efforts:

1. They pledge to scrutinize their operations and wherever possible, implement procedures that will minimize any adverse effects on the environment.
2. They agree to field-test new "environmentally kind" products and services to evaluate their potential impact on both company costs and the environment.

When was it started?

Redmond BEAT was founded in 1989. USA BEAT, which currently has 210 local chapters, was founded in 1987.

Why was it started?

The chartering of Redmond BEAT was spearheaded by long-time Redmond resident Art Synkrafts, President of Creative GlassWorks. Struck by the incongruity between his family's efforts to recycle household waste and the fact that his company was sending several dumpsters of garbage to the Redmond landfill every month, Synkrafts began looking for other ways to dispose of the packaging in which his company received raw materials. His questions caused one of his suppliers, Jordan Manufacturing, to explore alternative packaging methods. The result was less garbage in the Creative GlassWorks dumpsters at no additional cost and negligible other effects for either company. In the meantime, Synkrafts learned about USA BEAT, and a few months of persuasive campaigning later,

Redmond BEAT became the newest chapter of a rapidly growing national association.

Who can join?

Membership in Redmond BEAT is open to all companies licensed to do business in the city of Redmond.

Why should my company join?

Current members cite two main reasons for joining. Many companies are managed by people who were attracted to this area by its natural beauty and who want to be part of the effort to preserve it. Other companies stress the potential advantages in today's competitive markets of being perceived as a "green" company by consumers who are increasingly environmentally aware.

How can I find out more?

Come to a meeting. Redmond BEAT meets at 8:00 AM on the last Tuesday of every month at Towne Center. For more information, contact Ted Lee at 555-6789.

Chapter 2 showed you some ways to edit, reorganize, and polish the content of your Word documents. In this chapter, you will explore ways to create useful documents with Word's ready-made templates. We'll then discuss Word features that can give your documents a really professional look.

Using Word's Templates

A template is a pattern that includes the information, formatting, and other elements used in a particular type of document. Unless you specify otherwise, all new Word documents are based on the Blank Document template. But Word comes with several other templates that you can use as is or modify, or you can create your own templates (see the tip on page 57).

As part of the Microsoft Office installation procedure, a few templates and wizards were copied to the Templates subfolder of the Program Files\Microsoft Office folder on your hard drive. To preview these templates and wizards, follow these steps:

Wizards

In addition to templates, the New dialog box provides access to wizards that help you create ready-made documents, such as faxes. Wizards are tools that are incorporated into all of the Office applications to help you accomplish specific tasks. They work in the same basic way, regardless of the application or the task. They all consist of a series of dialog boxes that ask you to provide information or select from various options. You move from box to box by clicking the Next button, and you can move back to an earlier box by clicking the Back button. Clicking Cancel cancels the entire procedure, and clicking Finish completes the task with whatever settings currently exist in all the dialog boxes.

1. If necessary, start Word and check that nonprinting characters are displayed. (If they aren't, click the Show/Hide ¶ button.) We also turned off the ruler to enlarge the workspace.

2. Choose New from the File menu to display the multi-tabbed dialog box shown here:

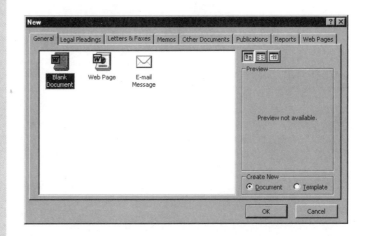

Word displays icons for all the template and wizards, organized by tab. The default selection is Blank Document on the General tab.

3. Click the Letters & Faxes tab and click the Fax Wizard once to highlight it. If this wizard is installed, the Preview box on the right displays a miniature version of the document it produces. If it is not installed and you want to create a fax, you can install the wizard by clicking OK. (See the tip below.)

4. Click other icons on the Letters & Faxes tab and then check out some of the other tabs. As you can tell from their names, the templates and wizards provide the basis for many common business documents.

5. When you are ready, click Elegant Memo on the Memos tab and either press Enter or click OK. Word switches to print layout view and displays this memo form on your screen:

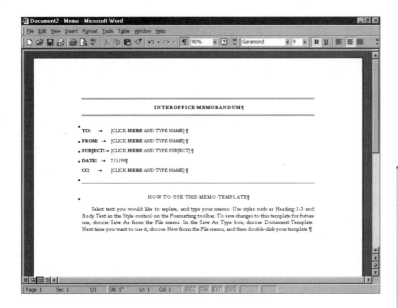

Install on demand

If a preview is not available for the template or wizard you select in the New dialog box, the item is not installed. You can easily install it by clicking OK and inserting the installation CD-ROM if prompted. When the installation is complete, Word loads the template or starts the wizard. This install-on-demand capability allows you to install items as you need them rather than storing items on your hard drive that you may never need to use.

As you can see, all the common elements of a memo have placeholders within square brackets, and Word has entered the current date (using the date stored by your computer—see the tip on page 56 for more information). To fill in the memo, follow the steps on the next page.

1. In the To section, click the placeholder text to select it, and type *Sandra Peters, Northwest BEAT*. (Do not type the period in these steps.) Because of the formatting applied to the place-holder text, the entries you type appear in all capital letters, regardless of how you enter them.

2. In the From section, type *Ted Lee* and in the subject section, type *Carson Awards*.

3. Finally, in the CC: section, type *Nathan Chou, Washington BEAT*.

4. Now select the title *How to Use This Memo Template* but not the paragraph mark, and replace it with *Tip Top Roofing Wins Carson Award for Recycling Program*.

Take a moment to admire your work. Without adding any formatting of your own, you've created a professional-looking header for a memo, as shown here:

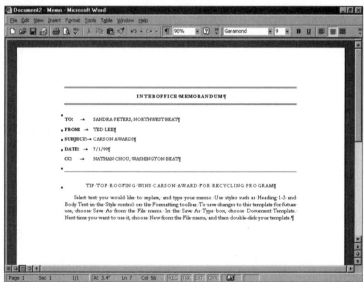

Date fields

When you create a new docu-ment based on the memo tem-plate, Word automatically enters the date stored by your system's clock/calendar. Why? Because the document contains a special code called a *field*. Fields can contain a variety of information; this particular field is an instruc-tion to get the current date and display it in the field's location. If you do nothing to this field, Word will insert the current date each time you open the docu-ment. To "freeze" the current date, click the field to select it, and then press Ctrl+Shift+F9. The field is converted to normal text that will not be updated and that can be edited. To insert a date field in a different docu-ment, choose Date And Time from the Insert menu, and in the Date And Time dialog box, se-lect a date format, click the Up-date Automatically check box to select it, and then click OK.

5. Choose Save As from the File menu and save the document with the name *Memo*.

Below the memo title, you need to enter the text of the memo. This information is essentially the same as that contained in the letter you wrote in Chapter 1. The beauty of a word processor like Word is that instead of retyping the information, you can borrow it from the letter and edit it to suit the purpose of the memo. Here's how:

1. Select the text of the main paragraph (but not the paragraph mark) and press the Delete key.

2. Now click the Open button on the toolbar, and in the Open dialog box, double-click Tip Top Letter to open the letter from Chapter 1 in its own window.

3. Select just the two paragraphs of the letter, including the paragraph mark between them and the paragraph mark at the end of the second paragraph. Click the Copy button.

4. Click the Memo button on the taskbar to switch to that document's window.

5. Make sure the insertion point is in front of the blank paragraph and click the Paste button to insert the copied text.

6. Edit the text of the memo so that it looks like the one shown below. (We've magnified the memo and temporarily turned off the ruler so that the text is more readable.)

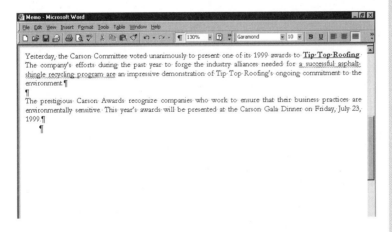

7. Print and save the document, and then close it.

8. Close Tip Top Letter, clicking No if Word asks whether to save any changes.

Creating custom templates

You can save any document as a template and then open a new document based on that template any time you need to create that type of document. Choose Save As from the File menu and then click the arrow to the right of the Save As Type box and select Document Template. Word displays the contents of the Templates subfolder. Assign a name to the template in the File Name edit box, and click Save. To use the new template, choose New from the File menu and select the template the same way you would select any of Word's built-in templates.

More About Formatting

As you saw in the last chapter, a well-designed document uses formatting to provide visual cues about its structure. For example, a report might use large bold type for first-level headings and smaller bold type for second-level headings. Summary paragraphs might be indented and italic. In this section, you'll explore some more formatting techniques as you combine the FAQ from Chapter 2 and the memo you created earlier in this chapter to make a flyer. Follow these steps:

1. Starting with a blank window, click the Open button on the Standard toolbar, and with the contents of the My Documents folder displayed, double-click Frequently Asked Questions.

2. To safeguard the original Frequently Asked Questions file, choose Save As from the File menu and change the name of the version now on your screen to *Flyer*.

Merging documents → 3. Press Ctrl+Home to be sure that the insertion point is at the top of the document, and choose File from the expanded Insert menu to display this Insert File dialog box:

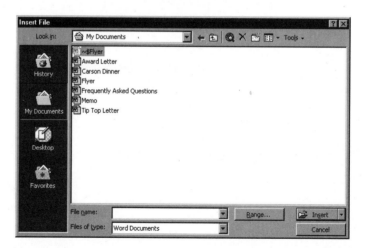

4. Select Memo and then click Insert to merge the file with Flyer.

5. Press Ctrl+Home to move to the top of the combined document. Then select and delete the memo heading (everything

up to and including the line below the CC: line). Finally, delete the blank paragraph at the end of the memo.

6. Click the Save button on the toolbar to save the combined document, which looks like the one shown here:

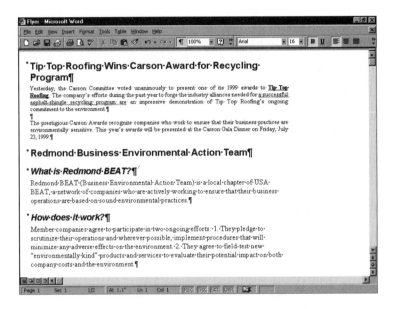

Notice that the Heading 1 style applied to the heading in the memo has adopted the Heading 1 style characteristics used in the FAQ. Also notice that the paragraphs of the memo have adopted the FAQ's formatting but with a smaller font size. You'll take care of this inconsistency in a minute, and you'll learn about controlling formatting with styles in more detail on page 68.

From now on, we won't tell you when to save the flyer, but you should do so at regular intervals to safeguard your work.

Making Titles Stand Out

As you know, you apply character formatting when you want to change the appearance of individual characters. Let's focus on the titles of the two "articles" in the new flyer:

1. Move to the top of the document, select the title of the memo, click the Center button on the Formatting toolbar to center the title, and change the font to Times New Roman.

Rebreaking titles and headings

As you create titles and headings for your Word documents, you may find that some of them would look better if they broke to multiple lines or broke in a different spot. To rebreak a title or heading (or any other line of text), click an insertion point where you want the break to occur and press Shift+Enter. Word then inserts a line break, which it designates on the screen with a broken-arrow symbol.

2. Select the *Redmond Business Environmental Action Team* heading including the paragraph mark. Center the title and change the font to Times New Roman.

3. With the title still selected, choose Font from the Format menu. Word displays the dialog box shown here:

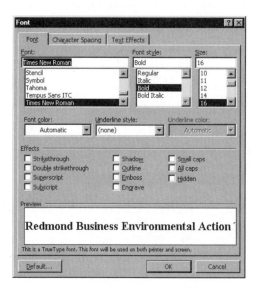

As you can see, the dialog box reflects the character formatting of the selected title. It also provides several formatting options not available on the Formatting toolbar.

4. Click Small Caps in the Effects section to format the title in small capital letters with large initial capital letters. Click OK.

If you want, you can experiment with some of the other options in the Font dialog box before moving on.

Adding Borders and Shading

For emphasis, you can draw lines above and below or to the left and right of a paragraph, or you can surround it with a box. Let's box the FAQ title:

1. With the title still selected, choose Borders And Shading from the Format menu. The Borders And Shading dialog box is displayed, as shown on the facing page.

Painting formats

To format a block of text with a set of formats that you have already applied to another block of text, you can copy all the formatting in a simple three-step procedure. Select the text whose formats you want to copy, click the Format Painter button on the Standard toolbar, and then select the text you want to format. Word duplicates the formatting for the new selection. To format multiple selections, simply select the text whose formats you want to copy, double-click the Format Painter button, and then select the text blocks you want to format. When you are finished, click the Format Painter button again, or press Esc.

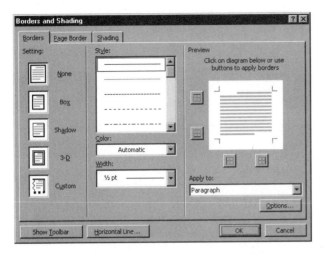

2. Click the arrow to the right of the Width box and select the 1½ pt single-line option.

Changing line styles

3. Click the Box setting. Word displays a preview on the right side of the dialog box.

Adding a border

4. Next click the Shading tab, and in the Fill section, click a light color. (We left the box white for legibility.) Then click OK.

Adding shading

5. Click anywhere to remove the highlighting and see the results, which look like this:

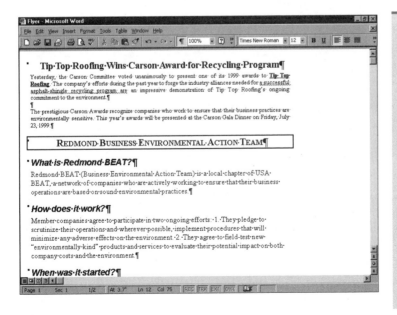

Web page dividers

If you are creating a document for viewing on the Web or an intranet, you can add fancy horizontal lines to separate information. Choose Borders And Shading from the Format menu and then click the Horizontal Line button to display the Horizontal Line dialog box, which has 72 line options. Click a design, and Word displays buttons that allow you to insert the line, preview it, add it to your list of favorites, or find other similar designs. Click the Clips Online button to access Microsoft's Clip Gallery for more design options.

If you want, experiment with the other possible border and shading options before moving on.

Setting Up Multiple Columns

Newsletters and flyers often feature multi-column layouts like those of magazines and newspapers. These layouts give you more flexibility when it comes to the placement of elements on the page, and they are often visually more interesting than single-column layouts. With Word, setting up multiple columns for an entire document couldn't be easier. You simply click the Columns button on the toolbar and select the number of columns you want. And as you'll see as you follow these next steps, when you want only part of a document to have a multi-column layout, you select that part of the document before clicking the Columns button:

1. Select the text from *What is Redmond BEAT?* to the period following the telephone number in the very last sentence (but not the paragraph mark).

The Columns button

2. Click the Columns button on the Standard toolbar's More Buttons palette. Word drops down this grid of columns:

3. Point to the first column, move the mouse pointer to the right to highlight three columns, click the third column, and then click away from the columns to deselect the text. Word switches to print layout view and puts a section break (a double dotted line) at the beginning and end of the selected text. It also reformats the text so that it snakes across the first page in three columns. The top of this part of the flyer now looks as shown on the facing page.

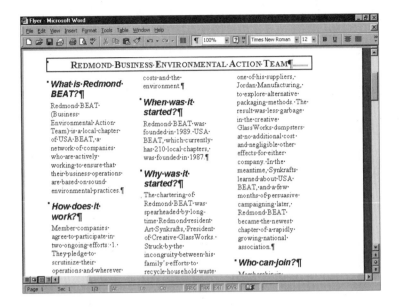

Creating Lists

The second paragraph of the FAQ contains two numbered items that would stand out better if they were set up as a list. Word has two built-in list formats: one for numbered lists and one for bulleted lists. Here's how to implement the numbered list format (the bulleted list format works the same way—see the tip on the next page for more information):

1. Use the scroll bar to move to the second paragraph of the FAQ, click an insertion point to the left of the number 1, and then press Enter.

2. Click an insertion point to the left of the number 2 and press Enter. Word recognizes that consecutive paragraphs starting with numbers comprise a numbered list, and responds by adding a 2 and a period in front of the new paragraph and giving both numbered paragraphs a hanging-indent format. This capability is called *AutoFormat As You Type* (see the adjacent tip).

3. Delete the extra 2, the period, and the space in the second numbered paragraph. The results are shown at the top of the next page.

AutoFormat As You Type

By default, Word automatically formats certain elements of your documents, such as numbered lists. If you want to turn this feature off, choose AutoCorrect from the Tools menu and then click the AutoFormat As You Type tab to view the settings available with this option. In the Apply As You Type section, deselect any of the features you want to turn off. In the Replace As You Type section, you can tell Word to turn straight quotes (" ") to smart quotes (" "), use superscript with ordinals (1st), use fraction characters (½), change symbol characters, apply formatting, and create hyperlinks for Internet and network paths. In the Automatically As You Type section, you can control the treatment of lists and styles.

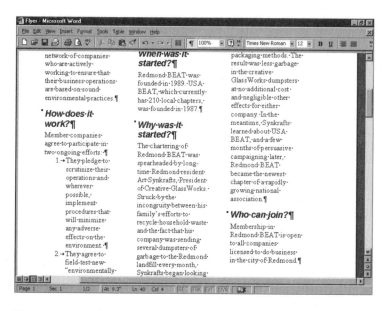

Creating a numbered list
from scratch

Bulleted lists

To create a bulleted list, select the paragraphs you want to be bulleted and click the Bullets button on the Formatting toolbar; or type an asterisk (*) and a space, and Word converts the paragraph to a bulleted list as soon as you press Enter at the end of the paragraph. (See the previous tip.) By default, Word precedes each paragraph with a large dot. To change the symbol, select the bulleted text, choose Bullets And Numbering from the Format menu, and select one of the standard symbols. To modify the format of bulleted and numbered lists, click the Customize button, make your changes, and click OK. You can also click the Picture button to insert graphical bullets appropriate for Web page use.

If you want to type a numbered list from scratch, type 1, a period, and a space, and press Enter after typing your text. Word then automatically formats the next paragraph as the next item of the numbered list. To return to regular paragraphs, click the Numbering button on the Formatting toolbar to turn the list off. (To turn off AutoFormat As You Type options altogether, see the tip on the previous page.)

You can also quickly convert existing text paragraphs to numbered lists by selecting the paragraphs and then clicking the Numbering button.

Adding Headers and Footers

The flyer is currently two pages long. For documents that are longer than one page, you'll usually want to add a header or footer, so we'll show you how to do that next.

Headers are printed in the top margin of the page, and footers are printed in the bottom margin. With Word, you have many header and footer options. For example, you can create identical headers and footers for every page, a different header and footer for the first page, different headers and footers for left (even) pages and right (odd) pages, or different headers and footers for each section of a document.

Suppose you want a header to appear on all pages of the flyer except the first. To create this type of header, first add another page to the flyer, like this:

1. Press Ctrl+End to move to the end of the document, and then choose Break from the Insert menu to display this dialog box:

Inserting a page break

2. Accept the default Page Break option by clicking OK. Your document now has three pages.

   You can also insert a page break by pressing Ctrl+Enter.

   Now let's tackle the header:

1. Press Ctrl+Home to move to the top of the document, and choose Header And Footer from the View menu. Word dims the document text, outlines the space in which the header will appear with a dotted box, and displays the Header And Footer floating toolbar, as shown here:

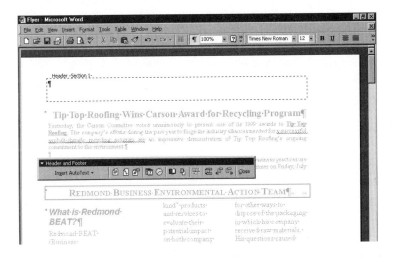

The Page Setup button

2. Click the Page Setup button on the Header And Footer toolbar to display the dialog box shown here:

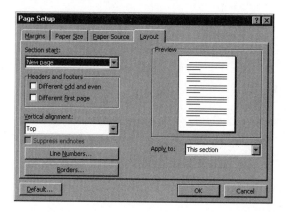

If the Layout tab is not already selected, click it to display its options.

3. In the Section Start area, select Continuous. In the Headers And Footers section, select the Different First Page check box. Then click OK. Word changes the header designation to read *First Page Header - Section 1-*.

The Show Next button

4. You're going to leave the first page header blank, so click the Show Next button on the Header And Footer toolbar to move to the next page, which begins section 2.

The Same As Previous button

5. Click the Same As Previous button to toggle it off, thereby indicating that you want this header to be different from the first one.

The Insert Page Number button

6. Now type *Redmond Business Environmental Action Team* as the second page header and press the Tab key twice. Then type *Page* and a space, and click the Insert Page Number button.

7. Select the entire header and click the Bold and Underline buttons. Then change the font size to 10.

8. Finally, press Home. The header should now look like the one shown at the top of the facing page.

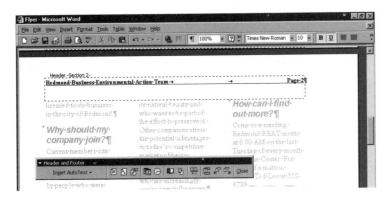

9. Click the Close button on the Header And Footer toolbar to return to print layout view.

Let's take a quick look at the flyer in print preview:

1. Press Ctrl+Home and click the Print Preview button. Then click the Multiple Pages button on the Print Preview toolbar to drop down a grid of "pages." Point to the first page in the top row, hold down the mouse button, and drag through the center page. When you release the mouse button, Word displays the first two pages of your document side by side, as shown here:

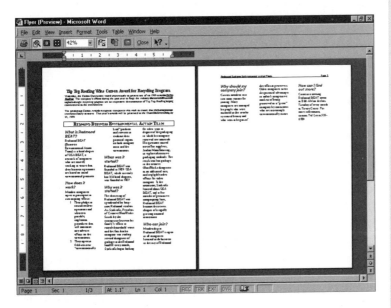

2. Press Page Down to see the blank third page, and then click the Close button on the Print Preview toolbar.

More about page numbers

If you want your headers or footers to contain nothing but page numbers, you don't have to create a header or footer. You can have Word perform this chore for you. First choose Page Numbers from the Insert menu, and in the Page Numbers dialog box, specify if the page numbers should appear at the top or bottom of the page, how they should be aligned, and whether a number should appear on the first page. Then click OK. Word inserts the page numbers in the document's header or footer. Whether you add page numbers this way or by clicking the Insert Page Number button on the Header And Footer toolbar, you can format them by clicking the Format button in the Page Numbers dialog box. You can select from five numbering schemes: Arabic numbers (1, 2, 3), lower or uppercase letters (a, b, c/A, B, C), and lower or uppercase Roman numerals (i, ii, iii/I, II, III). You can also specify whether chapter numbers should be included, and you can select a starting number.

Formatting with Styles

You can work through a document applying formats to headings and other special paragraphs one by one, but Word has an easier way: you can store custom combinations of formatting by defining the combination as a *style*. You can apply that combination to a text selection or a paragraph by selecting the style from the Style drop-down list on the Formatting toolbar.

The Normal style ⟶

Every paragraph you write has a style. When you open a new blank document, it is based on the Blank Document template, and Word applies that template's Normal style to all paragraphs unless instructed otherwise. The Normal style formats characters as 12-point regular Times New Roman and paragraphs as left-aligned and single-spaced. When you base a document on a template other than Blank Document, the styles included as part of that template become available, and as you saw earlier in this chapter, you can then create the document simply by filling in the paragraphs of the template.

Using Word's Predefined Styles

As you learned in Chapter 2, Word comes with nine predefined heading styles, one for each of the heading levels you can designate when using the Outlining feature. Word also has predefined paragraph styles for a number of other common document elements, such as index entries, headers and footers, and footnotes. However, Word does not list the other predefined styles unless the current document contains the corresponding elements. If you insert one of these elements in the document, Word applies the style to the element and adds the style name to the Style list. Try this:

Character vs. paragraph styles

Character styles affect only the selected text, and they apply their formats on top of any paragraph formats applied to the selected text. Paragraph styles affect the entire paragraph containing the insertion point. For example, you can apply a paragraph style that makes the font and size of an entire paragraph 12-point regular Arial and then select the first word and apply a character style that makes the font and size of just that word 18-point bold italic Arial. If you apply a character format before a paragraph format, it will also be applied on top of the paragraph format.

1. Click the More Buttons button on the Formatting toolbar and then click the arrow to the right of the Style box to drop down the Style list.

2. Scroll through the list. You'll see that Word has added the styles from the memo template, as well as a style for the headers you just created. Each style name is displayed with the formatting that will be applied to the selected paragraph if you select that style. To the right of the style name, Word displays the paragraph alignment, the font size, and whether

the style is a paragraph style or a character style. (Paragraph styles are indicated with a paragraph mark, and character styles are indicated with the letter *a*.)

3. Press the Esc key twice to close the list and the palette.

When Word applies one of its built-in styles to an element, it uses the predefined formatting for that element. Once the style is available on the Style list, you can apply it to other paragraphs. You can also redefine the style to suit the document you are creating, and you can create entirely new styles.

Creating Custom Styles

Although Word does a good job of anticipating the document elements for which you will need styles, you will often want to come up with styles of your own. For example, the spacing between the first two paragraphs of the flyer is controlled by a blank paragraph mark, and the second paragraph has no first-line indent. Let's create a style that specifies the spacing following the paragraphs (a more flexible way of controlling spacing), and indents the first line of each paragraph:

1. Delete the paragraph mark between the first and second paragraphs.

2. Click an insertion point in the first text paragraph and choose Paragraph from the Format menu to display this dialog box:

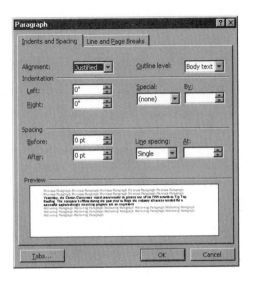

The Style dialog box

You can manage all the available styles, plus create new ones, by choosing Style from the Format menu. You can click the New button to define a new style or the Delete button to remove the selected style (you can delete only the styles you have created), and the Modify button to display a dialog box in which you can change the selected style. (See the tip on page 71 for more information on modifying styles.) If styles occur in a particular sequence in a document, you can specify that one style should automatically follow another, by selecting the first style, clicking the Modify button, and selecting a style from the Style For Following Paragraph drop-down list.

Notice that you can control alignment, indentation, the space above and below paragraphs, and line spacing (single-spaced, double-spaced, and so on), all from this one dialog box.

Indenting the first line

3. In the Indentation section, select First Line from the Special drop-down list. Word enters 0.5" in the By edit box as the default first-line indent, and in the Preview box below, shows how your text will look with this setting.

4. Change the setting in the By edit box to *0.15"*.

Adding space after paragraphs

5. Now change the After setting in the Spacing section to *6 pt* and click OK. Here are the results:

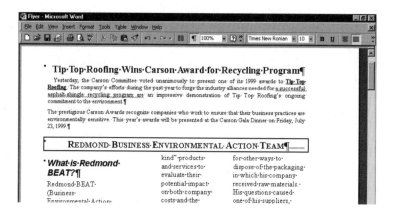

6. Select the paragraph and change the font size to 12.

Follow these steps to assign a different name to the new style:

Naming a style

1. With the insertion point located in the first paragraph of the flyer, click the Style box on the More Buttons palette to highlight the name in it.

2. Type *Indented Paragraph* as the name you want for this style, and press Enter. Word adds the style name and displays Indented Paragraph in the Style box to indicate that it is applied to the current paragraph.

Applying a style

3. Click an insertion point in the second paragraph of the flyer, drop down the Style list, and select the Indented Paragraph style. Word changes the style of the second paragraph so that its formatting is consistent with the first paragraph.

Now let's turn our attention to the FAQ part of the flyer. Suppose you want to add a little space before each paragraph and make the size of the characters slightly smaller. (Paragraphs with space before them are called *open paragraphs*.) Try this:

Open paragraphs

1. Click an insertion point in the first text paragraph of the FAQ and choose Paragraph from the Format menu.

2. In the Spacing section, type *3pt* as the Before setting and click OK.

3. Select the paragraph including the paragraph mark and change the font size to 10.

4. Now click Normal in the Style box to highlight it, type *Open Paragraph* as this style's name, and then press Enter.

5. In turn, select each text paragraph of the FAQ (including the numbered paragraphs) and then select Open Paragraph from the Style list to apply that style.

6. Now go back and select the second and third paragraphs under the *How does it work?* heading and click the Numbering button on the Formatting toolbar's More Buttons palette to apply the numbered-list format "on top of" the Open Paragraph style. Click anywhere to deselect the paragraphs. The results are shown on the following page.

The Numbering button

Modifying styles

To modify one of Word's default styles or one of your own, you select some text that uses the style you want to change and make the formatting changes. Then to redefine the style to include the changes you have made, select the style from the Style drop-down list. When Word displays the Modify Style dialog box, you can select the Update option to modify the existing style or the Reapply option to reapply the style's existing formatting to the paragraph. Click the Automatically Update check box if you want the style to be updated whenever you make a change to text that uses the style. (To turn off the Automatically Update option, choose Style from the Format menu, click Modify, deselect the Automatically Update check box, click OK, and then click Close.) Click OK to implement your choices or click Cancel to close the dialog box, leaving your formatting changes intact without redefining the style. Once you redefine the style, all other occurrences of that style in your current document are updated as well.

Copying styles

Once you have created a style for use in one document, you don't have to recreate it for use in others—you can simply copy the style to a new document or template. Choose Style from the Format menu and click the Organizer button. The Styles tab shows a list of styles available in the current document. Select the style you want to copy and click Copy to copy the style to the document or template selected in the Styles Available In box.

Now check the layout of the pages:

1. Click the Print Preview button.

2. If the text does not fit on just the first page, click Close and choose Page Setup from the File menu.

3. On the Margins tab, set both Top and Bottom to *0.75"*, select Whole Document from the Apply To drop-down list, and then click OK.

4. Check the document in print preview to verify that all the text now fits on the first page, and then close print preview.

Creating Tables

Creating tables in Word is a simple process. You specify the number of columns and rows and then leave it to Word to figure out the initial settings. To demonstrate how easy the process is, let's add a table to the flyer:

1. Press Ctrl+End to move to the end of the flyer. Because you inserted a page break on page 65, your insertion point is now at the top of page 2.

2. Type *AIR POLLUTANT SOURCES* as the table's title, press Enter, type *In Millions of Metric Tons*, and press Enter twice.

3. Make the title bold and 14 points and make the subtitle bold and italic. Then center both lines.

4. Press Ctrl+End and then click the Insert Table button on the Standard toolbar's More Buttons palette to drop down a column/row grid.

5. Point to the top-left cell (the intersection of the first column and the first row), hold down the mouse button, and drag the pointer across four columns and down six rows. The grid expands as you drag beyond its bottom edge, and Word shows the size of the selection below the grid. When you release the mouse button, Word inserts this table structure:

The table has four equal columns that span the width of the document's text column. The insertion point is in the first cell. To make an entry in this cell, all you have to do is type, like this:

1. To enter column headings, type *Contributor* in the first cell and press Tab. The insertion point moves to the cell to the right. Type *Sulfur Dioxide* and press Tab to move to the next cell. Next type *Carbon Monoxide* and press Tab. Finally, type *Nitrogen Oxides* and press Tab. (Pressing Tab at the end of the first row moves the insertion point to the first cell in the second row.)

2. Type the entries below, pressing Tab to move from cell to cell. (You can also use the Arrow keys or mouse to move around.)

Transportation	*0.9*	*41.2*	*8.1*
Industrial Emissions	*3.4*	*4.7*	*0.6*
Fuel Combustion	*16.4*	*7.6*	*10.8*
Solid-Waste Burning	*- -*	*1.7*	*0.1*
Miscellaneous	*- -*	*6.0*	*0.2*

3. After typing *0.2*, press Tab. Word adds a blank row to the table.

4. Type *TOTAL* and press Tab.

Changing column width

You can adjust column widths in several ways. If the ruler is displayed, you can click an insertion point in the table and move the pointer onto the ruler and over the grid marker to the left of the column you want to adjust. When the pointer changes to a two-headed arrow, drag the marker to the right or left until the column is the width you want it. You can also move a column border by pointing to it and dragging the two-headed pointer to the left or right until the column is the desired width. You can choose Table Properties from the Table menu to enter exact width measurements in the Preferred Width box on the Column tab of the Table Properties dialog box.

The Tables And Borders
button

The AutoSum button

5. Click the Tables And Borders button on the Standard toolbar to display the Tables And Borders toolbar. Then double-click the toolbar's title bar to dock it below the Standard and Formatting toolbars. (If the Office Assistant appears with a tip, click its Cancel button.)

6. Click the AutoSum button on the Tables And Borders toolbar. Word looks at the values above the current cell and totals them.

7. Press Tab and click the AutoSum button again. Then repeat this step for the final column.

8. Click anywhere in the first row, choose Select and then Row from the Table menu, and click the Center and Bold buttons.

9. Press Home to move to the first cell, and choose Select and then Column from the Table menu to select the first column. Then click the Bold button twice. (The first click turns off bold in the first cell.)

10. To center the values, point to the left of the 0.9 entry in the Sulphur Dioxide column, drag through all the cells containing values to select them, and click the Center button.

11. Click an insertion point anywhere in the table and choose Select and then Table from the Table menu. Then change the font size to 10.

12. Press Home to see the results shown on the facing page.

Deleting rows/columns

To delete one or more rows or columns, select the rows or columns and choose Delete and then Rows or Columns from the Table menu. (If you choose Delete and then Cells, Word displays a dialog box in which you can specify what you want to delete.) To delete the entire table, choose Delete and then Table from the Table menu.

Moving tables

You can move a table anywhere in your document. First click an insertion point in the table to select it. When Word displays a framed four-headed arrow in the upper left corner of the table, point to it, hold down the left mouse button, and drag the table to the desired location. (As you drag, Word displays a dotted frame indicating where the table will appear when you release the mouse button.) To modify the way text flows around the table, verify that the table is still selected and then choose Table Properties from the Table menu. On the Table tab, select the desired alignment option and click OK. To fine-tune the table's placement, click the Positioning button on the Table tab and enter measurements such as the distance of the table from the surrounding text.

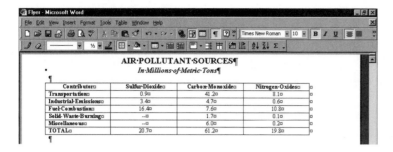

Before we wrap up this section, let's add gridlines to the cells and put a border around the whole table:

1. With the insertion point anywhere in the table, choose Select and then Table from the Table menu.

2. Click the arrow to the right of the Line Weight box on the Tables And Borders toolbar and select the 1½ pt single-line option from the drop-down list.

The Line Weight box

3. Click the arrow to the right of the Outside Border button on the Tables And Borders toolbar and then select All Borders from the palette of options. Press Home to see these results:

The Outside Border button

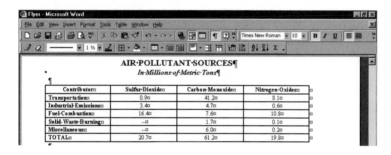

4. Check the flyer in print preview and then print it. The printout should look like the one shown at the start of this chapter.

5. Click Close, click the Tables And Borders button to turn off the Tables And Borders toolbar, and then save and close the Flyer document.

With the features you have explored in these first few chapters, you should have no trouble using Word to create useful documents for your work.

Other ways to create tables

To create a table with specific column widths, choose Insert and then Table from the Table menu and enter specifications in the Insert Table dialog box. You can also click the Draw Table button on the Tables And Borders toolbar to activate the drawing tool. Drag it diagonally to draw a box the size you want the table. Release the mouse button and draw horizontal and vertical lines to create rows and columns. Click the Eraser button and drag the Eraser tool over lines you want to erase. You can erase a cell's border to merge cells either vertically or horizontally. To turn off either the Draw Table or Erase tool, click the appropriate button to toggle it off. You can then edit and format the table.

4

Excel Basics

You build a simple worksheet as you learn how to enter, edit, and format information. Then you enter formulas that perform simple calculations, set up a calculation area, and experiment with more complex formulas. Finally, you print the worksheet.

The example for this chapter involves an income analysis for a company that sells a product or service. The sample worksheet can be adapted to any set of data that involves income, such as memberships or subscriptions.

Worksheet created and concepts covered:

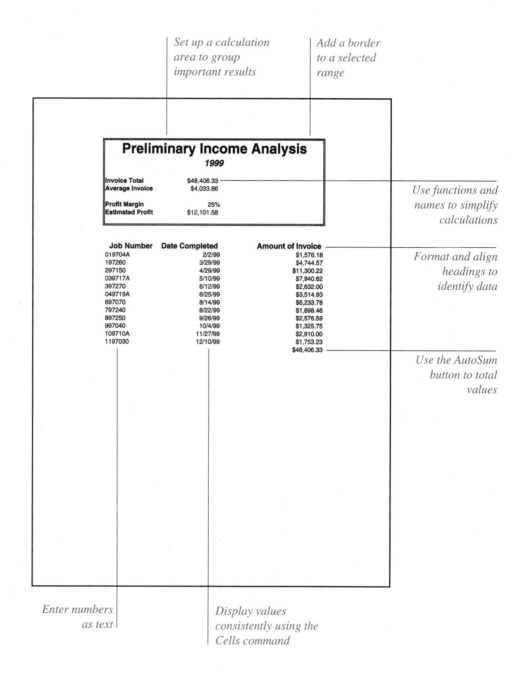

Set up a calculation area to group important results

Add a border to a selected range

Preliminary Income Analysis
1999

Invoice Total	$48,406.33
Average Invoice	$4,033.86
Profit Margin	25%
Estimated Profit	$12,101.58

Use functions and names to simplify calculations

Job Number	Date Completed	Amount of Invoice
019704A	2/2/99	$1,576.18
197260	3/29/99	$4,744.57
297150	4/29/99	$11,300.22
039717A	5/10/99	$7,940.62
397270	6/12/99	$2,632.00
049719A	6/25/99	$3,514.93
697070	8/14/99	$6,233.78
797240	8/22/99	$1,898.46
897250	9/26/99	$2,576.59
997040	10/4/99	$1,325.75
109710A	11/27/99	$2,910.00
1197030	12/10/99	$1,753.23
		$48,406.33

Format and align headings to identify data

Use the AutoSum button to total values

Enter numbers as text

Display values consistently using the Cells command

Microsoft Excel 2000, the Office spreadsheet component, is tailor-made for performing calculations on your data. If you want to maintain lists of information that you can summarize in reports, you should use Access rather than Excel. But if you need to analyze sales, calculate budgets, figure out loan or stock information, or compare two financial situations, Excel is the place to be. In this chapter, we give you an overview of Excel as you create a simple worksheet for Tip Top Roofing. Follow these steps:

Starting a new workbook

1. Choose Programs and then Microsoft Excel from the Windows Start menu.

2. If necessary, close the Office Assistant and maximize the window. Your screen now looks like this:

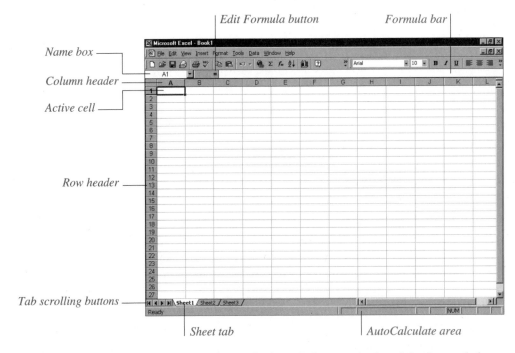

Taking up the majority of the screen is a blank *worksheet*, which as you can see, is laid out in a grid of *columns* and *rows* like the ledger paper used by accountants. There are 256 columns, lettered A through IV, and 65,536 rows, numbered 1 through 65536. (When you drag the horizontal or vertical scroll box, Excel displays the letter of the current column or the number of the current row, respectively.) The rectangle at the junction of each column and row is called a *cell*. To identify each of the 16 million plus cells on the worksheet, Excel uses an *address*, or *reference*, that consists of the letter at the top of the cell's column and the number at the left end of its row. For example, the reference of the cell in the top left corner of the worksheet is A1. The *active cell*—the one you're working with—is designated on the worksheet by a heavy border. Excel displays the reference of the active cell in the *name box* at the left end of the *formula bar*.

Cells

Cell references

The active cell

The name box and formula bar

The status bar at the bottom of the window includes an *Auto-Calculate area*, where Excel displays the sum of the entries in the selected cells. For more information about the AutoCalculate area, see the tip on page 92.

An Overview of Workbooks

The worksheet on the screen is just one *sheet* in the current file, which is called a *workbook*. By default, each new workbook contains three sheets. However, a single workbook file can store many sheets of different types including worksheets, chart sheets (where you can create graphs of your data), and macro sheets (which store automated ways of manipulating the data or the workbook). This workbook format allows you to store related data on separate sheets but in a single file.

Sheets

For each sheet in a workbook, Excel displays a *tab*, like a file folder tab, above the status bar at the bottom of the screen. These tabs are handy for moving from sheet to sheet. Let's see how to use them to move around the workbook:

Sheet tabs

1. Click the Sheet2 tab. Excel displays that sheet.

2. Next click the Sheet3 tab to display that sheet, and finish by selecting Sheet1.

Although you haven't entered any data in your workbook yet, let's go ahead and save it with the name *1999 Jobs*. As you'll see if you follow the steps on the next page, saving workbooks is just like saving other Office files.

The tab scrolling buttons

The number of sheets in the workbook may exceed the number of tabs Excel can display at the bottom of the worksheet window. You can use the tab scrolling buttons to the left of the Sheet1 tab to bring the tabs for hidden sheets into view without changing the active sheet. Click the First Sheet or Last Sheet button to display the tabs for those sheets and the Previous Sheet or Next Sheet button to move tabs into view one at a time.

Saving workbooks

1. Click the Save button. Because you have not yet assigned the workbook a name, Excel displays the Save As dialog box (see page 16).

2. Be sure the My Documents folder appears in the Save In box and then type *1999 Jobs* in the File Name edit box.

3. Leave the other settings in the dialog box as they are for now and click Save.

From now on, you can save this workbook by simply clicking the Save button.

Entering Data

Most worksheets consist of blocks of text and numbers in table format on which you can perform various calculations. To make your worksheets easy to read, you usually enter text as column and row headings that describe the associated entries. Let's try entering a few headings now:

Entering text

1. With cell A1 selected, type *Job Number*. As you type, the text appears in both the cell and the formula bar, and a blinking insertion point in the cell tells you where the next character you type will be inserted. A Cancel button (✕) and an Enter button (✓) appear between the formula bar and the name box. Meanwhile, the indicator in the status bar changes from Ready to Enter because the text you have typed will not be recorded in cell A1 until you "enter" it.

When you need more sheets

If you need to add sheets to a workbook, simply choose Worksheet from the Insert menu. Excel inserts a new sheet to the left of the active sheet and makes the new sheet active. If you frequently create workbooks with more than three sheets, you can change this default number by choosing Options from the Tools menu and increasing the Sheets In New Workbook setting on the General tab.

2. Click the Enter button to complete the entry. Excel enters the Job Number heading in cell A1, and the indicator changes to Ready. The entry is left-aligned in its cell. (Unless you tell Excel to do otherwise, it always left-aligns text.)

3. Click cell B1 to select it. The reference displayed in the name box changes from A1 to B1.

4. Type *Date Completed*, but instead of clicking the Enter button to enter the heading in the cell, press the Tab key. Excel completes the entry in cell B1 and selects cell C1.

5. Type *Amount of Invoice* and click the Enter button. Here's how the newly entered row of headings looks in the worksheet:

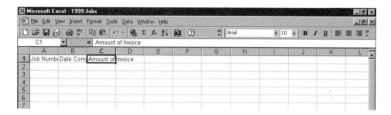

Notice that the headings are too long to fit in their cells. The Job Number and Date Completed headings are still intact, however. (If you're skeptical, click either cell and look at the formula bar.) After you have entered more information, you'll adjust the column widths to accommodate long entries (see page 90).

As you'll see in the next section, you can complete entries in several different ways, which we've summarized here:

To do this...	Use this...
Stay in the same cell	Enter button
Move down	Enter key or Down Arrow
Move up	Shift+Enter or Up Arrow
Move right	Tab key or Right Arrow
Move left	Shift+Tab or Left Arrow

Entering numeric values is just as easy as entering text. Follow these steps to enter the amount of each completed roofing job in column C:

1. Click cell C2 to select the first cell in the Amount of Invoice column and type *1576.18*. Press Enter to complete the entry, which Excel right-aligns in its cell.

2. Enter the amounts shown below and at the top of the next page in the indicated cells, pressing Enter after each one:

C3   *4744.57*
C4   *11300.22*
C5   *7940.62*
C6   *2632.00*

Correcting mistakes

If you make a mistake, you can click the cell containing the error and simply type the new entry. If you want to correct part of an entry, click its cell and press F2, or double-click the cell so that you can edit the entry directly in the cell. You can then press Home or End to move the insertion point to the beginning or end of the entry and press Right Arrow or Left Arrow to move the insertion point forward or backward one character. Press Backspace to delete the character to the left of the insertion point or Delete to erase the character to the right of the insertion point. Then type the correction and click the Enter button.

C7	35149.30
C8	6233.78
C9	1898.46
C10	2576.59
C11	1325.75
C12	2910.00
C13	1753.23

Don't worry for now that Excel does not display these values exactly as you entered them.

Now you're ready to enter the job numbers in column A. Normally, you want Excel to treat ID numbers as text rather than as values on which you might want to perform calculations. If the "number" includes not only the digits 0 through 9 but also letters and other characters (such as hyphens), Excel recognizes it as text. However, if the number consists of only digits and you want Excel to treat it as text, you have to explicitly tell Excel to do so. Let's see how Excel treats two types of job numbers:

Long numeric values

Excel allows a long text entry to overflow into an adjacent empty cell and truncates the entry only if the adjacent cell also contains an entry. However, Excel treats a long numeric value differently. By default, Excel displays values in scientific notation, and values with many decimal places might be rounded. For example, if you enter 12345678912345 in a standard width cell (which holds 8.43 characters), Excel displays 1.23457E+13 (or 1.23457 times 10 to the 13th power). And if you enter 123456.789 in a standard width cell, Excel displays 123456.8. In the latter case, Excel leaves the underlying value unchanged, and you can widen the column to display the value in the format in which you entered it. (Adjusting the width of columns is discussed on page 90.) Excel tries to automate the column-adjustment process by estimating the width needed for long numeric values so that they are fully displayed. If the program can't make the necessary adjustment, it displays pound signs (#) instead of the value you entered to indicate that the value is too large to display in the cell.

1. Enter these job numbers in the indicated cells:

A2	019704A
A3	0197260
A4	0297150
A5	039717A
A6	0397270
A7	049719A
A8	0697070
A9	0797240
A10	0897250
A11	0997040
A12	109710A
A13	1197030

You'll notice that Excel treats the entries that end with *A* as text and left-aligns them. However, Excel treats the entries that end with *0* as numeric values, dropping the leading 0 and right-aligning them. We show you how to tell Excel to treat all the entries as text on page 90.

Entering Dates and Times

For a date or time to be displayed correctly, you must enter it in a format that Excel recognizes as a date or time. Excel then displays the entry as you want it but stores it as a value so that you can perform date and time arithmetic (see the tip below). Let's see how Excel handles different date formats:

1. Enter these dates in the indicated cells:

B2	*Feb 2, 1999*
B3	*3/29/99*
B4	*Apr 29, 99*
B5	*5/10/99*
B6	*12-June-99*
B7	*6/25/99*
B8	*aug 14, 99*
B9	*8/22/99*
B10	*26-Sep-99*
B11	*10-4-99*
B12	*11/27/99*
B13	*December 10, 1999*

Again, don't worry if Excel displays the dates differently from the way you enter them. Later, you'll come back and make sure all the dates appear in the same format. As you can see below, you've now completed all the columns of this simple worksheet:

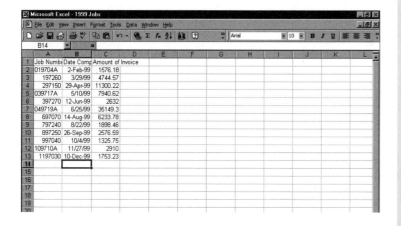

Date and time arithmetic

Each date you enter is internally recorded by Excel as a value that represents the number of days elapsed between that date and the base date of January 1, 1900, which is assigned the value 1. As a result, you can perform arithmetic with dates—for example, you can have Excel determine whether a payment is past due. Similarly, when you enter a time, it is internally recorded as a decimal value that represents the portion of the day that has elapsed between that time and the base time of 12:00 midnight.

Selecting Ranges

Ranges ➝

Range references ➝

In Chapter 1, we covered some techniques for selecting text. Here, you'll select blocks of cells, called *ranges*. Any rectangular block is a range, whether it includes two cells, an entire row or column, or the entire worksheet. *Range references* consist of the address of the cell in the top left corner of the rectangular block and the address of the cell in the bottom right corner, separated by a colon. For example, A1:B2 consists of cells A1, A2, B1, and B2. Follow these steps to select various ranges:

Selecting with the mouse ➝

1. Point to cell A1, hold down the left mouse button, and drag to cell C13. As you drag, the reference in the name box indicates the number of rows and columns in the selected range.

2. Release the mouse button when A1:C13 is highlighted. As you can see here, cell A1 (where you started the selection) is white, indicating that it is the active cell in the range:

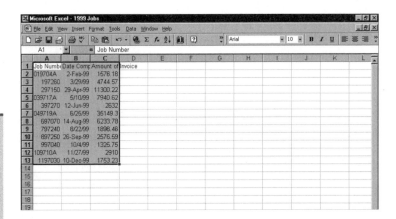

Other ways of selecting

To select a range with the keyboard, select the first cell, hold down the Shift key, and press the Arrow keys. To select all the cells in a column, click the column header (the gray box containing the column's letter). Similarly, select all the cells in a row by clicking the row header (the gray box containing the row's number). You can select a range that consists of more than one block of cells by selecting the first range, holding down the Ctrl key, selecting the next range, and so on.

3. Press Home to deselect the range and activate cell A1.

Editing Entries

In this section, we briefly cover some simple ways of revising worksheets. Up to now you have been working with one worksheet. In one of the following examples, you will copy data from one worksheet to another in the same workbook. But first let's see how to change individual entries.

Glancing at the Amount of Invoice column in 1999 Jobs, suppose you notice that the amount in cell C7 should be 3514.93, not 35149.3. To correct the entry without having to retype the whole thing, follow these steps:

1. Double-click cell C7 to select the cell and position an insertion point in the current entry.

Editing directly in a cell

2. Point between the 4 and 9 in the cell and click the left mouse button to reposition the insertion point. Then type a period.

3. Press the Right Arrow key once and press the Delete key to delete the second period.

4. Press Enter to confirm the corrected entry.

Copying and Moving Entries

You can copy an entry or group of entries anywhere within the same worksheet or in a different worksheet using the Copy and Paste buttons on the Standard toolbar or the Copy and Paste commands on the Edit menu. Similarly, moving entries is a simple cut-and-paste operation. Try this:

1. Select A1:C13 and click the Copy button.

2. Click the Sheet2 tab at the bottom of the worksheet window to display Sheet2, and with cell A1 selected, click the Paste button. Excel pastes in a copy of the range from Sheet1. (Notice that you don't have to select the entire paste area.)

You can also use drag-and-drop editing to copy and paste cells. Follow these steps:

1. With A1:C13 selected in Sheet2, move the pointer to the right border of the selected range.

2. Hold down the left mouse button and the Ctrl key, and drag the outline of the selection over the range D1:F13. As you drag, a small box displays the reference of the range that the selection will be copied into when you release the mouse button.

Checking spelling

If your worksheets will be seen by other people, you will probably want to spell-check them. You can easily accomplish this task by clicking the Spelling button on the Standard toolbar or choosing Spelling from the Tools menu. Excel then performs a spelling check similar to the one Word performs (see page 48). If you don't want to spell-check the entire worksheet, select the cells you want to check and then click the Spelling button.

3. Release the Ctrl key and the mouse button. Excel copies the selected cells into the designated area.

The result of dragging a copy is similar to using the Copy and Paste buttons or the equivalent commands, except that Excel doesn't place a copy of the selected range on the Clipboard.

You can also drag a selection to move it. Here's how:

Moving by dragging

1. With D1:F13 selected, point to the selection's right border.

2. Hold down the left mouse button and drag the outline of the selection over the range F1:H13. (Again, Excel displays the range reference in a box adjacent to the mouse pointer.)

3. Release the mouse button. Excel moves the entries to their new location, like this:

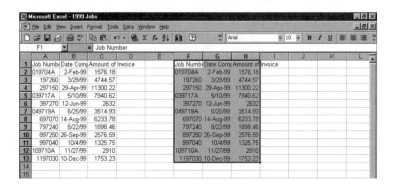

Dragging and Dropping Entries Between Worksheets

As you've already seen, you can copy and move entries between worksheets using the Copy, Cut, and Paste buttons (or the Copy, Cut, and Paste commands). You can also use drag-and-drop editing to copy and move entries between worksheets. Follow these steps:

1. With F1:H13 selected in Sheet2, point to the bottom border of the selection.

2. Hold down the Alt key and the left mouse button and drag the outline of the selection to the Sheet3 tab. Sheet3 opens.

3. While still holding down the Alt key and the left mouse button, drag the outline of the selection over the range A1:C13 and then release the Alt key and the mouse button. Now Sheet1, Sheet2, and Sheet3 all contain the same data.

To copy rather than move entries between worksheets using drag-and-drop editing, hold down Ctrl+Alt and the left mouse button.

Clearing Cells

Clearing cells is different from cutting entries. Cutting entries assumes you want to move the entries somewhere else, whereas clearing cells simply erases the entries. Follow these steps:

1. Click the column A header on Sheet3—the gray box containing the letter *A*—to select the entire column, and then choose Clear from the Edit menu. Excel displays a submenu something like this one:

The All option clears both the formats and contents of the selected cells. Formats clears only formats, and Contents clears only contents. Comments clears any comments attached to the selected cells (see the adjacent tip), leaving the formats and contents intact.

2. Choose All. The entries in the column disappear.

3. Now select B1:C13 and clear the cells by pressing the Delete key. (When you press Delete, Excel leaves any formats and comments intact.)

Attaching comments to cells

You might want to attach a comment to a cell for various reasons (to explain a formula or remind yourself to check an assumption, for example). Simply select the cell, choose Comment from the expanded Insert menu, and type the comment in the text box that appears. (The comment is "signed" with the name entered when Excel was installed on your computer. You can edit or delete this signature.) Click anywhere outside the cell and text box to enter the comment. Excel then places a red marker in the top right corner of each cell with a comment attached. To see a comment, just point to the red marker. To edit or delete a comment, simply right-click the cell and choose either Edit Comment or Delete Comment from the shortcut menu. (You can also remove comments attached to a selected cell by choosing Clear and then Comments from the Edit menu.)

4. Next click the Sheet2 tab, select A1:C13 and right-click the selection to display its shortcut menu. Choose Clear Contents to clear the selected cells.

5. Move to Sheet1 by clicking its tab.

Inserting and Deleting Columns

It is a rare person who can create a worksheet from scratch without ever having to tinker with its design—moving this block of data, changing that heading, or adding or deleting a column here and there. In this section, we'll show you how to insert and delete columns. Follow these steps:

Selecting multiple columns

1. Point to the column C header, hold down the left mouse button, and drag across the column D header to select the two columns.

2. Choose Columns from the Insert menu. Excel inserts two blank columns in front of the Amount of Invoice column, one for each column in the selection.

Inserting rows works the same way as inserting columns. You simply select the row headers—the boxes containing the row numbers—above which you want to insert the rows and choose Rows from the Insert menu (see the adjacent tip).

Now let's see how to delete columns:

Inserting and deleting cells

Rather than insert an entire row or column, you can insert a specified number of cells. Simply select a cell or range of cells and then choose Cells from the Insert menu. When the Insert dialog box appears, select the Shift Cells Right or Shift Cells Down option and click OK. Excel then inserts the cell(s), shifting the selected cell(s) to the right or down. (You can also insert an entire row above the selection or an entire column to the left of the selection using the last two options in the Insert dialog box.) Deleting cells is similar to inserting them except that you choose the Delete command from the Edit menu and make selections in the Delete dialog box.

1. Click the header for column D and choose Delete from the Edit menu. Excel deletes the column and moves the Amount of Invoice column over to take its place, as you can see here:

You can leave the empty column C where it is for now—you'll use it later.

Formatting Entries

Excel offers a variety of formatting options that let you empha-size parts of a worksheet and display data in different ways. For example, you can use a different font or style to distinguish different categories of information in the worksheet. Try this:

1. Select A1:D1, the range that contains the headings.

2. Click the Bold button and then change the font size to 12.

   As you know, by default Excel left-aligns text and right-aligns numeric values. You can override the default alignment by using the alignment buttons. Here's how:

1. With A1:D1 still selected, click the Align Right and Align Left buttons, noting their effects.

2. When you're ready, click the Center button, which is a typical choice for headings.

Changing the Display of Numbers

Earlier, you entered dates in column B in a variety of formats. Now we'll show you how to change the date format to reflect the needs of the worksheet. Follow these steps:

1. Select the range B2:B13, which contains the dates.

2. Choose Cells from the Format menu to display this dialog box:

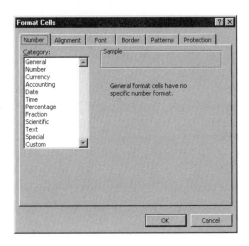

AutoFormats

An autoformat is a predefined combination of formatting that works well with certain kinds of worksheets. To apply an auto-format to a worksheet, first select the range of cells you want to for-mat and choose the AutoFormat command from the Format menu. When the AutoFormat dialog box appears, select an option from the list and then click OK. You can also customize an autoformat by clicking the Options button in the AutoFormat dialog box and selecting or deselecting the op-tions in the Formats To Apply section. It's worth setting up a worksheet and experimenting with autoformats so that you know what is available and which kinds of worksheets can take advantage of this one-stop formatting feature.

3. On the Number tab, select Date in the Category list, select 3/14/98 (or its equivalent) in the Type list, and click OK.

Displaying numbers as text → 4. Now format the entries in column A so that they look consistent. Select A2:A13, choose Cells from the Format menu, select the Text category, and click OK. (You can also tell Excel to treat an individual entry as text by beginning the entry with an apostrophe.)

Displaying numbers as currency → 5. To display the column D entries as currency, select D2:D13, right-click the selection, and then choose Format Cells from the shortcut menu to display the Format Cells dialog box. Select Currency in the Category list and accept the default settings by clicking OK. (Excel automatically adjusts the width of the column to accommodate the new formatting.)

Changing Column Widths

As a finishing touch for this worksheet, let's adjust the widths of columns A, B, and D so that all the headings are visible and fit neatly in their cells:

1. Move the mouse pointer to the dividing line between the headers of columns A and B. The pointer changes to a vertical bar with two opposing arrows.

2. Hold down the left mouse button and drag to the right until column A is wide enough to display the Job Number heading. (As you drag, the width is displayed in a box above the pointer.) Release the mouse button when you think that the heading will fit.

3. Now change the width of column B using the same method you used to widen column A.

Now you'll widen column D using a different method:

1. Select D1 and choose Column and then Width from the Format menu. Excel displays this Column Width dialog box:

Column width shortcuts

To adjust the width of a column to fit its longest entry, select the column and choose Column and then AutoFit Selection from the Format menu, or double-click the column header's right border. To change the standard width, choose Column and then Standard Width from the Format menu, type a new value in the Standard Column Width edit box, and click OK. (Columns whose widths you have already adjusted retain their custom widths, but all the other columns are now the new standard width.)

2. Type *20* and press Enter. Here are the results:

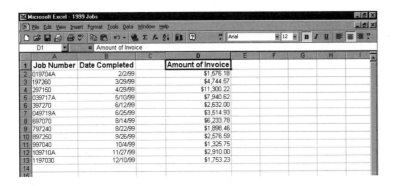

3. Save the worksheet.

You can adjust the height of rows the same way you adjust the width of columns. Simply drag the bottom border of the row header up or down or choose Row and then Height from the Format menu to make the row shorter or taller.

Simple Calculations

The whole purpose of building worksheets is to have Excel perform calculations for you. Excel has many powerful functions that are a sort of shorthand for various mathematical, logical, statistical, and financial calculations. However, the majority of worksheets involve simple arithmetic.

Doing Arithmetic

In Excel, you begin a *formula* (Excel's term for an *equation*) with an equal sign (=). In the simplest formulas, the equal sign is followed by a set of values separated by +, -, *, or /, such as =5+3+2. If you enter this formula in any blank cell in the worksheet, Excel displays the result 10.

Let's experiment with a few formulas. You'll start by inserting a couple of blank rows:

1. Select the headers for rows 1 and 2 to select the two rows.

2. Choose Rows from the Insert menu. Excel inserts two blank rows above the table, moving the table down so that it begins in row 3.

AutoComplete

If you have already typed a text entry, you don't have to type it again if you need to enter it a second time. When you type the first character or two of an entry you have already typed in the same column, Excel's AutoComplete feature finishes the entry for you. For example, if your entry in cell A1 is *North*, the instant you type *N* in cell A2, Excel enters *orth*. (You can either enter Excel's suggestion in the cell or continue typing your own entry.) You can also right-click the next cell in a column of text entries and choose Pick From List from the shortcut menu to display a drop-down list of the entries you've already typed. You can then simply select the next entry from the list rather than typing it.

Now you're ready to construct a formula in cell A1, using some of the values in the Amount of Invoice column. You tell Excel to use a value simply by clicking the cell that contains it. Follow these steps:

Constructing a formula

1. Click cell A1 and type an equal sign followed by an opening parenthesis.

2. Click cell D4. Excel inserts the reference D4 in cell A1 and the formula bar.

3. Type a plus sign and click cell D5. Excel adds the reference D5 to the formula.

4. Continue to build the formula by typing plus signs and clicking cells D6, D7, and D8.

5. Type a closing parenthesis, type / (the division operator), and then type 5. The formula now looks like this:

This formula tells Excel to first add the amounts in cells D4, D5, D6, D7, and D8 and then divide the result by 5, to obtain the average of the five amounts.

6. Click the Enter button. Excel displays the result of the formula, $5638.72, in cell A1.

You can use this technique to create any simple formula. Start by typing an equal sign, then enter a value or click the cell that contains the value, type the appropriate arithmetic operator, enter the next value, and so on. Unless you tell Excel to do otherwise, the program performs multiplication and division before addition and subtraction. If you need parts of the formula to be carried out in a different order, use parentheses as you did in this example to override the default order.

Displaying formulas

By default, Excel displays the results of formulas in cells, not their underlying formulas. To see the actual underlying formulas in the worksheet, first choose Options from the Tools menu, display the View options, select Formulas in the Window Options section, and then click OK. Excel widens the cells so that you can see the formulas. Deselect the Formulas option to redisplay the results.

Totaling Columns of Values

Although this method of creating a formula is simple enough, it would be tedious to have to type and click to add a long series of values. Fortunately, Excel automates the addition process with a very useful button: the AutoSum button.

Using the AutoSum Button

The AutoSum button will probably become one of your most often-used Excel buttons. In fact, using this button is so easy that we'll just show you what to do:

The AutoSum button

1. Click cell D16 and then click the AutoSum button. Excel looks first above and then to the left of the active cell for an adjacent range of values to total. Excel assumes that you want to total the values above D16 and enters a SUM function in cell D16 and in the formula bar. Your worksheet looks as shown here:

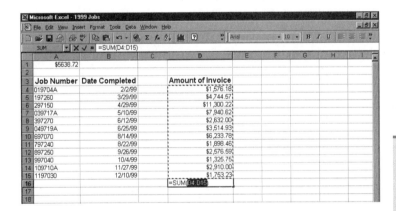

2. Click the Enter button to enter the formula in cell D16. Excel displays $48,406.33—the sum of the values in D4:D15.

That was easy. The AutoSum button serves you well whenever you want a total to appear at the bottom of a column or to the right of a row of values. But what if you want the total to appear elsewhere on the worksheet? Knowing how to create SUM functions from scratch gives you more flexibility.

Using the SUM Function

Let's go back and dissect the SUM function that Excel inserted in cell D16 when you clicked the AutoSum button, so that you can examine the function's components.

AutoCalculate

You can use the AutoCalculate area at the right end of the status bar to instantly see the results of certain functions. Right-click the AutoCalculate area to display a menu of functions, and choose the function you want. (The default function is SUM.) Next select a range of values on your worksheet. The result of the function that you selected appears instantly in the AutoCalculate area. For example, if you choose the AVERAGE function and then select a range of values, the average of the values appears in the AutoCalculate area.

With cell D16 selected, you can see the following entry in the formula bar:

=SUM(D4:D15)

Like all formulas, the SUM function begins with an equal sign (=). Next comes the function name in capital letters, followed by a set of parentheses enclosing the reference to the range containing the amounts you want to total. This reference is the SUM function's *argument*. An argument answers questions such as "What?" or "How?" and gives Excel the additional information it needs to perform the function. In the case of SUM, Excel needs only one piece of information—the references of the cells you want to total. As you'll see later, Excel might need several pieces of information to carry out other functions, and you enter an argument for each piece.

Arguments

Creating a SUM function from scratch is not particularly difficult. For practice, follow these steps:

Entering a SUM function from scratch

1. Press Ctrl+Home to move to cell A1 and type this:

   =SUM(

2. Select D4:D15 on the worksheet in the usual way. Excel inserts the reference D4:D15 after the opening parenthesis.

3. Type a closing parenthesis and click the Enter button. Excel displays in cell A1 the total of the values in the Amount of Invoice column—$48,406.33.

Referencing Formula Cells in Other Formulas

After you create a formula in one cell, you can use its result in other formulas simply by referencing its cell. Try this:

1. Select cell B1 and type an equal sign.

2. Click cell A1, which contains the SUM function you just entered, type / (the division operator), and then type *12*.

3. Click the Enter button. Excel displays the result—the average of the invoice amounts—in cell B1.

Entering function names

When you type a function name, such as SUM, in the formula bar, you don't have to type it in capital letters. Excel capitalizes the function name for you when you complete the entry. If Excel does not respond in this way, you have probably entered the function name incorrectly.

4. Press the Delete key to erase both the experimental formula and its result from cell B1.

Naming Cells and Ranges

Many of the calculations that you might want to perform on this worksheet will use the total you have calculated in cell A1. You could include a copy of the SUM function now in cell A1 in these other calculations, or you could simply reference cell A1. The latter method seems quick and simple, but what if you subsequently move the formula in A1 to another location? Excel gives you a way to reference this formula no matter where on the worksheet you move it. You can assign a name to the contents of cell A1 and then use the name in any calculations that involve the total.

You can assign a name to cell A1 by following these steps:

1. Select cell A1 and click the name box at the left end of the formula bar.

2. Type *Total* and press Enter. The name box now refers to the cell by the name you just entered, instead of by the reference A1. You can use either designation in formulas.

To see how Excel uses assigned names, try this:

1. Click cell D16, which currently contains the SUM function you inserted earlier in the chapter.

2. Type *=Total* and click the Enter button. The worksheet does not appear to change, but now instead of two SUM functions, the worksheet contains only one. You have told Excel to assign the value of the cell named *Total*, which contains the SUM function, to cell D16.

You can also assign names to ranges. Let's use a different method to assign the name *Amount* to the cells containing amounts in column D:

1. Select D4:D15 and choose Name and then Define from the Insert menu. Excel displays the dialog box shown at the top of the next page.

Name conventions

Certain rules apply when you name cells or ranges. Names can have up to 255 characters and can include capital letters. Although you can use a number within the name, you must start the name with a letter or an underscore. Spaces are not allowed within the name; instead you should use underscore characters to represent spaces. For example, you cannot use 1999 or Totals 1999, but you can use Totals_1999. Cell references cannot be used as names, and you also cannot have two names that are distinguished only by their capitalization.

Notice that the Names In Workbook list box contains Total, the name you assigned to cell A1 earlier. The range reference Sheet1!$D$4:$D$15 is displayed in the Refers To edit box. This absolute reference points to the selected range on Sheet1 of the current workbook. (For an explanation of absolute references, see page 112.)

2. Replace *Amount_of_Invoice*, the name Excel suggests in the Names In Workbook edit box, with *Amount* and click OK.

Now let's replace the range reference in the SUM function in cell A1 with the new range name:

1. Click A1 to select it and display its contents in the formula bar.

2. Drag through the D4:D15 reference in the formula bar to highlight it.

Pasting a name

3. Choose Name and then Paste from the Insert menu to display this dialog box:

4. Click Amount and then click OK. Excel replaces the range reference with the assigned name, and the formula now reads *=SUM(Amount)*.

5. Click the Enter button to redisplay the results of the SUM function in A1.

Efficient Data Display

When you create a worksheet, you are interested not so much in the individual pieces of information as in the results of the calculations you perform on the pieces. So before we discuss other calculations, let's look at ways to format worksheet information to make the results of your calculations stand out from your data. It's a good idea to design worksheets so that the results are easily accessible and in a predictable location. For these reasons, you will probably want to leave room in the top left corner of your worksheets for a calculation area.

Let's create an area at the top of Sheet1 of the 1999 Jobs workbook for a title and a set of calculations. Start by freeing up some space at the top of the worksheet:

1. Select A1:D16.

2. If necessary, point to the Formatting toolbar's move handle and then drag it to the right until the Cut button joins the Copy and Paste buttons on the Standard toolbar. Then click the Cut button.

3. Select A10 and click the Paste button to move the selection to A10:D25.

Now let's enter a title for the worksheet:

1. In cell A1, type *Preliminary Income Analysis* and click the Enter button.

2. Format the title by clicking the Bold button on the Formatting toolbar. Then click 10 in the Font Size box, type *22*, and press Enter. The height of row 1 increases to accommodate the larger font.

3. In cell A2, type *1999* and click the Enter button.

4. Format the subtitle by pressing Ctrl+B and then Ctrl+I—the keyboard shortcuts for bold and italic—and by selecting 14 from the Font Size list.

Calculation area advantages

Creating a calculation area at the top of your worksheet is a good habit to get into and offers the following advantages:

- You don't have to scroll around looking for the totals and other results.

- You can print just the first page of a worksheet to get a report of the most pertinent information.

- You can easily jump to the calculation area from anywhere on the worksheet by pressing Ctrl+Home to move to cell A1.

The Merge And Center button

5. To center the title above the calculation area, select A1:D1 and click the Merge And Center button on the Formatting toolbar's More Buttons palette. Excel centers the title over the selected area and merges the four cells, but the title is still stored in cell A1.

6. Repeat step 5 for the subtitle, using the range A2:D2.

Next you'll set off the calculation area. With Excel, you can get really fancy, using borders and color to draw attention to calculation results. Try the following:

Adding a border

1. Select A1:D9 and choose Cells from the Format menu.

2. In the Format Cells dialog box, click the Border tab.

3. In the Line section, select the last option in the second column of the Style box and select Outline in the Presets section.

Adding shading

4. Click the Patterns tab, select a light color from the palette, and click OK. (We left our calculation area white so that our graphics will be more legible.) Excel surrounds the calculation area with a border and fills it with the color you selected.

Now that you've created a calculation area, let's move the calculation in cell A10. Follow these steps:

1. Select cell A4, type *Invoice Total*, and press Enter.

Moving formulas

2. Select cell A10 and use the Cut and Paste buttons to move the formula to cell B4. (We'll show you how to quickly restore the color to cell B4 in a moment.)

Now let's add another touch:

Preformatting cells

1. Select A4:A9 and click the Bold button.

Why did we tell you to select the empty cells below Invoice Total before applying the bold format? Try this:

2. Select cell A5, type *Average Invoice*, and click the Enter button. The new heading is bold because you already applied the bold format to cell A5.

3. If necessary, choose Column and then AutoFit Selection from the Format menu to widen column A so that the headings fit within the column. (From now on, adjust the column width as necessary to see your work.)

You can also save time by applying number formats to empty cells. Here's how:

1. Select B4:B9 and choose Cells from the Format menu.

2. Click the Number tab, select Currency in the Category list, and select the third option in the Negative Numbers list. Be sure the Decimal Places setting is 2 and then click OK. Excel formats the selected cells with a dollar sign, a comma, and two decimal places.

3. To see the Currency format for negative values, select cell B5, type -*1234*, and click the Enter button. Excel displays the negative value in parentheses, aligning the value itself with the positive value above it.

4. To restore the background color to cell B4, make sure cell B5 is selected, click the Format Painter button on the Standard toolbar, and then click cell B4 to duplicate the formatting of B5 in B4. Here are the results:

The Format Painter button

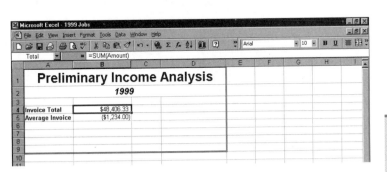

More Calculations

Now let's perform some more calculations on the data in 1999 Jobs, starting with the average invoice.

Averaging Values

To find the average amount for the invoices you've entered in this worksheet, you can use Excel's AVERAGE function.

Underlying vs. displayed

After you apply a format, the value displayed in the cell might look different from the value seen in the formula bar. For example, 345.6789 is displayed in its cell as $345.68 after you apply the Currency format. When performing calculations, Excel uses the value in the formula bar, not the displayed value.

You'll use the Paste Function button on the Standard toolbar to avoid errors and to make sure you include all the arguments Excel needs for the function. Here are the steps:

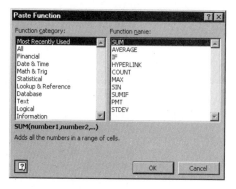

The Paste Function button

1. Select cell B5, press Delete, and click the Paste Function button. Excel displays this Paste Function dialog box:

(If necessary, click the Office Assistant's No button to decline its offer of help.)

2. Select AVERAGE in the Function Name list and click OK. Excel displays this dialog box:

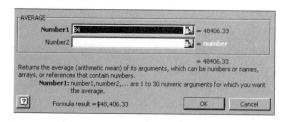

Conditional formatting

To monitor the activity of a worksheet, you can use conditional formatting, which works by highlighting a cell or cells that meet certain criteria. For example, you can change the color of the value in a particular cell to magenta when it falls between 100,000 and 200,000. To apply this type of formatting, first select the cell or cells and choose Conditional Formatting from the Format menu. In the Conditional Formatting dialog box, select a condition from the second drop-down list and enter the conditional parameters in the appropriate edit boxes. For example, select Between from the drop-down list and enter *100,000* and *200,000* in the adjacent edit box. Finally, click the Format button, select the formatting you want to use to highlight the cell (such as a color), and click OK twice. When the value in the selected cell meets the condition(s) you've set, Excel highlights the cell with the formatting you've selected. To delete conditional formatting from a cell, select the cell and choose Conditional Formatting from the Format menu. Click the Delete button, select the condition you want to delete, and then click OK twice.

The dialog box contains a definition of the function and its arguments. In the Number1 edit box, you can enter a number, cell reference, name, formula, or another function.

3. Click the button with the red arrow at the right end of the Number1 edit box to shrink the dialog box so that you can see more of the worksheet. Then select D13:D24 in the worksheet to add its reference to the formula.

4. Click the button with the red arrow again to enlarge the dialog box, which now looks like this:

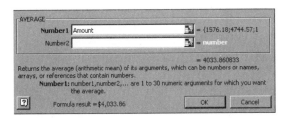

5. Click OK to enter the formula in cell B5 and press Ctrl+Home to see the results. Excel displays $4,033.86 in cell B5.

Calculating with Names

The last calculation you'll make with this set of data involves the Invoice Total value from cell B4. As a gross indicator of how well Tip Top Roofing fared in 1999, let's calculate the estimated profit:

1. In cell A7, type *Profit Margin* and press Tab.

2. Type *20%* and click the Enter button.

3. With cell B7 still active, click the name box. Assign the name *Profit_Margin* to the cell, and then press Enter.

Now for the formula that will calculate the profit:

1. Select cell A8, type *Estimated Profit* and press Tab.

2. With cell B8 selected, type the formula *=total*profit_margin* and press Enter. Excel multiplies the value in the cell named Total (B4) by the value in the cell named Profit_Margin (B7) and then displays the result, $9,681.27, in cell B8. (Notice

A function for every task

Excel provides many functions for common business and financial tasks—some of them quite complex. To obtain more information about a function, choose Microsoft Excel Help from the Help menu and display the Index tab. Type *worksheet functions* in the Type Keywords edit box and click Search to display a list of related topics. Scroll the list of topics and then click a specific function. Excel displays a description of the function, its syntax, and any other pertinent information.

that Excel displays the result of the formula in the Currency format because you preformatted the cell.)

3. Now select cell B7, type *25%*, and click the Enter button. Instantly, the value in cell B8 changes to reflect the new profit margin, as shown here:

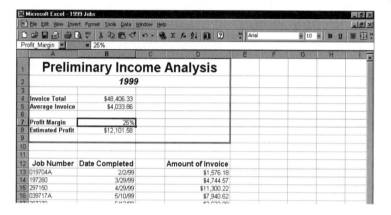

Adding headers/footers
By default, when Excel prints a worksheet, it does not print any header or footer text. If you want to add a header or footer, click the Setup button on the Print Preview toolbar to display the Page Setup dialog box, or choose Page Setup from the File menu. Next click the Header/ Footer tab and make your selection from the Header or Footer drop-down list. If none of these options meets your needs, click the Custom Header or Custom Footer button, and then enter text in the appropriate boxes. To format the text, select it, click the Font button (the A) in the middle of the dialog box, and then make your selections in the Font dialog box. Click the other buttons in the middle of the Header or Footer dialog box to add a page number, date, time, filename, or tab name to your worksheet.

If a hundred calculations throughout the worksheet referenced the cell named Profit_Margin, Excel would adjust all their results to reflect this one change.

Printing Worksheets

Usually, you'll want to preview worksheets before you print them to make sure that single-page documents fit neatly on the page and that multi-page documents break in logical places. Follow these steps to preview the worksheet:

1. Click the Print Preview button on the Standard toolbar. The Print Preview window opens, with a miniature version of the printed worksheet displayed.

2. To examine part of the page in more detail, move the pointer over that part, and when the pointer changes to a magnifying glass, click the mouse button. Excel zooms in on that portion of the page. Click again to zoom out.

Now let's adjust the data's position on the page:

1. Click the Setup button to display the Page Setup dialog box, and then click the Margins tab to display these options:

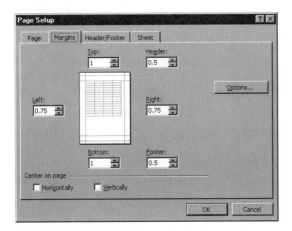

2. In the Center On Page section, click Horizontally to center the worksheet horizontally on the page. The worksheet diagram shows you the effects of your changes.

3. Click OK to enter your selection. Here's the finished product:

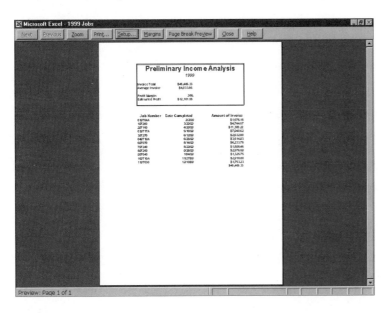

4. When you're ready, click the Print button on the Print Preview toolbar and then click OK in the Print dialog box to print the worksheet.

5. Save the workbook and quit Excel.

5 More About Excel

You work with multiple workbooks and explore more advanced features such as IF functions and consolidating data. You also set up a worksheet with links to data on a different worksheet. Finally, you create, format, and print a graph.

As with Chapter 4, the worksheets you create in this chapter can also be applied to other income sources, including interest and dividend payments.

Worksheets created and concepts covered:

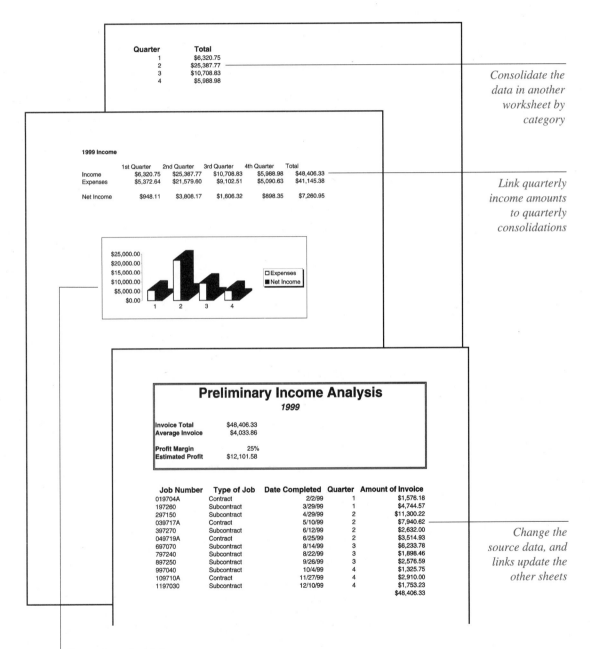

Quarter	Total
1	$6,320.75
2	$25,387.77
3	$10,708.83
4	$5,988.98

Consolidate the data in another worksheet by category

1999 Income

	1st Quarter	2nd Quarter	3rd Quarter	4th Quarter	Total
Income	$6,320.75	$25,387.77	$10,708.83	$5,988.98	$48,406.33
Expenses	$5,372.64	$21,579.60	$9,102.51	$5,090.63	$41,145.38
Net Income	$948.11	$3,808.17	$1,606.32	$898.35	$7,260.95

Link quarterly income amounts to quarterly consolidations

$25,000.00		
$20,000.00		☐ Expenses
$15,000.00		■ Net Income
$10,000.00		
$5,000.00		
$0.00	1 2 3 4	

Preliminary Income Analysis
1999

Invoice Total	$48,406.33
Average Invoice	$4,033.86
Profit Margin	25%
Estimated Profit	$12,101.58

Job Number	Type of Job	Date Completed	Quarter	Amount of Invoice
019704A	Contract	2/2/99	1	$1,576.18
197260	Subcontract	3/29/99	1	$4,744.57
297150	Subcontract	4/29/99	2	$11,300.22
039717A	Contract	5/10/99	2	$7,940.62
397270	Subcontract	6/12/99	2	$2,632.00
049719A	Contract	6/25/99	2	$3,514.93
697070	Subcontract	8/14/99	3	$6,233.78
797240	Subcontract	8/22/99	3	$1,898.46
897250	Subcontract	9/26/99	3	$2,576.59
997040	Subcontract	10/4/99	4	$1,325.75
109710A	Contract	11/27/99	4	$2,910.00
1197030	Subcontract	12/10/99	4	$1,753.23
				$48,406.33

Change the source data, and links update the other sheets

Create an embedded graph that is also linked to the source invoice data

You covered a lot of important ground in Chapter 4, and you now have a feel for Excel's potential power. In this chapter, we introduce you to more Excel techniques, such as how to work with multiple workbooks and how to create a link between two worksheets. We also give you lessons in consolidating and graphing.

Working with Workbooks

In Chapter 4, you moved a range of cells from one worksheet to another. You can also transfer data between two workbooks to compare the information in one workbook with that in another. For example, if the people at Tip Top Roofing kept their 1999 invoice analysis in one workbook and their 2000 invoice analysis in another workbook, they could quickly determine which year was more profitable by simply opening both workbooks side by side on the same screen.

Let's start by opening an existing workbook and a new one:

1. Start Excel, click the Open button on the Standard toolbar, and double-click 1999 Jobs to open that workbook. Because you have made no changes to the default Book1 workbook, Excel automatically closes it.

2. Click the New button. Excel displays a new workbook called Book2.

Displaying two workbooks simultaneously

3. To see both workbooks at the same time, drop down the Window menu, wait until the Arrange command appears, and choose Arrange to display this dialog box:

4. Click OK to accept the default Tiled option. Excel arranges Book2 and 1999 Jobs side by side on your screen.

Copying Entries Between Workbooks

In addition to using the Copy and Paste buttons (or the Copy and Paste commands) to copy between workbooks, you can use drag-and-drop editing. Try the following:

1. Activate 1999 Jobs by clicking its title bar.

2. Select A12:D24 and point to any border of the selection. (We pointed to the top border.)

3. Hold down the Ctrl key and the left mouse button. (A plus sign appears next to the pointer.) Then drag the outline of the selection until it is over the range A1:D13 in Book2.

4. Release both the Ctrl key and the mouse button. Here's the result:

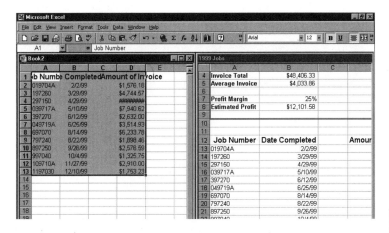

To move rather than copy entries between workbooks, you hold down only the left mouse button.

5. Press Home to move to cell A1.

Moving Sheets Between Workbooks

A sheet can easily be moved within a workbook or from one workbook to another. For this example, you'll move a worksheet from Book2 to 1999 Jobs, but first let's rename a couple of the worksheet tabs so that you can easily identify the worksheet you're going to move. Follow the steps on the next page.

Copying sheets

You can copy a sheet within your current workbook or to another workbook. Display the sheet you want to copy and choose Move Or Copy Sheet from the expanded Edit menu. In the To Book edit box of the Move Or Copy dialog box, specify the destination workbook. In the Before Sheet box, select the sheet that will follow the copied one. Then select the Create A Copy option and click OK.

Renaming sheets

1. Activate the 1999 Jobs window and then double-click the Sheet1 tab to select its name.

2. Type *Invoices 1999* and press Enter. Excel displays the new name on the tab.

3. Activate the Book2 window, double-click the Sheet1 tab, and enter *Invoices 2000* as the name.

Moving sheets

4. Point to the Invoices 2000 tab and hold down the left mouse button. The pointer becomes an arrow with a sheet attached to it.

5. Drag the sheet pointer until it sits between Invoices 1999 and Sheet2 of the 1999 Jobs workbook. Excel indicates with an arrowhead where it will place the selected sheet.

6. Release the mouse button. The Invoices 2000 sheet now appears in 1999 Jobs, as shown here:

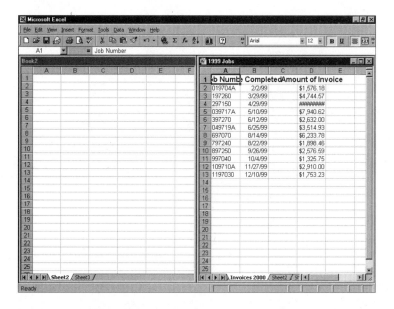

Deleting Sheets

Before deleting a sheet from a workbook, you should always display it. Excel permanently deletes the sheet, so it is wise to do a quick visual confirmation before sending a sheet into oblivion. In this example, you'll delete the sheet you just moved to 1999 Jobs and then close Book2. Follow these steps:

1. Right-click the active Invoices 2000 sheet tab and choose Delete from the shortcut menu. When you are warned that the sheet will be permanently deleted, click OK. Excel removes the Invoices 2000 sheet from the 1999 Jobs workbook.

2. Activate Book2 and close it by clicking the Close button at the right end of its title bar. When asked if you want to save the changes to Book2, click No.

3. Maximize the 1999 Jobs window, display the Invoices 1999 worksheet (if necessary, click the Previous Sheet button—see the tip on page 79), and press Ctrl+Home.

Formulas That Make Decisions

There will be times when you want Excel to carry out one task under certain circumstances and another task if those circumstances don't apply. To give this kind of instruction to Excel, you use the IF function.

In its simplest form, the IF function tests the value of a cell and does one thing if the test is positive (true) and another if the test is negative (false). It requires three arguments: the test, the action to perform if the test is true, and the action to perform if the test is false. You supply the arguments one after the other within the function's parentheses, separating them with commas (no spaces). Try this:

◄ ─────────────── The IF function

1. Select cell D4, type the following, and then press Enter:

   =IF(B4=0, "TRUE", "FALSE")

   Excel checks whether the value in cell B4 is zero (the test), and because it isn't zero, it ignores TRUE (the action to perform if the test is true) and displays FALSE (the action to perform if the test is false) in cell D4.

2. Double-click cell D4, drag through *=0* to highlight it, type *<100000*, and press Enter. The entry in cell D4 instantly changes from FALSE to TRUE because the value in cell B4 is less than one hundred thousand; that is, the test is true.

   In this example, the test Excel performed was a simple evaluation of the value in a cell. However, you can also build tests

Text values as arguments

When entering text values as arguments in a formula, you must enclose them in quotation marks. Otherwise, Excel thinks the text is a name and displays an error message. For example,

=RIGHT("Excel",2)

gives the value *el*—the two characters at the right end of the word *Excel*. However,

=RIGHT(Excel,2)

results in an error—unless the name Excel happens to be assigned to a cell on the worksheet.

that involve other functions. Suppose that the last character of the job numbers in column A of the worksheet indicates whether the roofing job is a contract (A) or subcontract (0) job, and you want to assign Contract and Subcontract entries to each job number so that you can compare the contributions of the two types of jobs to the Tip Top Roofing income. Follow these steps:

1. Delete the entry in D4.

2. Insert a new column between columns A and B by selecting B3:B24 and choosing Columns from the Insert menu. (The first two cells in column B have been merged to accommodate the title and subtitle, so you must exclude those cells.) Then use the Cut, Paste, and Format Painter buttons to restore the entries now in C4:C8 to B4:B8.

3. Enter the heading *Type of Job* in cell B12. Then select B13:B24, choose Cells from the Format menu, and on the Number tab, click General and then click OK.

Using functions as tests

4. Select cell B13, type the following, and click the Enter button:

   =IF(RIGHT(A13,1)="A","Contract","Subcontract")

   You have told Excel to look at the character at the right end of the value in cell A13 and if it's A, to enter *Contract* in cell B13. If it's not A, Excel is to enter *Subcontract*. Here's the result:

Logical operators

Here is a list of operators you can use with the IF function:

= <> <> >= <=

You can also use AND and OR to combine two or more tests. The function

=IF(AND(B4=0,B5>0),"Yes","No")

displays Yes only if both tests are true. The function

=IF(OR(B4=0,B5>0),"Yes","No")

displays Yes if either test is true.

Using Nested IF Functions

When constructing decision-making formulas, you can use IF functions within IF functions. Called *nested functions*, they add another dimension to the complexity of the decisions Excel can make. Here's a quick demonstration:

1. Select cell D12 and enter the column heading *Quarter*.

2. Select column D, choose Cells from the Format menu, and double-click General on the Number tab of the Format Cells dialog box.

3. Now select cell D13 and type this formula all on one line:

   =IF(MONTH(C13)<4,1,IF(MONTH(C13)<7,2,
   IF(MONTH(C13)<10,3,4)))

4. Check your typing, paying special attention to all the parentheses, and then click the Enter button.

You have told Excel to check the month component of the date in cell C13. If it is less than 4 (that is, before April), Excel is to display 1 in the corresponding cell in the Quarter column. If the month is not less than 4 but is less than 7 (that is, before July), Excel is to display 2 in the Quarter column. If it is not less than 7 but is less than 10 (that is, before October), Excel is to display 3. Otherwise, Excel is to display 4. If you have typed the formula correctly, Excel enters 1 in cell D13.

Copying Formulas

The IF functions you just entered are arduous to type, even for good typists. Fortunately, you don't have to enter them more than once. By using Excel's AutoFill feature, you can copy the formula into the cells below, like this:

1. Select B13 and position the pointer over the bottom right corner of the cell. The pointer changes to the black cross, called the *fill handle*.

2. Hold down the mouse button and drag down to cell B24. Excel copies the formula from B13 into the highlighted cells.

3. Select cell D13, point to the bottom right corner of the cell, hold down the mouse button, and drag down to cell D24. The worksheet now looks like the one on the next page.

The Fill command

You can use the Fill command to copy a single entry or a column or row of entries into a range of adjacent cells. Select both the cell(s) whose contents and formats you want to copy and the adjacent range, and then choose Fill from the Edit menu. How Excel copies the cell(s) is determined by the shape of the selection and the command you choose from the Fill submenu. For example, selecting cells below a single entry and then choosing Down copies the entry down a range; selecting cells to the right of an entry or entries and choosing Right copies the selection to the right; and so on. Three more complex commands are also available on this submenu. Try out the Across Worksheets, Series, and Justify commands to see their effects.

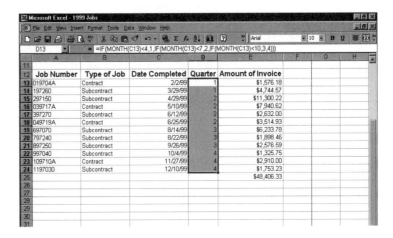

4. Select cell B14 and look at the formula in the formula bar. Excel has changed the original formula

=IF(RIGHT(A13,1)= "A", "Contract", "Subcontract")

to

=IF(RIGHT(A14,1)= "A", "Contract", "Subcontract")

Excel changed the reference so that it refers to cell A14 as its argument, not A13. Why?

Relative references

By default, Excel uses *relative references* in its formulas. Relative references refer to cells by their position in relation to the cell containing the formula. So when you copied the formula in cell B13 to cell B14, Excel changed the reference from A13 to A14—the cell in the same row and one column to the left of the cell containing the formula. If you were to copy the formula in cell B13 to E13, Excel would change the reference from A13 to D13 so that the formula would continue to reference the cell in the same relative position.

Absolute references

When you don't want a reference to be copied as a relative reference, as it was in these examples, you need to use an *absolute reference*. Absolute references refer to cells by their fixed position in the worksheet. To make a reference absolute, you add dollar signs before its column letter and row number. For example, to change the reference C4:C9 to an absolute reference, you would enter it as $C$4:$C$9. You could then copy a formula that contained this reference anywhere on the worksheet and it would always refer to the range C4:C9.

References can also be partially relative and partially absolute. For example, $C3 has an absolute column reference and a relative row reference, and C$3 has a relative column reference and an absolute row reference. ← **Mixed references**

Consolidating Data

You can use Excel to summarize data in a variety of ways. In this section, we'll show you how to use the Consolidate command to total the amounts in 1999 Jobs by quarter, enter the totals in another worksheet, and create a link between the totals and their source data. Follow these steps:

1. First name the destination worksheet by double-clicking the Sheet2 tab in 1999 Jobs, typing *Quarterly* as the name, and pressing Enter.

2. In cell A1 of the Quarterly sheet, type *Quarter*, and in cell B1, type *Total*. Make the headings bold, size 12, and centered.

Now for the consolidation:

1. Select cell A2 in the Quarterly sheet and then choose Consolidate from the expanded Data menu to display the dialog box shown here:

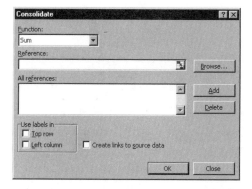

2. Click the Invoices 1999 tab to move to the worksheet that contains the data you want to summarize. Excel enters the name of the worksheet in the dialog box.

3. Shrink the Consolidate dialog box by clicking the button with the red arrow at the right end of the Reference edit box, and if necessary, move the dialog box so that you can see columns D and E.

4. Select D13:E24. Excel enters in the dialog box an absolute reference to the selected range.

5. Click the button with the red arrow again to redisplay the entire dialog box.

6. If Sum does not already appear in the Function edit box, select it from the Function drop-down list.

7. In the Use Labels In section, select the Left Column check box to tell Excel to use the entries in the Quarter column as labels in the summary worksheet. (Excel returns you to the Quarterly sheet at this point.)

8. Click the Create Links To Source Data check box to link the data in the Quarterly sheet to the data in the Invoices 1999 sheet, and then click OK to perform the consolidation. Here are the results after you widen columns A and C:

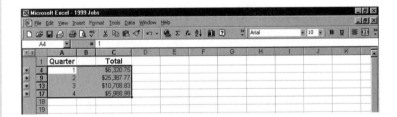

As you can see, Excel enters the column labels in the Quarter column and the quarter totals in the Total column, which is now column C. Excel inserted a column and outlined the worksheet to hide the mechanisms used to maintain the link between the totals and their source data. (The topic of outlining worksheets is beyond the scope of this book, but if you're interested, you might want to read the adjacent tip.) When you have time, you can practice consolidating data from several worksheets and using some of the other functions available in the Consolidate dialog box. In the meantime, let's use the consolidated quarter totals in another worksheet.

Outlining worksheets

Excel's outlining feature lets you view as little or as much of a worksheet as you want to see. To outline a worksheet, select all the cells containing data and choose Group And Outline and then Auto Outline from the expanded Data menu. Excel searches for what it considers to be the most important information (for example, the totals) and uses this information to create different row and column outline levels. Initially, an outlined worksheet displays all its levels. You use the Row Level buttons and Column Level buttons in the top left corner of the window to expand and collapse the outline. For example, clicking the Level 2 Rows button displays the first and second levels and hides any lower outline levels. You can also click the Hide Detail buttons (marked with minus signs) above and to the left of the worksheet to collapse an outline level. Excel deduces that the last row or column of a section is the "bottom line" of the collapsed section and displays only that row or column. Conversely, you can click the Show Detail buttons (marked with plus signs) to expand collapsed levels. Choose Group And Outline and then Clear Outline from the Data menu to exit outline mode.

Linking Worksheets

Before you can move on, you need to set up the following summary income statement for Tip Top Roofing:

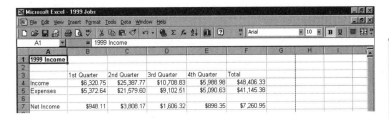

In the process, you'll link this worksheet to the Quarterly worksheet. Follow these steps:

1. Double-click the Sheet3 tab of 1999 Jobs and enter *Annual* as the sheet name.

2. In cell A1, type *1999 Income*, click the Enter button to enter the title, and click the Bold button to make the title bold.

3. In cell B3, type *1st Quarter* and click the Enter button. Using AutoFill, drag the fill handle to cell E3 (see page 116 and the adjacent tip for more information about AutoFill). Excel fills C3:E3 with the labels 2nd Quarter, 3rd Quarter, and 4th Quarter. Enter *Total* in cell F3 and *Income* in cell A4.

4. Select columns A through F, choose Cells from the Format menu, and double-click General on the Number tab to clear any existing number formats.

   To link the quarter totals on the Quarterly sheet to those on the Annual sheet, follow these steps:

1. Click the Quarterly tab, select C4 (the first quarter total), and then click the Copy button.

2. Click the Annual tab, select B4, and choose Paste Special from the Edit menu to display the dialog box shown on the next page.

More about AutoFill

You can copy information from one area of your worksheet to an adjacent area using three methods: AutoFill, dragging, and copy and paste. These methods produce similar results unless the cell you are copying contains a number that can be incremented, as with the 1st Quarter heading, or the cell contains an entry from a custom list. If the cell contains a number that can be incremented, using AutoFill copies the entry and increments the number—for example, 1st Quarter becomes 2nd Quarter, 3rd Quarter, and so on. (You may need to enter the first two entries—for example, 1, then 2—for it to recognize the entries as a series.) If the cell contains an entry from a custom list, using AutoFill fills the cells with other entries from that list. You define a custom list by choosing Options from the Tools menu, clicking the Custom Lists tab, clicking NEW LIST in the Custom Lists box, and typing the list's entries in the List Entries box. After you click OK, you can enter the list in consecutive cells of any worksheet by typing one of the entries and dragging the fill handle. This feature is invaluable if you frequently create worksheets involving lists of the same entries, such as part numbers or employee names.

3. Be sure the All option is selected in the Paste section and None is selected in the Operation section, and then click the Paste Link button to create a link between the totals in the Quarterly and Annual worksheets.

4. Repeat steps 1 through 3 for the 2nd, 3rd, and 4th quarter totals in the Annual sheet.

Now let's tackle the expenses:

1. Enter the following information in the indicated cells:

   A5   *Expenses*
   A7   *Net Income*
   B5   *= 0.85*B4*

2. Select B4:F7 and assign the Currency format (see page 90).

3. Use AutoFill to copy the formula in cell B5 to C5:E5.

4. Widen column A so that all its labels fit. Then drag through the headers for columns B through F, choose Column and Width from the Format menu, type *12* in the Column Width edit box, and click OK. The selected columns take on the new width.

Now let's compute the Total column and Net Income row:

1. Select cell F4 and click the AutoSum and Enter buttons. Then use AutoFill to copy the formula in cell F4 to cell F5.

2. In cell B7, type *=B4-B5* and click the Enter button. Excel enters the result, $948.11 as the 1st quarter's net income.

3. Use AutoFill to copy the formula in cell B7 to C7:F7. Your worksheet should now look like the one on page 115.

Testing Links

Earlier, when you consolidated the quarter totals, you created a link between the Quarterly sheet and the Invoices 1999 sheet. In the previous section, you used the Paste Special command to create a link between the Annual sheet and the Quarterly sheet. With these links in place, you can change the data in the original source worksheet—the Invoices 1999 sheet—and Excel will automatically update the data in the destination worksheets—the Quarterly and Annual sheets. To test the links you created, try the following:

1. Click the Invoices 1999 tab, select E20, type *100000*, and click the Enter button. The total in cell E25 is $146,507.87.

2. Next click the Quarterly tab and, if necessary, widen column C. The third quarter total in cell C13 is now $108,810.37.

3. Finally, click the Annual tab and note the changes Excel has made in the summary income statement.

As you can see, creating links between worksheets can really save you time because when you update the source worksheet, Excel updates any linked worksheets for you. Obviously, links help cut down on typographical errors, too.

Creating Graphs

Excel shares the graphing program, Microsoft Graph, with the other Office components. If you're new to Graph, this section is a good introduction to its features and flexibility. (In this discussion, we use the term *graph* to refer collectively to all types of graphs and charts.)

With Excel, you can create graphs in three ways: on the current worksheet, as a separate sheet in the current workbook, or in another workbook. In this section, we show you how to quickly plot a graph on the current worksheet. The advantage of this method is that you can print the graph and the underlying worksheet on the same page. Let's create a graph based on the income and expenses data in the Annual sheet by following the steps on the next page.

Noncontiguous ranges

The Chart Wizard button

1. Select A5:E5 in the Annual sheet. Then hold down the Ctrl key and select A7:E7.

2. Click the Chart Wizard button to display the first of four dialog boxes that lead you through the process of creating and customizing a graph. (If the Office Assistant appears, click the No option.)

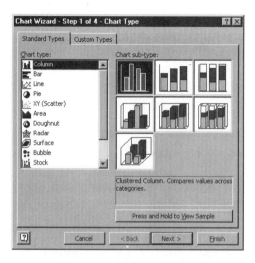

3. With Column selected in the Chart Type list, select the 3-D Clustered Column in the Chart Sub-Type list (the first option in the second row). Then click Next to display this dialog box:

Creating graphs on chart sheets

To create a graph on a separate chart sheet, first select the data and then click the Chart Wizard button. Build the graph in the Chart Wizard's dialog boxes as usual. When you reach the fourth Chart Wizard dialog box, select the As New Sheet option and click Finish. Excel places a sheet named Chart1 in front of the worksheet containing the selected data and plots a graph on the Chart1 sheet. To quickly build a graph in the default format on a separate chart sheet, simply select the worksheet data you want to plot and press the F11 key.

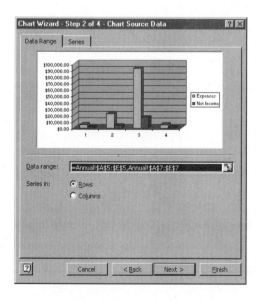

Graph displays how the selected range will look, with all labels and other information in place.

4. Accept the default settings and move to the dialog box shown below by clicking Next. (At any point, you can click the Back button to move back to a previous dialog box, so you can always select a different format if you change your mind.)

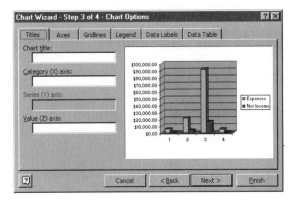

You can use the tabs in this dialog box to add and change titles, axes, gridlines, and so forth.

5. Click Next to accept the default settings and display the dialog box shown here:

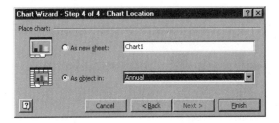

6. Click Finish to insert the graph in the Annual sheet.

7. Double-click the title bar of the Chart toolbar to "dock" it below the toolbar row. The column graph looks like the one on the following page.

The default graph format

Graph's default format is a two-dimensional column graph. To change the default format, choose Chart Type from Graph's Chart menu (you must first select a chart) and select a different type on the Standard Types or Custom Types tab of the Chart Type dialog box. Then click the Set As Default Chart button at the bottom of the dialog box. When Excel asks you to confirm your default graph selection, click Yes. Click OK in the Chart Type dialog box to have the new default graph type take effect immediately.

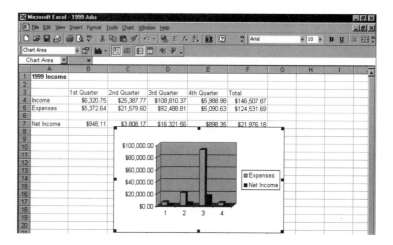

Data markers

As you can see, four groups of columns, called *data markers*, represent the four quarters of data you selected. Within each group, one data marker represents the expenses category and the other represents the net income category. The data markers are identified in the legend by the labels from column A of the selected range: Expenses and Net Income. Before moving on to the next section, take a moment to familiarize yourself with the various elements of a graph. When you point to an element, such as the legend, Graph displays the element's

Selecting chart objects

name in a box. (To select a specific element, you can click it once or select it from the Chart Objects drop-down list at the left end of the Chart toolbar.) Notice that because your new column chart is selected, as indicated by the black squares (called *handles*), the Microsoft Graph program is active and

Handles

has modified the menus on the menu bar to accommodate the commands appropriate for working with graphs.

Sizing and Moving Graphs

You don't have to worry about the precise size and location of a graph when you create it because you can always adjust it by dragging the handles around the graph's frame. Try this:

Adjusting the size

1. Point to the middle handle on the left side of the frame and drag it to the left to increase the graph's width.

2. Drag a corner handle diagonally inward to decrease both the height and the width.

3. Move the entire graph below the data of the Annual sheet by pointing just inside its frame and dragging in the direction you want to move.

Moving a graph

Updating Graphs

Graph has actively linked the column graph to its underlying data, so if you change the data, Graph will redraw the graph to reflect the change. As a demonstration, let's see what Graph does when you restore the original amount in cell E20 of the Invoices 1999 worksheet:

1. Click the Invoices 1999 tab and enter *1898.46* in cell E20.

2. Next click the Annual tab. The updated graph looks like this:

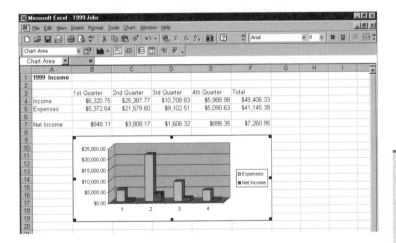

Changing the Type

No matter what type of chart or graph you need—area, bar, pie, line, and so on—Graph has a format that will probably do the job. You can always come up with impressive visual support for a worksheet by carefully selecting from among Graph's many predefined types. Let's try changing the type of the graph currently on your screen so that you can see the possibilities:

1. Be sure the graph is selected (surrounded by handles). If it isn't, click anywhere within the graph to select it.

Adding values to an existing series

If you add values to a set of data in a worksheet and want to update a graph you created earlier to reflect the new values, you can select the values and drag the selection to the graph. When you release the mouse button, Graph displays the Paste Special dialog box. Click New Point(s), select Rows or Columns, and then click OK to add the additional data points along the category axis. To add values to a graph located on a separate chart sheet, select the values and click the Copy button. Move to the chart sheet, select the graph, and then click the Paste button.

2. Choose Chart Type from the Chart menu to display a dialog box similar to the first Chart Wizard box (see page 118).

3. In the Chart Type list, select the Line option and click OK. Graph draws this graph, in which the expenses and net income data are represented as two separate lines on the graph:

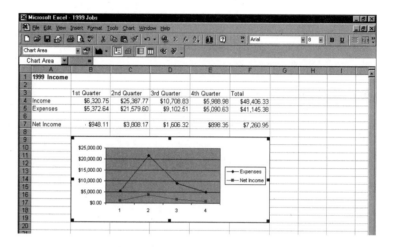

4. Click the Undo button to restore the previous type.

The Chart Type button

5. Now click the arrow to the right of the Chart Type button on the Chart toolbar to display this drop-down palette of graph types:

X axis and y axis

Graph uses the terms *x axis* and *y axis* in some of its dialog boxes. For clarification, here are a couple of definitions: The x axis shows the information categories—for example, expenses and net income; the y axis shows the data points (plotted values).

6. Select the 3-D Pie Chart option (the second option in the fifth row). The four quarters of expenses data are represented as colored wedges in a three-dimensional pie graph, as shown on the facing page. (You no longer see the net income data because a pie graph can display only one set of data.)

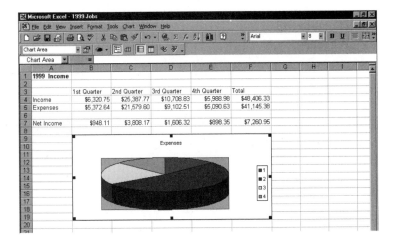

7. Select other graph types from the Chart Type dialog box or the Chart Type palette to get an idea of what's available. Then finish up with a simple two-dimensional column graph.

Using Custom Graph Types

Often, selecting one of the options on the Standard Types tab of the Chart Type dialog box will produce exactly the graph you need, but sometimes you might want something slightly different. Before spending time adjusting a graph's format, it's worth exploring Graph's custom types. Follow these steps:

1. With the graph selected, choose Chart Type from the Chart menu and click the Custom Types tab to display the options shown here:

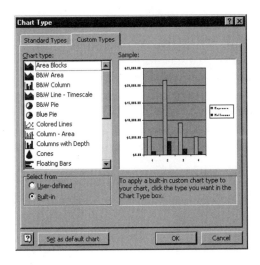

Adding notes

To add explanatory notes to a graph, select the graph, click an insertion point in the formula bar, type the note, and press Enter. Graph displays a text box containing the note in the middle of the graph. You can use the frame and handles around the text box to reposition it or resize it. To format the text box and the note it contains, choose Selected Object from the Format menu and make your selections on the tabs of the Format Text Box dialog box.

2. In the Chart Type list, select the types that interest you and then check the results in the Sample box.

3. When you are ready, select the Columns With Depth type and click OK. Here's the result:

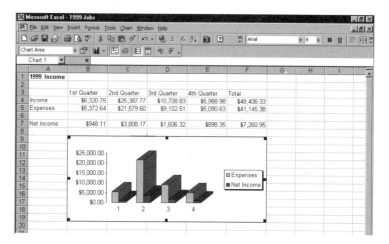

You might want to continue exploring some of the other available custom types. In particular, try creating a combination graph, which plots one type of graph on top of another as an "overlay" (see the adjacent tip).

Previewing and Printing Graphs

Previewing and printing graphs is much like previewing and printing worksheets. You can preview and print the worksheet data and graph together or just the graph. Follow these steps:

1. Click anywhere outside the graph to deselect it, click cell A1, and then click the Print Preview button. As you can see, one or two adjustments would improve the look of this page.

2. Click the Close button to return to the Annual worksheet. Adjust the position and size of the graph (see page 120) so that it is centered on columns A through F and separated from the worksheet entries by about five rows of blank cells.

3. Deselect the graph, click the Print Preview button again, and then click the Setup button on the Print Preview toolbar.

Combination graphs

To create a combination graph, select one of the combination graph types (for example, Line-Column) on the Custom Types tab of the Chart Wizard or Chart Type dialog box. You can plot your data as one graph type overlaid by another—for example, a column graph overlaid by a line graph. If your data includes series that span widely divergent ranges of values, you can plot the data against two y axes of different scales—for example, one series against a y-axis scale on the left of the graph ranging from 0 to 100 and another series against a y-axis scale on the right of the graph ranging from 100,000 to 1,000,000.

4. On the Margins tab, change the Top setting to *1.5*, and in the Center On Page section, select the Horizontally option.

5. Click OK to implement your changes. Here are the results:

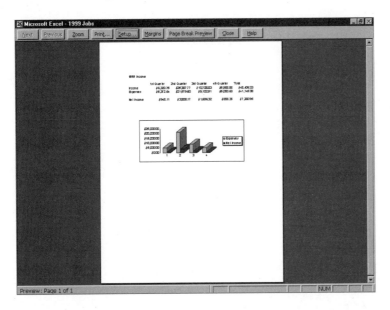

If you want, you can now click the Print button to create a paper copy of your graph.

To print a graph without its underlying worksheet, click the graph to select it and then click the Print button on the Standard toolbar. (Or choose Print from the File menu, be sure the Selected Chart option is selected in the Print dialog box, and click OK.)

Printing only the graph

Chapters 4 and 5 have given you a quick overview of Excel. Don't be shy about exploring the program further on your own and using its many features to create more sophisticated worksheets.

6
PowerPoint Basics

You use the AutoContent Wizard to create a presentation and investigate ways of refining the text provided by the wizard. Next you use a design template to create another presentation. Finally, you combine your two presentations.

The sample presentations are promotional materials for an environmental group. They can easily be adapted to presentations for any business, organization, or club.

Presentations created and concepts covered:

Let the AutoContent Wizard create a slide show that you can customize

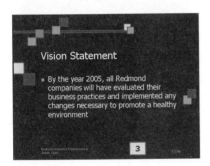

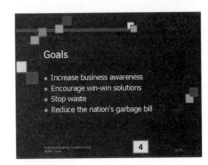

Pick a design and then create slides one by one

Microsoft PowerPoint 2000 is the presentation component of Office, and it's packed with all sorts of tools to simplify the task of creating presentations. From reliable transparencies to electronic slide shows with "flying bullets," PowerPoint does it all.

In this chapter, we cover the basic steps for developing a PowerPoint presentation. First we introduce you to the Auto-Content Wizard, which helps you decide on the text of a presentation. Then we show you how to get the look you want by creating a presentation based on one of PowerPoint's design templates.

Using the AutoContent Wizard

For your first presentation, you'll use the AutoContent Wizard, which asks a few questions to get the ball rolling and then lets you select one of several sample presentations as a starting point. Follow these steps:

Starting Microsoft PowerPoint

1. Click the Start button and choose Programs and then Microsoft PowerPoint from the Start menu.

2. If necessary, click the Start Using Microsoft PowerPoint option. Your screen should look something like this:

Bypassing dialog boxes

While going through the Auto-Content Wizard, as well as other wizards' dialog boxes, you can bypass sections of the wizard. In the "road map" on the left side of the dialog box, click the colored square next to the part of the process you want to display. You can move backward to a previous dialog box by using this method, or by clicking the Back button.

As you can see, you can start a new presentation in one of three ways, or you can open a presentation that already exists.

3. With the AutoContent Wizard option selected, click OK to display the first AutoContent Wizard dialog box. (If the Office Assistant reappears, click No to turn it off.)

4. Read the information in the dialog box and then click Next to move to this dialog box, where you select the type of presentation you want to create:

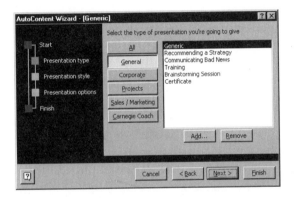

5. Click the buttons in the middle of the dialog box to see the presentation types available in each category. When you're ready, click the General button and select the Recommending A Strategy presentation type. Then click Next.

6. Check that On-Screen Presentation is selected as your output option and then click Next to display this dialog box:

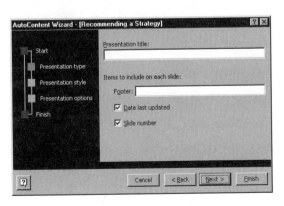

Presentation do's and don'ts

Using a program like PowerPoint won't ensure that your presentations will be successful. You have to use some common sense, too. Here are some tips for creating clear and concise presentations:

- Know as much as you can about your audience before you start creating your presentation and then tailor its tone, words, and graphics appropriately.

- What points do you want your audience to remember after your presentation? Come up with an overall theme that you can reinforce throughout the presentation.

- Make each slide convey only one main idea that can be interpreted at a glance.

- Cut the verbiage on each slide to the essentials. Never have more than six bulleted items on a slide. The more items per slide, the fewer words you should use in each item.

- Make sure your capitalization and punctuation are consistent. On any one slide, don't mix complete sentences and partial sentences.

- Above all, don't expect your slides to carry the entire weight of the presentation. To hold the attention of your audience, you must be poised and confident, and you must express your ideas clearly and persuasively.

The title slide

The information you enter in this dialog box will become the first slide, called the *title slide*, of the presentation. In the Presentation Title and Footer edit boxes, PowerPoint may have entered a title and company name used when the program was installed.

7. Type *Toward a Healthy Environment* in the Presentation Title edit box, and then type *Redmond Business Environmental Action Team* in the Footer edit box.

8. Check that the Date Last Updated and Slide Number boxes have been selected so that this information, in addition to what you typed in the Footer box, will be included on each slide. Click Next to display the AutoContent Wizard's final dialog box.

9. Click Finish. PowerPoint opens this presentation window:

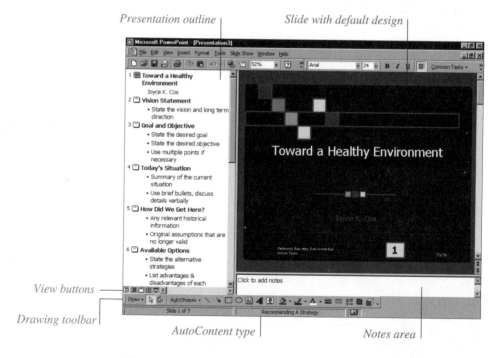

Presentation outline   *Slide with default design*

View buttons

Drawing toolbar

AutoContent type

Notes area

The name you see on the slide now on your screen is the one used when the program was installed. We show how to change this name on page 132.

Taking up most of your screen is your new presentation, which PowerPoint displays in *normal view* in the *presentation window*. Normal view divides the work area into three panes. On the left is an outline of the presentation. The first topic is the title-slide information you entered in the fourth AutoContent Wizard dialog box. The remaining topics are PowerPoint's suggestions as to the items you might want to cover when recommending a strategy. Each topic supplied by PowerPoint is designated by a number and a slide icon, which indicates that the topic will appear as the title of a slide. Subtopics are indented and bulleted to indicate that they will appear as bulleted items on their respective slides. Also in the work area is the first slide, which is displayed with the default design template for the presentation. (See page 138 for more information about templates.) Below the slide is an area where you can add notes as you work on each slide. These notes can then be printed out as speaker's notes to guide you as you deliver the presentation.

← Normal view

10. Save the presentation by clicking the Save button to display the Save As dialog box, typing *1 Redmond BEAT* in the File Name edit box, and clicking Save.

Editing Slides in Slide View

On the left above the Drawing toolbar is a row of buttons that you use to switch from one view of a presentation to another. Right now you are in normal view; you may notice that the Normal View button appears "pressed." We will introduce you to the other views as you work your way through the next two chapters. We'll start with *slide view*, where you can concentrate on the content of the presentation one slide at a time. Here's how to switch to slide view:

← The Normal View button

1. Click the Slide View button in the bottom left corner of the presentation window, or choose Slide from the View menu. Your screen now looks as shown on the next page.

← The Slide View button

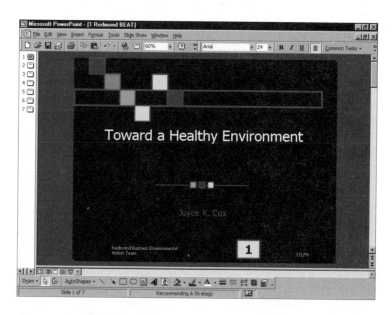

The Previous Slide and
Next Slide buttons

Occupying most of the window is your presentation's title slide. The vertical scroll bar has acquired a Previous Slide button and a Next Slide button, which you click to move backward and forward through the presentation's slides. The outline pane on the left has shrunk to display only the slide icons, which you can click to move from slide to slide. The notes area has disappeared.

You can work on different aspects of a presentation by viewing it in different ways. When it comes to editing the text of a presentation, you can use normal view, outline view, or slide view. We show you how to reorganize the slides in outline view on page 136, but in this section, you concentrate on editing text while working in slide view. Follow these steps:

1. On the title slide, PowerPoint has inserted a name below the title. Click next to the name to activate the *object area* where the name appears. PowerPoint surrounds the area with a shaded border.

2. Select the name and type *Ted Lee*.

3. Click the Next Slide button at the bottom of the vertical scroll bar to move to Slide 2, as shown on the facing page.

Moving among slides

In addition to the Previous Slide and Next Slide buttons, you can use the Page Up and Page Down keys to move from one slide to another. You can also use the scroll bar to move around your presentation. As you scroll, PowerPoint displays the number and title of the slide that will appear when you release the mouse button at that particular point. You can also click any icon in the outline pane to move to a specific slide.

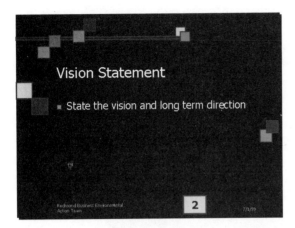

4. If you see a light bulb in the top left corner of the selected area, click it to display the Office Assistant and a tip about Auto ClipArt. This tip will appear every time you edit a new slide. For now, click the Don't Search check box and then click OK to tell the Office Assistant that you don't want to see the tip again. (From now on, check out the tips each time the light bulb appears.)

Office Assistant tips

5. On Slide 2, activate the object area by clicking an insertion point in the bulleted item.

6. Click the bullet to select its text and type this:

   By the year 2005, all Redmond companies will have evaluated their business practices and implemented any changes necessary to promote a healthy environment

7. Click the Save button to save the changes you have made.

   Slide 2 looks good, so let's move on to the next slide:

1. Click the Next Slide button to display Slide 3.

2. Activate the title area of the slide by clicking an insertion point to the right of *Goal*.

3. Type an *s* to turn *Goal* into *Goals*, and then delete the words *and Objective*.

4. Activate the object area of the slide by clicking anywhere in the slide's bulleted list.

The fewer bulleted items the better

The default slide template lets you enter eight single-line bulleted items on a slide, but eight is really too many. As we said in the tip on page 129, you will stand a better chance of making your point with your audience if you limit the number of bulleted items to no more than six single lines. The more bullets you have, the harder it is for your audience to focus on any one of the points you are trying to make. If you have many bulleted items, try to find ways of breaking them up into logical groups and use a different slide for each group.

5. Select the text of the first bulleted item and type *Encourage win-win solutions*.

6. Repeat step 5 to replace the second bulleted item with *Stop waste* and the third bulleted item with *Reduce the nation's garbage bill*.

Adding a bulleted item →

7. Press Enter. PowerPoint moves the insertion point to a new line, preceded by a bullet.

8. Type *Increase business awareness*. Here are the results:

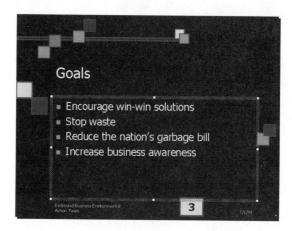

Adding Subordinate Points

To get a point across, you will sometimes need to add subordinate points below a main bullet, like this:

1. Click the Next Slide button to move to Slide 4, click the title to activate the title area of the slide, select *Today's Situation*, and type *About Redmond BEAT*.

2. In the object area, change *Summary of the current situation* to *Publishes On the BEAT newsletter* and press Enter to create a new bullet.

3. Type *Supports local recycling efforts* and press Enter.

4. Type *Chapter of USA BEAT* and press Enter.

The Demote button →

5. Now click the Demote button on the Formatting toolbar. (If necessary, click the More Buttons button and then click the

Demote button.) PowerPoint indents the line to show that this item is subordinate to the preceding bullet.

6. Next type *National office, Washington DC*, press Enter to create a second subordinate item, type *Chartered 1989*, and then press Enter.

7. To stop adding subordinate points and create a new main bulleted item, click the Promote button on the Formatting toolbar. PowerPoint moves the line back out to the margin.

The Promote button

8. Type *Maintains resource center* as the new first-level bullet.

9. Finally, delete the *Use brief bullets* item by selecting the text and pressing the Delete key. Slide 4 now looks like this:

Deleting bulleted items

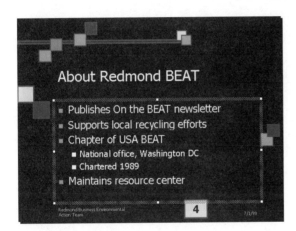

Deleting Slides in Slide View

You'll create the next four slides using a design template, so you need to dispose of Slides 5, 6, and 7, which were provided by the AutoContent Wizard. Follow these steps to delete Slide 5 (you'll take care of Slides 6 and 7 later):

1. Click the Next Slide button to move to Slide 5, which is titled *How Did We Get Here?*

2. Choose Delete Slide from the expanded Edit menu. In the outline pane, notice that Slides 6 and 7 are renumbered to take the place of the deleted slide.

Organizing Slides in Outline View

In outline view, you can see all the topics and bulleted lists of the presentation in outline form. You can edit slide text in outline view, but this view really shines when it's time to organize a presentation. Organizing is often a trial-and-error process. You start by evaluating the major topics, add and delete a few subtopics, and then move items around and change their levels. This task is easiest to accomplish in outline view because the Outlining toolbar puts the tools needed for organizing a presentation close at hand. Let's experiment:

The Outline View button

1. Click the Outline View button to switch to outline view. Then if necessary, right-click a toolbar and choose Outlining to turn on that toolbar. Your screen now looks like this:

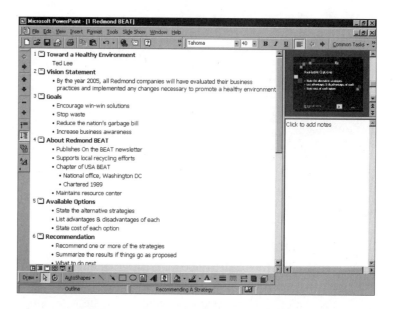

2. Under the *About Redmond BEAT* topic, click the bullet to the left of *Maintains resource center* to select that item.

The Move Up button

3. Click the Move Up button on the Outlining toolbar until the selected item sits above *Supports local recycling efforts*.

The Move Down button

4. Now click the bullet to the left of *National office, Washington DC*, and click the Move Down button once. The two subordinate points effectively switch places.

5. Click the bullet to the left of *Chapter of USA BEAT*. PowerPoint selects not only the text adjacent to the bullet but also its two subordinate items.

Selecting a bulleted group

6. Click the Move Up button three times. PowerPoint moves the main bullet and its subordinate items to the top of the *About Redmond BEAT* list.

Here's another way to rearrange bulleted items:

1. Under the *Goals* topic, click the bullet to the left of *Increase business awareness*.

2. Point to the selected text, hold down the left mouse button, drag the shadow insertion point until it sits to the left of the *E* in *Encourage*, and then release the mouse button. Power-Point moves the selection to its new location at the top of the bulleted list.

Reorganizing by dragging

As you scroll through the outline of the presentation, you might notice a slide or two that would work better in a different location. However, if an outline is too long to fit on your screen in its entirety, it is sometimes hard to decide on a precise order for the slides. The solution is to collapse the outline so that only the main topics are visible. Follow these steps to collapse the outline of your presentation:

1. Click the Collapse All button on the Outlining toolbar. All of the bulleted items are hidden and a gray line appears under each topic to indicate the presence of the hidden information, as shown here:

The Collapse All button

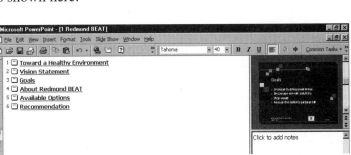

2. Click the slide icon next to the topic for Slide 4 to select the slide and its hidden text, and then click the Move Up button until *About Redmond BEAT* is the second topic in the outline.

The Expand button

3. Verify that the hidden text moved with the topic by clicking the Expand button. Here's the result:

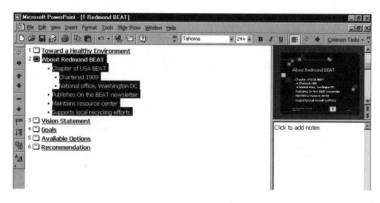

The Collapse button

4. Click the Collapse button to hide the bulleted items again.

Deleting Slides in Outline View

Deleting a slide in outline view is a simple editing process. Let's delete the last two slides in the presentation:

1. Click the slide icon next to the topic for Slide 5, hold down the Shift key, and click the icon next to the topic for Slide 6 to select both Slides 5 and 6.

2. Press Delete.

The Expand All button

3. Click the Expand All button to display the entire outline.

4. Save and close the presentation.

Using a Design Template

If you know exactly what you want to say but you need a little help coming up with a design for your presentation, you can bypass the AutoContent Wizard and instead start a presentation based on one of PowerPoint's design templates. And if you don't like the design you select, you can easily switch to a different template with just a few mouse clicks (see page 144). Follow the steps below to create a second presentation using a design template:

1. Choose New from the File menu to display the New Presentation dialog box and then click the Design Templates tab, which looks like this:

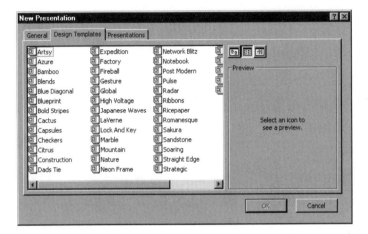

2. Click various template icons, checking the Preview box on the right to see how they look. (If a template is not yet installed, you can click OK to install it. See the tip on page 55.)

3. When you're ready, double-click the Capsules icon. Power-Point opens the New Slide dialog box shown here:

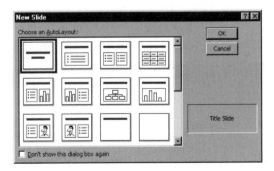

PowerPoint provides 23 predefined slide layouts, called *autolayouts*, and one blank slide that you can use to design a slide layout of your own. You can scroll the other autolayouts into view by using the scroll bar to the right.

Changing the bullet character

PowerPoint's Bullet command allows you to change the character preceding the bulleted text on a slide. Select the bulleted items and choose Bullets And Numbering from the Format menu. Then click Character, and in the Bullet dialog box, select a font in the Bullets From drop-down list, select a character, and then click OK. If you want to change the color or size of the bullet, you can use the Color and Size options in the Bullet dialog box.

4. Click the second autolayout in the top row and click OK to create a bulleted list slide.

5. Save the presentation with the name *2 Redmond BEAT*.

Slide 1 is now ready and awaiting your input. Follow these steps to add some text:

1. Click the title area and type *The Cost of Waste in the US* as the slide's title.

2. Click the object area and type *Today: $10 billion* as the first bulleted item.

3. Press Enter to start another bulleted item and then type *By the year 2005: $110 billion*. (By the way, these statistics are for purposes of demonstration only.)

Adding Slides

When you create a presentation based on a design template, PowerPoint provides only the initial slide. Obviously, you'll never create a one-slide presentation. Follow these steps to add three more slides to the presentation you're working on:

The New Slide button

1. Click the New Slide button on the Standard toolbar to display the New Slide dialog box.

2. With the Bulleted List autolayout selected, click OK to add a second slide to your presentation.

3. Click the title area of Slide 2 and type *How Much Waste?*

4. Type *Residences: 850 million tons* as the first bulleted item, press Enter to start the second bulleted item, and then type *Industry: 6.5 billion tons*.

5. Repeat steps 1 and 2 to add a new bulleted list slide and then type *Where Do I Start?* as the title.

6. Next click the object area of Slide 3 and type the bulleted items listed here:

- *Join Redmond BEAT*

- *Attend meetings at 8:00 AM on the last Tuesday of every month*

Repositioning text objects

You can use the mouse to reposition text objects on a slide. For instance, if you want to shift the title up a bit, click the title area to select it, point to the frame surrounding the area, hold down the left mouse button, and then drag the frame upward. You can use this same technique to reposition the object area on a slide. In addition, you can resize text objects by dragging the handles that appear when an object is selected (see the tip on page 141).

7. Add a fourth bulleted list slide and type *What Can I Do?* as the title. Then type the following bulleted items:

- *Start a recycling program*

- *Educate employees*

- *Buy post-consumer products*

- *Call Ted Lee at 555-6789 for more suggestions*

Moving Text Between Slides

If you take a look at Slide 4, you'll notice that the fourth bulleted item might be better suited for Slide 3. You can move the text to Slide 3 using a little cutting and pasting. Try this:

1. With the object area of Slide 4 activated, select the text of the fourth bullet.

2. On the Standard toolbar's More Buttons palette, click the Cut button to remove the text from the slide and store it temporarily on the Clipboard.

3. Click the Previous Slide button to move to Slide 3.

4. Now click an insertion point at the end of the second bulleted item, press Enter to create a new bullet, and then click the Paste button to paste the bulleted text onto Slide 3.

5. Press Backspace twice to remove the extra bullet. Here are the results:

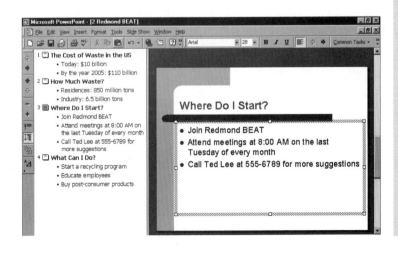

Selecting parts of a slide

You can use many of the standard Office text-selection techniques when editing text in both outline and slide views. For example, you can double-click a word to select it. In outline view, you can click a bullet to select that item and its subordinate bullets. Also in outline view, you can click the slide icon to the left of a topic to select the topic and all of its bulleted items. In slide view, you can select an entire text object, such as a bulleted list, by clicking the object and then either choosing Select All from the Edit menu or pressing Ctrl+A.

Merging Presentations in Slide Sorter View

Thumbnails →

In slide sorter view, you can see the slides of your presentation laid out visually. Sketches, called *thumbnails*, display the slides in enough detail that you can get a pretty good idea of how they look. You can then make adjustments to the presentation by adding or deleting slides or changing their order. Slide sorter view is also the place to merge two presentations, because you can see and control the process. Follow these steps to merge 2 Redmond BEAT with 1 Redmond BEAT:

The Slide Sorter View button →

1. Click the Slide Sorter View button in the bottom left corner of the presentation window. Your screen now looks like this:

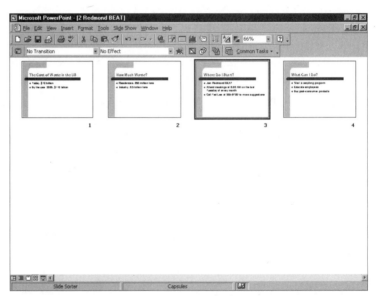

The Show Formatting button

The Show Formatting button appears at the right end of the Standard toolbar in Slide Sorter view. Clicking it removes the formatting, as well as the design template, from the current slides, leaving only the slide titles. Removing the formatting and design template can be a time-saver because PowerPoint does not have to "redraw" the slides every time you make a change to your presentation. To restore the formatting and design template, simply click the Show Formatting button again.

2. Now choose 1 Redmond BEAT from the bottom of the File menu and click the Slide Sorter View button. (If 1 Redmond BEAT is not one of the four most recently opened files and therefore is not displayed at the bottom of the File menu, use the Open command to open the file.)

3. Choose the Arrange All command from the expanded Window menu to place the presentations side by side. (The small slide icons below the slides in 1 Redmond BEAT indicate that a transition effect has been added to each slide of the AutoContent

Wizard's Recommending A Strategy presentation type. We
discuss transitions and other effects in the next chapter.)

4. To decrease the size of the slide thumbnails, click the arrow to
the right of the Zoom box on the Standard toolbar and select
33% from the drop-down list. Then activate the other window
and do the same thing. Here are the results:

The Zoom box

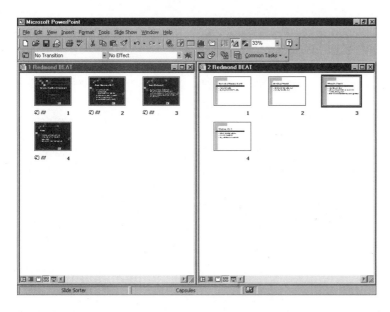

Now you can combine the two presentations:

1. Save the active 2 Redmond BEAT presentation, and then select its slides by choosing Select All from the Edit menu.

2. Point to any one of the selected slides, hold down the left
mouse button, and drag the vertical marker to just after Slide 4
in the 1 Redmond BEAT presentation.

3. Release the mouse button to drop all the 2 Redmond BEAT
slides into place. PowerPoint renumbers the merged slides
and overwrites the design template of 2 Redmond BEAT
with that of 1 Redmond BEAT.

4. Close the 2 Redmond BEAT window, clicking No when asked
whether you want to save your changes.

Reordering Slides in Slide Sorter View

Now that you've merged the two presentations, suppose you decide that Slides 7 and 8 need to be transposed. Here are the steps for reordering slides in slide sorter view:

Increasing the thumbnail size

1. Maximize the 1 Redmond BEAT window and then select 66% from the Zoom drop-down list to increase the size of the slide thumbnails.

2. Click a blank area of the Window to deselect any currently selected slides. Then click Slide 8 to select it, hold down the left mouse button, and drag the vertical marker to the left of Slide 7. When you release the mouse button, Slides 7 and 8 switch places, like this:

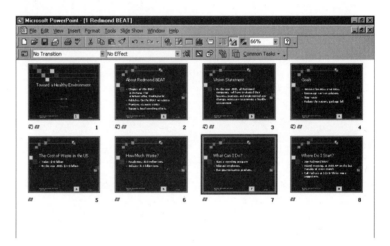

Applying Templates

The appearance of a presentation is controlled by its template, and you can change the entire look and feel of a presentation by simply switching to another template. As you saw in the New Presentation dialog box shown on page 139, PowerPoint offers a wide variety of design templates to choose from. Follow these steps to reapply the Capsules template:

1. With 1 Redmond BEAT displayed on your screen in slide sorter view, choose Apply Design Template from the Format menu to open the dialog box shown on the facing page.

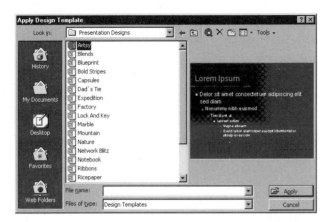

2. Double-click the Capsules icon to apply that template to your presentation, as shown here:

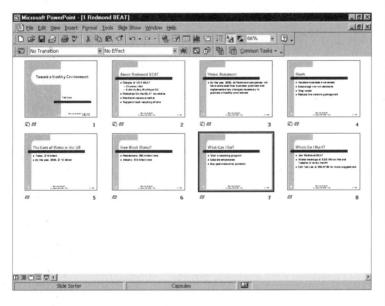

3. Save and close the presentation, and then close PowerPoint.

Now that you've learned how to create presentations using the AutoContent Wizard and a design template, you're ready to start exploring ways of enhancing presentations. In the next chapter, we show you how to add graphics, graphs, and special effects to your presentations so that you can wow your audiences with visual information.

Customizing your presentation

PowerPoint provides three formatting masters for customizing a presentation: slide, handout, and notes. To change the font of the slide master, choose Master and then Slide Master from the View menu. Click the title area on the master and choose Font from the Format menu. Change the font, style, and size to fit your needs, and click OK. Follow the same process to change the format of the object area and the subordinate items. To activate the handout master, which will help you get an idea of how your handouts look before they are printed, choose Master and then Handout Master from the View menu. The buttons on the Handout Master toolbar let you change the layout of your handouts. If you want to create a customized look for speaker's notes, you can enlist the help of the notes master. Choose Master and then Notes Master from the View menu, and then add headers, footers, the date and/or slide numbers to your speaker's notes. If you want the format of your title slide to differ from the rest of your presentation, you can create a new title master. Choose Master and then Title Master from the View menu. You can then make all your formatting changes using the techniques described in this chapter.

7

More About PowerPoint

You add clip art to your presentation and learn how to import graphics from other sources. Then you create a couple of graphs. Finally, you see how to add special effects to an electronic slide show and how to run it.

Graphics and graphs are important additions to any presentation, whether you are planning on creating transparencies or slides, or whether you will deliver your presentations as an electronic slide show.

Presentation created and concepts covered:

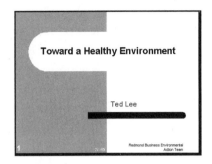

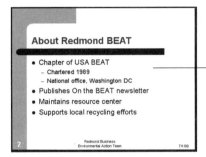

*Build slides
bullet by bullet
to maintain focus*

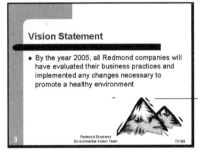

*Crop graphics to
show only the parts
you want*

*Use graphs to convey
numeric information
at a glance*

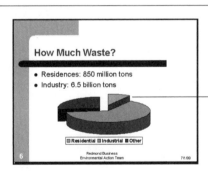

*"Explode" a pie graph
to emphasize each
part's contribution*

*Apply animation
effects to graphics
to add interest*

*Adjust a graphic's
colors so that overlying
text is readable*

Words and numbers are nice, but visual representations of information can make an audience sit up and take notice. There's nothing like a graphic to add pizazz to a slide, or a line graph to show the fluctuations in sales over the past six months. In this chapter, we cover adding graphics and graphs to your presentations, and we show you how to run an electronic slide show on your computer.

Adding Clip Art to Slides

You can add clip art to existing slides, or select the clip art autolayouts in the New Slide dialog box to create brand new slides with clip art placeholders. Using the 1 Redmond BEAT presentation you worked with in Chapter 6, we'll show you how to add clip art to an existing slide. (For information about creating a new slide with a clip art placeholder, see the tip below.) Follow these steps:

1. Start PowerPoint, click Open An Existing Presentation in the PowerPoint dialog box, and double-click the 1 Redmond BEAT entry in the list box to open it in slide sorter view.

2. Click Slide 7 and then click the Slide View button.

The Insert Clip Art button

3. Now click the Insert Clip Art button on the Drawing toolbar, or choose Picture and then Clip Art from the Insert menu. PowerPoint displays this Clip Gallery window:

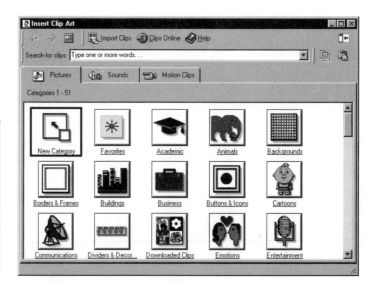

New clip art slides

If you want to create a brand new clip art slide, rather than add a clip art graphic to an existing slide, simply click the New Slide button on the Standard toolbar and select one of the clip art autolayouts in the New Slide dialog box.

4. Click a category to see its available graphics, and then click the Back button to return to the categories list. Repeat this step to explore other categories that interest you. (Some of the categories are empty. You can fill these with graphics from other sources, including those you download from the Web.)

The Back button

Instead of looking through all the categories on the Pictures tab, you can search for a specific clip art graphic. Let's find a graphic that symbolizes recycling and insert it on Slide 7:

1. Type *recycling* in the Search For Clips box and press Enter to see results something like these:

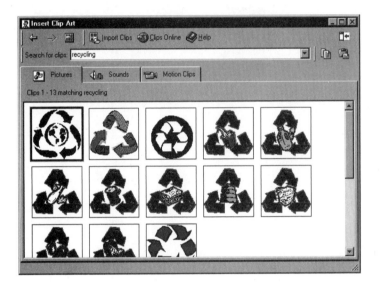

Any graphic that relates to recycling is displayed. (Don't worry if you see different or fewer graphics.)

2. Click a graphic. (We selected the third graphic in the second row of our dialog box.) This palette drops down:

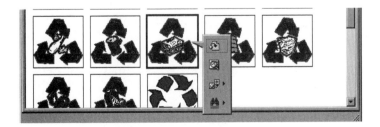

Importing graphics from other sources

PowerPoint can import any graphics file format for which the proper graphics filter is installed. In slide view, choose Picture and then From File from the Insert menu to display the Insert Picture dialog box. (If the Picture toolbar is displayed, you can click the Insert Picture From File button.) Select the correct file type from the Files Of Type drop-down list and move to the folder where the graphics file is located. Double-click the graphics file in the list box to insert the graphic on the active slide. You can then resize the graphic or add it to the slide's background. To add the graphic to the Clip Gallery, click the Insert Clip Art button and in the Clip Gallery window, click the Import Clips button. Select the graphic's file type from the Files Of Type drop-down list, move to the folder where the file is located, and then double-click the graphic's filename. Power-Point imports the file and then displays the Clip Properties dialog box. Enter keywords, separating them with commas. Select a category or click the New Category button to create a new category. Then click OK. Finally, click the Pictures tab to see the imported graphic in its designated category.

From this palette, you can insert the selected clip, preview it, add it to the Favorites category or another category on the Pictures tab, or find similar clips.

3. Click the Insert Clip button to add the graphic to Slide 7.

4. Close the Clip Gallery window and if necessary, dock the Picture toolbar at the bottom of the screen. Here are the results:

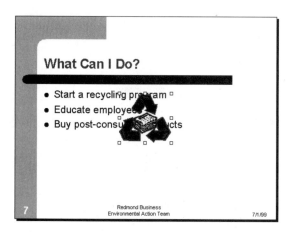

5. Click the Save button to save the presentation. (We won't tell you to save from now on, but you should save often.)

Sizing and Positioning Clip Art

Like other objects in PowerPoint, you can easily resize and relocate clip art graphics on a slide. Follow these steps to adjust the size and location of the recycling graphic:

1. If the graphic is not currently surrounded by handles to show that it is selected, click it once to select it.

2. Point to one of the graphic's bottom corner handles, and when the pointer changes to a double-headed arrow, hold down the left mouse button and drag downward until the graphic has about doubled in size.

3. Next point anywhere inside the graphic, hold down the left mouse button, and drag downward and to the right until the graphic sits in the bottom right corner of the slide.

4. Click outside the graphic to deselect it. Slide 7 looks like this:

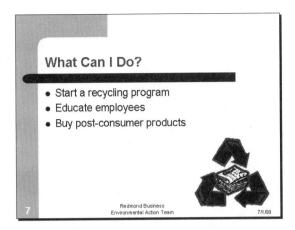

Cropping Clip Art

If you don't want to use all of a graphic, you can cut away the parts you don't want. Follow these steps to see how:

1. Move to Slide 3 and click the Insert Clip Art button.

2. Type *mountains* in the Search For Clips box and press Enter. Select the graphic of a mountain with a flag, click the Insert Clip button on the drop-down palette, and close the Clip Gallery.

3. Move the graphic to the bottom right corner, and with the graphic selected, click the Crop button on the Picture toolbar to activate the cropping tool.

The Crop button

4. Place the cropping tool over the graphic's top middle handle, drag down, and release the mouse button when the flag and its pole are cut off, as shown here:

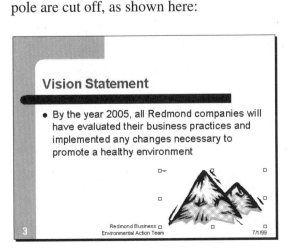

Adding borders

To add a border to any graphic object, select the object, and click the Format Picture button on the Picture toolbar. On the Colors And Lines tab, change the Color setting in the Line section to the desired color, select a style and weight for the border, and click OK.

The Reset Picture button

5. Click the Crop button again to deactivate the cropping tool.

You can easily restore a cropped graphic to its original state by clicking the Reset Picture button on the Picture toolbar.

Adding Clip Art to the Background

You can add a clip art graphic to the background of a slide so that the text flows over it. Follow these steps to add a graphic to the background of Slide 8:

1. In the outline pane, click the icon for Slide 8 to show that slide.

2. Next click the Insert Clip Art button, type *light bulb* in the Search For Clips box, and press Enter.

3. Select and insert the colorful light bulb graphic, close the Clip Gallery, and move the graphic to the bottom of the slide.

4. If necessary, resize the graphic so that it covers part of the text.

5. With the graphic selected, click the Draw button on the Drawing toolbar to show a menu of options. Choose Order and then Send To Back. The text of the slide overlays the graphic.

When you add a background graphic, your text may become difficult to read. Follow these steps to make the text of the last bulleted item more legible:

The Recolor Picture button

1. Click the Recolor Picture button on the Picture toolbar to display the dialog box shown here:

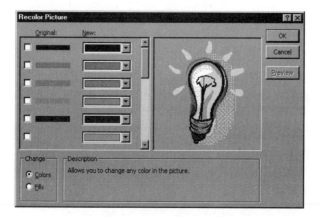

2. Check that the Colors option is selected in the Change section. (You select Fills if you want to change the graphic's background colors.)

3. Select the first Original check box (black). Then click the arrow to the right of the adjacent New box and select the third color in the bottom row of the drop-down palette. The preview box shows the effects of the change. Then click OK. Here's what Slide 8 looks like now:

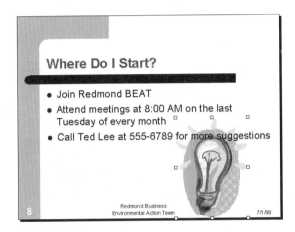

Adding Graphs

PowerPoint shares the graphing program Microsoft Graph with the other Office applications. In this section, we show you how to add a couple of graphs to the 1 Redmond BEAT presentation. You'll use a graph autolayout to add the first graph and the Insert Chart button to add the second graph. We'll also give you a few pointers about working with graph objects and manipulating a graph on a slide.

Using a Graph AutoLayout

Let's add a graph to the 1 Redmond BEAT presentation by changing the layout of Slide 5:

1. Move to Slide 5, choose Slide Layout from the Format menu, and when the Slide Layout dialog box appears, select the Text & Chart autolayout (the first autolayout in the second row) and click Apply. Slide 5 now looks like the one shown on the next page.

Changing a slide's layout

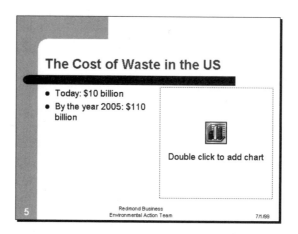

2. Double-click the graph placeholder to start Microsoft Graph. Your screen looks something like this:

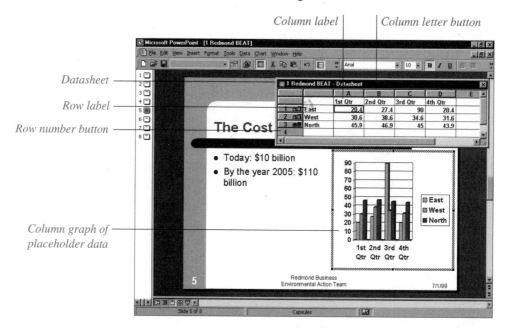

Column label   *Column letter button*

Datasheet

Row label

Row number button

Column graph of placeholder data

As you can see, Graph's menus and toolbars are now displayed. You can also see Graph's default *datasheet*, which resembles an Excel worksheet. Gridlines divide the datasheet into cells. In the leftmost column and topmost row are column and row headings, or *labels*. You can edit and format these labels like any other text in PowerPoint. Above the column labels and to the left of the row labels are column letter and row number buttons. Depending on whether the data is organized by column or by row (see the tip below), markers appear on the column letter or row number buttons to indicate the current graph type, which by default is a three-dimensional column graph. In the space allocated for the graph object on the slide behind the datasheet, Graph has plotted the datasheet's placeholder data.

You need to replace the placeholder data in the datasheet with your own information. (By the way, our data is fictitious and is used for demonstration purposes only.) Start with the labels:

1. Select the first cell in column A (the cell that contains *1st Qtr*) by clicking it with the mouse. (Be careful not to click outside the datasheet or graph. If you do, Graph automatically returns you to PowerPoint. You must then double-click the graph on the current slide to start Graph again.)

2. Type *1995*, press Tab to move to the first cell in column B, and type *2005*.

3. Select the first cell in row 1 (the cell that contains *East*), type *US*, press Enter to move to the first cell in row 2, type *Europe*, press Enter again, and type *Japan*.

To speed up the entry of the remaining data in the datasheet, try this technique:

1. Point to the second cell in column A, hold down the left mouse button, and drag to the third cell in column B to select the block of cells.

2. Now type *10*, press Enter, type *6*, press Enter, type *7.5*, and then press Enter again. In the next column, enter the data shown below:

   110

   57

   75

3. Choose Save from Graph's File menu to save your work.

By row or by column

You can arrange the data series in your datasheet by row or by column. Graph assumes that the series are arranged by row; if you have arranged the series by column, you can ensure that Graph will plot your data correctly by clicking the By Column button on Graph's Standard toolbar. If you later want to return to the by-row arrangement, click the By Row button. Graph places miniature markers on the row number buttons of the datasheet if the data series are arranged by row, and on the column letter buttons if the data series are arranged by column.

Now you are ready to plot the graph. You don't want to include the placeholder data in columns C and D, so first exclude it by doing this:

1. Click column C's letter button, hold down the Shift key, click column D's letter button, and release the Shift key.

2. With both columns selected, choose Exclude Row/Col from Graph's Data menu. (Notice that the columns are now shaded, indicating that they are inactive.)

The View Datasheet button

3. Click the View Datasheet button to remove the datasheet and display the new graph, which looks like this:

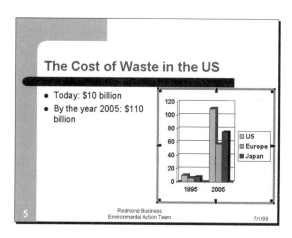

We'll show you how to size and move the graph on page 160.

Changing the Graph Type

With Graph, you can easily switch from one graph type to another if you're not satisfied with the way your data is displayed. For a clearer representation, change the type of the graph on Slide 5 by following these steps:

1. Choose the Chart Type command from Graph's Chart menu to display the dialog box shown on the facing page, where the current type, a clustered 3-D column graph, is highlighted.

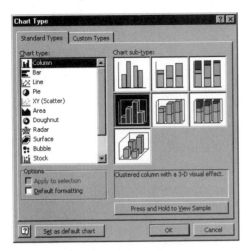

2. Select the first option in the Chart Sub-Type section (a clustered 2-D column graph), and then click OK. Graph changes the graph on Slide 5, like this:

Adding a Title

You can add a title to the graph as a whole, to the category (x) axis, to the value (y) axis, or to all three. Try adding a title to the column graph in 1 Redmond BEAT now:

1. With the graph still selected, choose the Chart Options command from Graph's Chart menu and, if necessary, click the Titles tab to display the options shown on the next page.

Adjusting column width

To increase or decrease the width of a column in a datasheet, first select the column (click its column letter button), then choose Column Width from Graph's Format menu, and enter a number in the Column Width dialog box. Click the Best Fit button in the Column Width dialog box to automatically adjust the column width to fit the longest entry in the column. You can also use the mouse to change the column width. Simply point to the border that separates adjacent column letter buttons, and when the pointer changes to a vertical bar with two arrows, hold down the left mouse button and drag to the left or right. If you double-click the border between two column letter buttons, the width of the column on the left is automatically adjusted to fit the longest entry. You can select multiple columns and use any of the methods described above to change the width of all the selected columns simultaneously.

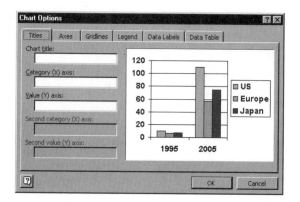

2. In the Chart Title edit box, type *In Billions of Dollars*. (As you type, the new title appears in the preview box.) Then click OK.

Repositioning the Legend

By default, Graph has added a legend to the column graph in 1 Redmond BEAT. (If a graph does not have a legend, you can always add one simply by using the Legend tab of the Chart Options dialog box.) Follow these steps to reposition the legend:

1. First click the legend once to select it. (Be sure that you have selected the entire legend, rather than just one of the legend entries or keys.)

2. Point to a blank area within the border surrounding the legend. (Be sure you are not pointing to an object or to one of the handles.) If you drag a handle, you will resize the legend instead of repositioning it.

3. Drag upward until the legend's top border is aligned with the graph's top gridline.

4. Click inside the graph's frame to deselect the legend. (Be careful not to click *outside* the graph's frame, or you'll wind up back in PowerPoint.) The graph now looks like the one shown on the facing page.

Adding an axis title

To add a title to a graph's axis, simply choose Chart Options from Graph's Chart menu, enter a title in the appropriate edit box on the Titles tab of the Chart Options dialog box, and then click OK. To rotate the title once it's in place, click it once (a border with handles will appear around it) and then choose Selected Axis Title from Graph's Format menu. Click the Alignment tab of the Format Axis Title dialog box, and then change the Degrees setting in the Orientation section.

Adding a Border

So that the graph, title, and legend appear as a unit on the slide, you can surround the chart area with a border. Try this:

1. Click a blank area of the graph to select the chart area, and then choose Selected Chart Area from Graph's Format menu to display this dialog box:

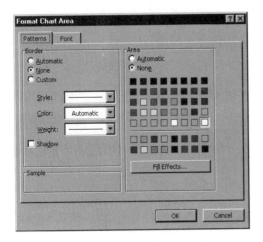

2. On the Patterns tab, click the arrow to the right of the Color edit box in the Border section to display a color palette, and select the first box in the first row below the line (pale green).

3. Next click the arrow to the right of the Weight edit box, select the last option (heavy), and click OK.

4. Click anywhere outside the chart area to return to PowerPoint. Your slide now looks like the one shown on the next page.

Changing label position

By default, Graph places tick-mark labels (the small marks used to group values or categories) next to their respective axes. You can change the position of the labels by selecting one of the Tick Mark Labels options on the Patterns tab of the Format Axis dialog box. (To open this dialog box, select an axis and then choose Selected Axis from Graph's Format menu.) Selecting the Low or High option places labels next to the minimum or maximum values of the other axis, respectively. If you select the None option, the labels are removed altogether.

Moving and Sizing Graphs

You don't have to open Graph to move and resize a graph. You can do these tasks in PowerPoint, like this:

1. Choose Ruler from the expanded View menu to turn on the rulers, which will serve as guides.

2. Click the graph on Slide 5 once to select it.

3. Point inside the graph's border and hold down the mouse button. When the dashed positioning box appears, drag to the left about ½ inch, using the horizontal ruler as a guide.

4. Now point to the right middle handle, and when the pointer changes to a double-headed arrow, drag to the right ½ inch.

5. Choose Ruler from the View menu to turn off the rulers and then deselect the graph to see the results shown here:

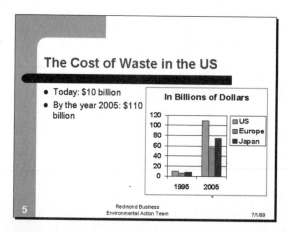

The Fill Color button

To quickly add color to any graph object, select the object, click the arrow to the right of the Fill Color button on Graph's Standard toolbar, and select the desired color.

Using the Insert Chart Button

The second method of adding a graph to an existing slide involves using the Insert Chart button. Follow these steps to add a 3-D pie graph to Slide 6:

1. Move to Slide 6 and click the Insert Chart button on the Standard toolbar's More Buttons palette.

The Insert Chart button

2. When the default datasheet appears, complete it as shown below (we used the mouse to widen column A so that the entire Residential heading is visible):

		A	B	C	D	E
		Residential	Industrial	Other	4th Qtr	
1	Waste	0.85	6.5	2.65	20.4	
2	West	30.6	38.6	34.6	31.6	
3	North	45.9	46.9	45	43.9	
4						

1 Redmond BEAT - Datasheet

3. Use the Exclude Row/Col command on Graph's Data menu to exclude rows 2 and 3 and column D from the graph.

4. Click the View Datasheet button to close the datasheet.

Now, instead of using the Chart Type dialog box to change the graph type, try the following:

1. Click the arrow to the right of the Chart Type button on the Standard toolbar to see the palette of options shown below. (If you don't see the button, click the More Buttons button.)

The Chart Type button

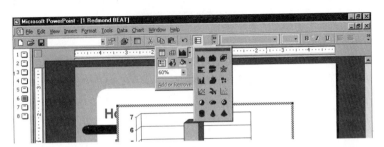

2. Click the 3-D Pie Chart option. (It is the middle option in the fifth row.) The graph now looks like the one shown on the next page.

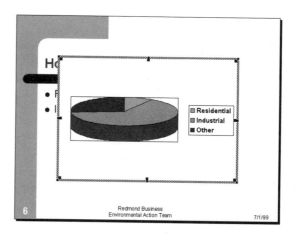

3. Point to the top middle handle of the pie's chart area and drag down until the graph no longer obscures the bulleted text of the slide. Then drag the other handles to enlarge the graph so that it fills the bottom of the slide, like this:

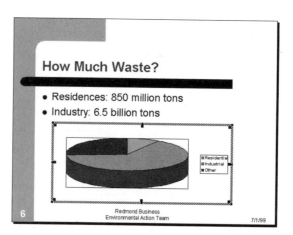

Rotating a pie graph

To rotate a three-dimensional pie graph, choose the 3-D View command from Graph's Chart menu. When the 3-D View dialog box appears, enter the number of degrees you want to rotate the pie in the Rotation edit box, and then click Apply. A preview of your pie graph is displayed so that you can see the effects of your changes. To implement your changes, simply click OK.

Separating Slices

In pie graphs, you can separate the individual markers, or slices, by simply dragging them with the mouse. As you'll see as you follow these steps, separating the slices helps to distinguish them:

1. Select the plot area (the rectangle containing the pie) and choose Selected Plot Area from the Format menu. Then in the Border section, select the None option and click OK.

2. Click the Residential marker to select it. (Selecting individual markers is a tricky process. You know that a single marker is selected when it's the only one surrounded by handles.)

3. Point to the marker and drag away from the center of the pie.

4. Repeat step 3 for the Industrial and Other markers.

5. Right-click the legend and choose Format Legend from the shortcut menu.   ← Repositioning the legend

6. On the Placement tab, select the Bottom option. On the Font tab, change the size to 18. Then click OK.

7. Deselect the graph to return to PowerPoint. Your graph looks like the one shown here:

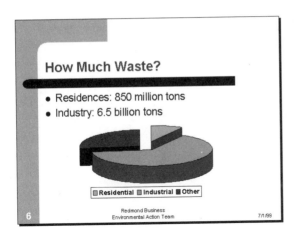

Adding Special Effects

To spruce up a presentation that you will run on your computer (rather than printing it out on transparencies or producing a set of 35mm slides), you can add special effects such as *animation effects* or *transitions*. Animation effects are visual or sound effects that you apply to specific objects on a slide, such as the title. Transitions are visual or sound effects that you apply to an entire slide to help move the audience smoothly from one slide to another. You can also apply preset animation effects to the bulleted items on a slide to help keep

Adding data labels

Instead of using a legend, you can add labels to the data markers. These labels can even show the value or percent of each marker and can include the legend key. Choose Chart Options from Graph's Chart menu and click the Data Labels tab. Select the Show Label And Percent option and click OK. The plot area of the pie graph shrinks to accommodate the labels, which now appear next to their respective data markers. You can then increase the size of the plot area and reposition the data labels.

the audience focused on a particular point. Let's add some special effects to the 1 Redmond BEAT presentation:

1. First turn off the Outlining toolbar.

The Animation Effects button

2. Move to Slide 1 and click the Animation Effects button on the Formatting toolbar's More Buttons palette to display a floating Animation Effects toolbar. Then dock the toolbar below the toolbar row.

The Laser Text Effect button

3. Select the slide's title area and click the Laser Text Effect button on the Animation Effects toolbar.

The Camera Effect button

4. Select the slide's object area and click the Camera Effect button on the Animation Effects toolbar.

5. Click the Slide Sorter View button at the bottom of the presentation window to switch to slide sorter view.

Applying slide transition effects

6. Choose Select All from the Edit menu to select all eight slides, click the arrow to the right of the Slide Transition Effects box on the Slide Sorter toolbar, and select Blinds Vertical from the drop-down list. PowerPoint demonstrates the effect of this transition on the first selected slide and puts a transition icon below each slide, as shown here:

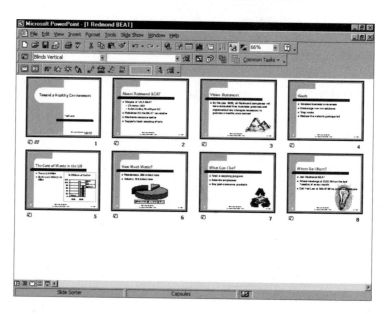

7. Hold down the Ctrl key and click Slides 1, 3, 5, and 6 to deselect them.

8. Click the arrow to the right of the Preset Animation box on the
   Slide Sorter toolbar and select Fly From Right from the drop-
   down list. Now the bulleted items on each selected slide will
   "fly in" when you click the left mouse button during an electronic slide show.

The Preset Animation box

   Now let's animate the graphic on Slide 7:

1. Click between the slides to deselect everything, click Slide 7,
   and then click the Slide View button.

2. Click the recycling graphic to select it, and click the Custom
   Animation button on the Animation Effects toolbar to display
   the dialog box shown below:

The Custom Animation
button

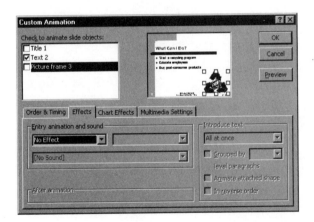

3. In the Check To Animate Slide Objects box, make sure Picture Frame 3 is selected.

4. On the Effects tab, click the arrow to the right of the first edit
   box in the Entry Animation And Sound section, and select
   Swivel from the drop-down list.

5. Click the Preview button to see the results, and then click OK
   to apply the animation.

   Now let's check out the special effects you've added by running the presentation as an electronic slide show.

Running an Electronic Slide Show

Printing a presentation

Making 35mm slides

To output a PowerPoint presentation on paper or on acetate (to create overhead transparencies), you can use the Print command. You can also send a PowerPoint file to a graphics service bureau if you want to output the presentation as a set of 35mm slides. However, to really impress an audience and simultaneously take advantage of the latest technology, you'll want to deliver your presentation as an electronic slide show that showcases the special effects you've added. In this section, you'll learn how to view an electronic slide show on your own computer. Let's get going:

The Slide Show button

1. With 1 Redmond BEAT open on your screen, move to Slide 1 and click the Slide Show button at the bottom of the presentation window, or choose View Show from the Slide Show menu. PowerPoint builds the title slide of the presentation using the effects you've specified. It then looks like this:

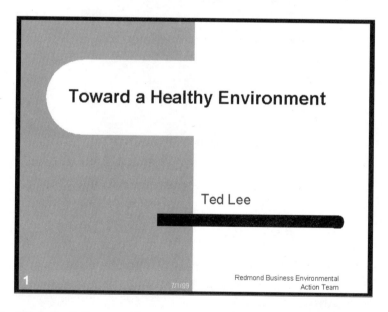

2. Click the left mouse button or press the N key to move to the next slide.

3. Click the mouse button four times to bring each bulleted item into view.

Building a bulleted list

4. Move the mouse pointer across the displayed slide. A button with an arrow and a slide icon appears in the bottom left corner. Click the button to display the slide show shortcut menu shown here:

Displaying the presentation tools

```
Next
Previous
Go                    ▶
Meeting Minder...
Speaker Notes
Pointer Options       ▶
Screen                ▶
Help
End Show
```

As you can see, the commands on this menu help you control an electronic slide show.

5. Choose Go and then By Title from the shortcut menu to display a drop-down list of slide titles.

Moving to a specified slide

6. Select Slide 3's title to move to that slide.

7. Click your way through all the slides so that you can see the special effects in action.

8. When you reach the end of the slide show, click the mouse button to return to slide view. (You can leave slide show view at any time by pressing Esc.)

9. Do a little experimenting with the other animation effects and transitions that PowerPoint offers, and then run through the slide show again.

Now that you have an understanding of how PowerPoint works, you can forge ahead on your own to create professional presentations.

8 Access Basics

We show you how to create a database and enter records in a table in both table and form views. Then you learn how to change the table's structure by setting its field properties, and how to find, move, and sort records.

The sample table stores information about employees of the Tip Top Roofing company. You can adapt the table for other groups of people, such as students in a class or members of a club.

Table created and concepts covered:

Set the maximum size for entries, depending on their type

Specify an input mask to control what can be entered and how it looks

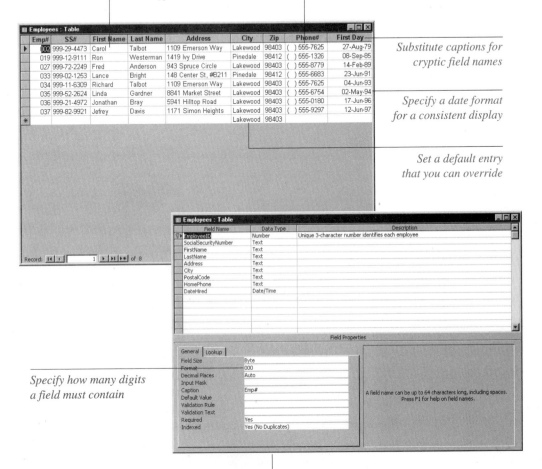

Substitute captions for cryptic field names

Specify a date format for a consistent display

Set a default entry that you can override

Specify how many digits a field must contain

Use a wizard to create database tables and then customize their structure

You are probably excited but nervous about learning to use a powerful database like Microsoft Access 2000. And you're probably hoping that, like the other Office applications, Access will be simple to use and yet offer you the tools you need to handle complex data. Well, relax. By the end of this chapter, you will be familiar enough with Access to be able to start creating databases to meet most of your needs.

Database concepts →

Before you load Access, let's discuss the concept of a database. The most basic component of an Access database is a *table*—a collection of information arranged in *records* (rows) and *fields* (columns). A database can consist of several tables of related data. For example, a client database might assign clients a number and list their names and addresses in one table and then list their numbers and credit references in another. Still another table might summarize account transactions for the last three years by client number. All the tables contain information about the clients, but different information is related by the client number in each table. All the information could be kept in just one table, but if only a few clients have active accounts, the part of the table devoted to account transactions would have only a few entries. So it's better to break the database into separate but related tables.

Other database components →

Tables are the basic building blocks of a database. In addition to tables, a database can include queries, forms, reports, and other components, all of which allow you to view and manipulate database information in a variety of ways. As you follow along with our examples, you will create a database for Tip Top Roofing that includes several of these components.

Setting Up a Database

Without any more preamble, let's fire up Access and set up the sample database, which is called Roofs. Access will then store all the tables, queries, forms, reports, and data access pages you create as you work your way through Chapters 8 and 9 in the Roofs database file. Follow the steps on the facing page.

Fields and records

The basic structure of a database is a combination of fields and records. Each field contains bits of similar information—for example, all the phone numbers in the phone book. Each record contains all the bits of information about a particular item such as a person, product, or event—for example, the name, address, and phone number for one person in the phone book.

1. Choose Programs and then Microsoft Access from the Start menu to open Access. Then, if necessary, click the Office Assistant's Start Using Microsoft Access option. You see a dialog box that looks like this:

2. Click the Blank Access Database option and then click OK to display the File New Database dialog box, which resembles the Save As dialog box because you must save your database with a name before you can begin working with it.

3. Type *Roofs* in the File Name edit box and click Create. Access opens this Database window:

Naming the database

As you can see, the Database window has a bar on the left that displays icons for the various database components, or objects. Clicking one of these icons displays in the workspace to the right a list of possible actions for that type. At the moment, the Tables icon is selected, and in the pane on the right you see various options for creating tables. Once you have created a table, it will be listed in this pane, making it easily accessible at any time.

Creating a Table

You want to create the first table in the database, which will be used to store information about Tip Top Roofing's employees. Follow these steps:

The Table Wizard →

1. In the Database window, with Tables selected on the Objects bar, double-click Create Table By Using Wizard. The Table Wizard displays the first of its dialog boxes so that it can lead you through the steps for creating the table's field structure:

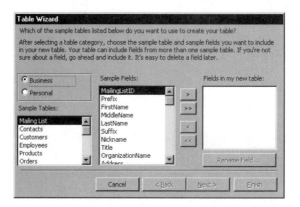

Ready-made business and personal tables

The first Table Wizard dialog box provides several business and personal tables, with the Business category selected by default. If you click the Personal category, Access displays a list of tables you can create for personal use. You may find some of these sample tables quite useful, so it's worth taking the time to explore the list.

2. In the Sample Tables list, click Employees. The Sample Fields list changes to reflect the kind of information usually stored in an employee database, with DepartmentName selected.

3. Select EmployeeID and then click the > button to add the EmployeeID field name to the Fields In My New Table list.

4. Add the SocialSecurityNumber, FirstName, LastName, Address, City, PostalCode (zip code), HomePhone, and DateHired field names to the Fields In My New Table list either by clicking each name and then clicking the > button or by

double-clicking each field name. (If you add a name by mistake, simply select it in the Fields In My New Table list and click the < button.) Then click the Next button to display the next wizard dialog box:

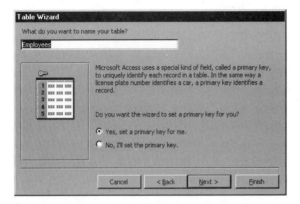

5. The name Access suggests for this database—Employees—is pretty logical, so don't change the entry in the edit box. However, you don't want Access to set the *primary key*, which is a field that distinguishes one record from another. When you enter field values in the table, no two entries in this field can be the same. In tables with keys, if you try to enter the same field value in two records, Access displays an error message and won't let you move to a new record until you change one of the duplicates. Click the No, I'll Set The Primary Key option and then click Next. This wizard dialog box appears:

The primary key

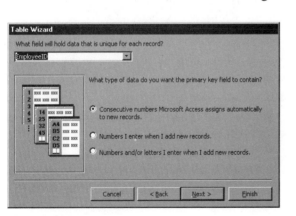

6. You want to use the default EmployeeID field as the primary key, but instead of allowing Access to enter consecutive

Allowing Access to create the primary key

If you allow Access to create the primary key, Access inserts an AutoNumber field as the first field of the table, designates that field as the primary key, and automatically enters a consecutive number as that field's value for each record.

numbers, you want to enter the numbers yourself. Click the second option and click Next. This dialog box appears:

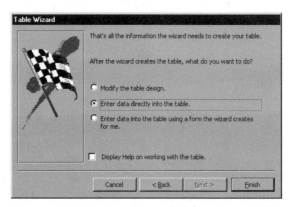

7. Click the Finish button to indicate that you want to enter data directly in the table. Access displays an empty Table window.

Entering and Deleting Records

Datasheet view

Form view

Each record in the Employees table will contain information about one employee. In Access, you can enter and edit records either directly in the table in *datasheet view*, which displays as many records as will fit on the screen in column/row format, or in a form in *form view*, which displays one record at a time. You'll look at both methods in this section.

Entering Records in a Table

The record selector

Because you told the Table Wizard that you want to enter data directly in the table, Access has already switched the new table to datasheet view. An insertion point sits blinking in the Employee ID field, ready for you to enter the first item of information, and an arrowhead in the *record selector* at the left end of the row indicates that the record is ready to receive data. Let's enter the first item now:

Fast navigation

When you are entering and editing data, using the keyboard to move around a window is often faster than using the mouse. You can easily navigate using the Arrow, Tab, Home, End, Page Up, and Page Down keys.

1. Type *2* as the first employee number. The arrowhead in the record selector changes to a pencil, indicating that the data in the record has been changed but not yet saved. (Access has added a second record with an asterisk in its record selector, indicating that the record is empty.) Press Enter to move the insertion point to the next field.

2. In the first record, enter the field values shown below, pressing Enter to move from field to field:

Field	Record 1
Social Security Number	*999294473* (Access inserts the hyphens)
First Name	*Carol*
Last Name	*Talbot*
Address	*1109 Emerson Way*
City	*Lakewood*
Postal Code	*98403* (Access adds a hyphen)

Don't worry that the data in the Address field doesn't fit in its column; you'll fix that in a minute.

3. Click the Home Phone field, click an insertion point after the area code to leave it blank, type *5557625,* and press Enter. (Access inserts the hyphen.)

4. In the Date Hired field, type *082779,* and press Enter. (Access inserts slashes.)

5. Enter records 2 through 5 as shown below, remembering to skip over the area code in the Home Phone field:

Field	Record 2	Record 3	Record 4	Record 5
Employee ID	*19*	*27*	*29*	*33*
Social Security Number	*999129111*	*999722249*	*999218635*	*999021253*
First Name	*Ron*	*Fred*	*James*	*Lance*
Last Name	*Westerman*	*Anderson*	*Murray*	*Bright*
Address	*1419 Ivy Drive*	*943 Spruce Circle*	*7921 Port Avenue*	*148 Center St, #B211*
City	*Pinedale*	*Lakewood*	*Lakewood*	*Pinedale*
Postal Code	*98412*	*98403*	*98403*	*98412*
Home Phone	*5551326*	*5558779*	*5555934*	*5556683*
Date Hired	*090885*	*021489*	*032291*	*062391*

The Employees table now looks like the one shown here:

Employee ID	Social Security	First Name	Last Name	Address	City	Postal Code	Hom
2	999-29-4473	Carol	Talbot	1109 Emerson	Lakewood	98403-	( ) 5
19	999-12-9111	Ron	Westerman	1419 Ivy Drive	Pinedale	98412-	( ) 5
27	999-72-2249	Fred	Anderson	943 Spruce Circ	Lakewood	98403-	( ) 5
29	999-21-8635	James	Murray	7921 Port Aven	Lakewood	98403-	( ) 5
33	999-02-1253	Lance	Bright	148 Center St, #	Pinedale	98412-	( ) 5

Now let's adjust the widths of a few fields:

Adjusting field widths

1. Double-click the border between the Address and City field names. The Address column widens to fit the longest entry. Repeat this step for the First Name, Last Name, and City fields.

Selecting multiple fields

2. Scroll the table to the right until the last three fields are visible.

3. Point to the Postal Code field name. When the pointer changes to a downward-pointing arrow, click to select that field in all records. Then point to the Date Hired field name, hold down the Shift key, and click to add the last two fields to the selection.

4. Choose Column Width from the Format menu to display the dialog box shown here:

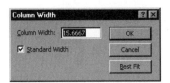

5. Type *15* and press Enter to change the widths of all three fields.

Entering Records in a Form

Instead of entering information in a table, you can enter it in a form. To display a form for the Employees table and to see how easy it is to enter records in a form, follow these steps:

The New Object button

1. Click the New Object button to display this form:

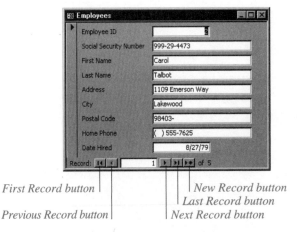

First Record button

Previous Record button

New Record button
Last Record button
Next Record button

2. Click the Next Record button at the bottom of the Form window to display the information for Ron Westerman.

3. Click the Last Record button to move to the last record and then click the New Record button to display a blank record.

4. Enter the sixth record shown below. After typing the last field value, press Enter to display a new blank record, enter the seventh record, and press Enter.

Field	Record 6	Record 7
Employee ID	34	35
Social Security Number	999116309	999522624
First Name	Richard	Linda
Last Name	Talbot	Gardner
Address	1109 Emerson Way	8841 Market Street
City	Lakewood	Lakewood
Postal Code	98403	98403
Home Phone	5557625	5556754
Date Hired	060493	050294

The table is complete for now, and you can view the records in form or datasheet view. Here's how to switch back and forth:

1. Click the arrow to the right of the View button at the left end of the toolbar to drop down a list of three views. Click Datasheet View. Instead of the form, you now see the table in the Form window.

2. Click the View button's arrow again and click Form View to switch back to the form.

3. Close the form by clicking the Form window's Close button, clicking No when asked if you want to save the design of the form. (The records are already saved because Access automatically saves each record when you move to another one.)

4. The Employees table is now visible, but it doesn't include the records you entered via the form. Update the table by choosing the Remove Filter/Sort command from the Records menu. Access then updates the table to show the last two records. (We discuss filters in the tip on page 185.)

The View button

Flexible buttons

The View button's picture icon changes depending on whether you are in form or datasheet view. If you are in form view, the View button displays the datasheet icon, because Access assumes that if you want to change views, you'll want to change to datasheet view. Similarly, the New Object button displays the icon of the last new object you created, because Access assumes you'll want to create that type of object again. If the icon displayed is the one you want, you can click the button instead of making a selection from the button's drop-down list.

Deleting Records

To delete a record, you simply select the record and choose the Delete command. Follow these steps to delete a record from the Employees table:

The Delete Record button

1. Select James Murray's record by clicking its record selector, and either choose Delete from the Edit menu, click the Delete Record button on the toolbar, or press the Delete key. Access displays this dialog box:

2. Click Yes. Access deletes the record and updates the table.

Changing a Table's Structure

When you used the Table Wizard to set up the Employees table, Access made a number of decisions about the table's basic design. But those decisions are not cast in stone. Let's examine the existing table structure and see how to change it:

1. Click the View button on the toolbar to switch to design view. Access displays the structure of the table in this window:

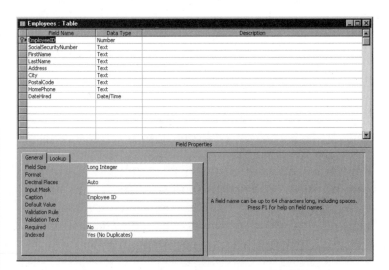

Delete with caution

Be careful when deleting records. If you make a mistake and delete the wrong record, you can't restore the record by clicking an Undo button or choosing Undo from the Edit menu after you've confirmed the deletion.

As you can see, the window is divided into two sections. The top half lists the table's field names (with no spaces) and their data type. (Specifying the data type determines what kind of information you can put in the field and how Access can work with the information.) The bottom half lists the properties assigned to the field selected in the top half.

Data types

2. Press Enter to move to the Data Type column for the EmployeeID field, and click the arrow that appears to display a list of the available data types.

3. Click Number to close the Data Type list without changing its setting, and press Enter to move to the Description column.

4. Type *Unique 3-character number identifies each employee.* When the table is displayed and this field is selected, this description will appear in the Access window's status bar.

After you define a field for a table, you can refine your field definitions in the Field Properties section. You will use some of these properties frequently, others rarely. Here, you'll explore the more common properties.

Setting the Field Size

You can set a field size for the text and number data types. For text fields, the size indicates the maximum number of characters you can enter in the field. You can specify up to 255 characters, which can include letters, numbers, and other characters such as &, %, and ?. If you try to enter, paste, or import a field value that is longer than the specified size, Access truncates the data. Follow these steps to set the size of the text fields of the Employees table:

1. Click anywhere in the SocialSecurityNumber field in the top table grid to display the default properties for that field in the Field Properties section.

2. Double-click 30 in the Field Size edit box to select it, and type *11* to indicate that the field can have up to eleven characters.

3. Repeat steps 1 and 2 to assign the field sizes shown on the next page.

Help with data types

Access is much more rigid about its data types than Excel is with its number formats. For example, specifying a Currency number format for a cell in Excel does not prevent you from entering text in that cell. In Access, you cannot enter text in a field that has been assigned the Number data type. For more information, choose Microsoft Access Help from the Help menu and search for the *data types* topic.

Field	Size	Field	Size
FirstName	10	City	12
LastName	12	PostalCode	10
Address	25	HomePhone	20

Number field size

For number fields, the size is determined by the complexity of the data type format selected. The options are:

Format	Description
Byte	Whole numbers between 0 and 255
Integer	Whole numbers between −32,768 and 32,767
Long Integer	Whole numbers between −2,147,483,648 and 2,147,483,647
Single	Single-precision floating-point numbers between −3.402823E38 and 3.402823E38
Double	Double-precision floating-point numbers between −1.79769313486232E308 and 1.79769313486232E308

Follow these steps to set the size of the table's number field:

1. Click anywhere in the EmployeeID field and then click the Field Size edit box in the Field Properties section.

2. Click the arrow to see a list of available sizes. You don't think the company will ever employ more than 255 employees, so select Byte.

Setting the Format

You use the Format property to specify how the characters entered in a field are to be displayed on the screen. The type of formatting you can set varies depending on the data type. For example, you can select one of several predefined formats for date/time fields, like this:

Predefined formats

1. Click anywhere in the DateHired field and then click the Format edit box in the Field Properties section.

2. Click the arrow to see a list of predefined formats and select Medium Date. The dates in the table will now be displayed in dd-mmm-yy format.

In addition to selecting predefined formats, you can specify custom formats for some data types. Follow these steps to tell Access to always display three digits in the EmployeeID field:

1. Click anywhere in the EmployeeID field and then click the Format edit box.

Custom formats

2. Type *000* to tell Access to enter three digits, using zeros unless you enter something else. Now if you enter an EmployeeID of *36*, Access will display the entry as *036*.

Specifying an Input Mask

Formats aren't the only way to control the display of data. You can also specify an *input mask*, or character pattern, that not only determines how your data looks on the screen but also what kind of data can be entered in a particular field. Because you used the Table Wizard to set up the Employees table, Access has already specified input masks for some fields. Let's take a look at a few of these input masks and make any necessary changes:

1. Click anywhere in the SocialSecurityNumber field. The entry in the Input Mask edit box is *000\-00\-0000*. The zeros are placeholders for digits that you must enter, and the backslashes indicate that the hyphens are literal characters that Access will insert for you.

2. Click the PostalCode field in the table grid. The entry in the Input Mask edit box is *00000\-9999*. Again, the zeros are placeholders for digits you must enter. The nines are placeholders for an optional, four-digit zip code extension. Access enters the hyphen whether or not you enter this extension.

3. Click an insertion point after the last 9 and press the Backspace key six times to delete all but the five zeros. Now Access will accept only five digits in this field. You can no longer enter a four-digit extension.

In case you want to experiment further, on the next page we list some common characters used in the Input Mask edit box, together with what they mean to Access.

Data integrity

Always stop and think before you change the field sizes and input masks for your data. Such changes can result in data losses that will seriously affect the usability of some fields. For example, if you have entered area codes in the HomePhone field, eliminating the area code from the input mask might result in the last three digits of the employees' phone numbers being chopped off.

Character	Action
L	Require a letter.
?	Allow any letter; if no letter is entered, leave blank.
&	Allow any character, but no blanks allowed.
0	Require a digit; if no digit is entered, insert 0.
#	Allow any digit; if no digit is entered, leave blank.
<	Convert all following characters to lowercase.
>	Convert all following characters to uppercase.
\	Insert the following character as entered.

You can remove an input mask at any time. For example, let's remove the input mask from the DateHired field:

Deleting an input mask → 1. Click anywhere in the DateHired field to display its properties.

2. Select the entry in the Input Mask edit box and press Delete.

Assigning a Caption

You use the Caption property to substitute text for the field name when you display the table. The caption may simply repeat the field name with spaces added for readability, or it may display something different. Let's change a few of the captions specified by the Table Wizard when you created the table. Follow these steps:

1. Click anywhere in the EmployeeID field to display its properties in the Field Properties section.

2. Click an insertion point to the right of the *p* in *Employee* in the Caption edit box, hold down the Shift key, and press the End key to highlight all but *Emp*. Then type #.

3. Repeat steps 1 and 2 to change the following captions:

   Social Security Number to *SS#*
   Postal Code to *Zip*
   Home Phone to *Phone#*
   Date Hired to *First Day*

When you display the table, the new captions will be displayed as field names above each column of information.

Setting a Default Value

The Default Value property lets you specify a field value that Access is to enter in the table automatically. Because Tip Top Roofing is small and most of the employees live in the same city, you can use this property for both the City and PostalCode fields to speed up data entry. Follow these steps:

1. Click anywhere in the City field to display that field's properties in the Field Properties section.

2. In the Default Value edit box, click to display an insertion point, and then type *Lakewood* as the default city name.

3. Repeat steps 1 and 2 for the PostalCode field, this time specifying *98403* as the default value.

Now every record you enter in the database table will have Lakewood as its City field value and 98403 as its PostalCode field value, unless you replace them with something else.

Requiring Entries

If you leave the table's field structure as it is, it would be possible to create incomplete employee records. To ensure that key information is always entered, you can specify that a field must have an entry. Try this:

1. Click the EmployeeID field, click the Required edit box, click the arrow, and then click Yes.

2. In the Required edit box for all the other fields, double-click the word No to quickly change it to Yes.

Other Properties

When you made the EmployeeID field the primary key for the table, Access changed that field's Indexed property to Yes (No Duplicates), meaning that the field is indexed and no duplicate values will be allowed. Only text, number, currency, and date/time fields can be indexed. When a field is indexed, Access can process queries, searches, and sorts based on that field more quickly. (If a few values will be repeated often in a

The Indexed property

field, as is the case with the City and PostalCode fields, then indexing the field doesn't save much processing time.) Data entry and editing may be slower with indexed fields because Access must maintain the index as well as the table.

The Validation Rule property

You set the Validation Rule property for a field when you want Access to allow only specific field values to be entered in the field. The kind of rule you can set up varies with the field's data type. You can specify that a text field should contain one of a set of values—for example, the City field should contain only Pinedale or Lakewood. You can specify that a date field should contain only the current date or a date that falls within a certain range. With number fields, you can specify that Access should accept only a specific value, or you can use the greater than (>) and less than (<) signs to specify that field values must fall within a range. You can also specify that the values in a field must match the values in the same field in another table. When you set a validation rule for a field, you can use the Validation Text property to display a message when an unacceptable value is entered.

The Validation Text property

The Allow Zero Length property

You will rarely need to use the Allow Zero Length property (available for text fields). When this property is set to Yes, you can enter " " in a field to indicate that the field doesn't apply for this record. For example, you could enter " " to indicate that an employee doesn't have a phone; simply skipping the field indicates that you don't know the phone number.

Testing the Changes

Now let's return to the table to see the effects of your changes:

Saving in Access

You don't need to worry about saving the data in a database table. Access updates the table file one record at a time as you enter or edit records. But, you do have to explicitly save any changes you make to the table's structure in design view or to the way your records are displayed in datasheet view.

1. Click the View button on the toolbar to switch to datasheet view. Access warns you that you must save the table before switching views.

2. Click Yes. When warned that some data may be lost, click Yes. Then click Yes again to test the data against the new rules (properties). Access then displays the table.

3. Decrease the widths of the fields so that you can see all the employee data at once, as shown on the facing page.

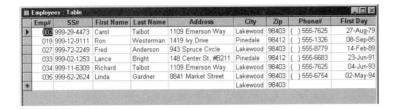

The table reflects all the visual changes you made to its structure. The Emp# field displays three digits, and *Lakewood* and *98403* have been entered by default in the blank record at the bottom of the table. Let's add more employees to try everything out:

1. Click the Emp# field of the blank record at the bottom of the table, type *36*, and press Enter. Access enters *036* in the field.

2. Type the information below in the indicated fields (press Enter to skip over the City and Zip fields). As you enter the field values, notice the effect of the field properties specified as part of the table's structure.

Field	Record 7	Record 8
Emp#		*37*
SS#	*999214972*	*999829921*
First Name	*Jonathan*	*Jefrey* (use this spelling)
Last Name	*Bray*	*Davis*
Address	*5941 Hilltop Road*	*1171 Simon Heights*
Phone#	*5550180*	*5559297*
First Day	*06/17/96*	*06/12/97*

3. Press Enter to complete and save the eighth record.

Working with Records

In Chapter 9, we show you some fairly sophisticated ways of working with records. Here, we'll cover some simple methods of manipulating data so that you can locate information.

Finding Specific Records

You often need to find either a particular record in a table or all the records that have something in common, so Access provides an easy way to locate records. As a demonstration,

Filtering records

When dealing with a very large table, you can temporarily focus on a subset of the records in the table by using filters. For example, if you select Talbot and then click the Filter By Selection button, Access displays the subset of records that have the value Talbot in the Last Name field. (To redisplay all the records, choose Remove Filter/Sort from the Records menu.) Filters are closely related to *queries*, which you'll learn about in Chapter 9.

let's search the Employees table for a record that has Talbot in the Last Name field:

1. Select the Last Name field of any record by pointing to the left of the field value and, when the pointer changes to a fat plus sign, clicking to highlight the field.

2. Click the Find button on the toolbar to display the Find And Replace dialog box shown here:

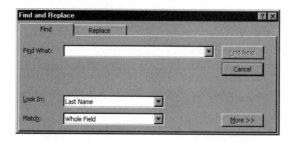

3. Point to the Find And Replace dialog box's title bar, and drag the dialog box downward so that you can see all the table's records.

4. Type *Talbot* in the Find What edit box and click the Find Next button. Access highlights the first field value below the selection that matches your specification.

5. Suppose this is not the employee record you need to examine. Click the Find Next button in the dialog box to find the other record with Talbot in the Last Name field.

6. Click the Close button to close the dialog box.

Hiding/unhiding fields

Sometimes you might want to simplify the display by hiding a field. Select the field's column and then choose Hide Columns from the Format menu. To redisplay the field, choose Unhide Columns from the Format menu, click the check box next to the field you want to redisplay, and then click Close.

Moving Fields

By default, the fields are displayed in the order in which you entered them when you designed the table. You can change the field order by selecting a field's column and dragging it to a new position. For example, if you want to look up an employee's phone number, it might be useful to see the Phone# field next to the employee names. Follow these steps to move the Phone# field:

1. Click the Phone# field name to select the entire column.

2. Point to the Phone# field name and drag the field to the left. As you move the field, Access highlights the divider lines between columns to indicate the new position of the Phone# field.

3. When the divider line to the right of the Last Name field is highlighted, release the mouse button. As you can see here, the Phone# field moves to its new position:

Emp#	SS#	First Name	Last Name	Phone#	Address	City	Zip	First Day
002	999-29-4473	Carol	Talbot	( ) 555-7625	1109 Emerson Way	Lakewood	98403	27-Aug-79
019	999-12-9111	Ron	Westerman	( ) 555-1326	1419 Ivy Drive	Pinedale	98412	08-Sep-85
027	999-72-2249	Fred	Anderson	( ) 555-8779	943 Spruce Circle	Lakewood	98403	14-Feb-89
033	999-02-1253	Lance	Bright	( ) 555-6683	148 Center St, #B211	Pinedale	98412	23-Jun-91
034	999-11-6309	Richard	Talbot	( ) 555-7625	1109 Emerson Way	Lakewood	98403	04-Jun-93
035	999-52-2624	Linda	Gardner	( ) 555-6754	8841 Market Street	Lakewood	98403	02-May-94
036	999-21-4972	Jonathan	Bray	( ) 555-0180	5941 Hilltop Road	Lakewood	98403	17-Jun-96
037	999-82-9921	Jefrey	Davis	( ) 555-9297	1171 Simon Heights	Lakewood	98403	12-Jun-97
*						Lakewood	98403	

Employees : Table

4. For more practice, move the Phone# field back to its original position between the Zip and First Day fields.

Moving fields in datasheet view does not affect the data or change the basic structure of the table.

Sorting Records

The Employees table is short enough that you can view all of its records on the screen at one time. But you may need to work with tables, such as mailing lists, that contain several hundred or even several thousand records. In those tables, one way to easily locate a specific record or set of records is to sort the table on a particular field. Try this:

1. Click the Last Name field name to select that column.

2. Click the Sort Ascending button on the toolbar to sort starting with A or the lowest digit, or click the Sort Descending button to sort starting with Z or the highest digit.

The Sort Ascending and Sort Descending buttons

3. To return the data to its original order, choose the Remove Filter/Sort command from the Records menu.

Restoring the original order

4. Close Access, clicking Yes if asked whether to save your changes to the look of the table.

9

More About Access

You create more tables and establish relationships between them. Then you design a custom form and construct queries to extract information. Finally, you share your data in two ways: by creating printed reports and by creating data access pages for Web viewing.

The techniques you learn for extracting information and sharing data in this chapter can be applied to the tables you might need to create for any business, school, or community group.

Components created and concepts covered:

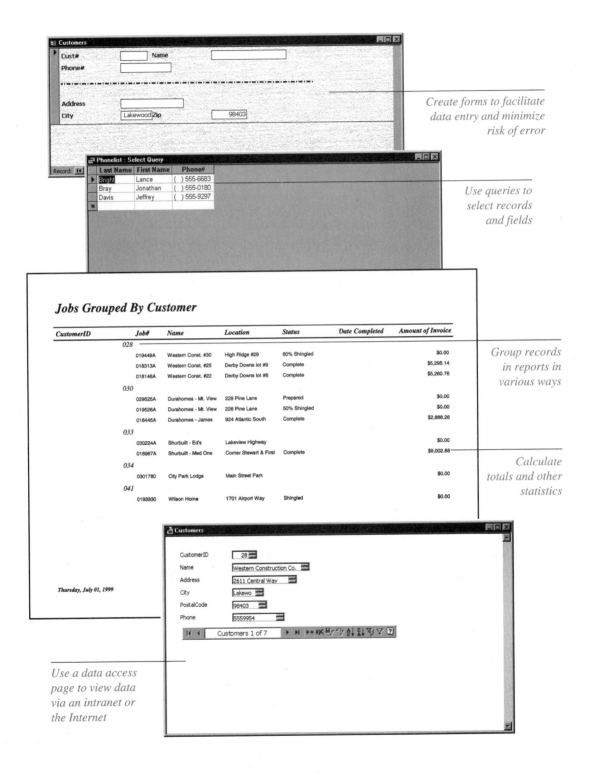

Create forms to facilitate data entry and minimize risk of error

Use queries to select records and fields

Jobs Grouped By Customer

CustomerID	Job#	Name	Location	Status	Date Completed	Amount of Invoice
028						
	019449A	Western Const. #30	High Ridge #29	80% Shingled		$0.00
	018313A	Western Const. #25	Derby Downs lot #9	Complete		$5,295.14
	018146A	Western Const. #22	Derby Downs lot #8	Complete		$5,260.76
030						
	029525A	Durahomes - Mt. View	228 Pine Lane	Prepared		$0.00
	019526A	Durahomes - Mt. View	226 Pine Lane	50% Shingled		$0.00
	018445A	Durahomes - James	924 Atlantic South	Complete		$2,888.26
033						
	030224A	Shurbuilt - Ed's	Lakeview Highway			$0.00
	018967A	Shurbuilt - Med One	Corner Stewart & First	Complete		$9,002.88
034						
	0301780	City Park Lodge	Main Street Park			$0.00
041						
	0193330	Wilson Home	1701 Airport Way	Shingled		$0.00

Group records in reports in various ways

Calculate totals and other statistics

Thursday, July 01, 1999

Use a data access page to view data via an intranet or the Internet

imple tables like the one you created in Chapter 8 will probably meet many of your needs. However, relational databases like Access enable you to manipulate tables so that you can easily access the information they contain. In this chapter, you will look at more ways to work with Access.

Creating One Table Based on Another

Databases often consist of several tables with the same general characteristics. For example, the database for the roofing company might include one table with information about employees and another with information about customers. You don't want to spend a lot of time recreating the structure of the Employees table for the Customers table, and with Access you don't have to. You can copy the structure of an existing table to create a new one. Here's how to copy the Employees table structure to create the Customers table:

1. Click the Start button and choose Roofs from the Documents submenu to start Access and open the Roofs database.

2. With Tables selected on the Objects bar and Employees selected in the Database window, click the Copy button on the Standard toolbar.

3. Click the Paste button on the Standard toolbar to display the Paste Table As dialog box.

4. In the Table Name edit box, type *Customers*, select the Structure Only option, and click OK. Access adds the Customers table to the list in the Database window.

5. With Customers selected, click the Design button on the window's toolbar to display the new table in design view.

Now you need to make some field adjustments:

1. Change the *EmployeeID* field name to *CustomerID*, change the word *employee* in this field's Description column to *customer*, and change this field's Caption property to *Cust#*.

Copying records

When you want to copy a record from one table to another, you can use the Copy and Paste buttons, provided that the fields in the two tables are compatible. If Access has a problem when pasting the record, it puts the record in a Paste Errors table. By scrutinizing the Paste Errors table, you can usually discover the problem and fix it. You can then cut and paste the record from the Paste Errors table into the desired table.

2. Select the SocialSecurityNumber field by clicking its row selector, and press the Delete key to delete it. Then delete the FirstName and DateHired fields.

3. Change *LastName* to *Name*, change the field size to *30*, and then change the Caption property to *Name*.

4. Change the *HomePhone* field name to *Phone*. The table structure now looks like this:

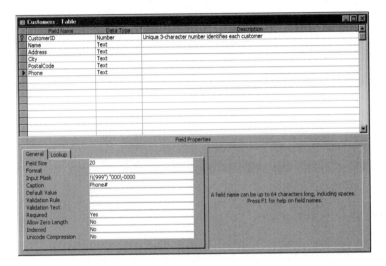

5. Click the View button to switch to datasheet view, and when prompted to save the table, click Yes.

Creating Forms

In Chapter 8, you saw how you can use a form to enter and view the information in a database table one record at a time. When we introduced forms, we mentioned that you can create different kinds of forms to accomplish different kinds of tasks. You can also design custom forms. A detailed discussion of customization is beyond the scope of this book, but we do want to give you a taste of it here. Create a form for entering information in the Customers table by following the steps on the next page.

Copy with caution

Copying the structure of simple tables is relatively easy, but as you begin to create more complex tables, you'll need to consider carefully such characteristics as primary keys and validation rules, as well as the applicability of other Access table features such as referential integrity, which we discuss on page 196.

1. Close the Customers table, and then with Customers selected in the Database window, click the arrow to the right of the New Object button on the toolbar and select Form.

The Form Wizard ───────▶ 2. In the New Form dialog box, select Form Wizard and then click OK to display this dialog box:

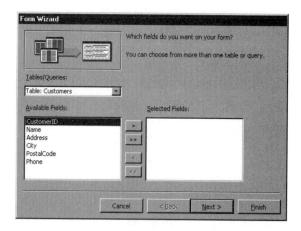

3. With CustomerID selected in the Available Fields list, click the >> button to move all the field names to the list on the right. Then click the Next button.

Selecting the layout ───────▶ 4. You need to select the form's basic layout. Click the various options to see how they look in the sample on the left. Then select Columnar and click Next to display another dialog box:

Graphing Access data

Graphs are sometimes the most logical way to present data because they enable people to quickly make visual comparisons. In Access, you graph data in a form. You select the table you want to work with, click the arrow to the right of the New Object button on the toolbar, select Form, and double-click Chart Wizard. (You may need to install the feature first.) The Chart Wizard then helps you plot your data.

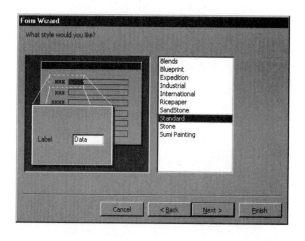

5. Access asks you to choose a style for your form. Select each of the styles listed on the right in turn, noticing their effect in the window to the left. Then select Sumi Painting and click Next to display the last dialog box:

Selecting the style

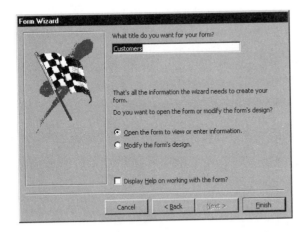

6. If you wanted to work with the default form, you could just click the Finish button, but you want to make a few adjustments to the form's design before you start using it. So click the Modify The Form's Design option and then click Finish.

7. Dock the Toolbox toolbar at the left edge of the screen, which looks like this:

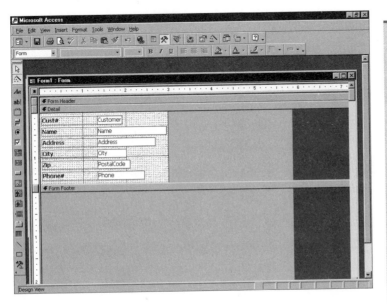

Creating forms from scratch

You can create a blank form by clicking the arrow to the right of the New Object button on the toolbar, selecting Form, and then double-clicking Design View in the New Form dialog box. Access switches to design view and displays a form containing only the Detail section, ready for you to add the controls you want. To add Form Header and Form Footer or Page Header and Page Footer sections, choose the corresponding command from the View menu.

8. Save the form by clicking the Save button on the toolbar.

The Form window →

Labels and controls →

The Form window is divided into three sections: the Form Header section, which can contain information such as a title or date that you want to appear at the top of the form; the Detail section, which displays transparent boxes called *labels* and white boxes called *controls* for each of the fields you selected for inclusion in the form; and the Form Footer section, which, like the Form Header, can contain information such as a title or date that you want to appear at the bottom of the form. Two other sections, Page Header and Page Footer, are not visible in the form now on your screen. They contain elements you want to appear on every page of a multi-page form. The window also displays horizontal and vertical rulers and gridlines that help you position controls on the form.

Let's customize the Customers form so that its fields are grouped more logically:

1. Scroll the Access window and point to the Form window's bottom border. When the pointer changes to a double-headed arrow, drag upward to decrease the height of the Form window. Then scroll back to the top of the Access window.

2. Click the Name control. Small handles appear around the control's border.

Two types of hands

To move a control and its label on a form so that they maintain their relative positions, select the control and drag the black open hand that appears when you point to the control's border. To move a control independently of its label, select the control and drag the black pointing hand that appears when you point to the large handle in the control's top left corner. To move a label independently of its control, select the label and drag the large handle's pointing hand.

3. Point to the border of the selected control. When the pointer changes to a small, open hand, drag the control and its label to the right of the CustomerID control. (Use the rulers to help align the controls.)

4. Next select and drag the Phone control and its label under the CustomerID control.

5. Drag the City control down into the space formerly occupied by the Phone control, and drag the PostalCode control down to the right of the City control. Then drag the Address control down so that it sits just above the City control. The fields are now arranged in two groups on the form, as shown on the facing page.

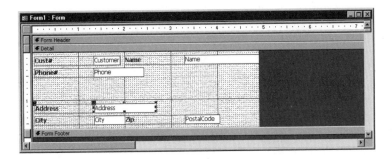

6. Select all the labels by holding down the Shift key and clicking each in turn. Then click the Align Right button on the Formatting toolbar.

Now let's draw a line to separate the two groups:

1. First click the Line button on the Toolbox toolbar and then position the cross-hair pointer next to the ¾-inch mark on the vertical ruler.

The Line button

2. Hold down the left mouse button and drag a straight line to the 5½-inch mark on the horizontal ruler.

3. Click the Save button to save your changes to the form.

4. Click the View button to switch to form view, where the form looks as shown here:

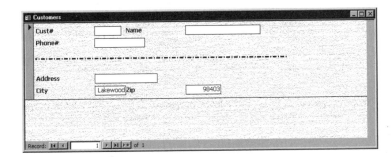

5. Now enter the customer records shown at the top of the following page, pressing Tab to move from field to field and to start a new record.

The Toolbox toolbar

The Toolbox provides many tools with which you can customize forms. You might want to practice adding elements to forms to explore these tools. If you need help, choose What's This from the Help menu, point to the tool you want to know more about, and click.

Cust#	Name	Address	City	Zip	Phone#
28	Western Construction Co.	2611 Central Way			5559954
30	Durahomes	4969 Market St. #211	Pinedale	98412	5557965
33	Shurbuilt	966 8th Street			5558742
34	Lakewood City Const. Dept.	28 Central Way			5557865
35	James Bready	511 Shoreline Drive	Pinedale	98412	5558121
41	Marcus Wilson	1701 Airport Way			5553882
45	Roberts Construction	734 Stewart Road			5551044

6. Close the Customers form, saving the form design.

Establishing Table Relationships

With Access, you can create relationships between tables so that you can combine the data from more than one table in forms, queries, and reports. The relationships involve tables in which the primary key of one table matches a field called the *foreign key* in another table. Usually the values in the foreign key field don't have to be unique, but each one must match a value in the primary key field. Access provides a method called *referential integrity* for ensuring that the field values match. As a demonstration, let's create a new table called Jobs:

Referential integrity →

1. With Tables selected on the Objects bar, click New on the window's toolbar, select Design View and click OK. Then create the table structure shown below. (You can type the first letter of the data type, and Access will complete it.)

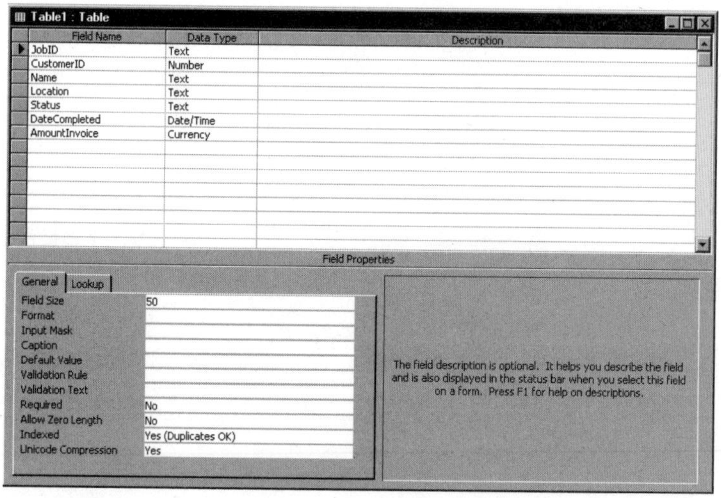

Field name rules

The field names in any one table must be unique and cannot be longer than 64 characters. You can use any combination of characters except periods, exclamation marks, and square brackets.

2. Click the row selector of the JobID field and click the Primary ←
Key button on the toolbar to make this field the table's primary key. (See page 173 if you've forgotten what the primary key is.)

The Primary Key button

3. Assign the fields these properties:

Field	Field Size	Format	Caption	Required
JobID	8		*Job#*	Yes
CustomerID	Byte	000	*Cust#*	Yes
Name	25			
Location	25			
Status	25			
DateCompleted		Short Date	*Date Completed*	
AmountInvoice			*Amount of Invoice*	

4. Click the Close button to close the window, and save the new table with the name *Jobs* when prompted.

Now let's create a referential integrity relationship between the Customers and Jobs tables:

1. With the Database window active, click the Relationships ←
button on the Standard toolbar to display the Show Table dialog box shown here:

The Relationships button

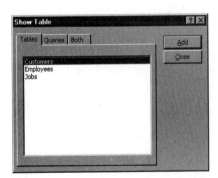

2. In the Tables list, Access has selected the Customers table. Click the Add button to add a Customers box to the blank window behind the dialog box.

3. Click Jobs, then Add, and then Close. You see the window shown on the next page.

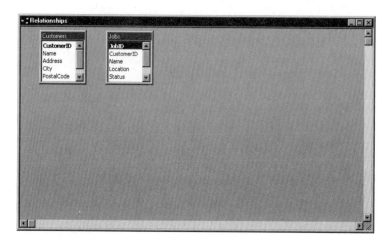

4. In the Customers box, point to the CustomerID field name. Hold down the left mouse button, drag the field icon to the CustomerID field name in the Jobs box, and release the mouse button. Access displays this dialog box:

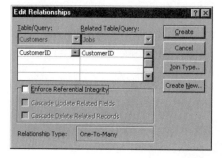

At the bottom of the dialog box, notice that the relationship type is listed as One-To-Many. This means that for each record in the parent table (Customers), there can be many records with a matching field value in the child table (Jobs).

5. Click the Enforce Referential Integrity check box to tell Access to require that values in the CustomerID field in the Jobs table match values in the same field in the Customers table.

6. Click the Create button to create the new relationship between the tables. Access draws a line connecting the two fields in the Relationships window, as shown at the top of the facing page.

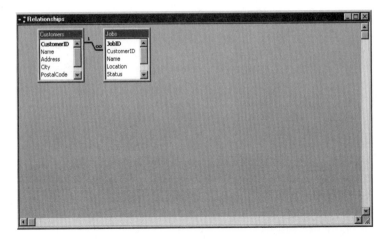

7. Close the Relationships window, saving the changes to the database when prompted.

Here's the acid test:

1. Open the Jobs table and enter the data shown here:

Testing referential integrity

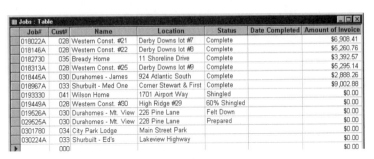

2. Try entering an incorrect customer number. You can type any number in the field, but Access won't let you leave the record until a correct customer number is in place.

3. When you have entered all the data, close the Jobs table.

As you created the Jobs table, suppose you realized that you need to track the current job assignments of all employees. You can't add an EmployeeID field to the Jobs table because several employees might be assigned to the same job. Instead, you will have to modify the Employees table to include a JobID field. This process involves changing the design of the Employees table, adding another relationship, and entering the job numbers. Follow the steps on the next page.

1. In the Database window, click Employees and then click the Design button to open the table in design view.

Adding a field

2. Select the FirstName field by clicking its row selector, and press the Insert key to add a new blank row above FirstName.

3. Type *JobID* as the new field name, specify Text as the data type, and assign a field size of *8* and a caption of *Job#*.

4. Close the Employees table, saving the changes when prompted.

Now let's add another relationship to the database:

1. Click the Relationships button on the toolbar.

The Show Table button

2. When the Relationships window appears, click the Show Table button, select Employees, click the Add button, and then click the Close button.

3. Next drag the JobID field in the Jobs box to the JobID field in the Employees box, click Enforce Referential Integrity in the Edit Relationships dialog box, and then click Create to add this one-to-many relationship to the database.

4. Close the Relationships window, clicking Yes to save your changes.

Now all you have left to do is enter the job numbers in the Employees table:

1. Open the Employees table and enter the job numbers shown here, leaving the field for Carol Talbot blank because she works in the office:

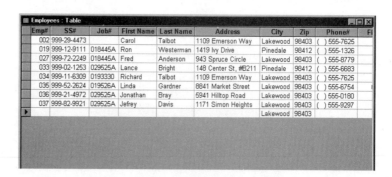

Emp#	SS#	Job#	First Name	Last Name	Address	City	Zip	Phone#	Fi
002	999-29-4473		Carol	Talbot	1109 Emerson Way	Lakewood	98403	( ) 555-7625	
019	999-12-9111	018445A	Ron	Westerman	1419 Ivy Drive	Pinedale	98412	( ) 555-1326	
027	999-72-2249	018445A	Fred	Anderson	943 Spruce Circle	Lakewood	98403	( ) 555-8779	
033	999-02-1253	029525A	Lance	Bright	148 Center St, #B211	Pinedale	98412	( ) 555-6683	
034	999-11-6309	0193330	Richard	Talbot	1109 Emerson Way	Lakewood	98403	( ) 555-7625	
035	999-52-2624	019526A	Linda	Gardner	8841 Market Street	Lakewood	98403	( ) 555-6754	
036	999-21-4972	029525A	Jonathan	Bray	5941 Hilltop Road	Lakewood	98403	( ) 555-0180	
037	999-82-9921	029525A	Jefrey	Davis	1171 Simon Heights	Lakewood	98403	( ) 555-9297	
						Lakewood	98403		

2. Close the table.

Viewing Hierarchical Data

Access reflects table relationships in a way that allows you to see the linked information with a single mouse-click. Follow these steps to see what we mean:

1. Open the Customers table, which now has a column of plus signs on the left, as shown here:

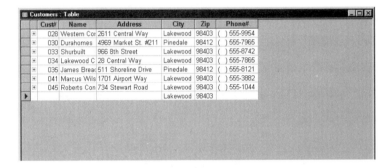

The plus signs indicate the availability of additional data that "belongs" to each of the customer records.

2. Click the plus sign for Durahomes to see a *subdatasheet* of information from the Jobs table, like this:

Subdatasheets

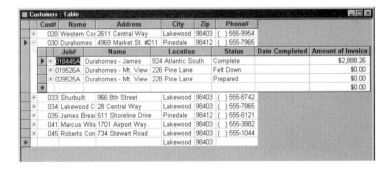

This subdatasheet contains only the records for Durahomes' jobs from the Jobs table. Each of these records also has a plus sign.

3. Click the plus sign for job 018445A to see its subdatasheet which, as you can see on the next page, contains records from the Employees table.

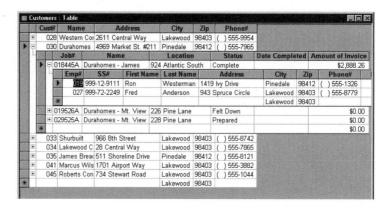

4. Close the Employee subdatasheet by clicking the minus sign for 018445A in the Jobs subdatasheet.

Now test the link by making a change in a subdatasheet. Follow these steps:

Editing data in subdatasheets

1. Select the entry in the Status field for the 019526A record, type *50% Shingled*, and press Enter.

2. Click the minus sign for Durahomes to close the Jobs subdatasheet, and then close the Customers table.

3. Now open the Jobs table to verify that job 019526A reflects the change you just made. Then close the table.

Using Queries to Extract Information

In Access, you use queries to ask questions about your data, to extract complete or partial records from the tables, and even to edit records. Queries that find and extract information from a database are called *select queries*, and queries that perform an action such as updating or deleting records are called *action queries*.

Select queries

Action queries

Selecting Specific Fields

Suppose Tip Top Roofing's job supervisor has asked you for a list of the phone numbers of company employees. He is not interested in any other information about the employees; all he wants is names and phone numbers. You can create the list by following the steps on the facing page.

1. In the Roofs Database window, click the Queries icon on the Objects bar and then click New. In the New Query dialog box, select Simple Query Wizard and click OK. The Simple Query Wizard displays the dialog box shown here:

The Simple Query Wizard

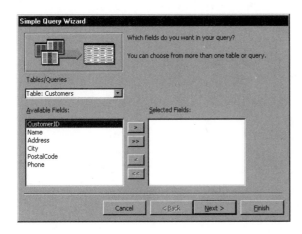

2. Select Table: Employees from the Tables/Queries drop-down list. Access displays the available fields for the Employees table in the list below.

3. Double-click LastName, FirstName, and then HomePhone to move these fields to the Selected Fields list. Then click Next.

4. Give the query the name *Phonelist* and then click Finish. The result is the datasheet shown here:

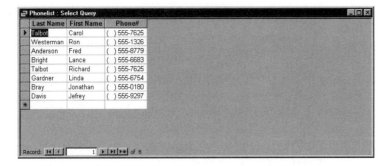

5. Print the query datasheet by clicking the Print button on the toolbar. You can then give the list of phone numbers to the job supervisor.

Printing the datasheet

6. Close the Select Query window.

Rerunning queries →

The Database window now lists Phonelist as an existing query. When you want to access the datasheet of the names and phone numbers of the roofing company's employees, you can select this query and click Open. Access runs the query again and opens a new datasheet. If you have made changes to the Employees table, these changes will be reflected in the datasheet.

Selecting Specific Records

What if you want Access to select fields only from specific records? For example, let's suppose that the shingles for job 029525A are going to be delivered late and you need the employees assigned to that job to report to the office in the morning instead of the job site. Follow these steps to modify the Phonelist query so that Access will include in the query datasheet only the names and phone numbers of the employees assigned to job 029525A:

Changing a query's structure →

1. With Phonelist selected in the Database window, click the Design button to display the query in design view. Access displays the Select Query window shown here:

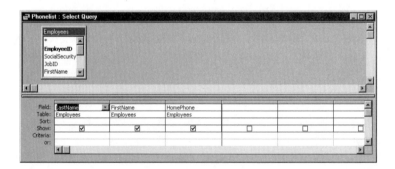

The Employees box lists the fields in the Employees table. (The * at the top of the list represents the entire table.) Below

The query by example grid →

is a table grid called the *query by example (QBE) grid*, in which you can visually structure the query.

Adding fields →

2. Double-click JobID in the Employees box to add it to the QBE grid, and click the Show box for the JobID field to deselect it.

Adding criteria →

3. In the Criteria row of the JobID column, type *029525A*. The query now looks like the one shown on the facing page.

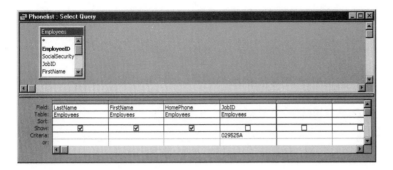

You are telling Access to give you the names and phone numbers from the records that have the value 029525A in the JobID field. (The JobID field value will not appear in the query datasheet because that field's Show box is not selected.)

4. Run the query by clicking the Run button on the Standard toolbar. Access displays this new Phonelist datasheet:

The Run button

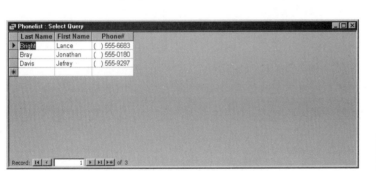

Editing Data in Query Datasheets

If you entered the information for employee number 37 exactly as it is shown on page 185, the datasheet now on your screen indicates a typo in the third record (*Jefrey* should be *Jeffrey*). Correcting the record in the query datasheet will automatically correct it in the table. Follow these steps:

1. Click an insertion point to the right of the *f* in *Jefrey*, type *f*, and press Enter to complete the record.

2. Close the Select Query window without saving the changes to the Phonelist query.

Using wildcards

When you want to select fields based on only part of their entries, you can use the wildcards * and ? before, after, and between characters as placeholders for unknown or varying characters. For example, to find all entries that include *School* or *Schools*, you can use *School? as the criterion. The * wildcard stands for any number of characters of any type, and the ? wildcard stands for any one character of any type. When you use wildcards, Access precedes the criterion with the *Like* operator to indicate that you do not want to look for an exact match.

3. In the Database window, click the Tables icon, select Employees, and click the Open button. In the table, employee number 37 now has a First Name field value of *Jeffrey*.

4. Close the Table window.

Using Logical Operators

You can narrow down the data Access pulls from a database table by specifying criteria in more than one field of the QBE grid. Sometimes you might want to extract records that meet all the criteria in all the fields (this *And* that), and sometimes you might want to extract records that meet any criterion in any field (this *Or* that). Let's look at an example that uses the And operator.

Suppose you need to know which of the Durahomes jobs is complete so that you can bill the customer; that is, you want to see records that are both for Durahomes and complete. In Access, the And operator is implied whenever you use more than one criterion in a single row of the QBE grid. Follow these steps to extract the required record:

1. In the Database window, highlight the Jobs table, click the New Object button's arrow on the toolbar, and select Query to open the New Query dialog box.

2. Double-click Design View to display the Jobs box in a Select Query window.

3. Add the JobID, CustomerID, Location, and Status fields to the QBE grid, type *Complete* as a criterion in the Status field, and type *30* as a criterion in the CustomerID field. The Select Query window now looks like the one shown here:

The And criterion →

The Or criterion →

The Or operator

When you want to find records that meet any of two or more criteria, you use the Or operator. Enter the criterion for the first field in the Criteria row and enter all the criteria for the other fields in the Or row. If you want to find records that meet any of two or more criteria in the same field, you enter the criteria under each other in that column of the QBE grid. (Although only one row is designated as the Or row, the Or operator is implied for all the rows below the Or row.)

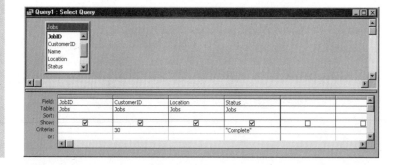

4. Run the query. Access displays the record for one completed Durahomes job:

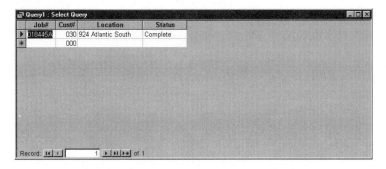

5. Save the query by clicking the Save button on the toolbar and typing *Complete Jobs* in the Query Name edit box.

If the roofing company has many customers, you might want to include the customers' names in the query results, instead of just their numbers. However, the customers' names are not part of the Jobs table; they are stored only in the Customers table. To get the information you want, you must use both tables in a query, like this:

Using more than one table

1. With Complete Jobs still open, use the View button on the toolbar to switch to design view and display the query in the Select Query window.

2. Click the Show Table button, double-click Customers, and close the Show Table dialog box. The window now contains boxes for both tables. Because you have created a relationship between these tables (see page 196), Access indicates the relationship in the Select Query window by drawing a line between the CustomerID fields in the two boxes.

3. In the Customers box, double-click the Name field to add it to the QBE grid.

4. In the QBE grid, deselect the Show box for CustomerID.

5. Run the query. Access displays the job number, job location, status, and customer name, as shown at the top of the following page.

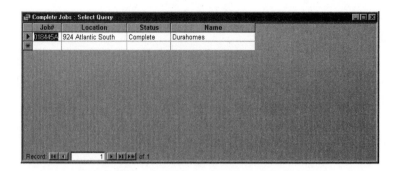

6. Close the Select Query window, clicking Yes to save the query.

All the queries you've run so far have been select queries, which provide information in datasheets. Unless you save this type of query, the information in the datasheet is temporary; it goes away when you close the Select Query window. Now let's explore action queries, which you can use to modify the information in your tables and even to create new tables.

Updating Records

From time to time, you may want to change a field value in several records in a table. For example, suppose the Post Office has assigned a new zip code to Pinewood, and you need to update the Employees table to reflect the change. You could update each record in turn, but an easier way is to use an update query. Follow these steps:

1. With the Tables icon selected in the Database window, select Employees, click the arrow to the right of the New Object button on the toolbar, and select Query.

2. In the New Query dialog box, first double-click Design View and then double-click the PostalCode field to add it to the QBE grid.

The Query Type button

3. Click the arrow to the right of the Query Type button on the toolbar and select Update Query to add an Update To row to the QBE grid.

4. In the Update To row, type *98415* in the PostalCode field.

5. In the Criteria row, type *98412* in the PostalCode field and then press Enter.

6. Run the query. Access advises you of the number of records to be updated.

7. Click Yes to complete the changes.

8. Click the Database Window button on the toolbar and open the Employees table, where the records for the two employees who live in Pinedale have been updated with the new zip code.

The Database Window button

For a small table, it may be faster to make changes like this one manually. For large tables, using an update query is faster and ensures that all the affected records are changed.

Moving Records

The data you keep in tables is rarely static, and it is often easier to keep current data in one table and archive old data in another. Tip Top Roofing's Jobs table is a good example. If you keep all the jobs the company has ever worked on in one table, the table will soon become too large to use on a daily basis. The solution is to have a separate table for the records of jobs that are complete.

To set the stage for the next example, you need to change the Status field values of two records in the Jobs table to *Closed*, indicating not only that the work is complete but that payment has been received. You also need to create a new table to contain the records for closed jobs. Let's get going:

1. To keep your desktop neat, close all windows except the Database window without saving anything. Then open the Jobs table.

2. Change the Status values for the records with job numbers 018022A and 0182730 to *Closed*, enter *2/1/99* and *3/1/99* in the Date Completed field of those records, and close the table.

3. With Jobs highlighted in the Database window, click the Copy button on the toolbar.

4. Now click the Paste button on the toolbar, and in the Paste Table As dialog box, name the table *Closed Jobs*, click Structure Only, and then click OK. Access adds the new table to the list in the Database window.

More logical operators

Access allows you to use the following operators as criteria: = (equal to), < (less than), > (greater than), <= (less than or equal to), and >= (greater than or equal to). These operators are often used for such tasks as identifying employees whose salaries fall within a certain range or locating high-volume customers.

5. Open the Closed Jobs table in design view and delete the Status field by clicking its row selector and pressing Delete.

6. Close the table, saving the changes when prompted.

You are now ready to move the closed records from the Jobs table to the Closed Jobs table. Follow these steps:

1. Select the Jobs table in the Database window, click the arrow to the right of the New Object button on the toolbar, and then select Query.

2. In the New Query dialog box, double-click Design View.

3. Add all the fields from the Jobs box to the QBE grid by double-clicking the Jobs title bar, pointing to the selection, dragging the image of the fields to the first column of the grid, and releasing the mouse button.

4. Type *Closed* in the Criteria row of the Status field.

5. Click the arrow to the right of the Query Type button on the toolbar and select Append Query. When Access displays the Append dialog box, type *Closed Jobs* as the name of the table to which you want to add the results of the query and click OK.

6. Run the query, and when Access advises you that it will append two rows, click Yes to proceed with the query.

7. Close the Append Query window, saving the query as *Append Closed Jobs* so that you can run it whenever you need to append records from the Jobs table to the Closed Jobs table.

8. Open the Closed Jobs table to see the two closed records:

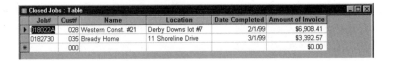

Subdatasheets are not available for this table unless you create relationships between it and the other tables in the database. However, that's not necessary here, because no one ever works on closed jobs.

You have copied the closed records to the Closed Jobs table, but they still exist in the Jobs table. Let's delete them now:

1. Close the Closed Jobs table and open the Jobs table. Click the record selector for job 018022A, press Delete, and click Yes to delete the record.

2. Repeat step 1 for job 0182730 and close the Table window.

Sharing Your Information

Now that you can use Access to manage your data, we'll show you two ways to share your results: on paper and electronically. Let's discuss printing reports first.

Using Reports to Print Information

The purpose of a query is to extract information from a database and display it on the screen. The purpose of a report, on the other hand, is to extract information and show it on the printed page. So when you need a neatly formatted hard copy of sorted and grouped information, consider using a report.

To start exploring reports, follow the steps below to create a single-table, single-column report based on the Jobs table:

1. In the Database window, select Jobs in the Tables list, click the New Object button's arrow on the toolbar, and click Auto-Report. After a few seconds, Access displays this report:

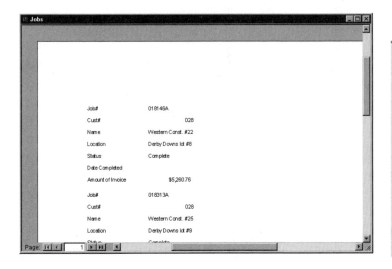

Creating reports from scratch

You can create a blank report by clicking the Reports icon in the Database window, clicking New, and then double-clicking Design View in the New Report dialog box. Access opens a new Report window containing Page Header, Detail, and Page Footer sections. You can then add controls to design the report.

Because reports are usually created to produce printouts, Access displays the report in print preview so that you can see what it will look like on the page.

The Zoom button

2. Click the Zoom button on the toolbar to zoom out for a bird's-eye view, as shown here:

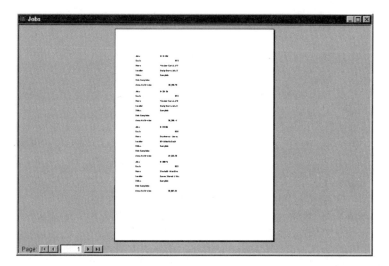

3. Click the Zoom button again to zoom back in. Then, using the page scrolling buttons in the bottom left corner of the window, scroll the page to see how the report will be printed.

As you scroll, notice that the records will be printed in job order. Suppose you want to sort the records by customer instead of by job. Follow these steps:

1. Click the Report window's Close button to close the window, and then click No to discard the report.

2. With Jobs selected in the Database window's Tables list, click the New Object button's arrow and select Report.

3. In the New Report dialog box, make sure that Jobs is selected in the table list, click Report Wizard, and then click OK. You see the first Report Wizard dialog box, shown at the top of the facing page.

Preview before printing
You can identify layout problems, such as text length and/or width exceeding the page's capacity using print preview. You can then change the document's design or modify the page setup before committing the document to paper. Choose Page Setup from the File menu to open the Page Setup dialog box. Here, you can adjust the margins, alter page orientation, and select your printer. When you are finished, click OK to apply the new settings. Preview the changes you've made, and when you are satisfied with the layout, print your document.

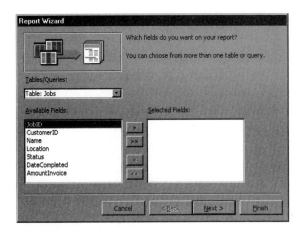

4. Make sure the entry in the Tables/Queries box is Table: Jobs. Then click the >> button to move all the available fields to the Selected Fields box, and click Next.

5. Click Next in the Report Wizard's second and third dialog boxes without making any changes to the default selections. (Note that in this case, Access automatically sorts the records by CustomerID.) Access then displays the Report Wizard's fourth dialog box, shown here:

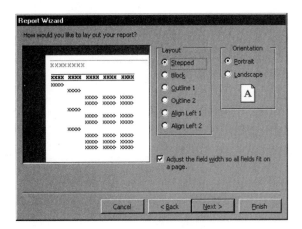

6. Make sure the Stepped option is selected in the Layout section, click Landscape in the Orientation section, and then click Next to display the fifth dialog box, shown at the top of the next page.

Customizing reports

Just as you can create custom forms to tailor the input of data, you can create custom reports to tailor its output. Customizing reports is beyond the scope of this book; however, you might want to create a report and then switch to design view to play around with it. (Choose the Design View command from the View menu to switch to design view.) To get a feel for some of the possibilities, try moving controls around, formatting labels, or using the buttons on the Toolbox toolbar to add new controls. (Use the structure of the existing controls as a guide.)

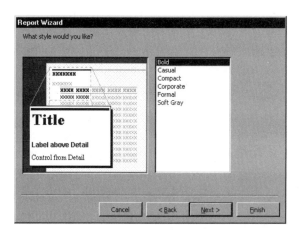

Creating mailing labels

To create mailing labels using database information, select the table you want from the Tables list in the Database window. On the toolbar, click the New Object button's arrow, select Report, click Label Wizard, and click OK to see the wizard's first dialog box. You can select a label format by company product number (the default company is A-ONE; select others from the Filter By Manufacturer drop-down list) or by size and number of labels in a row. (The available formats vary, depending on your printer's capabilities.) Select a label size, click Next, format the labels as you want, and click Next again. Double-click the FirstName field or other appropriate field, press the Spacebar, double-click the LastName field, and press Enter to create a second line. Continue adding fields using the appropriate punctuation and pressing Enter to start new lines. Click Next, move the field with which you want to sort the labels to the Sort By box, and click Next. Assign a name to your report and click Finish to display the labels in print preview. Make any necessary adjustments, and then click the Print button to print your labels.

7. Select Corporate as the style for the report and click Next to display the final Report Wizard dialog box.

8. Type *Jobs Grouped By Customer* as the title for the report and then click Finish to see these results:

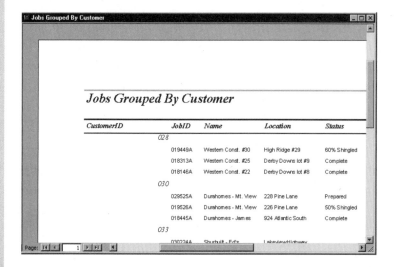

9. Click the Report window's Close button to return to the Database window.

To access the report later, click the Reports icon in the Database window and then double-click the report's name.

Creating Data Access Pages

You can provide quick access to your data for people in distant locations by publishing *data access pages* that allow your data to be viewed via an intranet or the Internet. Data access pages are forms that have been coded with HyperText Markup Language (HTML) so that they can be viewed using a Web browser such as Microsoft Internet Explorer. As a demonstration, let's convert an existing form to a data access page:

1. Select Customers in the Database window's Tables list, click the New Object button's arrow, and select Page.

2. In the New Data Access Page dialog box, make sure that Customers is selected in the table list and then double-click Page Wizard. ← The Page Wizard

3. In the wizard's first dialog box, click the >> button to move all the available fields to the Selected Fields box and then click Next.

4. Click Next in the Page Wizard's second and third dialog boxes to accept the default selections.

5. With *Customers* specified as the title for the page, click the Open The Page option, and click Finish. Access opens this data access page:

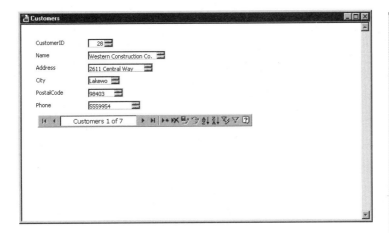

Creating data access pages from scratch

You can create a new data access page by clicking the Pages icon on the Objects bar, clicking the New button, and then double-clicking either Page Wizard or Design View in the New Data Access Page dialog box. Depending on your selection, Access opens a series of dialog boxes or a new Data Access Page window with a title area, a body text area, and a section to which you can add controls.

Rather than explore further in Access, let's take a look at how the page works in a Web browser. Follow these steps:

1. First close the Data Access Page window, saving the page as *Customers*. Then close Access, clicking Yes when prompted to empty the Clipboard.

2. Double-click the Internet Explorer icon on your desktop and choose Work Offline from the File menu.

3. In the Internet Explorer window, choose Open from the File menu to see this dialog box:

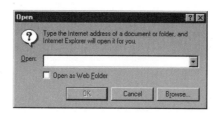

4. Click the Browse button, navigate to the folder where the Customers data access page is stored, select the file, and click Open. Then click OK. Your screen now looks like this:

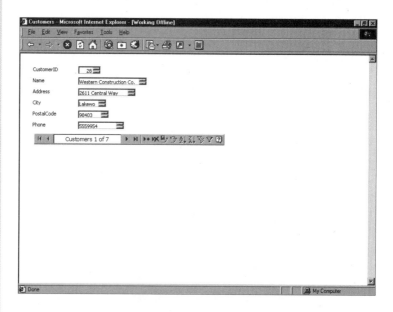

5. Try out the navigation bar by clicking the Next Record or Last Record button. Then return to the first record.

ReadOnly data access pages

By default, Access allows viewers to enter records in a database through the data access page, provided they have permission to change the database. But you can set a data access page so that users can read it, but not alter the underlying page. Click the Pages icon on the Objects bar and then double-click the data access page you want to modify. Click the View button to switch to design view, and right-click the first control to display its shortcut menu. Choose Properties, click the Other tab, and click an insertion point in the ReadOnly edit box. Now click the arrow, and select True from the dropdown list. Leaving the Properties dialog box open, select each of the controls in turn and set their ReadOnly properties to True. Then close the dialog box. If you designate a data access page as ReadOnly, then you don't need the New Record, Delete Record, Save Record, or Undo Record buttons on the navigation bar. Select the bar, click the Properties button on the Standard toolbar, and set these buttons to False on the Other tab of the Properties dialog box.

6. Select Western Construction Co. in the Name control and click the Sort Ascending button. Move through the records to verify the new sort order. Return to the original order by double-clicking any customer number and clicking the Sort Ascending button.

7. Now double-click Lakewood in the displayed record to select it and click the Filter By Selection button. The navigation bar shows that only five records have the value Lakewood in the City field.

The Filter By Selection button

The Remove Filter button

8. Click the Remove Filter button.

9. Close Internet Explorer.

In Chapters 8 and 9, we have given you an idea of ways you can use Access to store and manipulate essential business data. Now we'll leave you to explore further on your own.

10

Communicating with Outlook

We show you how to use the Inbox to send and receive e-mail, and how to organize your messages. Then you learn how to use Contacts to manage information about the important people in your life, and to streamline your communications work.

E-mail is becoming the communication mode of choice in business, education, and personal life. The examples in this chapter can be used as models for the efficient handling of all your electronic communications.

Tasks performed and concepts covered:

Quickly jump from one component to another using the Outlook bar

Respond to and forward messages quickly

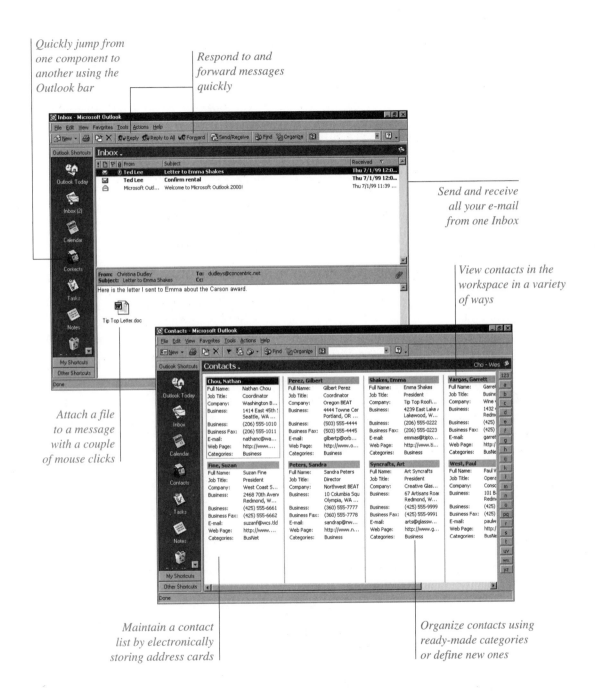

Send and receive all your e-mail from one Inbox

View contacts in the workspace in a variety of ways

Attach a file to a message with a couple of mouse clicks

Maintain a contact list by electronically storing address cards

Organize contacts using ready-made categories or define new ones

You can use Microsoft Outlook 2000 to handle your electronic correspondence and to manage the crucial personal and business information that you might keep in an assortment of address books, appointment books, and notebooks. In this chapter, we cover Outlook's two communication components: Inbox and Contacts. In Chapter 11, we discuss its two scheduling components: Calendar and Tasks. Outlook is very flexible and offers many ways to tailor its components to meet your personal organizational preferences. After we've given you an idea of some of the possibilities, you'll want to take the time to explore the components and their features more thoroughly on your own.

Let's take a look at Outlook now. Follow these steps:

The Microsoft Outlook icon

1. On the Windows desktop, double-click the Microsoft Outlook icon to start the program. (You can also click the Start button and choose Programs and then Microsoft Outlook from the Start menu.) Several things might happen:

   - If you are the first person to open Outlook 2000 on this computer, the Outlook 2000 Startup Wizard may appear to walk you through the process of setting up the program.

   - If e-mail is not yet set up on your computer, the Internet Conection Wizard may appear to help you with this task. The wizard will ask you several questions, starting with your choice of information services. If you are working on a network, contact your network supervisor for information about setting up your e-mail account. If you are working on a stand-alone computer, see the adjacent tip.

   - If e-mail is set up on your computer and you are working on a network, Outlook connects to your e-mail server and checks for new messages. If you have only Internet e-mail, Outlook may or may not connect to your server, depending on your setup. Don't worry if no connection is made. You can still proceed, and we will show you how to manually make the connection on page 225.

2. If you are asked whether you want Outlook to be your default contact manager, click Yes.

Setting up Internet e-mail

If you are working on a stand-alone computer, you can't send or receive Internet e-mail in Outlook until you set it up. You will need to obtain the names of your outgoing and incoming e-mail servers from your ISP. Then fill in the appropriate information in the Internet Connection Wizard. As you work through the dialog boxes, you will need to enter information such as your e-mail address, account name, password, and connection type. If you need help with this setup, contact your ISP for specific instructions. If you already have a Dial-Up Networking connection to your ISP, you may need to add the Internet E-Mail service to your Outlook profile. See Outlook's Help feature for more information.

3. If necessary, click the Office Assistant's Start Using Microsoft Outlook option and then hide the Office Assistant. Maximize the Outlook window, which looks something like this:

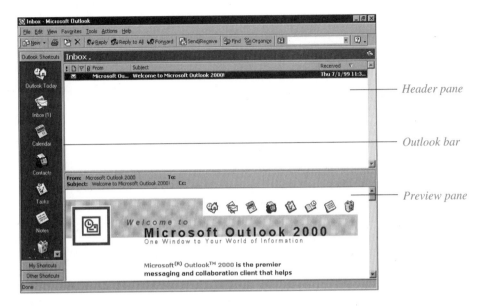

Header pane

Outlook bar

Preview pane

As you can see, the Outlook window is divided into a workspace on the right and a bar on the left, called the *Outlook bar*, that displays one of three groups of shortcuts. Currently the Outlook Shortcuts group, which contains icons for Outlook's various components, is displayed. You change the contents of the workspace by clicking these icons. Clicking the down arrow at the bottom of the bar brings more icons into view. Clicking the My Shortcuts button at the bottom of the bar closes the Outlook Shortcuts group and displays icons for the e-mail folders instead. Similarly, clicking the Other Shortcuts button closes the open group and displays icons for various folders on your computer.

4. Click various icons in the Outlook Shortcuts group to jump from one component to another, and then try the icons in the other two groups to get an idea of how the Outlook bar works.

Now that you have a feel for how to move around in Outlook and have a sense of the convenience of working with various types of information in one place, let's look at some of the individual components.

Customizing the Outlook bar

You can hide the Outlook bar by right-clicking it and choosing Hide Outlook Bar from the shortcut menu. Then to move from one Outlook component to another, click the arrow to the right of the name in the workspace title bar and select the desired component from the drop-down list. Redisplay the Outlook bar by choosing it from the View menu. You can display large or small icons in the Outlook bar by right-clicking it and choosing the appropriate command. You can make the Outlook bar wider or narrower by pointing to its right border and dragging to the right or left.

Using the Inbox

Electronic mail

Outlook is set up to work with several popular e-mail (for *electronic mail*) programs, so you can use Outlook's Inbox as an all-purpose e-mail service from which you can send and receive messages to colleagues down the hall or clients on the other side of the world. We'll give you an idea of how Outlook's Inbox works in the following sections.

Composing Messages

As we said, with Outlook, you both send and receive e-mail through the Inbox. We'll look at the sending side of the equation first. For this example, imagine that you are planning a meeting with the local Chamber of Commerce and you want to remind yourself to confirm the rental of the facilities first thing tomorrow morning. Follow these steps:

The Inbox icon

1. If necessary, click the Inbox icon to display your Inbox, which divides the workspace into a *header pane* and a *preview pane*, as shown on the previous page.

The New Mail Message button

2. Click the New Mail Message button on the toolbar to display a window like the one shown here:

Address books

You can click the Address Book button on the toolbar to access your network's Global Address List or the e-mail and fax information in your contact list. (You create a contact list on page 231.) Double-click a name to enter the corresponding e-mail address in the To box. Other information in the contact list is not available while creating an e-mail message, but is available when you click the Address Book button in some applications. For example, your contact list is available when you create mailing labels in Word.

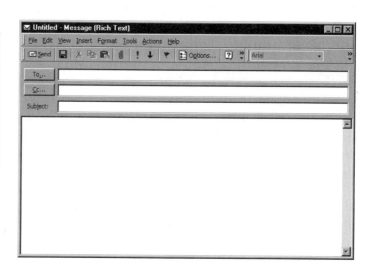

3. In the To edit box, type your e-mail address and press Tab. (To send a message to someone else, enter his or her address. To send the same message to more than one person, enter their addresses one after the other, separated by semicolons.)

4. To send a courtesy copy of the message, you can enter the name of the recipient in the Cc edit box. For this message, leave the Cc edit box blank and press Tab.

Sending courtesy copies

5. In the Subject edit box, type *Confirm rental* and press Tab.

Specifying the subject

6. Next enter the message itself. Type *Check on meeting hall rental (555-0111). Be sure to tell them I will be there at 8:00 AM to set up the presentation.* Your screen now looks like this:

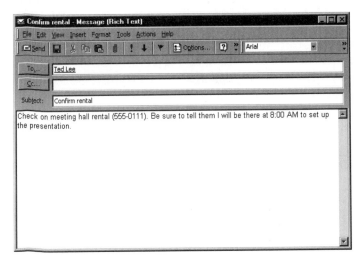

The Send button

7. Send the message by clicking the Send button. Outlook closes the Message window and does one of two things:

- If you are connected to your e-mail server, Outlook transfers the message to your Outbox and then sends it on its way.

- If you are not connected to your e-mail server, Outlook stores the message in your Outbox until your next connection. The Outbox icon in the My Shortcuts group on the Outlook bar then displays a number in parentheses to tell you how many messages are waiting to be sent.

8. If you are in the latter group, confirm that the message is waiting to be sent by opening the My Shortcuts group and clicking the Outbox icon to display its window.

The Outbox icon

9. Redisplay the Inbox's contents by clicking the Inbox icon.

Attaching Files to Messages

With Outlook, you can send files along with your messages. For example, suppose you want to send a letter you have written in Word to a colleague. Follow these steps, which use your own e-mail address instead of a colleague's:

1. With the Inbox active, click the New Mail Message button and then type your address in the To edit box.

2. In the Subject box, type *Letter to Emma Shakes*. In the message area, type *Here is the letter I sent to Emma about the Carson award.* Then press enter a couple of times.

The Insert File button

3. Click the Insert File button on the toolbar to display the Insert File dialog box, shown earlier on page 58.

4. If necessary, navigate to the My Documents folder. Then double-click the icon for *Tip Top Letter*. Outlook inserts a file icon, as shown here:

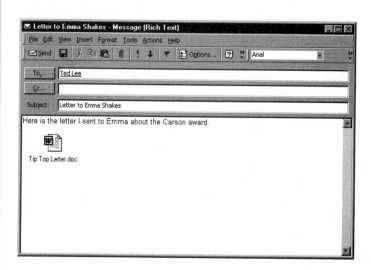

5. Click the Send button.

Sending and Receiving Messages

If you are connected to an internal or Internet e-mail server, you now have at least two message headers displayed in the workspace (not including any *Welcome to Microsoft Outlook 2000* messages). If you aren't connected, you need to log on

---

Message options

When composing a new message, you can set message options by clicking the Options button on the toolbar. You can set the importance level to High, Normal, or Low. (High displays an exclamation mark in the message's header.) You can set the sensitivity level to Normal, Personal, Private, or Confidential. You can select Encrypt Message Contents And Attachments to make a message's contents readable only by its recipients, and you can select Add Digital Signature to prove that you sent the message. You can also set voting options, notification options, and delivery options. You can assign a message to a category by clicking the Categories button and making a selection. You can save a message as RTF (Rich Text Format), Text Only, Outlook Tempate, or Message Format. (See Outlook's Help feature for more information.)

and send the messages stored in Outbox. You also want to check whether you have any new mail. Follow these steps to see how to send and retrieve messages:

The Send/Receive button

1. Click the Send/Receive button on the toolbar. (If Outlook is set up for more than one e-mail service, choose Send/Receive from the Tools menu and then either choose the service you want or choose All Accounts.) Outlook tells you it is checking for new messages and sending outgoing messages. (Internet e-mail users may have to enter a user name and password first.)

2. After Outlook retrieves new messages, it displays their headers in the header pane and puts the number of new messages in parentheses next to the Inbox icon on the Outlook bar. The header pane now looks like this:

New message alert

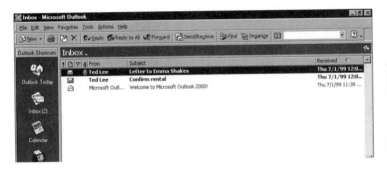

Next to the new messages, closed envelope icons indicate that you have not yet read or previewed the messages (see the adjacent tip for more information). The sender's name, the subject, and the date and time the message was received are all summarized. If AutoPreview is turned on, you also see up to three lines of the message itself below the header. Icons to the left of the message header tell you more about the message. An exclamation point means a message is urgent, and a paper clip indicates that a file is attached to the message. (You can also flag a selected message by choosing Flag For Follow Up from the Actions menu.) Follow these steps to read the *Emma Shakes* message:

1. Double-click the *Letter to Emma Shakes* header to display the message in a window, as shown on the next page.

Previewing messages

To turn off the preview pane, choose Preview Pane from the View menu. You can then choose AutoPreview from the View menu to display the first three lines of a message immediately below its header. If you don't want Outlook to mark your previewed (but unopened) messages as read, choose Options from the Tools menu, click the Other tab, and click the Preview Pane button. Then select the desired option in the Preview Pane dialog box and click OK. When the preview pane is turned on, you can adjust the relative amount of space allocated to the panes by dragging the border between them up or down. You can also adjust the size of the columns in the header pane by dragging the column heading borders.

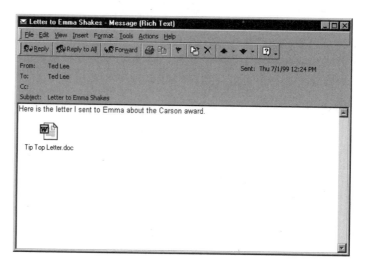

Reading attachments →

2. Double-click the attachment's icon. If Outlook displays a message about the possibility of a virus and asks whether to open the file or save it to disk, select Open It and click OK (see the tip below). Outlook opens the file in the program in which it was created (in this case, Word). Close the Word window.

Replying to Messages

Suppose this message is from a colleague and requires a response. Follow these steps to send a reply:

The Reply button →

1. Click the Reply button. Outlook opens a RE: window like this:

Handling attachments

Here, you open the message attachment because you sent it to yourself. If you receive an attachment from anyone else, you should save it in a folder and then scan it with a virus-detecting program before opening it. The likelihood that you will "catch" a virus is not great, but the consequences of an infection are bad enough that it's not worth taking chances.

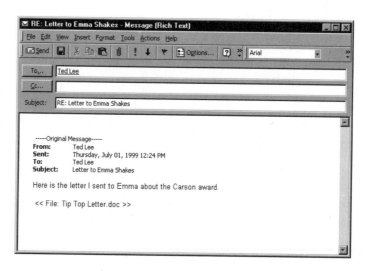

(To send the response to the sender of the message and to all recipients of courtesy copies, you would click the Reply To All button.) Notice that the To and Subject edit boxes are already filled in. Also notice that the original message appears below the blinking insertion point. (If you prefer not to display the original message in your responses, read the tip on the next page.) The attachment is represented by its name in chevrons, indicating that the attachment will not be sent back with the message.

The Reply To All button

2. Type *Thanks for the letter. That should work!* Click the Send button to either send the message or to transfer it to the Outbox. Back in the original message's window, Outlook indicates that you have responded to the message and gives you the opportunity to jump directly to the reply, as shown here:

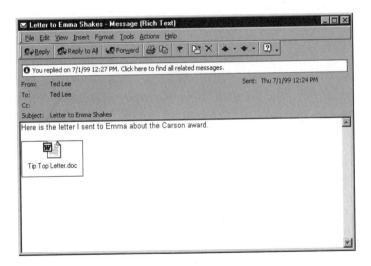

Forwarding Messages

If you receive a message that you think will be of interest to a colleague, you can forward the message with a few mouse clicks. Follow these steps to try it:

1. With the Emma Shakes message still displayed in its window, click the Forward button on the toolbar to display the FW: window, as shown on the next page.

The Forward button

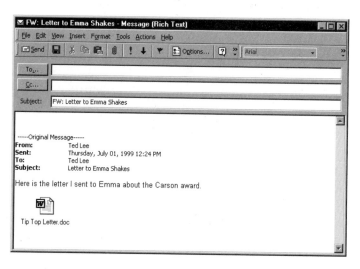

No message in replies and no sent messages

If you don't want Outlook to display the original message at the end of your reply, choose Options from Inbox's Tools menu and then click the E-mail Options button on the Preferences tab. Next click the arrow to the right of the When Replying To A Message box, select Do Not Include Original Message, and click OK twice. (Notice also that you can change the way the original message appears within a forwarded message using this dialog box.) To keep your Outlook files from growing too big, you can turn off the option that automatically saves a copy of all your outgoing messages in the Sent Items folder. Choose Options from the Tools menu, and click the E-Mail Options button on the Preferences tab. Deselect the Save Copies Of Messages In Sent Items Folder check box in the Message Handling section and click OK twice. If you later want to save a particular outgoing message in the Sent Items folder, simply click the Options button in the Message window before you send the message, select the Save Sent Message To check box, designate a location, and click Close.

2. For demonstration purposes, type your own e-mail address in the To box and click the Send button. In the original message's window, Outlook replaces the reply information with the more recent forward information.

3. To view the two new messages, close the message window and if necessary, click the Send/Receive button. Then open each new message after Outlook retrieves them from your e-mail server.

Notice that after you read or preview a message, an open envelope appears to the left of its header, and that the envelope of the forwarded message has a forward arrow attached to it.

Managing Messages

In addition to the Inbox, Outlook maintains three "folders" to help organize your messages: Sent Items, Outbox, and Deleted Items. You can move messages between folders and even create new folders by working through the following sections.

Deleting Messages

After you have read most of your messages, you will probably want to delete them. As a demonstration of how to delete messages, let's clean up the Sent Items folder, but bear in mind that the procedure is the same for any Outlook e-mail folder. Follow these steps:

1. To see messages you have already sent, open the My Short-cuts group and click the Sent Items icon to display its contents in the workspace, like this:

The Sent Items icon

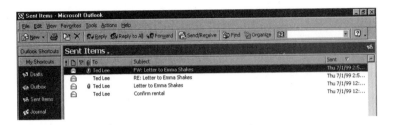

(By the way, if you want to switch the My Shortcuts group to large icon display, see the tip on page 221.)

2. Choose Select All from the Edit menu and then click the Delete button on the toolbar. Instead of actually deleting the messages, Outlook transfers them to the Deleted Items folder, giving you another opportunity to change your mind about deleting them.

The Delete button

3. Click the Deleted Items icon in the Outlook Shortcuts group to display that folder's contents.

The Deleted Items icon

4. You really do want to delete these files, so right-click the work-space title bar (the gray bar displaying the Deleted Items title). Choose Empty "Deleted Items" Folder from the shortcut menu and click Yes when asked whether you want to get rid of the items for good.

If you want to permanently delete messages and other items without having to later deal with them in the Deleted Items folder, you can choose Options from the Tools menu, click the Other tab, and select the Empty The Deleted Items Folder Upon Exiting option in the General section. Then Outlook will erase the folder's contents every time you exit the program.

Creating New Folders

To organize your mail, you can create folders for storing related messages. For example, turn the page to see how to create a new folder in which to store messages related to the Chamber of Commerce meeting.

Saving messages and attachments

To save a message, select it in the Inbox window, choose Save As from the File menu, navigate to the desired storage location, name the file, and designate the file type. To save an attachment to an e-mail message as a separate file, select the message header, choose Save Attachments from the File menu, and designate the storage location of the file. You can also right-click an attachment in a message and choose Save As from the shortcut menu.

1. Click the Inbox icon to display its contents.

2. Choose New from the File menu and then Folder from the expanded submenu to display this dialog box:

3. In the Name box, type *Chamber Of Commerce* and click OK. If you are asked whether you want to create an Outlook bar shortcut for the new folder, click Yes. An icon for the new folder appears at the bottom of the My Shortcuts group.

4. Now select the *Confirm rental* message you sent to yourself earlier, display the My Shortcuts group, and drag the message to the Chamber Of Commerce icon in the My Shortcuts group. (You may want to widen the Outlook bar so that it is easier to see the new icon. See the tip on page 221.)

5. You won't be sending and receiving messages for a while, so if necessary, disconnect from your e-mail server.

We'll leave you to experiment with folders as you receive mail from your colleagues. While you work, you will probably want to minimize Outlook so that it continues to run in the background and you can receive messages as they are sent to you. Alternatively, you can quit the program, knowing that your messages will be stored by your e-mail server until you make your next connection.

The folder list

To see a complete list of Outlook component folders, you can click the arrow to the right of the component name in the workspace title bar. If you decide to keep the folder list displayed, simply click the push pin in the top right corner of the list.

Managing Contacts

The Contacts component of Outlook lets you keep important addresses, e-mail addresses, and phone numbers handy at all times. You can look up addresses when sending e-mail or regular letters in Word, and you can even have your computer dial a selected phone number for you. What's more, you can automatically track activities related to your contacts (see page 266). In this section, we'll take a look at Contacts and then leave you to explore how you might put it to work.

Creating Address Cards

Follow these steps to make some entries in your contact list:

1. Click the Contacts icon in the Outlook Shortcuts group to display a contact list like this one in the workspace:

The Contacts icon

If you haven't used Contacts before, your list may be blank. If you have used Contacts before, your list may contain entries, called *address cards*. You may also have two additional cards that have been created by Outlook: one labeled *Welcome to Contacts* and one for a generic Microsoft customer.

Address cards

The New Contact button

2. Click the New Contact button on the toolbar to display this Contact window:

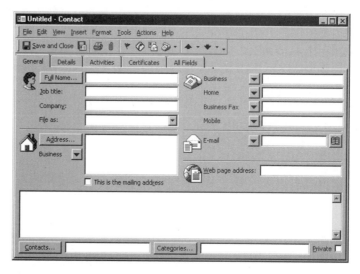

3. Enter the information shown below, entering the phone numbers without parentheses or hyphens (Outlook adds them for you automatically). If prompted to enter your phone information, complete the dialog box and click OK.

Other ways to add new contacts

If you are working in another Outlook component and want to quickly add a new contact, you can click the arrow to the right of the New button on the toolbar and select Contact, or choose New and then Contact from the File menu. If you have installed the Office shortcut bar (see page 371), you can click its New Contact button. If you prefer to use keyboard shortcuts, simply press Ctrl+N to enter a new contact from within the Contacts component or press Ctrl+Shift+C to enter a new contact from another Outlook component.

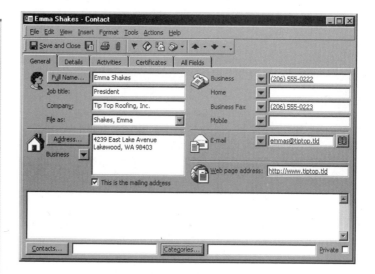

4. Click the Categories button at the bottom of the window to display the dialog box on the facing page.

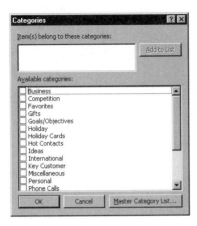

5. Click the Business check box and then click OK to designate Emma Shakes as a business contact.

6. Click the Save And New button to save the current address card and display a blank Contact window.

The Save And New button

7. Create address cards for the new contacts shown below, assigning them to the Business category by clicking the Categories button, clicking Business, and clicking OK. Click the Save And Close button after the last card.

Field	Card 2	Card 3
Name	*Sandra Peters*	*Gilbert Perez*
Job Title	*Director*	*Coordinator*
Company	*Northwest BEAT*	*Oregon BEAT*
Business Phone	*3605557777*	*5035554444*
Business Fax	*3605557778*	*5035554445*
Address	*10 Columbia Square Olympia, WA 98567*	*444 Towne Center Portland, OR 97208*
E-mail	*sandrap@nwbeat.tld*	*gilbertp@orbeat.tld*
Web Page Address	*www.nwbeat.tld*	*www.orbeat.tld*

Field	Card 4	Card 5
Name	*Nathan Chou*	*Art Syncrafts*
Job Title	*Coordinator*	*President*
Company	*Washington BEAT*	*Creative GlassWorks*
Business Phone	*2065551010*	*4255559999*
Business Fax	*2065551011*	*4255559991*
Address	*1414 East 45th Street Seattle, WA 98149*	*67 Artisans Road Redmond, WA 98052*
E-mail	*nathanc@wabeat.tld*	*arts@glassworks.tld*
Web Page Address	*www.wabeat.tld*	*www.glassworks.tld*

The Contacts workspace now looks like this:

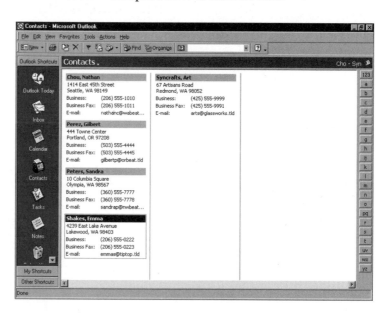

Editing and Adding Information

Once you add an address card to your contact list, you can easily edit the information on the card by double-clicking the card in the workspace to redisplay its Contact window. Looking over the address cards now in the workspace, suppose you discover an error in the Gilbert Perez card. Here's how to edit existing contact information:

Displaying an address-card window

1. Double-click Perez, Gilbert to display his address card.

2. Change *444 Towne Center* in the address to *4444 Towne Center*, and then click the Save And Close button.

You may have noticed that the Contact window is multi-tabbed. You used the General tab to fill in the information shown earlier. If you want to add more information about a contact, such as an assistant's name or a birthday, you can use the Details tab. Let's add some personal information for Nathan Chou, who is not only a colleague, but a friend. Follow these steps:

1. Double-click Chou, Nathan and then click the Details tab to display these options:

More about entering birthdays

When you enter a contact's birthday or anniversary, the date is recorded in the Calendar component of Outlook. (We discuss Calendar in Chapter 11.) Because of this feature, you'll no longer have to record special occasions in several places, and you'll never forget these important dates again!

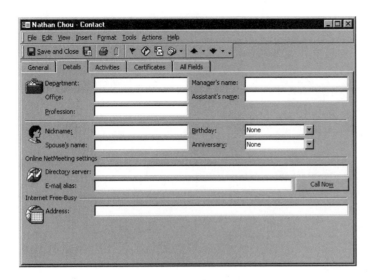

2. Click the arrow to the right of the Birthday box to display a small calendar. Then use the arrows on either side of the current month's name to navigate to December, and click 28.

3. Now change the Anniversary setting to August 7.

4. Click an insertion point in the Spouse's Name edit box and type *Chris*. Then click the Save And Close button.

Deleting Contacts

To keep your contact list up to date, you may need to delete address cards. Try this:

1. If your contact list includes a Welcome To Contacts address card, click its header to select it and click the Delete button.

2. Delete any other contacts you don't want, leaving only the five you just entered.

Organizing Contacts

As your contact list grows, you will probably want to organize it so that it is easier to use. In this section, we'll look at organizational options that are relevant to the Contacts component.

Before you experiment with organizing contacts, let's add some more address cards. Then you'll have more contacts to organize. Follow the steps on the next page.

More contact details

You can create custom forms to track your contacts. Choose Forms and then Design A Form from the Tools menu. In the Design Form dialog box, select Contact from the Standard Forms Library and then click Open. Outlook then displays the Contact window in design view and opens the Field Chooser dialog box. Click the (P.2) tab to display a blank tab. You can then drag fields from the Field Chooser dialog box onto the blank form or create new fields. To name the new tab, choose Rename Page from the Form menu. To save the custom form, click the Publish Form button on the Design toolbar and enter a name in the Display Name edit box. Verify that Outlook Folders is displayed in the Look In box and that Contacts is displayed in the header above the empty list box. Then click Publish. To fill in a custom form, choose New *file name* from the Actions menu and complete the form's tabs as usual. For more information about custom forms, see Outlook's Help feature.

1. Click the New Contact button to display the Contact window shown earlier.

2. Enter the names and addresses below, clicking the Save And New button to start a new address card and clicking the Save And Close button after the last entry:

Field	Card 6	Card 7	Card 8
Name	*Suzan Fine*	*Garrett Vargas*	*Paul West*
Job Title	*President*	*Business Manager*	*Operations Manager*
Company	*West Coast Sales*	*The Wine Cellar*	*Consolidated Messenger*
Business Phone	*4255556661*	*4255558787*	*4255557654*
Business Fax	*4255556662*	*4255558788*	*4255557655*
Address	*2468 70th Avenue*	*1432 NE Cleveland Street*	*101 Barclay Square*
	Redmond, WA 98052	*Redmond, WA 98052*	*Redmond, WA 98052*
E-mail	*suzanf@wcs.tld*	*garretv@cellar.tld*	*paulw@conmess.tld*
Web Page Address	*www.wcs.tld*	*www.cellar.tld*	*www.conmess.tld*

Creating New Categories

You've completed all the address cards, and now you need to fine-tune their categories. The contacts you just added are members of a professional organization you belong to. Let's create a new category for them:

1. Double-click Fine, Suzan and then in the Contact window, click the Categories button.

2. Click the Master Category List button in the bottom right corner to display this dialog box:

Jotting down notes

The Notes component of Outlook is a place to record simple reminders or ideas that don't fit in any other component. After clicking the Notes icon on the Outlook bar, you create a note by clicking the New Note button on the toolbar. Then simply type your note and click the Close button to close it. You can right-click the note to assign it to a category or color-code it. Then you can view notes by category or by color by selecting those options from the Current View box's drop-down list. You can also view notes as icons or in a list, and you can restrict the display to notes created in the previous seven days.

3. In the New Category edit box, type *BusNet* and click Add. Outlook adds the new category to the list.

4. Click OK to return to the Categories dialog box. Then click the BusNet check box to select it and click OK.

5. To save your changes, click Save And Close.

6. Double-click Vargas, Garrett and click the Categories button. Select BusNet and then click OK. Finally, click Save And Close.

7. Repeat step 6 for Paul West's card.

Switching Views

By default, Outlook displays the contact list in address cards view. Because this list is small, you can easily scroll through the cards. However, as a contact list grows, viewing the list in a different way may be more efficient. Let's explore the other available views now:

1. Choose Current View and then Detailed Address Cards from the View menu. The contacts information now looks like this:

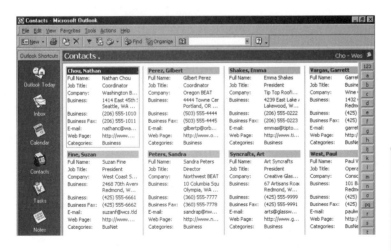

In this view, Outlook displays all the information that was entered on the General tab of the Contact window.

2. Choose Phone List from the Current View submenu to display your contacts as shown on the next page.

Sorting in table views

You can sort the information in a table view by clicking the header at the top of the column by which you want Outlook to sort. An arrow appears in the header, pointing up if the column is sorted in ascending order or down if it is sorted in descending order. Clicking the header again reverses the order.

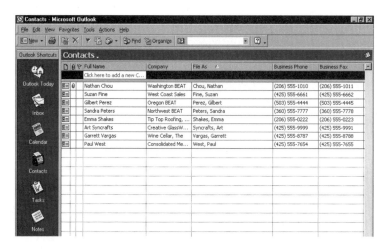

This table view displays identifying information for each contact as well as four phone columns, two of which currently contain no numbers. In a table view, you can see that the contact list is really a database, where the information about a particular contact is stored in a record (row) and an individual item of information is stored in a field (column).

3. Try each of the remaining table views and then switch to address cards view.

Using Your Contact List with E-mail

As an example of how you might use your contact list, let's send an e-mail message to one of your contacts:

1. Add a new address card for yourself to your contact list, entering your e-mail address in the appropriate edit box.

The New Message To Contact button

2. Select your address card in the contacts workspace and click the New Message To Contact button on the toolbar. Outlook displays a Message window like the one shown on page 222, with your e-mail address already entered in the To edit box.

3. Send yourself a message by completing the edit boxes in the Message window and then clicking the Send button. If you are connected to your e-mail server, you will soon see (1) next to the Inbox icon on the Outlook bar, announcing the arrival of your message.

Contacts from messages

If you drag a message header from the Inbox's header pane to the Contacts icon on the Outlook bar, Outlook opens a new Contact window and fills in the name and e-mail fields. You can then fill in the remaining information.

Tracking Contacts

We'll finish up this chapter by showing you how Outlook tracks your activities with each contact. Follow these steps:

1. In your contact list, double-click the header for your own address card. In the Contact window, click the Activities tab to display these options:

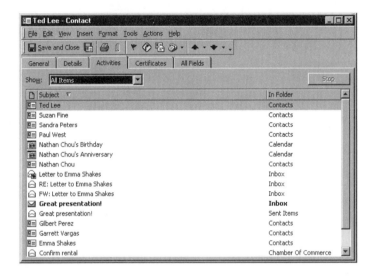

Outlook has recorded all your activities during this session, including the fact that you sent messages to yourself. (Both the sent messages and the received messages have been logged.)

2. Click the arrow to the right of the Show box to display a drop-down list of all the activities Outlook logs for each contact. You can filter the list of activities by selecting an option from this list to see, for example, only your e-mail correspondence with this contact.

3. Press Esc to close the drop-down list without changing the All Items selection, and then close the Contact window.

4. If you want to take a break, close Outlook. However, bear in mind that some of the program's features—such as message notification—can work only when Outlook is running. If you are working on a network, you might want to start Outlook and then minimize it at the beginning of each work session, quitting the program only when you're ready to quit for the day.

Printing the contact list

Using Outlook eliminates some of the need for paper printouts, but when you want a printout of your contact list, choose Print from the File menu to display the Print dialog box. Here you can select from several layout choices in the Print Style section, and you can click the Page Setup button to make adjustments on the Format, Paper, or Header/Footer tabs. On the Paper tab of the Page Setup dialog box, you can change the Type setting in the Paper section to various types of Avery labels or FiloFax, and you can change the Size setting in the Page section to fit special formats for Franklin Planners, Day Timers, or Day Runners. In the Print dialog box, you can also click the Define Styles button to make permanent edits to a particular style or to copy a style. When you are ready to print, simply click OK in the Print dialog box.

11

Managing Your Time
with Outlook

We show you how to use Outlook's Calendar and Tasks components to manage your time more effectively. You learn how to track appointments and events, plan a meeting with your colleagues, keep a to-do list, and delegate tasks.

Although the schedule and to-do list we use as this chapter's examples are business-oriented, you can use these techniques to plan your personal time as well.

Tasks performed and concepts covered:

Sort tasks by due date or by any other column

Classify tasks to make them easier to prioritize

Designate tasks as complete and then delete them when you're ready

View an entire week or month at a time

Move to the date you need by using date navigator

Quickly scan your to-do list while scheduling your time

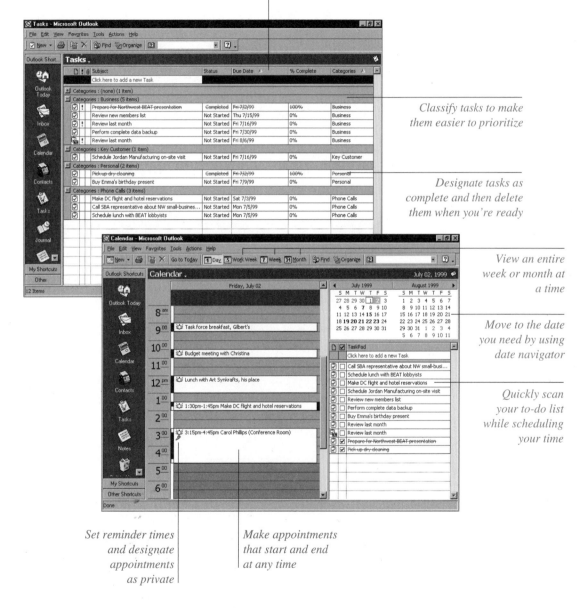

Set reminder times and designate appointments as private

Make appointments that start and end at any time

As your schedule becomes increasingly busy, you may have trouble juggling the many tasks you need to accomplish during the day and remembering appointments and events. In the past, you probably kept track of the things you needed to do either in your head or on paper (with varying degrees of legibility). Now you can use Outlook's Calendar and Tasks components to manage the demands on your time with one convenient program.

Using the Calendar

The Calendar component of Outlook is designed to take the hassle out of time management by enabling you to keep track of your schedule. If you are working on a network that uses Exchange Server, some of the information in your Calendar can be viewed by colleagues who need to know your availability (see page 253 for more information). When you set up an appointment, by default Outlook reminds you of the appointment a few minutes ahead of time. For this reminder feature to work, Outlook must be running when the specified time arrives, so you might want to automatically start Outlook every time you start your computer (see the tip below).

Follow these steps to begin working with the Calendar:

The Calendar icon

1. Start Outlook and then click the Calendar icon on the Outlook bar. The workspace now looks as shown on the facing page.

Outlook Today

Outlook Today gathers information about the current day's activities from Calendar, Tasks and the Inbox and summarizes them on one screen. To display Outlook Today, click its icon on the Outlook bar. From this screen, you can mark tasks as complete and jump to other components by clicking the appropriate section heading.

Automatic Outlook start-up

To have Outlook (or any other program) start automatically every time you turn on your computer, you can add an Outlook shortcut to the StartUp submenu. Right-click a blank area of the Windows taskbar and choose Properties from the shortcut menu. When the Taskbar Properties dialog box appears, click the Start Menu Programs tab, click the Add button to start the Create Shortcut Wizard, and then click the Browse button in the wizard's first dialog box. Navigate to the Program Files\Microsoft Office\Office folder, double-click Outlook, and then click Next. In the wizard's second dialog box, select the StartUp folder at the bottom of the list and click Next. Finally, click Finish in the wizard's last dialog box. Click OK to close the Taskbar Properties dialog box. Now the next time you start Windows, Outlook will be ready and waiting for you.

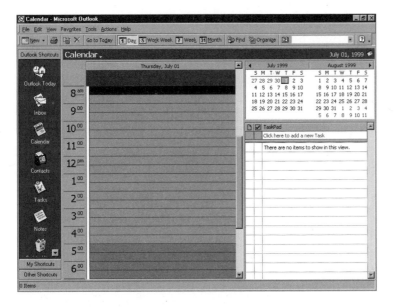

On the left side of the workspace is the appointment pane, divided into half-hour intervals. In the top right corner is the date navigator pane, which displays calendars for the current month and next month. (You can cycle through the months by clicking the right and left arrows on the calendar headers.) In the bottom right corner is the TaskPad, a miniature version of the pane where you keep your to-do list (see page 257). By default, Outlook displays your calendar for today.

2. Click the Week button on the toolbar and then click the Month button to see how the calendar view changes.

The Week and Month buttons

3. Click the Day button to return to the default view.

The Day button

Scheduling Your Time

The half-hour intervals in the appointment pane designate *time slots*. You use these time slots to schedule appointments for the day.

Entering Appointments

Suppose you have a meeting with David Perry at 3:00 this afternoon. You expect the meeting to last half an hour. Follow the steps on the next page to enter the appointment.

Computer dating

Outlook obtains the date and time from your system clock. If this clock is wrong, Outlook keeps an inaccurate calendar and reminds you of appointments at the wrong time. To set the correct date and time, right-click the clock at the end of the taskbar, choose Adjust Date/Time from the shortcut menu, and make the appropriate adjustments to the date or time.

1. In the appointment pane, click the 3:00 time slot.

2. Type *David Perry* and press Enter.

That's all there is to it. Today's date is now bold in the date navigator, indicating that you have an appointment today. The time slot holding the appointment indicates to anyone viewing your schedule that you are unavailable at that time. The bell in the time slot tells you that Outlook will remind you of the appointment 15 minutes ahead of time.

Now suppose you need to schedule an interview with a prospective employee named Carol Phillips at 4:15 PM tomorrow. The interview will probably last an hour and a half. Follow these steps:

1. Click tomorrow's date (or the next working day) in the date navigator. That day's schedule now appears in the appointment pane.

2. Because the Calendar time slots are in half-hour intervals, you need to make a special entry for Carol Phillips. Double-click the 4:00 time slot to display this Appointment window in which you can tailor your appointments:

Using AutoCreate

Outlook's AutoCreate feature lets you create appointments or tasks based on e-mail messages you receive. To use AutoCreate, select the message header in the Inbox and then drag it to the Calendar or Tasks icon on the Outlook bar. Outlook displays an Appointment or Task window with the contents of the message displayed in the message area at the bottom and the message's subject displayed in the Subject edit box. Fill in the remaining information to complete the appointment or task, and then click Save And Close. You can also drag tasks to the Calendar icon or appointments to the Tasks icon.

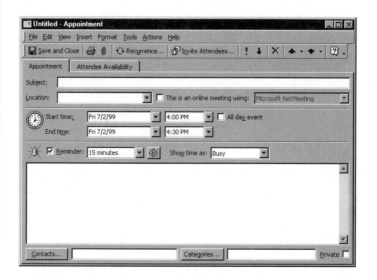

3. In the Subject edit box, type *Carol Phillips*, and in the Location edit box, type *Conference Room*.

4. To change the Start time, select 00 in 4:00 PM and type *15.* Then click the second End Time box, click its arrow, and select 5:45 PM (1.5 hours) from the drop-down list.

Specifying the start time

5. Make sure the Reminder check box is selected, then change the amount of warning time from 15 Minutes to 10 Minutes, and click Save And Close. You return to the Outlook window, which now looks like this:

Setting reminders

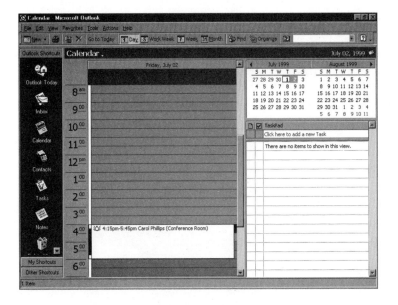

6. If you are working on a network, right-click the appointment and choose Private from the shortcut menu. A key icon in the time slot now indicates that other people viewing your schedule will find that you are busy during this time but won't see the appointment's description.

Private appointments

7. Click the Go To Today button on the toolbar or click today's date in the date navigator to move back to the appointment pane for today.

Go to Today

The Go To Today button

Entering Recurring Appointments

Unless you specify otherwise, appointments you schedule are nonrecurring. If you designate one as recurring, Outlook marks that engagement throughout your appointment book.

For example, suppose you meet with the Washington BEAT Coordinator, Nathan Chou, every other Wednesday from 12:00 to 1:00 PM. Here's how to schedule this recurring appointment:

1. Click next Wednesday's date in the date navigator and drag through the time slots for 12:00 and 12:30 to select them.

2. Choose New Recurring Appointment from the Actions menu to display this dialog box:

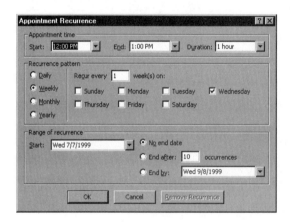

By default, Outlook assumes you want the meeting to occur weekly on the same day of the week, starting and ending at the times you selected, with no end date.

3. In the Recurrence Pattern section, enter *2* in the Recur Every edit box to change the appointment to every other week.

4. To add an end date, click the End By option in the Range Of Recurrence section and use the drop-down calendar to change the date to July 5, 2000. Then click OK. Outlook closes the dialog box and opens the Appointment window.

5. Type *Progress Report* in the Subject edit box and *Conference Room* in the Location edit box.

6. Change the reminder time for the appointment to 30 Minutes and then click Save And Close. The result is shown on the facing page.

Changing workday default times

By default, Outlook uses an 8:00 AM to 5:00 PM, Monday through Friday workweek and displays these hours in the appointment pane in yellow with all other hours of the day dimmed. But if your schedule is different, you can change the default times and days. Choose Options from the Tools menu and click the Calendar Options button on the Preferences tab. In the Calendar Work Week section, enter the start and end times of your workday. To change the days worked, click the desired days' check boxes. Then click OK twice.

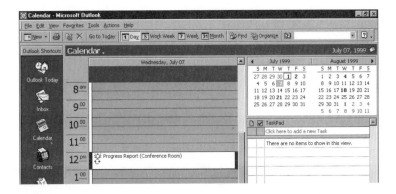

Outlook has entered the recurring appointment in the specified time slot for next Wednesday and for every other Wednesday thereafter, designating it with a circling arrow icon.

Scheduling Events

Sometimes appointments last for an entire day or even longer. Outlook refers to these long appointments as *events*. For example, you might need to schedule a day-long presentation at a new client's office or attend a week-long conference in another city. Scheduling events is similar to scheduling regular appointments. Here's what you do:

1. Click a date two weeks from now on the date navigator, and double-click the blank space below the date at the top of the appointment pane to tell Outlook that you want to enter an event. Outlook displays this Event window:

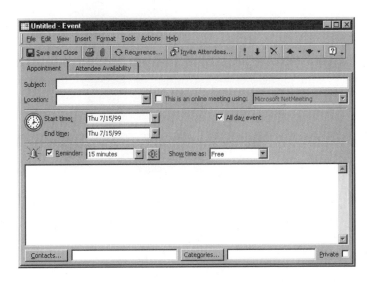

Making existing appointments recur

To turn an existing appointment into a recurring one, double-click the appointment in the appointment pane and click the Recurrence button. Outlook displays the Appointment Recurrence dialog box, where you can select the recurrence options you want. When you finish, click OK and then click Save And Close.

2. Next type *Presentation* in the Subject edit box, type *Jordan Manufacturing* in the Location edit box, change the Reminder setting to 0.5 Days, and change the Show Time As option to Out Of Office. Notice that Outlook has selected the All Day Event check box.

3. Click Save And Close to display the event in the appointment pane, like this:

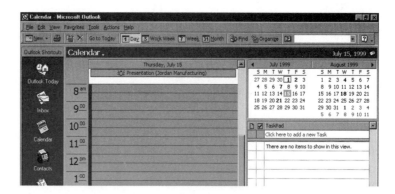

Now suppose you want to enter a week-long event for a conference you will attend in Washington, DC. Try this:

Entering week-long events

1. Click the Monday following the presentation at Jordan Manufacturing in the date navigator and then choose New All Day Event from the Actions menu to display the Event window.

2. Type *USA BEAT Conference* in the Subject edit box, then type *Capitol Convention Center* in the Location edit box, and finally, change the Show Time As option to Out Of Office.

Printing calendars

To print a calendar, choose Print from the File menu or click the Print button on the toolbar, select a print layout (and any other options) in the Print dialog box, and click OK. If you're not sure what type of layout you want to print, select one of the layout options and click the Preview button. You can also specify the dates you want to print in the Print Range section of the Print dialog box.

3. Click the arrow to the right of the End Time edit box and block out the entire week by selecting the Friday of the week you have chosen. Outlook displays a warning message at the top of the tab stating that you already have another appointment entered during this time (the recurring progress report meeting).

4. Click Save And Close.

5. Notice in the date navigator that the entire week is now marked in bold. Click one or two of the dates in the designated week to check that Outlook has entered the conference correctly.

Editing Appointments

Sometimes you will need to change an appointment to either fix errors or update details. Usually, you can double-click the appointment to open its Appointment window and then edit the appropriate area, but for certain changes you can take shortcuts. Let's try some shortcuts now as you change the appointment time for the interview with Carol Phillips:

1. First display the calendar for the day on which you scheduled Ms. Phillips' interview.

2. Click the 4:15 PM appointment to select it. Point to the blue border on the left side of the appointment, hold down the mouse button, and drag upward to the 3:00 PM time slot.

3. When the top of the appointment box is even with the 3:00 PM time slot, release the mouse button. Outlook moves the appointment and adjusts the times displayed in the box to reflect the fact that the appointment still starts at the quarter-hour, as shown here:

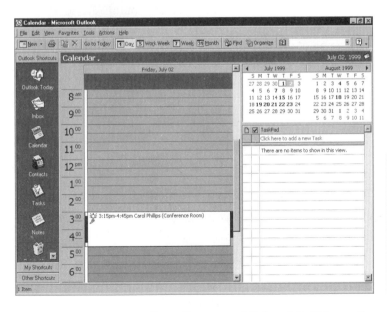

Now suppose you need to allow an additional half-hour for David Perry's appointment. Turn the page to see how to change the appointment in the appointment pane.

Adding holidays

If you work with clients or customers in other countries, you may want to track the national holidays of those countries in Calendar. To do so, choose Options from the Tools menu, click Calendar Options on the Preferences tab, and then click the Add Holidays button. You can then select the holidays of various countries as well as those of certain religions to add them to your calendar.

1. Display the David Perry appointment and point to the bottom border of its time slot.

2. When the pointer turns into a double-headed arrow, drag downward through the 3:30 PM time slot and then release the mouse button. The appointment is now scheduled for a full hour.

You can change an appointment to a different date in the appointment pane as well. Let's move Mr. Perry's appointment to Monday of next week:

1. Select the David Perry appointment, point to the left blue border, and drag it to the correct date on the date navigator.

2. Release the mouse button. Outlook displays the new date in the appointment pane and enters the appointment in the same time slot.

Editing Recurring Appointments

Editing a recurring appointment works the same way as editing any other type of appointment, except that Outlook gives you the option of changing just one occurrence of the appointment or all of them. Suppose the next progress report meeting, which occurs every other Wednesday, will take place in your office instead of the Conference Room. Follow these steps:

1. Click the date of the next progress report meeting and then double-click its box. You see this message box:

Editing one occurrence ──▶ 2. With the Open This Occurrence option selected, click OK. Outlook displays the Recurring Appointment window.

3. Change Conference Room to *My Office* in the Location edit box and then click Save And Close.

Canceling Appointments

In addition to editing appointments, you will sometimes need to delete them altogether. Suppose David Perry has called to cancel his meeting. Follow these steps to delete the appointment from Calendar:

1. Click the David Perry appointment once to select it.

2. Click the Delete button on the toolbar. Outlook instantly removes the appointment. (If you delete an appointment by mistake, you can choose Undo Delete from the Edit menu to move it back to the appointment pane.)

The procedure for canceling a recurring appointment is much the same as the one for canceling an individual appointment, except that you must decide whether to delete one occurrence of the appointment or all occurrences. You can also convert a recurring appointment to a onetime event. Suppose you have decided that after the next progress report meeting, reports will be added to the agenda of the monthly BEAT meeting instead of being addressed separately. Here's how to make this change:

1. Move to the first appointment of the recurring series and then double-click it. Outlook displays the message box shown on the previous page.

2. Select the Open The Series option and click OK. Outlook displays the Recurring Appointment window.

3. Click the Recurrence button to display the Appointment Recurrence dialog box shown earlier on page 246, and then click the Remove Recurrence button.

4. Back in the Appointment window, the series' Location setting has reverted to Conference Room, so reselect My Office from the Location drop-down list and then click the Save And Close button on the toolbar.

Be aware that you cannot undo this operation. The only way to restore the recurring appointment is to display its Appointment window, click the Recurrence button, and reenter its information.

Attaching files to appointments

If a file is associated with an appointment you have scheduled, you can attach the file to the appointment—for example, to remind you to print it beforehand. After scheduling the appointment in the Appointment window, click an insertion point in the message area at the bottom of the window and click the Insert File button on the toolbar. Outlook displays the Insert File dialog box shown earlier on page 58, where you navigate to the file you want to attach, select it, and click Insert. By default, the file is inserted as an attachment. You can click the arrow to the right of the Insert button to insert the file as text or to insert a shortcut to the document on your hard drive.

Finding Appointments

As your calendar begins to fill up, you may find it increasingly difficult to locate a particular appointment, meeting, or event. If you have a good idea of what you're looking for, you can use the Find button. Follow these steps:

The Find button

1. Click the Find button on Calendar's toolbar to display a Find area at the top of the workspace, as shown here:

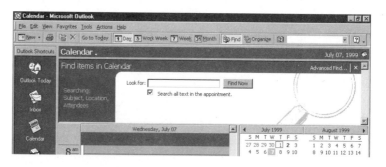

2. In the Look For edit box, type *Carol Phillips*. Outlook indicates that it will look for what you've typed in the Subject and Location boxes of the Appointment window and the Attendees box of the Meeting window (which we'll discuss in a minute).

3. Click Find Now. Outlook looks for an appointment that contains the specified words and displays the results in active appointments view, as shown here:

Advanced searches

You can carry out more complex searches in the Find area by clicking Advanced Find. Outlook displays an Advanced Find dialog box. On the Appointments And Meetings tab, you can enter more search criteria. By default, Find searches the currently active Outlook component, but you can change the component by selecting a different option from the Look For drop-down list. The More Choices and Advanced tabs of the Advanced Find dialog box offer still more ways to search. Once you finish entering your search criteria, click Find Now to begin the search.

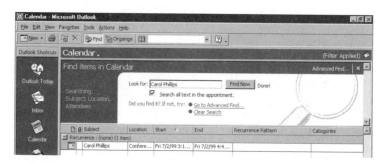

If your search is unsuccessful, you can click Go To Advanced Find (see the adjacent tip) to refine the search, or you can click Clear Search to begin again.

4. Click the Find area's Close button to return Calendar to its default view.

Planning a Meeting

The advent of programs such as Microsoft NetMeeting (see the adjacent tip) means that you no longer have to be physically present at a meeting to be able to participate. Nevertheless, the face-to-face meeting is still the most common means of collective communication in the workplace. Whether a meeting is electronic or face-to-face, it needs to be scheduled. If you are working on a network that uses Exchange Server, you can use electronic communication to take some of the hassle out of setting up meetings. With the help of Outlook's Calendar component, you can check other people's calendars to determine an appropriate time and place for a meeting. You can also send out meeting requests to potential attendees without the back-and-forth usually involved in such a task.

Sending Meeting Requests

Suppose you want to set up a meeting for next Wednesday. For this example, you will coordinate schedules and send out a meeting request to just one person, but you will see how the procedure could easily be applied to several meeting attendees. (If you are not working on a network that uses Exchange Server, simply read along so that you can get an idea of the procedure.) Let's get started:

1. With Calendar's contents displayed in the workspace, click next Wednesday's date in date navigator and then choose Plan A Meeting from the Actions menu. Outlook opens the Plan A Meeting dialog box shown here:

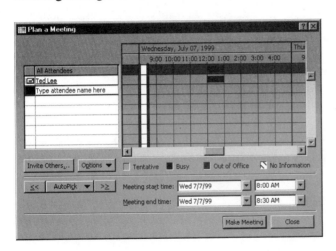

Online meetings

If you have set up Microsoft NetMeeting 2.1 or later on your computer, you can use Outlook to schedule an online meeting. (If you have Microsoft Internet Explorer installed on your computer, you also have NetMeeting.) NetMeeting allows you to communicate with one or more people over the Internet or on an intranet using both video and audio. Other communication capabilities include sharing documents, chatting, transferring files, and drawing on an electronic whiteboard. (For more information about NetMeeting, see the Help feature.)

The timeline on the right side of the dialog box shows Wednesday's date, displaying any appointments you have scheduled for that day blocked out with colored lines representing the type of appointment.

Selecting attendees

2. To invite someone to attend the meeting, click the Invite Others button. Outlook displays this dialog box, with your name already entered in the Required box:

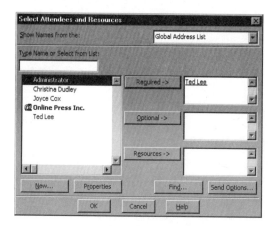

You can change the setting in the Show Names From The box to display the contents of a different address book. (See the tip on page 222 for more information about address books.)

3. Locate and select the name of the person you want to invite from the address book list.

Other ways to request a meeting

You can also create a meeting request by choosing New Meeting Request from the Actions menu. Instead of displaying the Plan A Meeting dialog box, Outlook displays the Meeting window. You then fill in the information as you would normally. To invite people to the meeting and to check their schedules using this method, use the window's Attendee Availability tab.

4. Click the Required button. Outlook moves the selected name to the Required list box. (If you want to invite someone to the meeting whose presence is desired but not necessary, select his or her name from the address book list, and then click the Optional button. Outlook then moves the selected name to the Optional list box.)

5. Click OK. Outlook adds a row to the timeline displaying the schedule of the person you want to invite, like the one shown at the top of the facing page.

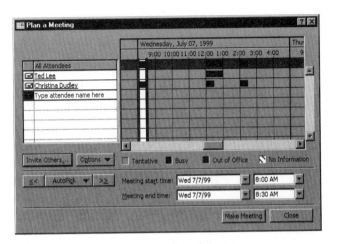

6. Select the time slot you want by simply clicking it, by clicking the AutoPick >> button to move to the slot, or by selecting a time in the Meeting Start Time box.

7. To send a meeting request to the person you selected, first click the Make Meeting button. Outlook displays a Meeting window, like this one:

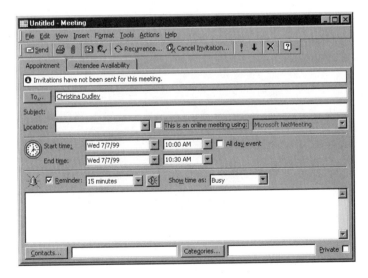

8. Notice that the selected person's name or e-mail address is in the To edit box. For purposes of demonstration, replace this e-mail address with your own.

◄—— Sending meeting requests

Recurring meetings

To create a new recurring meeting, first choose New Recurring Meeting from the Actions menu. Fill in the Appointment Recurrence dialog box as usual and click OK. Next fill in the necessary information on the Appointment and Attendee Availability tabs and click Send. To turn an existing meeting into a recurring one, double-click its box in the appointment pane, click the Recurrence button to display the Appointment Recurrence dialog box, fill in the information, and then click OK. In the Recurring Meeting window, click the Send Update button so that you can notify all participants of the change.

9. Type *Membership Update Meeting* in the Subject edit box and select Conference Room from the Location drop-down list. Then change the time in the End Time edit box so that the meeting will last 1 hour.

10. Click an insertion point in the blank note area at the bottom of the window and type *Hope this time will work for you*.

11. Click the Send button. Outlook sends an e-mail message to the designated address, requesting the meeting at the specified time.

Responding to Meeting Requests

Now that you know how to request a meeting, you need to see how things work on the receiving end. Because you sent the meeting request to yourself, follow these steps to check for the meeting request:

1. Display the contents of the Inbox in the workspace and, if necessary, click the Send/Receive button to check for new messages.

2. Double-click the Membership Update Meeting header to open the message in a window like this one:

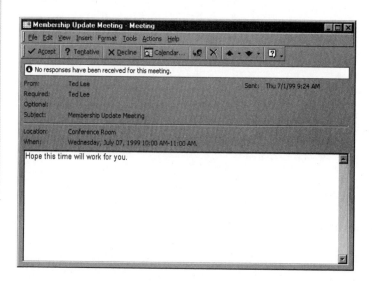

At the top of the window, Outlook displays a message that no responses have been received for the meeting. (If a conflict in

Canceling meetings

If you need to cancel a meeting, first open the meeting in its Meeting window. Then choose Cancel Meeting from the Actions menu. Outlook displays a message box, giving you the option of deleting the meeting and sending cancellation notices to all attendees or deleting the meeting without sending the cancellation notice. Select the option you want and then click OK. If you are sending cancellation notices, be sure to click the Send button in the Meeting window before closing it. If you receive a meeting cancellation notice, you can click the Remove From Calendar button to remove the meeting from your calendar.

your Calendar schedule means the requested meeting time won't work for you, Outlook also informs you of the conflict.) Toolbar buttons provide three options for responding to the meeting request. You can accept, tentatively accept, or decline.

The Calendar button

3. Click the Calendar button to open a Calendar window, check whether the meeting fits with your schedule, and then click the Membership button on the Windows taskbar to redisplay the Meeting window.

The Accept button

4. Click the Accept button. Because you are the meeting organizer, Outlook displays a message saying no response is needed. (Obviously, this message would not appear if you were responding to a real meeting request.)

5. Click OK to close the message box.

6. Close the Meeting window and delete the meeting request from the Inbox before moving on. You might also want to cancel the meeting by following the instructions given in the facing tip.

Keeping a To-Do List

Using the Tasks component of Outlook, you can create, prioritize, and manage a to-do list. If necessary, you can "schedule" time for specific tasks in Calendar so that other people will know that you are unavailable during the time you plan to work on a task. In the following sections, we discuss how to create entries and how to deal with tasks in their various stages. We also show you how to organize tasks and how to electronically delegate tasks to colleagues.

Adding Tasks

Let's start by adding a couple of tasks to your to-do list. You'll first add a simple one and then a high priority task with a deadline:

The Tasks icon

1. Click the Tasks icon to open the to-do list, which is displayed in simple list view as shown on the following page. (If necessary, choose Current View and then Simple List from the View menu.)

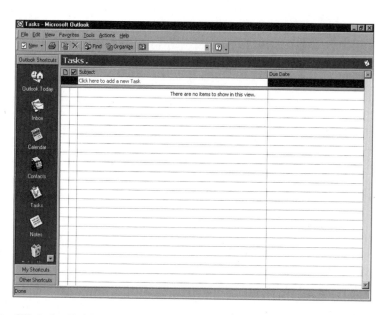

2. Click the Subject slot marked Click Here To Add A New Task and type *Pick up dry cleaning*. Then click None, which has appeared in the Due Date column, click the arrow, select tomorrow's date from the drop-down calendar, and press Enter.

The New Task button

3. To add a second task, click the New Task button on the toolbar to display this Task window:

Other ways of adding tasks

To add a task while working in another Outlook component, you can click the arrow to the right of the New button and select Task, press Ctrl+Shift+K, or choose New and then Task from the File menu. If you have installed the Office shortcut bar (see page 371), click the New Task button. In Word, Excel, or PowerPoint, you can create a new task that is linked to the open document. Display the Reviewing toolbar and click the Create Microsoft Outlook Task button to display a Task window.

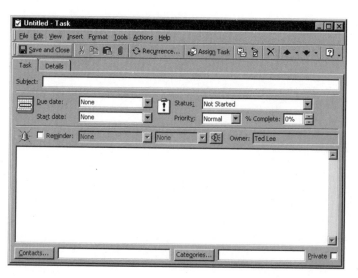

4. Type *Prepare for presentation* in the Subject edit box of the Task tab.

By default, the task has no due date and has not yet started. You can enter start and due dates and assign a priority level. For example, suppose this task is very important and must be completed by tomorrow afternoon. Follow these steps to assign dates and change the priority:

1. Click the arrow to the right of the Due Date edit box, and when the calendar appears, click tomorrow's date.

2. Change the Priority setting to High.

Setting a priority level

3. Click Save And Close. As you can see here, the tasks pane now lists your two tasks:

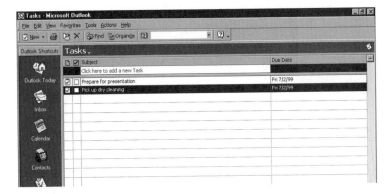

Adding Recurring Tasks

Now suppose that on the first Friday of every month, you have to review a report of the previous month's activities. Here's how you add a recurring task to the to-do list:

1. Click the New Task button on the toolbar and type *Review last month* in the Subject edit box.

The Recurrence button

2. Click the Recurrence button on the Task window's toolbar to display a dialog box similar to the one shown on page 241.

3. Select Monthly and change the entries in the adjacent section to the first Friday of every month. Then select the Start entry and change it to the first Friday of the current month. The dialog box now looks like the one shown on the next page.

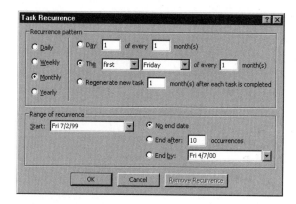

4. Click OK to close the Task Recurrence dialog box.

Setting reminders

5. Back in the Task window, change the Reminder time to 1:00 PM and click Save And Close.

Editing Tasks

The Details tab

You use the Details tab of the Task window to keep track of additional information about a task. Outlook fills in the Date Completed field when you mark the task as complete. (Outlook assumes that the day you mark the task is the date you complete it.) In the Total Work field, enter the number of hours you think the task will take to complete, and in the Actual Work field, enter the number of hours it took. You use the remaining four fields to track mileage, billing information, and contacts or companies associated with the task. If you are working on a network that uses Exchange Server and you use Tasks to assign tasks to coworkers (we explain how on page 265), the Update List section lists all people whose task lists must be updated if a change is made to the task.

After creating a task, you may sometimes notice a typographical error that needs to be fixed or an item of information, such as a due date, that needs to be changed. You can make some changes directly in the to-do list, or you can reopen the Task window. Let's try both methods:

1. Click the presentation task and then click an insertion point before the word *presentation*.

2. Type *Northwest BEAT* and a space and press Enter.

Suppose you're told that, because of database problems, the monthly review can't be completed for another two weeks. However, it is required by USA BEAT before the end of the conference. Let's change its due date and priority level:

1. Double-click the review task to display its Task window.

2. Change the due date to the third Friday of the month (or the Friday before the USA BEAT conference) and then reset the Priority to High.

3. Click Save And Close to update the task. When Outlook tells you that you have changed one occurrence of a recurring task, click OK. Outlook then creates a new task to reflect the

changes you just made, and updates the recurring task to start the following month.

Designating Tasks as Complete

Adding tasks to the to-do list is only the first step if you want to manage your time effectively. You must also keep the status of your tasks up-to-date. Outlook's Tasks component provides several methods for showing that a task is complete.

Suppose you have picked up the dry cleaning and finished the Northwest BEAT presentation. Let's try a couple of different methods to show that these tasks are complete:

1. Click the check box in the second column of the dry cleaning task to designate the task as finished, and then click elsewhere to deselect the task and see these results:

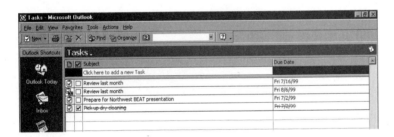

When you mark a task as complete, Outlook displays a check mark in the check box, changes the type color to gray, and crosses out the task text. It does not delete the task from the list. This way, you can view the list and double-check that you did in fact complete the task. (If Outlook simply erased the task, you might not remember whether you ever added it to the list in the first place.)

2. Next double-click the presentation task to display its Task window and then click the Mark Complete button on the toolbar. Outlook closes the window and changes the display of the task in the to-do list to show that it is complete.

The Mark Complete button

You can change the Status edit box in the Task window to Completed and then click Save And Close. You can also change the % Complete field to 100. To update this field, display the Task window, or make changes directly in the % Complete field in detailed list view.

Deleting Tasks

Follow these steps to see how to remove a completed task from the list:

1. In the Tasks list, quickly create a task you can experiment with. Then click the new task's check box in the second column. Outlook checks the box and draws a line through the task to indicate that it is complete.

2. With the completed task selected, click the Delete button on the toolbar to remove the task from the list, and then delete any other tasks created by Outlook.

   Like deleted items in other components, Outlook moves deleted tasks to the Deleted Items folder, where they remain until you erase a specific item from the folder or empty the folder completely.

Managing Tasks

Now that you know how to add, edit, and delete tasks, you need to know how to categorize and organize them for maximum efficiency. As with other Outlook components, you can change the view of the to-do list. But before you take a look at the different views available for the Tasks component, we'll show you a quick way to reorganize the list. Follow these steps:

1. First add a few more tasks to your to-do list using any of the methods we've discussed, so that you have a longer list to work with. Your to-do list then looks something like this:

Setting reminder times

By default, reminder times for tasks are set for 8:00 AM. However, if you would prefer to be reminded at a different time of day, you can change the default setting. Choose Options from the Tools menu, and in the Tasks section of the Preferences tab, type a new time in the Reminder Time edit box or click the arrow to the right of the box to select a time from the drop-down list. Then click OK.

In the current view, tasks are listed in the order in which you entered them, with the most recent entry at the top of the list. You might find it more useful, however, to list them in due date order.

2. Click the Due Date column header once to quickly reorganize the list chronologically by due date. Notice that Outlook has reorganized the list in descending order, symbolized by the down arrow in the column header.

Sorting tasks

3. To switch to ascending order, simply click the column header again. The list now looks like this:

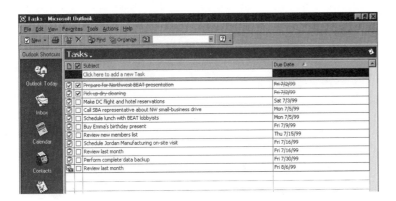

Now let's take a look at other Tasks views. (In the following pages, you choose views from the View menu, but you can also use the Current View button on the Advanced toolbar.)

1. Choose Current View and then Detailed List from the View menu to display the to-do list like this:

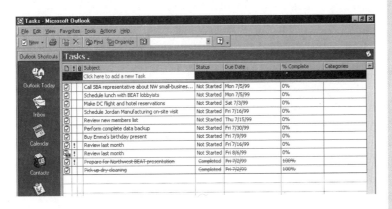

Using the Journal

Outlook's Journal component can be used to log the tasks you perform on your computer, including work done with Office applications. You can record your own journal entries and track interaction with certain contacts. And you can use Journal to archive Outlook files. To display the Journal, click its icon in the My Shortcuts group of the Outlook bar. For more information, check Outlook's Help feature.

This view displays the Type, Priority, Attachment, Subject, Status, Due Date, % Complete, and Categories fields. Notice that high priority tasks are flagged with an exclamation mark in the Priority column.

Before you look at the next view, you need to assign all the tasks to categories. Being able to categorize tasks is particularly useful if you work concurrently on different projects or if you like to keep track of personal as well as business tasks. Let's categorize the tasks now:

1. Right-click the first task and choose Categories from the shortcut menu to display the Categories dialog box shown earlier on page 233.

2. Select the appropriate category from the list and click OK.

3. Repeat this procedure for the remaining tasks. When you finish, your to-do list looks something like this:

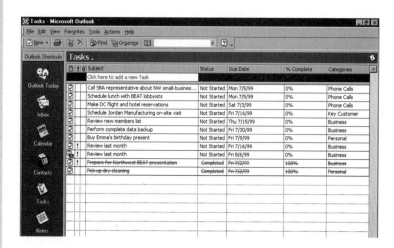

Now you're ready to use the by category view to look at the to-do list. Follow these steps:

1. First choose Current View and then By Category from the View menu.

2. Next click the plus sign next to each category to display its contents, as shown on the facing page.

Other Tasks views

You may want to experiment with other Tasks views to help organize your day. The active tasks view displays the same fields as the detailed list view but displays only the tasks that have not been designated as complete. The next seven days view focuses on the immediate tasks by displaying only the ones with due dates within the next week. With the overdue tasks view, you can focus on any tasks that have slipped through the cracks. The assignment view displays the tasks you have given to others but that you track with an updated copy. (We discuss assigning tasks to others on page 265.) The by person responsible view is similar to the assignment view but groups the tasks you track by the people who now own them. The completed tasks view allows you to see what you have accomplished. Finally, the task timeline view displays your tasks in the appropriate section of a timeline. It shows the start date and due date of a task if that information was entered in the Task window, and when both dates are known, a gray bar indicates the interval between them.

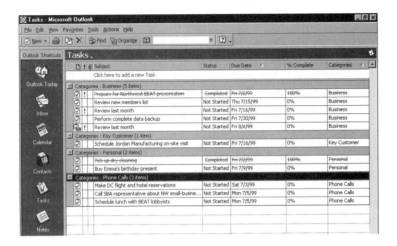

This view displays the same fields as the detailed list view but it rearranges the tasks by category.

3. Experiment with some of the other task views (see the tip on the facing page) and then return to the simple list view.

Delegating Tasks

Before we wrap up this discussion of the Tasks component, we want to quickly discuss one more potentially useful feature. If you are using Outlook on a stand-alone computer, you can skip this section because it pertains only to those of you who are working with Outlook on a network that uses Exchange Server.

If you are a manager or supervisor, part of your job is to delegate tasks to ensure that your organization's business is carried out efficiently and economically. And you will probably need to keep tabs on the status of the tasks you delegate. Outlook's Tasks component can help you with these chores. Although we don't recommend eliminating face-to-face communication with your colleagues, we do suggest you experiment with this feature to see if it can help you manage projects better. Let's try it now:

1. Choose New Task Request from the Actions menu to display a window similar to the standard Task window.

2. Type the e-mail address of the person to whom you want to delegate the task in the To edit box. (You can also click the To

Owning tasks

Every time you create a new task, Outlook automatically designates you as the "owner" of the task unless you specify otherwise by assigning the task to someone else. If someone else accepts the task, he or she becomes the new owner even though you were the one who initially created the task. Also, bear in mind that when you assign a task to several people, Outlook designates the first person listed in the To edit box as the owner of the task.

button to display the Select Task Recipient dialog box, which works like the Select Attendees And Resources dialog box shown on page 254.)

3. In the Subject edit box, type *Finish reviewing conference materials.*

4. Click the arrow to the right of the Due Date edit box and assign a date two weeks from today.

5. Change the Status setting to In Progress, the Priority setting to High, and the % Complete setting to 25%. Then assign the task to the Business category. The task now looks something like this:

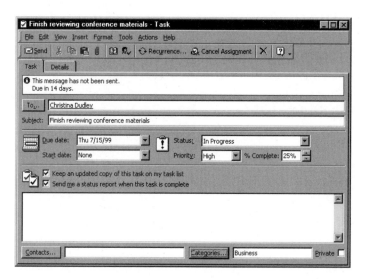

Notice the two check boxes above the message area of the window. If the Keep An Updated Copy check box is selected, Tasks tracks the progress of the task on a copy of it on your to-do list even if you assign the task to someone else and no longer "own" it. If the Send Me A Status Report check box is selected, the task recipient (the new "owner") can easily keep you posted on the task's status by clicking the Send Status Report button in the Task window to create a status report addressed to you (the original "owner"). If these check boxes are not selected, the task is removed from your to-do list after you delegate it.

Assigning existing tasks

To assign an existing task of your own to someone else, first open the task to display its window. Next click the Assign Task button on the toolbar. The standard Task window is then converted into a Task Request window, and you can fill in the information as usual and click Send.

6. To send the task, you would click the Send button. You won't actually send this task, so click the Close button and then click No when asked if you want to save your changes.

When someone receives a task request from you, it shows up in his or her inbox with a hand attached to its icon. After the recipient opens the request and accepts or declines the task, notification shows up in your Inbox. Double-clicking the notification displays the Task window with the recipient's response. If the task is declined, you can return the open task to your own to-do list by choosing Return To Task List from the Actions menu.

Dealing with a Task Request

If someone else delegates a task to you, you receive the task request in your Inbox just like a meeting request or an e-mail message. (The task is also added to your to-do list.) You can respond to the request by opening its window and using the Accept, Decline, or Assign Task buttons on the window's toolbar. When you accept or decline a task, Outlook displays a dialog box giving the option of either editing the response or sending the response immediately.

If you accept a task, it remains in your to-do list, and you become its owner, meaning you can make changes to its status, deadline, and so on. If you decline a task, the task is returned to the original owner, who can then reassign it. If you assign the task to someone else, either in the original request message or after accepting it, you follow the procedure for assigning an existing task described in the tip on the facing page.

That ends our discussion of Outlook's Calendar and Tasks components. The more diligent you are about using and updating your schedule and to-do list, the more Outlook can help you keep your life on track. Also remember that the usefulness of Outlook's Tasks component is augmented by the fact that a small version of the to-do list is displayed in the Calendar, which makes it easy to schedule time slots for specific tasks so that nothing slips through the cracks.

12

Publisher Basics

You use one of Publisher's wizards to get started, and then we show you how to move around a publication and work with text. Next you learn about frames, and finally, you take a look at some of Publisher's formatting capabilities.

The postcard and flyer you create in this chapter are useful for promoting any kind of business or organization, and you can apply what you learn about design and color schemes to other promotional materials as well.

Publications created and concepts covered:

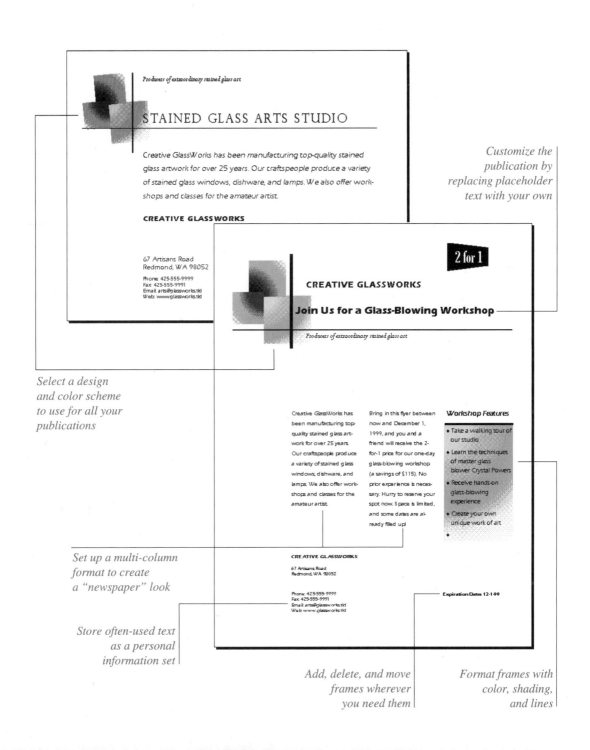

Customize the publication by replacing placeholder text with your own

STAINED GLASS ARTS STUDIO

Producers of extraordinary stained glass art

Creative GlassWorks has been manufacturing top-quality stained glass artwork for over 25 years. Our craftspeople produce a variety of stained glass windows, dishware, and lamps. We also offer workshops and classes for the amateur artist.

CREATIVE GLASSWORKS

67 Artisans Road
Redmond, WA 98052

Phone: 425-555-9999
Fax: 425-555-9991
Email: arts@glassworks.tld
Web: www.glassworks.tld

CREATIVE GLASSWORKS

Join Us for a Glass-Blowing Workshop

Producers of extraordinary stained glass art

2 for 1

Select a design and color scheme to use for all your publications

Creative GlassWorks has been manufacturing top-quality stained glass artwork for over 25 years. Our craftspeople produce a variety of stained glass windows, dishware, and lamps. We also offer workshops and classes for the amateur artist.

Bring in this flyer between now and December 1, 1999, and you and a friend will receive the 2-for-1 price for our one-day glass-blowing workshop (a savings of $115). No prior experience is necessary. Hurry to reserve your spot now. Space is limited, and some dates are already filled up!

Workshop Features

- Take a walking tour of our studio
- Learn the techniques of master glass blower Crystal Powers
- Receive hands-on glass-blowing experience
- Create your own unique work of art

Set up a multi-column format to create a "newspaper" look

CREATIVE GLASSWORKS

67 Artisans Road
Redmond, WA 98052

Phone: 425-555-9999
Fax: 425-555-9991
Email: arts@glassworks.tld
Web: www.glassworks.tld

Expiration Date: 12-1-99

Store often-used text as a personal information set

Add, delete, and move frames wherever you need them

Format frames with color, shading, and lines

icrosoft Publisher 2000 is the desktop-publishing component of some editions of Office. Publisher makes creating a variety of publications a breeze because you can focus on your message and let the program handle many of the aesthetic details. In fact, Publisher can help with virtually every facet of creating a professional-quality publication. At the same time, you can tailor various components to your own needs and tastes, and you're never constrained by the program's ideas of what a particular publication should look like.

In this chapter, you create a postcard and flyer for Creative GlassWorks, a company that creates stained glass art as well as offers classes and workshops. Let's get started:

Starting Microsoft Publisher

1. Choose Programs and then Microsoft Publisher from the Start menu to open the program.

2. If necessary, close the Office Assistant by right-clicking it and choosing Hide from the shortcut menu. Publisher then displays this Catalog dialog box:

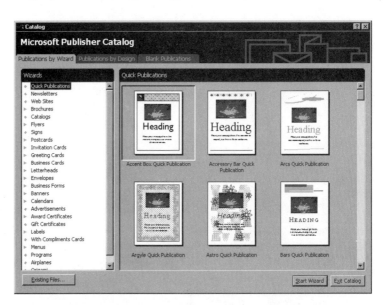

Which Office editions include Publisher?

Microsoft Office 2000 comes in five different editions, four of which include Publisher: the Professional, the Premium, the Small Business, and the Developer editions.

You see this directory of publication designs every time you start Publisher. The Publications By Wizard tab, which is currently displayed, lists publications by type, such as flyers, newsletters, and business cards. Selecting a publication type from the list on the left displays miniature pictures of the designs available for that type on the right. These designs are consistent across types, so you can create a collection of publications that all have the same look. You use the other two tabs to open a publication based on its design or to open a blank publication so that you can build it from scratch. To open an existing publication, click the Existing Files button in the bottom left corner of the dialog box.

Consistent designs

Using a Wizard to Create a Publication

Suppose you have decided to create an informational postcard that promotes Creative GlassWorks. For this publication, you're going to let one of Publisher's wizards be your guide. Follow these steps to see how to use a wizard to create a professional-looking publication:

1. With the Catalog dialog box open on your screen, click Postcards in the Wizards list in the left pane to expand the list to show all the available postcard types.

Selecting a publication type

2. Click Event in the list of postcard types to display pictures of the postcard designs for events in the right pane of the Catalog dialog box.

3. Now click Informational in the list of postcard types to display pictures of the postcard designs for giving information in the right pane.

Selecting a design

4. Use the right pane's scroll bar to move down in the list until you see the Tilt Informational Postcard.

5. Click the Tilt Informational Postcard once to select it and then click the Start Wizard button in the bottom right corner of the dialog box. Publisher closes the dialog box, starts the Postcard Wizard, and checks for a *personal information set* that stores information about you and your organization. If you haven't yet created a personal information set, Publisher displays a message that it needs to collect this information for use wherever it's needed in the publications you create.

The Postcard Wizard

6. Click OK. You see the dialog box shown on the next page.

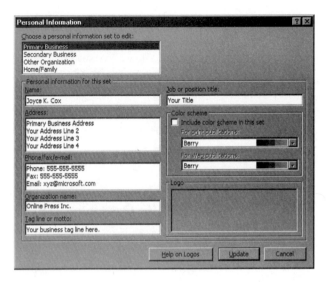

7. Leaving Primary Business selected as the information set, re-place the entry in the Name edit box with *Art Synkrafts*. Replace the entry in the Job Or Position Title edit box with *President*.

8. Fill in the boxes so that the dialog box looks like this:

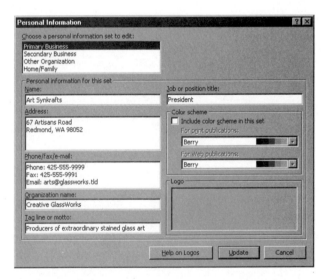

In a hurry?

You can use Publisher's *quick publications* to create a one-page document in seconds. Start the Quick Publication Wizard from the Catalog window by double-clicking the layout you want. Indicate by selecting from the list whether you want to have pictures, headings, sidebars or messages, and where you would like each item. Finish the wizard and edit the objects as usual.

9. You want all the publications you create for Adventure Works to have the same color scheme. Click the Include Color Scheme In This Set check box to turn it on, click the arrow to the right of the For Print Publications box, and select Glacier from the drop-down list. Then change the For Web Publications set-ting to Glacier as well.

10. Click the Update button to close the Personal Information dialog box. Your screen now looks like this:

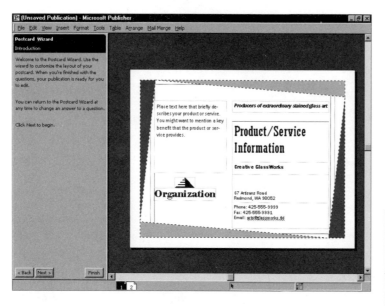

You can now work with the Postcard Wizard to create your first publication. Follow these steps:

1. Read the information in the wizard's pane on the left and click Next at the bottom of the pane. The wizard's pane then displays a list of color schemes.

2. Click some of the color schemes and notice their effect on the postcard in the right pane. Then with Glacier selected, click Next. The wizard asks you to select either a quarter-page or half-page postcard.

3. Leave the quarter-page option selected and click Next. The wizard displays options for the back of the postcard.

4. You want to be able to mail these postcards, so check that Only Address is selected and click Next.

5. Check that One In The Center Of The Page is selected as your print specification and click Next.

6. Check that Primary Business is the personal information set and click Finish to see results something like those shown on the next page.

Other personal information sets

Publisher can maintain up to four personal information sets: Primary Business, Secondary Business, Other Organization, and Home/Family. For each set, Publisher stores eight items of information. By default, Publisher uses the Primary Business set when you create publications. To use a different personal information set, choose Personal Information from the Edit menu, select a set from the list box at the top of the Personal Information dialog box, review the information in all the edit boxes, and click Update. (You also use this command to change an item of information.) To insert a particular item from the active personal information set in a publication, choose Personal Information and then the desired item from the Insert menu. Once an item has been inserted in a publication, you can add to it or delete parts of it without affecting the way it is stored in the personal information set.

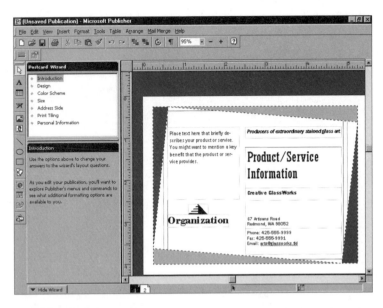

7. As you can see, Publisher leaves the wizard displayed on the left side of the screen so that you can modify the postcard if needed. Click the Hide Wizard button below the wizard's pane to give the postcard more space on the screen, as shown here:

Hiding the wizard

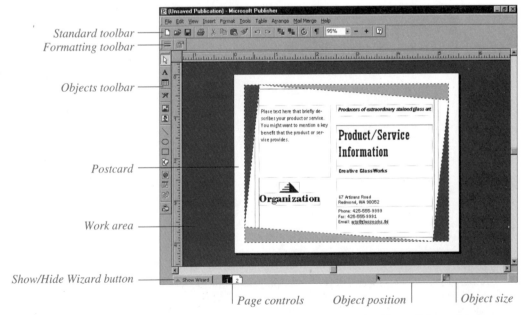

Standard toolbar
Formatting toolbar
Objects toolbar
Postcard
Work area
Show/Hide Wizard button
Page controls   *Object position*   *Object size*

The Hide Wizard button becomes the Show Wizard button so that you can easily display the wizard again at any time.

Taking up most of the window's work area is your new post-card. Notice that the organization name and other information from the personal information set has already been entered in the relevant places.

The status bar at the bottom of your screen displays messages and a selected object's size and position on the page. At the left end of the status bar are the Show/Hide Wizard button and the *page controls* for moving among pages in your publication.

Before you go any further, save the publication:

1. Choose Save As from the File menu.

Saving a publication

2. Type *Glass Postcard* in the File Name edit box, and click Save.

Moving Around a Publication

Before you can proceed with customizing the postcard, you need to know how to move around a publication. If a page of a publication is bigger than the window, you can bring hidden parts into view by using the scroll bars. To display a different page of a publication, you can use the page controls at the bottom of the window, like this:

1. Click the Page 2 icon. Publisher shows the back of the postcard:

The Page 2 icon

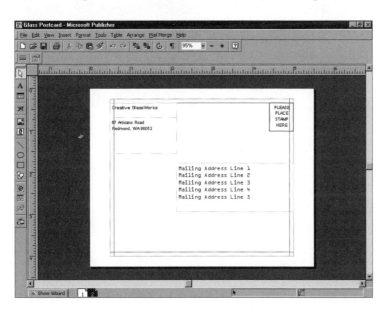

You can also choose Go To Page from the View menu to display its dialog box, type *2* and click OK.

The Page 1 icon

2. To return to the first page, click the Page 1 icon. (If the hidden taskbar gets in your way, move your pointer slowly when at the bottom of the screen. If you keep the pointer within the frame of the window, you won't activate the taskbar. If necessary, you can point to a blank area of the taskbar and drag it to the right side of the screen, where it won't get in your way.)

Zooming In and Out

In addition to scrolling around a large page and moving to different pages of a multi-page publication, you will also want to zoom in for a closer look at a particular element or zoom out to get an overview of an entire page. With Publisher, you can zoom in and out in several ways. Before you start working on the text of the postcard, let's experiment with zooming:

1. Click the arrow to the right of the Zoom box on the Standard toolbar and select 200% from the drop-down list to enlarge the postcard like this:

2. Next choose Zoom and then 100% from the View menu.

3. Right-click the Object Position or Object Size indicator to display a shortcut menu. You can choose the Whole Page command, which you use to view the entire page, the Page Width command, which expands the object to fit the width of your workspace, and the Actual Size command, which displays the page in its printed size. If you select an object on the page, Publisher adds a Selected Objects command to the shortcut menu. Choosing this command zooms the window to the percentage that allows full viewing of the selected object.

Changing the page magnification

4. Choose Whole Page from the shortcut menu.

5. To change the magnification to the next lowest increment, click the Zoom Out button on the toolbar. Publisher switches the view so that you see more of the page.

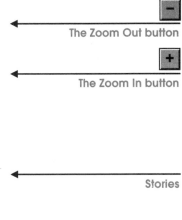

The Zoom Out button

6. Click the Zoom In button to return to 100%.

The Zoom In button

Working with Text

Unlike text in a Word document, text displayed in a Publisher publication must be contained in a text frame. Publisher refers to the text in a frame as a *story*. We discuss working with frames on page 285. For now, we'll just show you how to deal with the text that is currently in the postcard's existing frames, some of which contain placeholder text. You need to select the placeholder text and then replace it with your own words. Let's get going:

Stories

1. Click anywhere in the Product/Service Information placeholder text. (If Publisher displays a tip about the selection, read it and then click it to turn it off.) Publisher selects all the text in the frame to indicate that you must replace all the information. Publisher also displays an Ungroup Objects button below the selected frame. Although you can't see it very well, the frame has a line above it, and the frame and line have been grouped so that if you move, size, or delete one, the other will be moved, sized, or deleted as well. (We talk more about lines on page 292 and about grouping objects on page 318.)

The Ungroup Objects button

2. With the text selected, type *Stained Glass Arts Studio*.

Adding a line

3. In the Phone/Fax/E-Mail frame, click an insertion point to the right of the e-mail address and press Enter to add a new line of text to the frame. (If you have trouble seeing the text, use one of the zooming techniques described on page 276 to change the zoom magnification.)

4. Type *Web: www.glassworks.tld.*

Now enter the description of the company's services in the text frame on the left:

1. Move the pointer over the *Place text here* placeholder and click once to select both the text and the frame. Publisher may display the Connect Frames toolbar to the right of the Standard toolbar so that, if necessary, you can continue the text of this frame in another frame elsewhere in the publication.

2. With all the placeholder text selected, type this paragraph:

Creative GlassWorks has been manufacturing top-quality stained glass artwork for over 25 years. Our craftspeople produce a variety of stained glass windows, dishware, and lamps. We also offer workshops and classes for the amateur artist.

3. You may have already responded to Publisher's prompting and saved your work, but to be on the cautious side, save it now by clicking the Save button on the Standard toolbar. Be sure to save frequently as you continue working through this chapter. (See the adjacent tip for more information about saving options.)

Sometimes you will want to delete a placeholder without replacing it with anything. (Always delete placeholders for elements you don't want to use; otherwise, they appear just as they are when you print the final publication.) You can delete text in the usual way, by selecting it and then pressing the Delete key. If you want to delete a frame as well as the text it contains, you must use another method. Delete the logo placeholder on the left side of the postcard using this technique:

1. Click the word *Organization* in the Logo placeholder to select it. (The logo's frame should be surrounded by handles.) Because a wizard is associated with the logo, a Wizard button appears.

Saving options

By default, Publisher reminds you to save your files every 15 minutes. To change the frequency of the reminders or to turn off the feature altogether, first choose Options from the Tools menu and click the User Assistance tab. Change the setting in the Minutes Between Reminders box or click the Remind To Save Publication check box to remove the check mark and turn the feature off. Then click OK to implement your changes. To save only the text of a publication, select the format you want from the Save As Type drop-down list at the bottom of the Save As dialog box. To save a publication so that it can be accessed as a template, select the Publisher Template option in the Save As Type box. (Publisher saves templates in the C:\Windows\Application Data\ Microsoft\Templates subfolder.) Finally, to retain the previous version of the file as a backup copy each time you save a new version, select Save With Backup from the Save button's drop-down list. (Publisher names the backup copy "Backup of *name*.pub.")

2. With the logo frame selected, choose Delete Object from the expanded Edit menu. The postcard now looks like this:

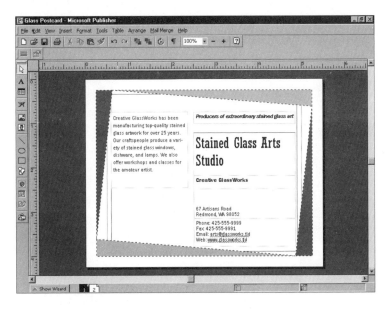

Using a Wizard to Make Design Changes

You've seen how to simplify the task of creating a publication by using one of Publisher's wizards. Obviously, adding text is easier when the text frames for all the elements are already in place. But what if you decide you don't like the arrangement or color scheme associated with the design you chose? Do you have to start all over again? No. You can simply call on the wizard to make these sorts of changes in one quick step.

Changing the Basic Design

Suppose you've decided that the Tilt design doesn't quite fit the image you want for Creative GlassWorks. Let's open the wizard again and look for something more appropriate:

1. With the postcard still displayed on your screen, open the wizard's pane by clicking the Show Wizard button at the left end of the status bar at the bottom of the window. An outline of the process by which the Postcard Wizard created the publication is displayed at the top of the pane, and the instructions for the step selected in the process are displayed at the bottom, as shown on the next page.

Using Word to edit text

You can use Word to edit your Publisher text, which is handy for longer publications or if you prefer to use Word for text editing. Select the frame that contains the text you want to edit, right-click the frame and then choose Change Text and then Edit Story In Microsoft Word from the shortcut menu. Word starts and displays the text in a document window. When you finish editing the text, you can close the document and update the Publisher file by choosing Close And Return from Word's File menu. Then exit Word.

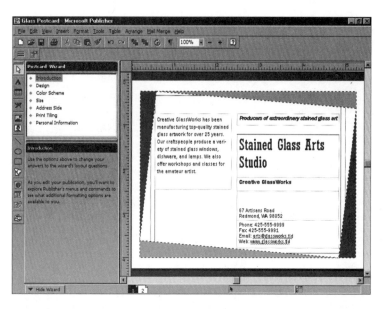

2. Click Design in the outline to display the wizard's instructions for that step. (Notice that you can change the postcard's type as well as its design.)

3. If necessary, scroll the list upward so that you can see all the designs that are available for the Informational type. Click the Blends design and then click the Hide Wizard button to display the postcard with its new design, as shown here:

Resetting designs

If you don't like some of the changes you have made to a publication, you can restore the original settings. First display the wizard for the open publication and click Design in the top part of the wizard's pane to display the list of available designs in the bottom part of the pane. Then with the current design selected, click the Reset Design button. Publisher displays the Reset Design dialog box where you can click various check boxes to reset the original formatting (including the color scheme. You can also restore deleted objects and reestablish the original layout, as well as remove objects and pages you have added and restore text and pictures you have changed. Click OK to reverse the specified design changes.

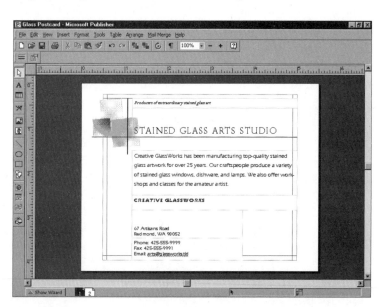

Notice that the Web address does not show up in the Phone/ Fax/E-Mail text frame because the text is too large. Let's quickly fix that by adjusting the text size:

1. Click the text frame containing the phone/fax/e-mail information to select it. Publisher displays the Text In Overflow indicator at the bottom of the frame to warn you that not all of the story fits in the frame. (Publisher puts the extra text in a hidden place called the *overflow area*.)

The Text In Overflow indicator

2. Choose Highlight Entire Story from the expanded Edit menu, or press Ctrl+A to select the frame's story. Then select 6 in the Font Size box. Publisher adjusts the font size, and there is now enough room for the Web address line to fit in the frame.

Selecting a story

Changing the Color Scheme

If you are going to print your publication in color, you need to carefully consider its color scheme. Choosing colors that are appropriate for the message you want to send is important. If you understand how colors work together and their effects on your audience, you may have no trouble devising your own color schemes. The rest of us can be thankful that Publisher provides several preset color schemes for us to choose from.

Glacier is an attractive color scheme that uses pleasant, cool colors, but you want something a bit more lively. Follow these steps to see if you can find another scheme that will jazz up the postcard a bit:

1. Click the Show Wizard button to redisplay the wizard's pane and then click Color Scheme in the top pane.

2. Scroll through the list and select any color schemes that catch your eye, noting their effect on the postcard in the pane on the right. When you finish experimenting, click Wildflower.

3. Click the Hide Wizard button to close the wizard and get a better look at the postcard's new colors.

4. Save Glass Postcard and then close it by choosing Close from the File menu.

Closing publications

Using a Design Set to Create a Publication

Most businesses and organizations use a common design and color scheme for all their printed promotional materials so that when people see one of the pieces, they immediately identify it with the business or organization. To make this practice easier, Publisher provides several *design sets*, which organize the publication wizards by design.

Suppose Creative GlassWorks has decided to use the Blends design for all its publications. You have already created an informational postcard using this design, and now you want to create a flyer to promote a special offer. Follow these steps to access the Flyer Wizard from the Publications By Design tab of the Catalog dialog box:

1. Choose New from the File menu to display the Catalog dialog box and then click the Publications By Design tab to display the options shown here:

Publisher lists all of its basic designs in the Master Sets section, as well as other design sets that have specific themes (see the adjacent tip for more information).

Special design sets

In addition to the design templates in the Master Sets list, you can access several specialized design sets via the Publications By Design tab. (All the special design sets on this tab can also be accessed via the Publications By Wizard tab.) Special Event Sets and Fund-Raiser Sets each offer three designs geared for special events or for fund-raisers. Holiday Sets has a group of three designs geared for winter holiday occasions. We've Moved Sets has four designs used for change of address announcements or housewarming invitations. Restaurant Sets provides two designs used for menus and other restaurant-related publications. Finally, Special Paper Sets displays nine designs that are available through a company called PaperDirect, a producer of colored and patterned paper. If you use one of these designs for a publication, Publisher shows you what the publication will look like when printed on the corresponding paper.

2. Click Blends in the Master Sets list and then scroll the right pane downward, checking out all the publication wizards that can use the Blends design template.

3. Double-click Blends Special Offer Flyer to start its wizard. ← **The Flyer Wizard**

4. Click Next in the wizard's pane to display the list of color schemes, select Wildflower, and click Next.

5. Click No to remove the graphic placeholder and then click Next. (We discuss working with graphics in Chapter 13.)

6. Make a note of all the special elements you can add to a flyer, then check that None is selected in the list, and click Next.

7. Click No when the wizard asks if you want to leave a placeholder for a customer address, and then click Finish.

8. Click the Hide Wizard button to close the wizard and display the new flyer in Publisher's window, as shown here:

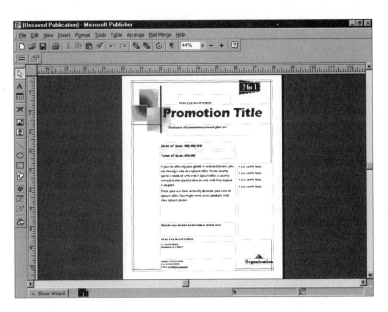

9. Choose Save As from the File menu and save the file as *Glass Flyer* in the My Documents folder.

Changing Personal Information

Notice that Publisher has added the company name, phone, and tag line stored in the Primary Business personal information set to this publication, but that the Web address, which you entered manually in the postcard, has not been added. Here's now to change the personal information set to include this information:

1. Choose Personal Information from the Edit menu to display the dialog box shown earlier on page 272.

2. In the Phone/Fax/E-mail box, click an insertion point to the right of the e-mail address, press Enter to add a line, and type *Web: www.glassworks.tld.*

3. Now change both the print and Web color schemes to Wildflower and click Update.

4. Back in the Publisher window, click the Phone/Fax/E-Mail frame. The Text In Overflow indicator tells you that more text is stored in the overflow area, but it can't be displayed because the frame is too small. You'll take care of that problem in a moment.

Before you begin the next section, you need to enter some of the flyer's text. Follow these steps:

1. Change the zoom setting to 100% and, if necessary, scroll to the section of the page that displays the Promotion Title placeholder.

2. Select the placeholder's text and then type *Join Us for a Glass-Blowing Workshop*. (Publisher uses *automatic copyfitting* to make the text fit in the frame. See the adjacent tip for more information.)

Reusing Text from Another Publication

Often, you will want to recycle the text from an existing publication into a new one. Suppose you want to use the text from

---

Copyfitting text

If you enter more text than will fit in a frame, the text is stored in the overflow area. Selecting the frame displays the Text In Overflow indicator shown earlier on page 281. You can make the text fit in its frame using several methods. You can manually decrease the text size until everything fits (as you did on page 281), or you can have Publisher perform this task for you by choosing AutoFit Text and then Shrink Text On Overflow from the Format menu. Publisher reduces the size of the text until there is no more text in the overflow area. If you resize the frame and want to make the text fit the new size, you can choose AutoFit Text and then Best Fit. Choosing either of these commands toggles them on for the selected frame so that Publisher automatically adjusts the text as you edit it. To turn off automatic copyfitting, choose AutoFit Text and then None from the Format menu.

the postcard as the basis for the text in the flyer. Follow these steps to copy and paste the text between publications:

1. Click the main text frame below the time-of-sale frame and with all the placeholder text in the frame selected, remove the text by pressing Delete.

2. You can't have more than one file open at a time in Publisher, so close the Glass Flyer publication, saving any changes.

3. Click the Open button on the Standard toolbar and double-click Glass Postcard to open the publication.

4. Select the text that describes the company and click the Copy button on the Standard toolbar.

5. Open the flyer by choosing Glass Flyer from the bottom of the File menu.

6. Press F9 to zoom to actual size (100%) and click an insertion point in the empty text frame below the time-of-sale frame.

7. Click the Paste button to paste the text from the postcard into the frame.

8. Press Enter and then type the following paragraph:

   Bring in this flyer between now and December 1, 1999, and you and a friend will receive the 2-for-1 price for our one-day glass-blowing workshop (a savings of $115). No prior experience is necessary. Hurry to reserve your spot now. Space is limited, and some dates are already filled up!

9. Select both paragraphs and change the font size to 11.

Working with Frames

You've entered the main text of the flyer, and Publisher has entered information about the company using the Primary Business personal information set. You now want to customize the flyer, but first you need to learn how to work with frames. In this section, you'll see how to size, delete, move, and add frames.

Special mouse pointers

By default, Publisher displays a special mouse pointer when you move the pointer over certain elements of a publication. You have already seen the resize arrows with the word *RESIZE*, and you may have seen a moving van with the word *MOVE*. You might find these pointers a little too cute and want to turn them off. While you are learning to use Publisher, we recommend that you leave them turned on—it is easy to find yourself moving a frame when you want to resize it, and vice versa. To turn off this feature later, choose Options from the Tools menu, deselect the Use Helpful Mouse Pointers check box on the User Assistance tab, and click OK.

Sizing Frames

On page 281, you decreased the size of some text so that it would fit in its frame. But often, you will want to increase the text's size so that it is more legible. When making the text larger means that the text frame is no longer big enough to display all the text, you can resize the frame. As a demonstration, let's increase the size of the company name and then increase the size of its text frame:

1. Select the company name at the top of the page and change the font size to 16. Publisher displays the Text In Overflow indicator shown earlier on page 281.

2. Point to the left middle handle of the frame. The pointer displays arrows showing the directions in which you can resize the frame, and the word *RESIZE* appears below the pointer. On the ruler at the top of the window's work area, guides attached to the pointer indicate the frame's position on the page.

3. To enlarge the frame, hold down the left mouse button and drag the left middle handle to the left until the pointer guide sits at the 2½-inch mark on the horizontal ruler. The company-name text frame now looks like this:

More about resizing text frames

If you drag a text frame's corner handles, Publisher resizes both the height and width of the frame. To resize both dimensions proportionally, hold down the Shift key as you drag. When the frame reaches the size you want, release the mouse button and then the Shift key. (This works only for text frames.)

Now let's do some more resizing by adjusting the Address and Phone/Fax/E-Mail frames so that the Web address line is displayed:

1. Scroll to the bottom of the page, select the Address text frame, and then drag the bottom middle handle up to the 9½-inch mark on the vertical ruler.

2. Next select the Phone/Fax/E-Mail text frame, point to the top middle handle and drag to the 9½-inch mark on the vertical ruler. The Web address is now visible.

3. Save your work.

   On page 279, you deleted the logo frame from the postcard. Before you move on, you need to delete that logo again, as well as other frames you don't want. Follow these steps:

1. In the bottom right corner of the flyer, select the logo place-holder and choose Delete Object from the Edit menu.

2. Right-click the location-description frame below the main text frame and choose Delete Object from the shortcut menu.

3. Also delete the time-of-sale frame above the main text frame using one of these procedures.

Moving Frames

Now the flyer includes only the frames you want, but some of the frames would look better in different locations. Follow these steps to move a couple of the frames:

1. Select the text in the date-of-sale frame and type *Expiration Date: 12-1-99*.

2. Change the font size to 9 and then resize the frame so that it is just wide enough to display its text.

3. Point to the frame's top border, but not at one of the border's handles. The pointer changes to a four-headed arrow with a moving van and the word *MOVE* attached.

4. Hold down the left mouse button and drag toward the bottom right corner of the page. When you reach the bottom of the window, continue dragging so that Publisher scrolls the hidden part of the page upward into view. As long as you hold down the mouse button, guides on the vertical and horizontal rulers indicate the position of the mouse.

5. Release the mouse button when the top of the frame sits at the 9½-inch mark on the vertical ruler and the 6⅛-inch mark on

Ruler options

By default, Publisher displays horizontal and vertical rulers in its window to help you position objects on the page. To see a bit more of the page, you can turn off the rulers by toggling off the Rulers command on the View menu. To redisplay them, choose the command again. To move a ruler, point to it and when the mouse pointer changes to a double-headed arrow, drag to the new position. To move both rulers at the same time, drag the box where they intersect. To return the rulers to their original positions, you just drag them back. You can move the zero point of a ruler, which normally corresponds to the top left corner of the page. Simply point to the location on the ruler where you want the new zero point to be, and when the mouse pointer changes to a double-headed arrow, hold down the Shift key and click the right mouse button. To return the zero point to its default position, double-click the ruler. To use a measurement unit other than inches, choose Options from the Tools menu, click the arrow to the right of the Measurement Units edit box on the General tab, and select the measurement unit you want to use. Publisher then updates the rulers and all dialog boxes that use units of measure.

the horizontal ruler. At a zoom setting of 45%, the flyer looks like this:

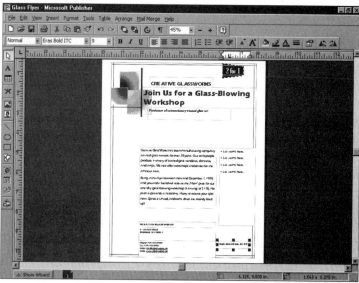

Now let's use a more precise method to move the Organization Name frame at the top of the page to the left so that it aligns better with the Tag Line frame:

1. Select the Organization Name frame at the top of the page and choose Size And Position from the expanded Format menu to display this dialog box:

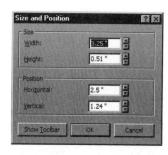

2. In the Position section, click the down arrow to the right of the Horizontal box until it reads *2.4"*. Publisher adjusts the frame's position on the page so that you can immediately see the results of the new setting. (You may need to move the dialog box.) The frame looks good, so click OK. The frame now aligns with the Tag Line frame below it.

Adding Frames

Before you move on to experiment with more complex text formatting, you need to add a subheading above the bulleted list on the right side of the page. Any text you want to add to a publication must be contained in a frame. To help position the new frame, you will display some ruler guides. Follow these steps:

1. Press F9 and select the bulleted-list frame on the right side of the page. (You will enter text in this frame on page 296.)

2. Resize the frame so that the top border of the frame is at the 5¼-inch mark on the vertical ruler. Then click outside the frame to deselect it.

3. Choose Snap To Ruler Marks from the Tools menu to toggle the command off.

4. Point to the horizontal ruler and hold down the Shift key. When the pointer changes to a double-headed arrow and the word *ADJUST* appears, drag downward. A green ruler guide is now attached to the pointer. When the guide aligns with the top border of the flyer's main text frame, release the mouse button and the Shift key.

Displaying ruler guides

5. Repeat step 4, this time pointing to the vertical ruler to add a guide that aligns with the left side of the bulleted-list frame.

6. Now add a new frame by clicking the Text Frame Tool button on the Objects toolbar. When you move the pointer over the work area, it changes to a cross hair, waiting for you to draw the frame.

The Text Frame Tool button

Ruler guides vs. layout guides

By default, Publisher displays blue and pink lines on the page as layout guides. Pink lines designate the page margins, and blue lines form a grid that repeats on each page of a publication. You use layout guides to position frames consistently from page to page and from publication to publication. To adjust the layout guides, choose Layout Guides from the Arrange menu and make changes to the margins (pink guides) or number of columns or rows (blue guides). Ruler guides, on the other hand, are displayed in green and appear only on the page on which you create them. To hide all guides so that you can get a better idea of how a page will look when printed, choose Hide Boundaries And Guides from the View menu. To redisplay them, choose Show Boundaries And Guides.

7. Position the cross hair at the intersection of the green ruler guides. (It turns pink when exactly aligned with them.)

8. Hold down the left mouse button and drag down and to the right until the new frame is about ½ inch tall and the same width as the bulleted-list frame below it. When the frame is the correct size, simply release the mouse button to insert the frame, as shown here:

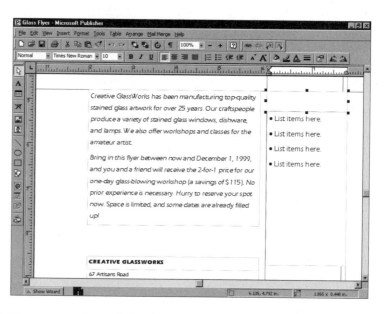

9. To remove the ruler guides, choose Ruler Guides and then Clear All Ruler Guides from the expanded Arrange menu. (You can also point to a ruler guide, hold down the Shift key, and drag toward the appropriate ruler. When you release the Shift key and the left mouse button, the green ruler guide disappears.) Then type *Workshop Features* in the new frame.

By default, the font of the text you enter in a new frame is Times New Roman, its size is 10 points, and it is aligned horizontally on the left and vertically at the top of the frame, with no other formatting. In the next sections, we show you how to add your own formatting to get the look you want.

Adding frames quickly

You can add a text frame to a page with just a couple of mouse clicks. Click the Text Frame Tool button on the Objects toolbar and click the page. Publisher instantly draws the frame, and you can then resize and reposition it as necessary. You can use this same technique to quickly add any of the other objects associated with the buttons located on the Objects toolbar. If you find yourself frequently creating objects by mistake, you can turn off this instant-object feature. Choose Options from the Tools menu, deselect the Use Single-Click Object Creation check box on the Edit tab, and click OK.

Changing the Look of Words and Paragraphs

When you use one of Publisher's wizards to create a publication, the program makes a lot of decisions for you about how various elements will look. However, as you just saw, when you add a new text element to a publication, Publisher applies very little formatting, assuming that you will want to control the appearance of the new element yourself. In this section, we look at a variety of methods for changing the look of words and paragraphs. (Many text formatting methods in Publisher are similar to or the same as the methods used in Word or PowerPoint.)

Formatting Headings

Headings are the most important elements in promotional publications. Since their job is to grab the attention of your readers, draw them in, and make them want to read further, headings should always be formatted in such a way that they catch your reader's eye. In the previous section, you added a new heading to the flyer. As it is, the heading would likely go unnoticed. Follow these steps to spruce it up a bit:

1. Select the Workshop Features heading and then change the font to Eras Medium ITC so that it matches other headings in the flyer.

2. Change the font size to 14 and then click the Bold button to make the selected text bold.

Now apply some formatting to other headings in the flyer so that they stand out better:

1. Select the *Join Us* heading (you may have to scroll upward), and make the text size 20 so that it fits on one line.

2. With the text still selected, choose Align Text Vertically and then Center from the Format menu to align the text vertically in the center of the frame. The heading now looks like the one shown on the next page.

Picas and points?

Picas and points are the standard units of measurement used in the publishing world. If you send your publications to a printing service, you may need to use picas and points instead of inches for certain elements. (A pica is $\frac{1}{6}$ inch and there are 12 points in a pica, so a point is $\frac{1}{72}$ of an inch.) You might also want to use these units of measurement on your ruler and in dialog boxes instead of inches or centimeters. (See the tip on page 288 for more information.) Font sizes are always measured in points from the top of ascending letters, such as h, to the bottom of descending letters, such as p.

Adding Lines and Shading

In Chapter 3, we showed you ways to add borders and shading to paragraphs in Word in order to emphasize them. Similarly in Publisher, you can emphasize a particular frame by adding borders or shading. Follow these steps:

1. Select the Workshop Features frame and click the Line/Border Style button on the Formatting toolbar to display a submenu of options. Then choose More Styles from the submenu to display this dialog box:

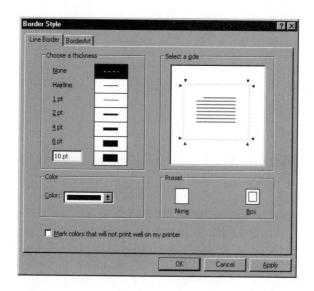

Character spacing

The spacing between characters is called *kerning*. Tighter kerning pulls characters together, and looser kerning pushes them apart. Awkward character spacing is more evident with large text, so by default, Publisher adjusts the kerning of certain character pairs when the size is greater than 14. You can change this setting or turn it off by choosing Character Spacing from the Format menu. In the Automatic Pair Kerning section, adjust the size at which kerning kicks in or deselect the Kern Text At check box to turn off automatic kerning altogether.

2. In the Select A Side section, point to the bottom left corner of the frame and click once. In the diagram, Publisher displays arrows on either side of the frame's bottom border.

3. Click the 4 pt line option in the Choose A Thickness section. Publisher adds a line to the bottom of the frame in the diagram. Then click OK.

Now let's add some shading to the bulleted-list frame. Try this:

The Fill Color button

1. Select the bulleted-list frame and then click the Fill Color button on the Formatting toolbar to display this submenu:

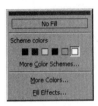

2. Click the third box (gold) in the Scheme Colors section to apply that color to the selected frame.

3. Click the Fill Color button again and then choose Fill Effects to display this dialog box:

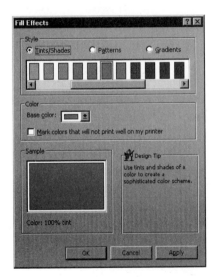

Here, you can change the tint or shade of the selected color and apply a pattern or gradient to the shading.

4. To match the pattern used at the top of the flyer, click the Gradients option, select the seventh gradient pattern, and click OK.

Painting formats

You can use the Format Painter button to copy formatting from one block of text to another. You can also copy the formatting from one block of text to another on the same page by selecting the formatted text, holding down the right mouse button, and dragging to the text you want to format. When you release the mouse button, choose Apply Formatting Here from the shortcut menu that appears. (If you prefer menu commands, use the Pick Up Formatting and Apply Formatting commands on the Format menu.)

5. Click outside the frame to display the results shown here:

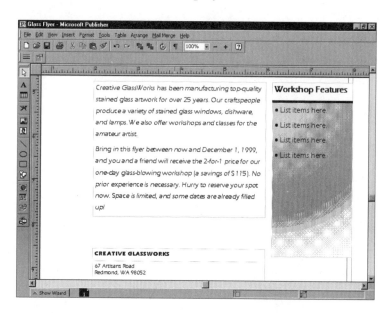

Changing Text Colors

When you add a border or shading, the formatting affects the entire frame. But when you change the color of text, it affects only the selected text. Let's change the title's color:

The Font Color button

1. Scroll the *Join Us* heading into view, select the text, and then click the Font Color button on the Formatting toolbar. Publisher displays a submenu similar to the one shown on the previous page, which you can use to apply formatting in much the same way you apply formatting to a frame. You can select one of the scheme colors, select a color from a different color scheme, select a custom color, or add fill effects.

2. If you want, try experimenting with some of the text effects and then finish by clicking the fourth box (blue) in the Scheme Colors section.

Setting Up Multiple Columns

On page 62, we showed you how to create a multi-column format in Word. You use this type of format in Publisher for the same reasons you use it in Word, but the way you apply the format is somewhat different. Let's change the main text frame of the flyer to a two-column format:

1. Click the flyer's main text frame once to select it. Then click the Text Frame Properties button on the Formatting toolbar to display this dialog box:

The Text Frame Properties button

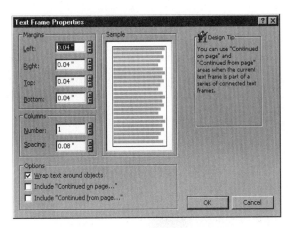

2. In the Columns section, change the Number setting to *2* and the Spacing setting to *0.28"* to set up two columns with 0.28 inch of space between them. Click OK.

3. To force the second paragraph to begin at the top of the second column, click an insertion point to the left of *Bring* and press Ctrl+Shift+Enter. Then resize the frame so that all of the text fits. Here are the results:

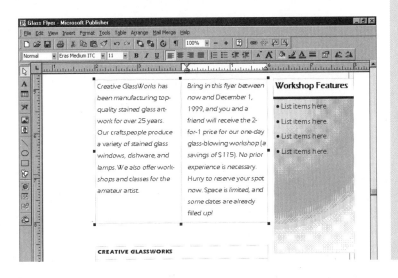

More text frame properties

In addition to changing the number of columns in a frame, you can make other adjustments in the Text Frame Properties dialog box. In the Margins section, you can adjust the amount of space between the frame and its contents. In the Options section, you can select or deselect options that determine whether text in the frame wraps around other objects, and whether a "Continued on page" or "Continued from page" area appears in the frame to help readers move through a multi-frame story.

Working with Lists

The text frame on the right side of the flyer contains four bulleted items that are waiting for your text. Like Word, Publisher has two built-in list formats: one for bulleted lists and one for numbered lists. Here's how to work with a list:

1. Select the bulleted-list text frame and if the bulleted text is not already selected, choose Highlight Entire Story from the Edit menu.

Creating a bulleted list

2. Type the following, pressing Enter after each line except the last to add a new bulleted item:

- *Take a walking tour of our studio*

- *Learn the techniques of master glass blower Crystal Powers*

- *Receive hands-on glass-blowing experience*

- *Create your own unique work of art*

Choosing a bullet style

3. Press Ctrl+A to select all the bulleted items in the frame and choose Indents And Lists from the Format menu to display this dialog box:

You can select a bullet shape or change the alignment, size, and indent settings. (You can also click the New Bullet button to select a different bullet symbol. The New Bullet dialog box works like the Insert Symbol dialog box; see the tip on page 305 for more information.) To switch to a numbered list, click the Numbered List option in the Indent Settings section. The dialog box changes to display numbered-list options, such as the numbering format and the separator type (a period, for example). To convert the list to regular text, click the Normal option in the Indent Settings section. (To quickly convert existing text paragraphs to a bulleted list, you simply select the paragraphs and click the Bullets button.)

← Switching to a numbered list

← Switching to normal text

4. Select the diamond shape to change the style of the bullets and click OK.

5. Resize both the Workshop Features frame and the bulleted-list frame so that they occupy the same amount of space as the main text frame. Here are the results:

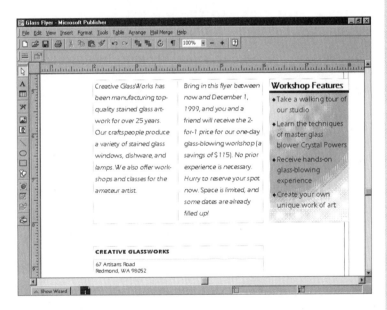

6. Save and close Glass Flyer.

You should now have a good grasp of how to work with text and text frames, and of the many ways you can customize these elements to get the results you want. In the next chapter, you'll look at how to add graphics and other visual elements to your publications to give them extra pizazz!

Hyphenating stories

By default, Publisher hyphenates the text in the flyer's main text frame as needed. To turn hyphenation on or off for a particular frame, select the frame, choose Language and then Hyphenation from the Tools menu, select or deselect the Automatically Hyphenate This Story check box, and click OK. You will want to turn automatic hyphenation on if the text is justified, because it eliminates big gaps between words. For left-aligned paragraphs, you can change the hyphenation zone (the space between the right margin and the end of the text) by displaying the Hyphenation dialog box and entering a new measurement in the Hyphenation Zone edit box. To manually hyphenate text, deselect the Automatically Hyphenate This Story check box and click the Manual button. Publisher then shows you each word that can be hyphenated. Click Yes to hyphenate the selected word or click No to leave the word unhyphenated.

13

More About Publisher

In this chapter, we show you ways to spruce up a publication by adding visual elements. You create a logo, a couple of tables, and a fancy WordArt title. Then you insert graphics from the Clip Gallery and use the drawing tools to create a simple graphic of your own.

The brochure you create here can be adapted to present any group's message or product in an attractive way, and you can use the same techniques to design other promotional materials to fit your needs.

Publication created and concepts covered:

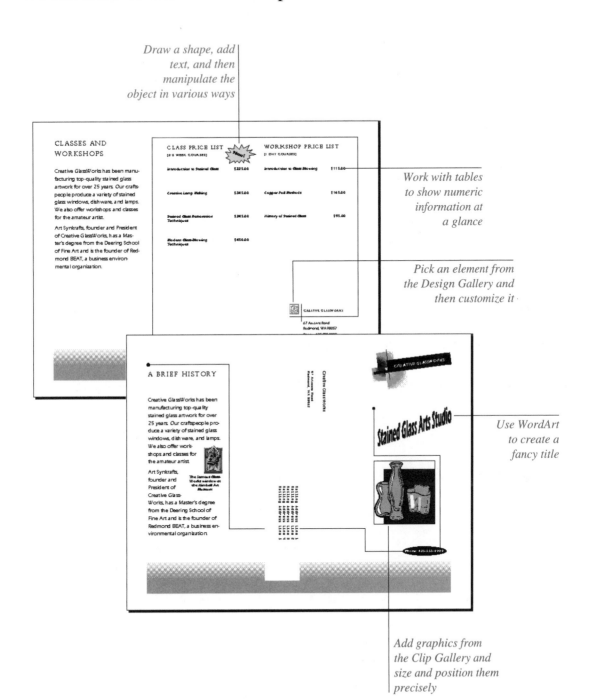

Draw a shape, add text, and then manipulate the object in various ways

Work with tables to show numeric information at a glance

Pick an element from the Design Gallery and then customize it

Use WordArt to create a fancy title

Add graphics from the Clip Gallery and size and position them precisely

While following the examples in the preceding chapter, you learned a lot about working with text and text frames, and about combining formats to create professional-looking publications. However, words alone are often not enough to get your point across. Most promotional materials include visual elements, either to provide information or to catch the reader's eye.

In this chapter, you create a brochure for Creative GlassWorks using the Brochure Wizard. We show you how to create special effects with text as you generate a company logo, a price-list table, and a fancy title. Then we demonstrate how easily you can incorporate graphics into your publications. We end the chapter with a discussion of Publisher's drawing tools, which you can use to create your own graphic elements. Let's get started with the brochure:

1. Start Publisher and when the Catalog dialog box appears, check that the Publications By Wizard tab is displayed.

2. In the left pane, click Brochures and then click Price List to display the designs available for price list brochures in the right pane.

The Brochure Wizard ⟶ 3. Double-click the Blends Price List Brochure in the right pane to start the Brochure Wizard.

4. Click Next to display the color schemes, check that Wildflower is selected, and click Next.

5. Click Yes to add a placeholder for a customer address, and then click Next.

6. Check that None is selected for the Forms option, and then click Next.

7. Check that Primary Business is selected as the personal information set and click Finish.

8. Click the Hide Wizard button to display the brochure shown on the facing page. (If necessary, hide the Office Assistant.)

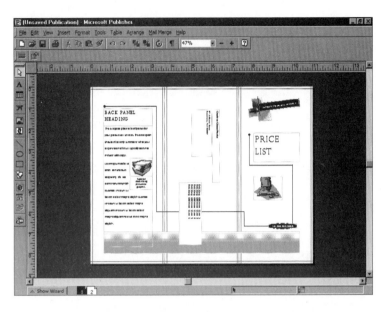

Publisher displays the three outside panels of the brochure. To view the three inside panels, you can click the Page 2 icon in the page controls.

9. Save the new publication as *Glass Brochure* in the My Documents folder.

Before you can get started on the visual elements of the brochure, you need to do some quick setup work by adding a little text, some of which you can copy from the postcard. Follow these steps:

1. Change the zoom setting to 100% and scroll the left panel on the first page into view.

Adding text

2. Select the *Back Panel Heading* placeholder at the top of the panel and type *A Brief History*. (Because of the font applied to the placeholder, the words appear in capital letters even though you type them with only initial capitals.)

3. Click anywhere in the frame that contains the *This is a good place* placeholder, and press Delete.

4. Save Glass Brochure.

5. Open Glass Postcard, copy the main text paragraph, and then reopen Glass Brochure.

6. Zoom to 100%, click an insertion point in the empty frame below the *A Brief History* heading, and click the Paste button.

7. Press Enter and then type the following paragraph:

   Art Synkrafts, founder and President of Creative GlassWorks, has a Master's degree from the Dearing School of Fine Art and is the founder of Redmond BEAT, a business environmental organization.

Changing the line spacing

8. Select both paragraphs and change the font size to 12. Then choose Line Spacing from the Format menu to display this dialog box:

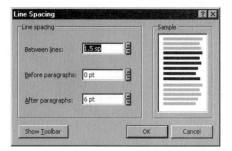

9. Change the Between Lines setting to *1.25* and click OK.

Now let's move on to the first panel inside the brochure:

1. Click the Page 2 icon and display the top of the left panel.

2. Select the *Main Inside Heading* placeholder and type *Classes and Workshops*.

3. Select the text frame below the heading and press Delete.

4. To simulate the text in this panel, copy the two paragraphs from the first page and paste them into the empty text frame.

5. Now scroll to the right panel on the first page, select the text in the blank oval below the graphic, and type *Phone: 425-555-9999*. Save your work.

The gibberish in the second paragraph

The second paragraph is a placeholder that is traditionally used in layout work. It gives you an idea of how the publication will look when the real text is in place, without distracting you with words you can actually read. We have been unable to discover the origins of this tradition, other than that this block of random Latin words has been used for this purpose for centuries. Interestingly, though the words are Latin, this type of placeholder is known as *greeked text*.

Adding Visual Text Elements

In the previous chapter, you learned how to format text to make it more visually appealing. But sometimes this type of text formatting won't be enough. Here, we'll look at a couple of techniques for giving publications more pizazz. You can then experiment on your own with different ways of combining effects to create the look you want.

Creating a Logo

In addition to wizards that help you create different types of publications, Publisher has a Design Gallery of elements that you might want to use in more than one publication. Here, you take a look at the Design Gallery, insert one of its logo designs, and customize it for Creative GlassWorks. Try this:

The Design Gallery

1. Move to the third panel of the inside of the brochure and zoom the bottom half into view.

2. Now right-click the black box containing *Creative Glass-Works* and choose Delete Object from the shortcut menu.

The Design Gallery Object button

3. Click the Design Gallery Object button on the Objects toolbar to display the Design Gallery dialog box, which is similar to the Catalog dialog box:

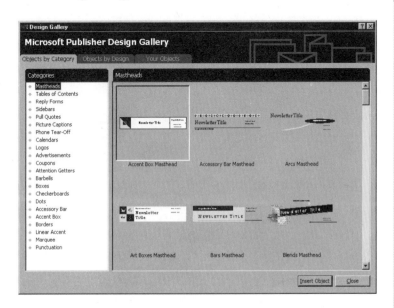

Saving objects in the Design Gallery

You can save objects on the Your Objects tab of the Design Gallery. Select the object, display the Design Gallery, and click the Your Objects tab. Click the Options button and choose Add Selection To Design Gallery from the shortcut menu. In the Add Object dialog box, type a name for the object in the Object Name edit box. Then select a category from the Category drop-down list or create your own category and click OK. To access the object later, open the Design Gallery Object and display the Your Objects tab.

4. In the Categories list in the left pane of the Objects By Category tab, experiment by clicking various categories and checking out the options in the right pane.

Inserting a generic logo

5. Click Logos in the left pane and double-click Crossed Corner Logo in the right pane to insert the object on the page, as shown here:

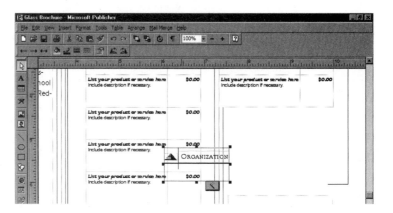

Customizing the logo

6. Select the Organization placeholder and then type *Creative GlassWorks*.

7. Change the font of the company name to Felix Titling and the color to blue.

8. Drag the top right handle up and to the right about ½ inch to increase the size of the logo.

9. Move the logo until its horizontal line connects with the horizontal line in the right panel of the brochure, like this:

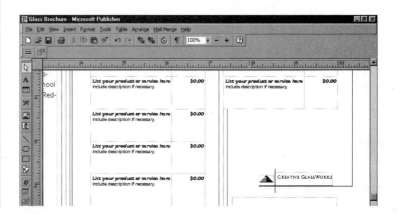

The Wizard button

Some of the objects that you add to your publications from the Design Gallery have accompanying wizards (such as the logo). To access the wizard to make changes to a Design Gallery object, select the object and click its Wizard button. Publisher displays the appropriate wizard and lists the parts of the object that you can change. When you finish making your changes, simply click the wizard's Close button.

On page 315, we show you how to change the logo's graphic placeholder and how to change the graphic's color, so leave the logo as it is for now. Here, let's quickly reformat the address and phone information that appears below the logo:

1. Select the address text and click the Align Left button on the Formatting toolbar.

2. Resize the Phone/Fax/E-Mail frame so that it is big enough to display the Web address. Then select all the text in this frame and click the Align Left button.

3. Resize and move both frames so that they look like this:

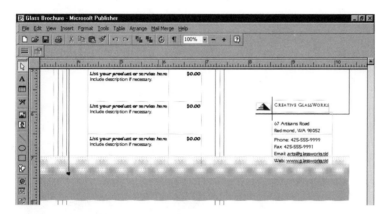

Using WordArt for Fancy Type Effects

The cover of the brochure needs a title that grabs your reader's attention, so we'll introduce you to WordArt, a program that comes with Office. You use this handy program to mold text into shapes that fit the mood of your publication or to flow text around other elements on the page. Follow these steps to jazz up the cover of the brochure:

1. Move to the right panel on the first page of the brochure.

2. Select the Price List frame and choose Delete Object from the Edit menu to delete the frame and its text. (You don't need this frame because you will use a WordArt frame instead.)

Inserting special symbols

You can insert special symbols, such as an accent mark or a pointing hand to grab the reader's attention. Position the insertion point where you want the symbol and then choose Symbol from the Insert menu. Different fonts have different symbols, so you first need to select the font you want. (Wingdings is a good choice if you're looking for cute little pictures.) Then select the symbol and click Insert.

The WordArt Frame Tool button

3. Click the WordArt Frame Tool button on the Objects toolbar.

4. Point to the right of the top of the vertical black line that is part of the L shape. Drag the cross-hair pointer to draw a frame 1¼ inches by 2 inches. When you release the mouse button, WordArt starts, and your screen looks like this:

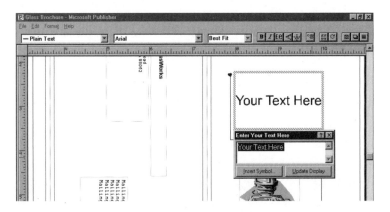

5. Type *Stained Glass Arts Studio* and click the arrow to the right of the Shape box at the left end of the WordArt toolbar. (The box currently contains the words *Plain Text*.) Publisher displays the palette of options shown here:

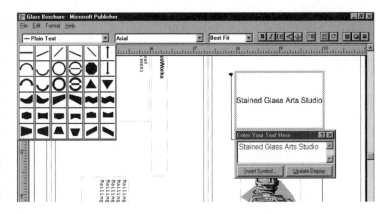

More WordArt options

The WordArt toolbar comes with a variety of buttons, but Screen-Tips doesn't work in WordArt, so you may have trouble deciphering what a particular button will do to your text without actually using the button. Some buttons are toggles, so if you don't like their effects, you can simply click the button again. Other buttons display dialog boxes in which you give more specific instructions for carrying out the task. Some of the effects that can be added to text by clicking the buttons on the WordArt toolbar include equalizing the height of uppercase and lowercase letters, changing the character spacing, rotating the text by varying degrees, applying shading, applying a shadow, or adding a border around each character.

6. Select the fifth shape in the last row (Slant Up). Publisher adjusts the text to reflect the new shape.

Now let's apply some formatting to the text to jazz it up a bit. Follow the steps on the facing page.

1. Change the font to Eras Bold ITC and then click the Shadow button to display this dialog box:

The Shadow button

2. Select the second shadow option from the left and click OK.

3. Next click the Shading button to display this dialog box:

The Shading button

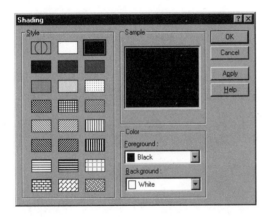

4. Click the arrow to the right of the Foreground box and select Blue to coordinate the color of the WordArt text with the publication's color scheme. Then click OK.

5. Click the Stretch To Frame button to expand the text.

The Stretch To Frame button

6. Click anywhere outside the WordArt frame and dialog box to close that program and return to the Publisher window. The title now looks like this:

Editing WordArt objects

To make changes to a WordArt object after you have inserted it in a publication, double-click the object. Then edit the text or use the toolbar buttons to make adjustments. When you're finished, click anywhere outside the WordArt frame and dialog box to close the program and update the object in your publication.

Not bad, but the WordArt text looks a little squished. Let's resize the frame:

1. Click the frame to select it and display its handles.

2. Use the right middle handle to make the frame wider by about ¼ inch, until it looks something like this:

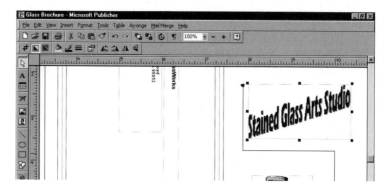

WordArt's capabilities far exceed those demonstrated here, so be sure to take the time to experiment on your own.

Working with Tables

When you first created the Creative GlassWorks brochure, you selected the Price List Brochure design template. The price list brochure includes ready-made tables with place-holder text, which you can alter to quickly create a price list. Tables are not as exciting as fancy text and graphics, but they are an important type of visual element. In this section, you'll see how to fill in and modify tables to meet a specific need. Follow these steps:

Modifying existing tables

1. Move to page 2 of the brochure and display the top of the middle panel.

2. Click an insertion point to the left of the *Price List* place-holder and add the word *Class*. Then press End to move to the end of the title, press Enter, and type *(6-8 Week Courses)*.

3. Select the second line of text and change the font size to 7.

Now add some text to the brochure's table by following these steps:

1. Click once in a blank area of the first *List your product* frame to select the table, as shown here:

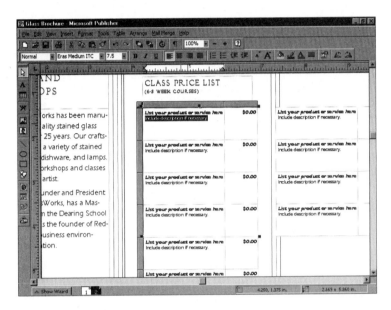

Publisher shows that the table is selected by adding horizontal and vertical bars.

2. Select the first line of text in the first cell and replace it with *Introduction to Stained Glass*.

3. Select the description placeholder and press Delete.

4. Press Tab to move to the next cell in the same row. Publisher highlights the price placeholder. Type *$225.00* and press Tab to move to the first cell of the second row.

5. Continue filling in the price list by typing the entries shown below, pressing Tab to move from cell to cell. (You can move around the table using the same techniques you use in Word—see page 72.)

Creative Lamp Making	*$345.00*
Stained Glass Restoration Techniques	*$245.00*
Modern Glass-Blowing Techniques	*$450.00*

Adding tables from scratch

To create a completely new table, click the Table Frame Tool button on the Objects toolbar and draw a frame. Publisher displays the Create Table dialog box, where you can specify the number of rows and columns and select a table format. When you click OK, Publisher inserts a blank table, ready for you to enter your data.

You don't need the last four rows in the price-list table, so here's how to delete them:

Deleting rows

1. Point in the vertical bar to the left of the first placeholder row. When the pointer changes to a pointing hand, hold down the left mouse button and drag through the other placeholder rows.

2. Choose Delete Rows from the Table menu.

For aesthetic or other reasons, you'll sometimes want to alter the line breaks of your text. As a finishing touch for this table, follow these steps to rebreak the lines in some of the cells:

Rebreaking lines

1. In the first cell of the third row, click an insertion point to the left of the word *Techniques* and press Shift+Enter to move the entire word to the second line. Repeat this step for the fourth row.

2. Next click anywhere outside the table to admire the results shown here:

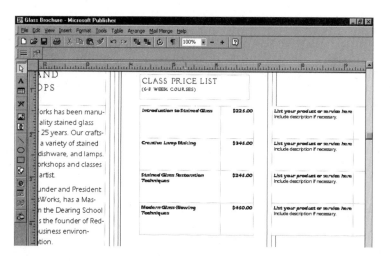

Now let's quickly fill in the second table, which appears in the third panel. Follow these steps:

Copying elements

1. To add a title above the second table, select the first table's title frame and click the Copy button.

2. Click the Paste button and drag the pasted frame above the second table so that it left-aligns with the pink boundary line and top-aligns with the first title frame.

3. Replace *Class* with *Workshop* and *6-8 Week* with *1 Day*.

4. Now fill in the rest of the table with these entries:

Introduction to Glass Blowing	*$115.00*
Copper Foil Methods	*$165.00*
History of Stained Glass	*$95.00*

5. Select the last row, choose Delete Rows from the Table menu, and click outside the table to display these results:

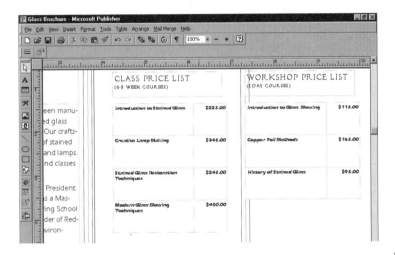

Adding Graphics to a Publication

Publisher can access the Clip Gallery that comes with Office 2000. We'll use a couple of the Clip Gallery graphics in the brochure to demonstrate how easy it is to import them.

To begin, let's place a graphic on the first panel of page 1 of the brochure. Follow these steps:

1. Move to page 1, scroll to the first panel and click the graphic placeholder (the stack of papers) to select it. Publisher selects both the graphic and its caption because they are grouped together. (We discuss grouping objects on page 318.)

2. Double-click the graphic placeholder to display the Clip Gallery window, which displays previews of any graphics similar to the one you double-clicked.

Adding graphics from scratch

Publisher's wizards often insert graphic placeholders in publications, and you can then replace the placeholder and customize the graphic to meet your needs. If you want to add a graphic to a page that doesn't have a placeholder, click the Clip Gallery Tool button on the Objects toolbar and use the cross-hair pointer to draw a frame on the page where you want the graphic to appear. When you release the mouse button, Publisher displays the Clip Gallery. After you select and insert a graphic, you can move, resize, or customize it as usual.

The All Categories button

3. If necessary, click the All Categories button. Then click the Nature category and scroll the graphic previews to check what's available.

4. Click the first leaf graphic, click the Insert Clip button, and close the Clip Gallery to see the graphic in place, as shown here:

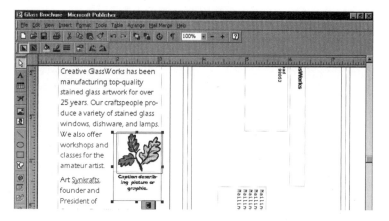

This graphic isn't quite what you had in mind, so let's track down a different image:

1. Double-click the leaf graphic to show the Clip Gallery window.

2. Type *stained glass* in the Search For Clips edit box and press Enter to display the results shown here:

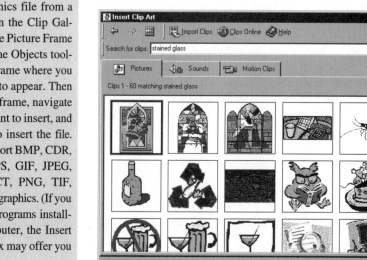

Importing graphics from other sources

To insert a graphics file from a source other than the Clip Gallery, first click the Picture Frame Tool button on the Objects toolbar and draw a frame where you want the picture to appear. Then double-click the frame, navigate to the file you want to insert, and double-click it to insert the file. Publisher can import BMP, CDR, CGM, EMF, EPS, GIF, JPEG, PCD, PCX, PICT, PNG, TIF, WMF, and WPG graphics. (If you have additional programs installed on your computer, the Insert Picture dialog box may offer you more choices.)

3. Click a stained glass window graphic and click the Insert Clip button to insert the graphic in the brochure. (You may have to insert your installation CD-ROM.) Then close the Clip Gallery dialog box.

4. Select the placeholder caption and type *The famous GlassWorks window at the Kimball Art Museum.*

If the results of a search don't identify a graphic you can use, you can always return to the Clip Gallery window and enter a different word or words in the Search For Clips edit box.

Sizing and Positioning Graphics

Like other objects in Publisher, you can easily resize and relocate the graphics you insert in a publication. Follow these steps to add a graphic to the brochure's cover and then change its size and location:

1. Move to the right panel on page 1 and double-click the graphic placeholder (the computer).

2. Search for graphics using the keyword *vase.*

3. Scroll through the previews, select an artistic vase, and insert it in the brochure. (Again, you might need to insert the installation CD-ROM.)

4. To increase the graphic's size, point to the bottom right handle. When the pointer changes to a double-headed arrow, drag the handle downward and to the right about 1 inch.

5. Next point anywhere inside the graphic. When the moving van appears, hold down the left mouse button and drag up and to the right until the graphic is about ⅛ inch below and to the left of the black horizontal and vertical lines.

To fine-tune the placement of the graphic, you can use the Size And Position dialog box as described earlier on page 288. You can also nudge the frame. Follow these steps to try the second method:

1. Choose Nudge from the Arrange menu to display the dialog box shown on the following page.

Microsoft's Clip Gallery Web page

If you have access to the Internet, you can click the Clips Online button at the top of the Clip Gallery window to access additional clips available on Microsoft's Web site. After you click OK in the message box that appears, Publisher starts your Web browser and then connects you to Microsoft's Web site. Read through the License Agreement and then click the Accept button to display the Clip Gallery page. Search for the graphic you want by keyword or category and then click the download icon to download your selection. The graphic is then automatically added to the Downloaded Clips category and any other applicable categories of the Clip Gallery.

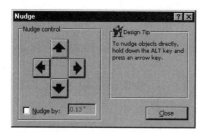

2. If necessary, move the dialog box by dragging its title bar until you can see the graphic.

3. Next use the appropriate arrow buttons to nudge the graphic frame so that its right edge is exactly where you want it.

4. Click the Close button to close the Nudge dialog box.

5. Click outside the graphic to deselect it. You can then see the results shown below:

Instead of using the Nudge dialog box to ease objects into place, you can hold down the Alt key and then press the appropriate Arrow key.

Adding Borders

Suppose you want to surround the graphic on the brochure's cover with a border so that it stands out even more. Follow these steps:

1. Select the graphic and click the Line/Border Style button.

2. Choose Hairline. The results are shown below:

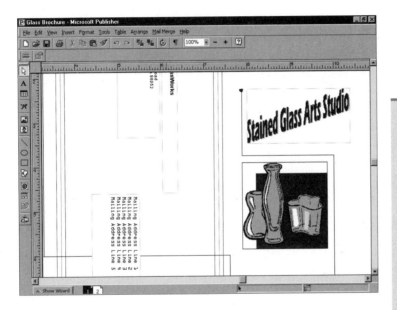

Changing Graphic Colors

On page 304, you added a logo to the inside page of the brochure. However, you still need to replace the logo's graphic placeholder and change its color. Follow these steps:

1. Move to page 2, display the logo, and double-click the graphic placeholder (the pyramid) to open the Clip Gallery.

2. Type *rose* in the Search For Clips box.

3. Select the stylized, green rose (you may need the installation CD-ROM). Then click Insert Clip and close the Clip Gallery dialog box.

Flowing text around graphics

When you insert a graphic in a publication, you can specify how text behaves in relation to the graphic's frame. By default, text flows around the frame. To ignore the frame and have the text flow around the actual graphic, select the graphic and click the Wrap Text To Picture button on the Formatting toolbar. You can then click the Edit Irregular Wrap button on the Formatting toolbar and use the handles around the graphic to fine-tune how the lines of text break. To return to the default settings, click the Wrap Text To Frame button. You can also adjust the margins of a frame or graphic to determine how close text can get to it. Select the frame and click the Picture Frame Properties button on the Formatting toolbar. With the Entire Frame option selected, you can adjust the margin of any side of the frame; with the Picture Only option selected, you can adjust the margin for the entire graphic.

4. With the graphic still selected, right-click it and choose Change Picture and then Recolor Picture to display this dialog box:

Putting borders around objects and pages

You can use BorderArt to put graphic borders around an object. Select the object's frame, click the Line/Border Style button on the Formatting toolbar, and click More Styles. In the Border Style dialog box, click the BorderArt tab. Select a border graphic from the Available Borders list and adjust the border's size and color as necessary, noticing the effects in the preview window on the right. If none of the styles fit your needs, click the Create Custom button to select a graphic from the Clip Gallery or another source. Give the new custom border a name and then click OK to add it to the Available Borders list. You can also delete or rename any borders in the list by selecting them and clicking the appropriate button. You can put a border around each page of a publication by clicking the Rectangle Tool button on the Objects toolbar and drawing a rectangle around all the objects on the page. When you release the mouse button, Publisher adds a black, 1-point border. To customize the border, follow the steps above. To repeat a border on every page, copy and paste the first border to all subsequent pages.

5. Click the arrow to the right of the Color edit box and select red. (Publisher displays a sample in the left pane.) Then click OK. The results are shown here:

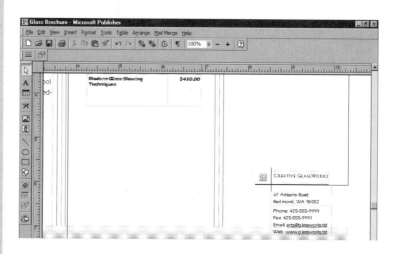

Don't worry that the graphic is a bit small. On page 319, you'll use the grouping feature to resize it.

Drawing Your Own Graphics

For those times when you need a small graphic shape to draw attention to part of a publication, you can use buttons on the Objects toolbar to create the shape on the fly. As an example, you'll add a starburst shape to draw attention to the new Creative GlassWorks classes. Let's get going:

1. On page 2, scroll the top of the first table in the second panel into view.

2. Resize the table title frame so that it is just wide enough to display its text.

3. Click the Custom Shapes button on the Objects toolbar to display a palette of shape options.

The Custom Shapes button

4. Click the fifth shape in the fifth column and then position the cross-hair pointer at the 6¼-inch mark on the horizontal ruler and about the ¾-inch mark on the vertical ruler.

5. Drag down and to the right until the shape looks something like this:

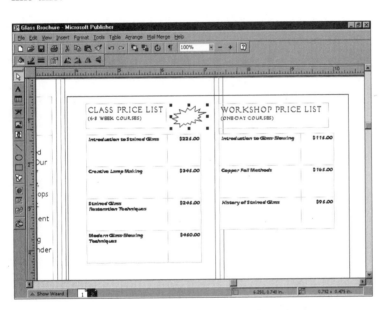

More about drawing shapes

You can draw ovals, rectangles, and lines using buttons on the Objects toolbar. If you hold down the Shift key while you use the Oval Tool, Rectangle Tool, or Line Tool buttons, you can draw circles, squares, or straight lines. To create arrows, first draw a line with the Line Tool button and then add an arrowhead by choosing the appropriate arrow button on the Formatting toolbar. To fine-tune the arrow, click the Line/Border Style button and then click More Styles to adjust the thickness, color, and arrow type. If none of the shapes you can create from the Objects toolbar meet your needs, you can use Microsoft Draw. Choose Picture and then New Drawing from the Insert menu to start Draw and display a blank frame. Use the Line, Arrow, Rectangle, and Oval buttons on the Drawing toolbar and the buttons on the AutoShapes toolbar to create shapes. Use other buttons on the Drawing toolbar to manipulate the drawing in a variety of ways—for example, you can change its color and orientation on the page. To return to the publication, click outside the Draw frame. Publisher inserts the new drawing object in a frame, which you can then move and resize like any other frame. To edit the object, double-click the frame to restart Draw.

Grouping Objects

When you want to be able to move, resize, or rotate two or more objects simultaneously, you can group them together. In this case, you want to add a text frame in the middle of the starburst and then group the shape and the text frame together. Follow these steps:

1. Click the Text Frame Tool button on the Objects toolbar and drag the cross-hair pointer to create a text frame in the middle of the starburst.

2. With the insertion point in the new frame, type *New!*. Then format the text as Eras Bold ITC and resize the frame until the text is fully displayed.

Selecting multiple frames

3. Now select the starburst frame by clicking one of the graphic's lines. (If necessary, enlarge the starburst so that the text box inside it does not obscure the star's edges.) Then add the text frame to the selection by holding down the Shift key and clicking inside the text frame. The objects look like this:

The Group Objects button

4. Click the Group Objects button attached to the selection to group the two frames. The objects are now surrounded by one frame, and it is no longer possible to select the graphic frame without selecting the text frame, and vice versa. (The Group Objects button has become the Ungroup Objects button, which you can click if you decide the two objects no longer need to be grouped.)

5. With the grouped objects selected, click the Fill Color button on the Formatting toolbar and select gold. Publisher fills in both the starburst shape and the text frame.

When you want to work with just one component of a grouped object, you must first ungroup the object. For example, suppose you want to resize the logo's graphic without changing any other component. Follow these steps:

1. Scroll to the logo at the bottom of the right panel, click it once to select it, and choose Ungroup Objects from the Arrange menu. Then click Yes in the message box. The objects that make up the logo are now no longer grouped and can be resized separately.

Ungrouping objects

2. Click outside the logo to deselect it and then click the logo's graphic.

3. Resize and move the graphic until it looks like this:

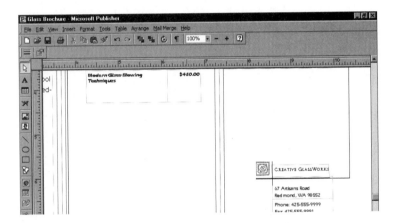

4. To regroup the logo objects, hold down the Shift key and select the graphic frame, the text frame, and both lines. Then click the Group Objects button.

Rotating Objects

What if you want to rotate an object so that it sits at a slight angle? Easy! Try this:

1. Move back to the starburst shape in the middle panel of the brochure.

2. Select the starburst shape and then click the Custom Rotate button on the Standard toolbar to display the dialog box shown on the next page.

The Custom Rotate button

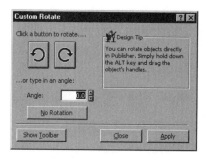

You can click one of the directional arrow buttons to rotate the object, or you can enter a precise rotational angle in the Angle edit box. To straighten a rotated object, click the No Rotation button.

Straightening a rotated object

3. If necessary, move the dialog box so you can see the object. Then click the right directional arrow button two times and click Close.

Manually rotating an object

4. How about rotating the object a little further? Instead of using the Custom Rotate dialog box, hold down the Alt key, point to one of the object's handles, and drag clockwise to rotate the object to the right.

5. Click outside the object to deselect it, choose Hide Boundaries And Guides from the View menu, and press F9 to zoom to full page view. The starburst looks something like this:

Flipping objects

In addition to rotating an object, you can flip it all the way over horizontally or vertically. Simply select the object and click the Flip Horizontal or Flip Vertical button on the Formatting toolbar. To quickly rotate an object 90 degrees to the right or left, click the Rotate Right or Rotate Left button on the Formatting toolbar.

6. If you want, click the Print button to see the results of all your hard work on paper.

7. Save and close the Glass Brochure file.

8. To get a better overview of the brochure's layout, place the two printed pages back to back and fold the brochure into three panels.

For more complex printing jobs, you might want to send your publication to an outside printing service. Consult the service about how to set up your publication, and be sure to tell them you are using Publisher 2000. When your publication is ready, Publisher can help you prepare the file for delivery. Choose Pack And Go and then Take To A Commercial Printing Service from the File menu to start the Pack And Go Wizard. The wizard can help you split large files across several disks, include linked graphics, embed fonts, and even create four-color separations that your printer may need.

Sending a publication to a printing service

Using WordArt, the clip art supplied by Office, the drawing tools, and graphics from other applications, you shouldn't have any trouble adding a dash of excitement to your publications. Just remember to keep things simple; otherwise, your audience might start paying more attention to your artwork than to the content of your publications.

14

FrontPage Basics

In this chapter, we introduce you to FrontPage, Microsoft's Web authoring program. First you use a wizard to create a simple site. Then you learn how to organize and link pages, add and edit text, and insert and manipulate graphics.

Our example is for a non-profit group. However, you can use FrontPage to create Web pages for a community or campus organization, your company's intranet, or even for yourself.

Web pages created and concepts covered:

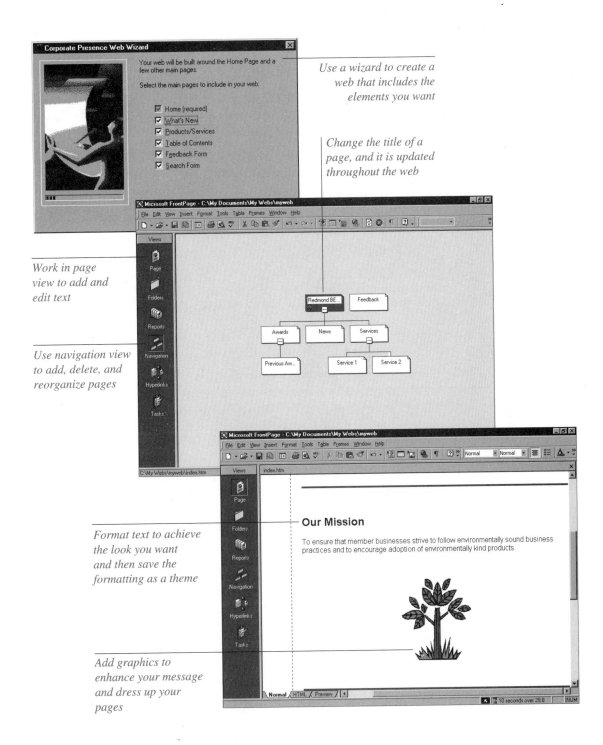

Use a wizard to create a web that includes the elements you want

Change the title of a page, and it is updated throughout the web

Work in page view to add and edit text

Use navigation view to add, delete, and reorganize pages

Format text to achieve the look you want and then save the formatting as a theme

Add graphics to enhance your message and dress up your pages

FrontPage 2000, Microsoft's Web authoring program, is included in some editions of Microsoft Office. That shouldn't surprise you. Only a short time ago, Web design was considered a job for programmers who were skilled in HyperText Markup Language (HTML). Now Web authoring is becoming a mainstream business skill, just like working with spreadsheets and creating electronic presentations. Any business, organization, or individual can use FrontPage to create and maintain a professional, up-to-date presence on the World Wide Web or on an intranet.

Web Site Concepts

Local webs vs. Web sites

In FrontPage terminology, a *web* is a Web site that you are building locally on your machine. It does not become a full-fledged Web site until it is stored on a Web server and is accessible for viewing by other people. In this book, we follow FrontPage's lead and refer to the site you are building locally as a *web* (with a lowercase *w*) and the *Web* (with an uppercase *W*) as anything related to the World Wide Web, the graphical component of the Internet.

Hyperlinks

A web is a collection of individual pages that include graphics, text, and other elements. The pages are usually linked together by *hyperlinks*, and are often linked in the same way to other Web sites. (We discuss hyperlinks in Chapter 15.)

Creating a Web

Just like any other task, creating a FrontPage web can be simple, or it can be fairly complicated. Whatever approach you take, you can be sure that using FrontPage for the job is a lot easier than producing Web pages using traditional HTML tools. FrontPage creates the HTML tags in the background; all you have to do is make decisions about how you want each item on your web to look and operate.

Deciding What Information You Need

Deciding what you want on each page is the most important step in producing a web; it's also the most overlooked. Most people are too eager to jump in and get going. But planning is important to any process, and it is crucial in developing your presence on an intranet or the Internet. You don't have to make every decision ahead of time because FrontPage makes it easy to make changes either during the creation process or afterwards. However, you should have a solid concept of what information you want to share, including graphics and links. Planning methods include drawing a flowchart on paper, using file cards (each with a notation that represents a page), or actually storyboarding the web.

Using a Wizard

Once the planning decisions have been made, the simplest way to create a web is to use one of FrontPage's built-in wizards. So let's get started:

1. Click the Start button and choose Programs and then Microsoft FrontPage from the Start menu.

2. If FrontPage asks whether you want to make FrontPage your default web page editor, click Yes.

3. Click OK if FrontPage needs to check your computer's settings, and click OK again when the settings have been checked. Your screen now looks as shown below. (We've arranged the Standard and Formatting toolbars on one row. Click More Buttons to display the buttons you need as you follow along.)

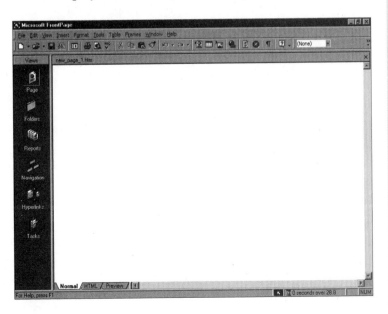

Web design considerations

If you have a lot of information to share with visitors to your web, you will want to split the information between related pages. By carefully planning the structure of your web, you can direct how a visitor interacts with your site, as well as the information you present. If you want to place pictures, graphics, or other images on your pages, be aware of the time it takes for a browser to download those images to a viewer's computer screen. (You can check the estimated download time of a particular page by displaying the page and looking at the time displayed in the status bar.) Your goal should be to give your viewers all the information you want to provide without overwhelming them with excessive reading or creating a page that loads so slowly that viewers give up and move elsewhere. Smaller pages load faster, so you will want to limit the size of pages that contain graphics, sound files, or other memory-intensive features.

The Page icon

The New Page button

4. If your screen looks different from ours, click the Page icon on the Views bar to switch to page view.

Now let's enlist the help of a wizard to create a web:

1. Click the arrow to the right of the New Page button on the Standard toolbar and select Web from the drop-down list to display the dialog box shown here:

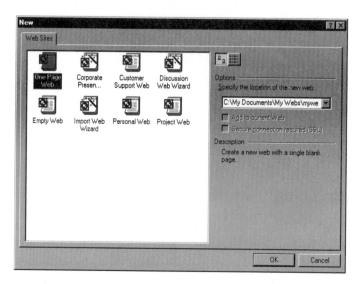

2. Click the Corporate Presence Wizard icon, check that C:\My Documents\My Webs\myweb is displayed in the Specify The Location Of The New Web edit box, and then click OK. FrontPage then displays the first dialog box of the Corporate Presence Web Wizard.

FrontPage has created a hierarchy of folders on your C: drive as subfolders of My Documents. The My Webs folder will hold all the webs you create on this computer in separate subfolders called *Myweb*, *Myweb2*, *Myweb3*, and so on. You can rename these subfolders as something more meaningful, but avoid renaming any of the other folders FrontPage creates to keep track of your web's pages and links.

Now follow these steps to set up your web's pages:

1. Read the information in the wizard's first dialog box and then click Next to display the dialog box shown at the top of the facing page.

Options for creating a new web

The New dialog box offers several wizards and templates that you can use to create a new web. (Refer to Chapter 3 if you need a refresher on the difference between wizards and templates.) The available options allow you to create one-page webs and empty (blank) webs, as well as webs for customer support, discussions, personal information, or projects. You can also use the Import Web Wizard to import a web that has already been created by another program.

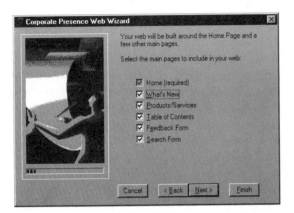

2. Deselect the Table Of Contents and Search Form check boxes so that those pages will not be included in your web. Then click Next.

Setting up the pages

3. For the home page, select the Introduction and Company Profile check boxes so that all the topics will be included, and then click Next.

4. For the What's New page, deselect Web Changes, select the Articles And Reviews check box, and then click Next.

5. For the Products/Services page, enter *0* in the Products box, verify that *3* is entered in the Services box, and click Next.

6. For the Feedback Form page, check that Information Request Form is the only check box selected and then click Next.

7. Select all the check boxes so that you can collect as much information as possible about your visitors. Then click Next.

8. You do not want your feedback file to use a tab-delimited format, so click No and then click Next.

9. To specify what you want to appear at the top of each page, select Page Title and Links To Your Main Web Pages. For the bottom of the page, select E-mail Address Of Your Webmaster and Date Page Was Last Modified. Then click Next.

10. You don't want to use an Under Construction icon, so click No and then click Next.

Using a tab-delimited format

If you want to be able to merge the information you receive from the Feedback Form page into a database or spreadsheet program for analysis, click Yes when asked whether the feedback file should use a tab-delimited format. That way, the items of information will be separated by tabs and can easily be interpreted into records and fields.

Now the wizard asks for information about your organization. Complete these steps:

Entering company
information

1. Enter *Redmond BEAT* as the name of the company and *BEAT* as the one-word version. Enter *14000 Willows Road, Redmond, WA 98052* as the address and then click Next.

2. Enter the contact information shown below in the appropriate edit boxes and then click Next:

   Phone Number: *425-555-6789*
   Fax Number: *425-555-1234*
   Webmaster E-mail Address: *tedl@redbeat.tld*
   General E-mail Address: *info@redbeat.tld*

To give your web distinction, you can apply a theme. Try this:

Choosing a theme

1. In the dialog box currently displayed on your screen, click the Choose Web Theme button to display this dialog box:

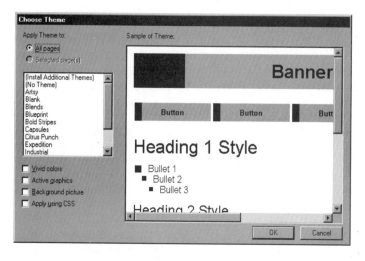

2. Experiment with the various themes and check out the effects of selecting and deselecting the check boxes in the bottom left corner. (See the adjacent tip for more information.)

3. When you're ready to move on, select the Blank theme and select both the Background Picture and Active Graphics check boxes. Click OK, click Next, and then click Finish in the wizard's last dialog box. FrontPage switches to tasks view, as shown on the facing page.

Theme options

You can use the check boxes in the bottom left corner of the Choose Theme dialog box to apply additional elements to the themes listed in the box above. For example, if you select the Active Graphics check box, FrontPage applies active bullets and other graphics that move when viewed in a Web browser. If you select the Background Picture option, FrontPage applies a textured, graphical background to your web instead of a solid background color. To look at more preset themes, select Install Additional Themes at the top of the themes list and click OK. (Insert the installation CD-ROM if prompted.) FrontPage then installs several more themes on your hard drive. (For information about how you can modify themes, see page 343.)

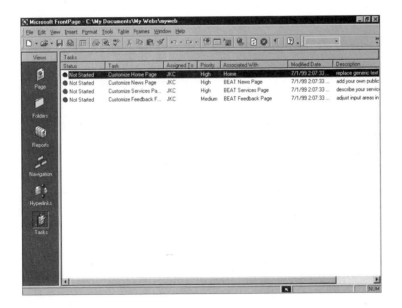

In this view, you can take a look at each page of your web and check items such as its status and priority. (You may notice that this view is similar to the tasks list in Outlook.) If you want to begin work on or change a particular page from tasks view, you can select the page, right-click it, and choose either Start Task or Edit Task from the shortcut menu. You can also mark tasks as complete, or you can delete them. (To return to this view at any time, simply click the Tasks icon on the Views bar.) Before you begin entering information in your pages, though, you need to do a little reorganizing.

The Tasks icon

Reorganizing a Web

Using a FrontPage wizard makes the creation of a web much easier. Unfortunately, the wizards don't always organize your web exactly the way you want. So after setting up a web using a wizard, you will probably want to look over its structure and make some adjustments by moving, adding, or deleting some pages. The best way to complete this sort of reorganization is by looking at the web in navigation view. Follow these steps:

1. Click the Navigation icon on the Views bar to display your web as shown on the following page.

The Navigation icon

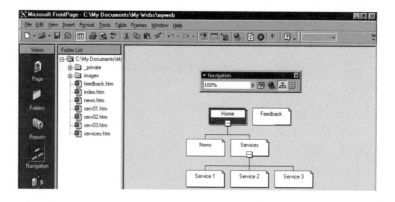

FrontPage displays the present layout of your web in a familiar flowchart format (like a PowerPoint organization chart). It also displays the Navigation toolbar and the folder list, which lists all of the folders and files of your web in its own pane between the Views bar and the navigation pane. (The folder list can be viewed in its own window by clicking the Folders icon on the Views bar.)

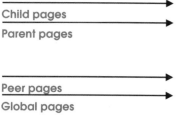

The Folders icon

Each of the boxes in the navigation pane represents a page of your web. The home page is identified by the small icon in the lower left corner of the Home box. Clicking a plus sign (+) on a box displays that page's *child pages*; clicking a minus sign (−) on a box hides the child pages, leaving only the *parent page* visible and giving you a more compact view of your web. Boxes that are connected by lines, such as the News and Services boxes, are considered *peer pages*; boxes with no connecting lines, such as the Feedback box, are *global pages*. Every page that displays navigation bars is linked to the web's global pages. (We discuss navigation bars on page 356.)You can move any of the boxes using standard drag-and-drop methods.

Child pages

Parent pages

Peer pages

Global pages

Changing the navigation view

By using the buttons on the Navigation toolbar, you can alter the appearance of your web in navigation view. Use the Zoom box to change the view magnification. (This feature is handy if your web contains several pages and you want to see them all on the screen at once.) Click the Portrait/Landscape button to change the orientation of your web layout. Select a box and then click the External Link button to attach a hyperlink to the page, or click the Included In Navigation Bars button to add or remove the page from the web's navigation bars. (See page 356 for more information about navigation bars.) Finally, click the View Subtree Only button to display only the subtree of a selected box.

2. To view more of the navigation pane, click the Folder List
button on the Standard toolbar to toggle it off. Then click the
Close button on the Navigation toolbar to turn it off.

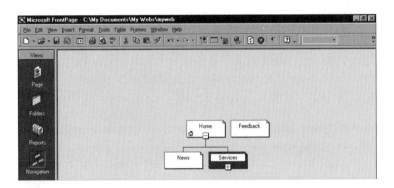
The Folder List button

3. Click the minus icon on the Services box to collapse its three
child pages, as shown here:

Collapsing pages

4. Next click the minus icon on the Home box to close all of its
child pages. (The Feedback page remains open because it is a
global page.)

5. Click the Undo button to restore the previous view.

6. Next redisplay the three Service pages by clicking the plus
icon on the Services box.

Expanding pages

Deleting Pages

Now that you know how to move around in navigation view,
let's start the reorganization process by deleting a page you
don't need. Follow these steps:

1. Right-click the Service 3 box and choose Delete from the shortcut menu. FrontPage displays this dialog box:

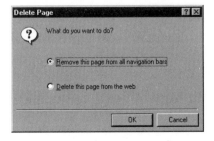

Deleting vs. removing pages

When you delete a page while in
navigation view, you can either
remove the page from all navigation bars or delete the page from
the FrontPage web. (See page 356
for more information about navigation bars.) If you select the
first option, the page is removed
from the structure displayed in
the navigation pane and from the
navigation bars, but not from
your web. So if you later decide to
use that page, it is still available.
But if you select the second option, the page is actually deleted
from the web itself.

2. Select the Delete This Page From The Web option and then click OK.

Adding Pages

One of the changes you will undoubtedly want to make to your web is to add pages to it. You saw in the previous steps how easy it is to delete pages, and adding pages is just as simple. Follow these steps:

1. With the Service 2 box selected, click the New Page button on the Standard toolbar. FrontPage adds a New Page 2 box as a child page of the Service 2 page.

2. Add a child page to the New Page 2 box by choosing New and then Page from the File menu. Your screen now looks like this:

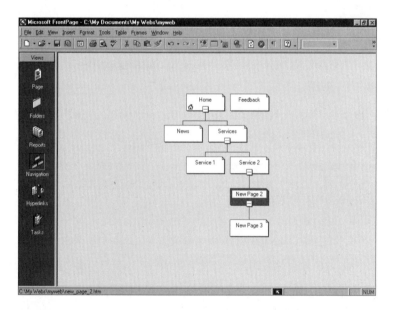

Now let's change the position of these new pages:

Changing page position

1. Point to the New Page 2 box and then drag it below the Home box. When a line appears, indicating that the page will become a child page of the home page, release the mouse button. Both the New Page 2 box and its child page (New Page 3) move to their new positions, as shown at the top of the facing page.

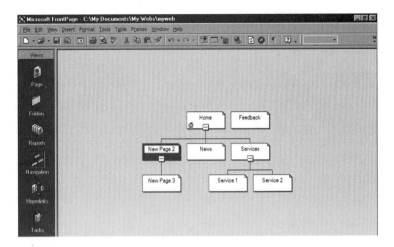

2. Click New Page 2's title once to select all the text in the title box. Then type *Awards* and press Enter to retitle the page. (The underlying filename does not change, but the title that appears on the page is updated.)

Changing a box's title

3. Next change the title of New Page 3 to *Previous Awardees* and press Enter.

4. Finally, change the Home box's title to *Redmond BEAT*. Here are the results:

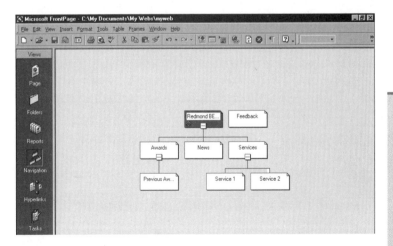

Name vs. title

When you rename a page, as you did in the exercise above, you are changing its title, not its name. The name of a web page is its filename, which serves as part of the address of the page; a computer uses the address to find the page on a server. The page's title is what visitors see when they view the page. Each title should be descriptive enough to tell viewers what that page is about.

Now that you have laid out the basic structure of your web, it is time to actually put some information on those pages! To do that, you will switch to page view.

Working in Page View

When working in page view, you can easily add, edit, and format text. You can also insert and manipulate graphics, tables, and other elements. This view is also where you define the features of your web, such as the buttons, hyperlinks, and bookmarks that you create. Page view provides a familiar word processor environment where you use editing techniques, such as manipulating and formatting text, that are similar to those you use in Word. Let's switch to page view now and then start adding information to the Redmond BEAT web:

Switching to page view

1. Double-click the Redmond BEAT box to both switch to page view and open the home page of the Redmond BEAT web, complete with the background and other attributes of the Blank theme that you chose earlier on page 328.

2. If necessary, click the Folder List button to close the folder list. Your screen now looks like this:

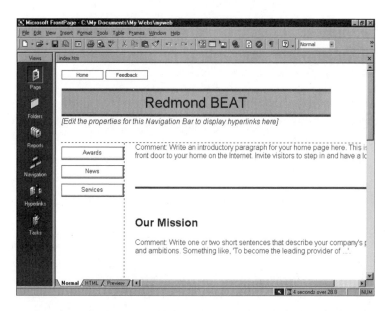

The home page includes two navigation bars. The first consists of the three buttons on the left with the titles Awards, News, and Services, which represent the child pages of the Home page. These are hyperlinks that allow your visitors to jump directly to one of those three pages by clicking its

Jumping between pages

respective button. The second navigation bar consists of the two buttons at the top with the titles Home and Feedback. These hyperlinks are available on all the pages of your web, allowing visitors to jump to either one of those pages from any other page.

3. Take a few moments to scroll through the home page and notice the headings, which you included during the design phase. The text after each heading recommends what you might include in each section. Toward the bottom of the page is the contact information that you entered earlier, including the Send Mail To and Last Modified features.

Adding and Editing Text

Now that you have a feel for what the page looks like, you are ready to begin adding and editing text. First you'll change the text of the opening paragraph. Follow these steps:

1. Scroll to the top of the page and select the text of the paragraph that begins *Comment:* by pointing anywhere in the paragraph and clicking once. (When an element has been predefined by FrontPage, you can select it using this single-click method.) Notice that the pointer changes to the properties symbol.

2. Type the following paragraph to replace the highlighted text:

   Redmond BEAT (Business Environmental Action Team) is a local chapter of USA BEAT, a network of companies who are actively working to ensure that their business operations are based on sound environmental practices.

3. Select the paragraph below the Our Mission heading and type this sentence:

   To ensure that member businesses strive to follow environmentally sound business practices and to encourage adoption of environmentally kind products.

4. Click the Save button to save your work. (If FrontPage asks if you want to mark the task as completed, click No.) Turn the page to see the results so far.

Reusing text from another source

You may recognize the text you type in step 2 as text from the FAQ you created in Chapter 2. You could have opened the FAQ and used standard copy-and-paste techniques to copy the text and paste it into your web. If you want to reuse an entire file from another source for your web, you can easily insert it. First click an insertion point where you want the file to appear. Then choose File from the Insert menu and double-click the file you want to insert. (Be sure that the Files Of Type setting is correct for the file you want to insert.) FrontPage then converts the file to HTML formatting and inserts it at the location of your insertion point.

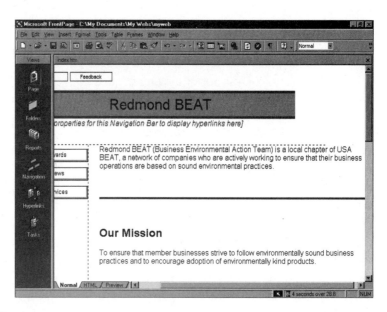

5. Delete the Company Profile heading, the paragraphs beneath it, and the horizontal bar below the paragraphs by selecting them and pressing Delete.

You aren't going to add text below the Contact Information heading, but you don't need to delete the placeholder paragraph. Follow along with the next section to find out why not.

Using the Page Tabs

You may have noticed that page view provides three tabs (Normal, HTML, and Preview) at the bottom of the workspace similar to the tabs in an Excel workbook. These tabs provide three different ways of looking at a page in your web. The

The Normal tab →

Normal tab, which is currently active, is where you add and edit items on your pages. The HTML tab displays the underlying HTML coding of your pages, and the Preview tab displays your pages as they will look in a Web browser. Let's take a closer look:

The Preview tab →

1. Click the Preview tab to simulate viewing your Home page in a Web browser. Your screen looks like the one shown at the top of the facing page.

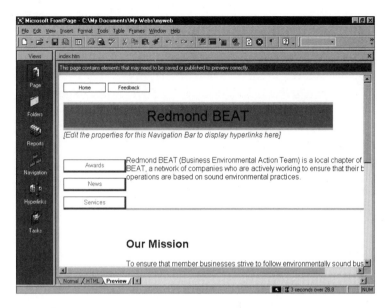

2. Scroll down the page and look at the Contact Information section. Notice that the placeholder paragraph below the heading is not displayed. Only text you have typed in a wizard dialog box or directly in page view is visible.

3. Next click the HTML tab to view the home page's underlying coding, which looks like this:

The HTML tab

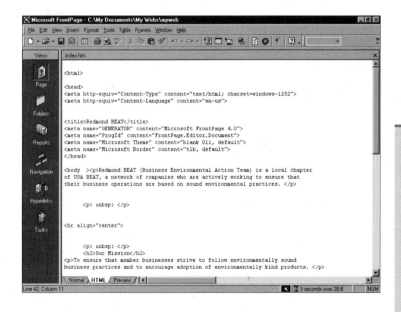

More about HTML

HyperText Markup Language is a coding system that controls how information is interpreted and displayed by a Web browser such as Internet Explorer or Netscape Navigator. HTML is the standard for all Web documents and relies on an array of codes, or *tags*, that tell the browser how to display text, graphics, and other elements.

Unless you are familiar with HTML, you won't need to use this view, especially while you are still learning the program. However, you can see from a glance at this tab that using Front-Page instead of creating your web from scratch by inserting HTML codes is a much more user-friendly way to go!

Formatting Text

Now that you have most of the information you need on your home page, you can go ahead and make changes to its appearance. Some of these techniques will be familiar to you because you have worked with the other Office applications. Follow these steps:

1. Click the Normal tab and then select the first paragraph of text that describes Redmond BEAT.

2. Click the arrow to the right of the Font Size box on the Formatting toolbar and select 4(14 pt) from the drop-down list.

3. Select only the words *Redmond BEAT* in the first paragraph. Click the arrow to the right of the Font Color button on the Formatting toolbar and select red in the second row.

Changing the Paragraph Alignment

By default, FrontPage left aligns paragraphs when you set up your web pages. However, sometimes you will want to realign a paragraph or text selection. Let's center the paragraph at the bottom of the page:

1. Scroll to the bottom of the page and click an insertion point anywhere in the paragraph that begins *Send mail to*. Front-Page displays borders around this and two other sections on the page because they are designated as shared borders and appear on every page of the web. (See the tip on page 356 for more information about shared borders.)

2. Click the Center button on the Formatting toolbar. Now this text appears centered on every page.

Using unusual fonts

When changing fonts in your web, bear in mind that in order for a visitor to see a font on your web page, they must have that font installed on their computer. Otherwise, the browser they are using substitutes a similar font. Be careful about using fonts that are unusual or whose design probably can't be easily emulated by the fonts that are standard on most people's computers.

Changing Paragraph Spacing

When you enter text in page view, pressing Enter creates a new paragraph just like it does in the other Office applications. However, it also adds a blank line between the previous paragraph and your new paragraph. When you don't want the extra space between the two paragraphs, you need to use a line break instead of a new paragraph, like this:

1. Scroll to the top of the page, click an insertion point at the end of the introductory paragraph, and press Enter.

2. Now type the following text:

   If you like what you see here, tell others.

3. Hold down the Shift key and then press Enter. The insertion point moves to the next line without inserting extra space. Now type the following:

   If you don't, tell us!

   Inserting a line break

Creating Numbered and Bulleted Lists

You can add two types of lists to your pages in FrontPage: numbered lists or bulleted lists. These lists are sometimes referred to as *unordered* lists. In this section, you will create a bulleted list on the Previous Awardees page of your web, but bear in mind that the procedure for creating a numbered list is the same. Follow these steps:

   Unordered lists

1. Click the Open button on the Standard toolbar to display the Open File dialog box. Then double-click new_page_3 to display that page in page view.

   Opening another page in a web

2. Without moving the insertion point, enter these names, pressing Enter after each one:

   Forrest Greene
   Dolly Finn
   Heather Busch

Adding bullets

3. Select all three names and click the Bullets button on the Formatting toolbar. FrontPage places a bullet in front of each name, changes the line spacing, and adjusts the text size to match the size of the bullet.

The style of bullets is determined by the Blank theme you chose earlier. However, you can change the bullets fairly easily. Follow these steps:

Changing the bullet character

1. Right-click the selected bulleted items and choose List Properties from the shortcut menu to display the List Properties dialog box.

2. On the Picture Bullets tab, select the Specify Picture option in the Picture section and then click the Browse button.

3. In the Select Picture dialog box, click the Clip Art button to display the Clip Gallery window shown on page 312.

4. Scroll through the categories and then click the Web Bullets & Buttons category.

5. Select an option; we chose the dual-tone diamond.

6. Click Insert Clip, and then click OK in the List Properties dialog box. The results are shown below:

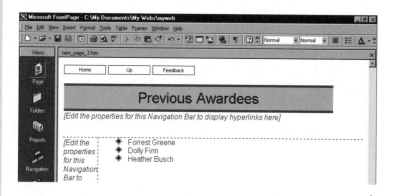

Positioning graphics

To reposition a graphic, select it, right-click it, and then choose Picture Properties from the shortcut menu. Then click the Appearance tab to change the alignment and the horizontal and vertical spacing around the graphic. In the Size section, you can click the Specify Size check box and enter an exact width and height. You can display the Positioning toolbar and enter an absolute position for the graphic on the page. To make the graphic appear in front of or behind any overlapping text, click the Bring Forward or Send Backward button.

Adding Clip Art and Graphics

One of the most attractive features of many Web pages is the inclusion of colorful graphic images and even photographs. You will most likely want to dress up your web with images to illustrate a point, sell an idea, or simply enhance its overall look. Let's add some graphics to the Redmond BEAT web right now:

1. Navigate back to the home page by choosing Index.htm from the Window menu.

2. Click an insertion point at the end of the paragraph that follows the Our Mission heading and press Enter twice.

3. Click the Center button to center the new paragraph.

4. Choose Picture and then Clip Art from the Insert menu to display the Clip Gallery window.

5. Click the Nature category, click the first tree graphic you see, and click the Insert Clip button. The home page now looks like the one shown here:

Not bad. But the graphic is a little large. Let's fix that now:

1. Click the graphic to select it. FrontPage displays the Picture toolbar along the bottom of the window.

2. Drag the handle in the bottom right corner upward and to the left until the graphic is about 1½ inches long.

The Picture toolbar

You can use buttons on the Picture toolbar to change a graphic's layout orientation, its contrast and brightness, and its position on the page. Click the Auto Thumbnail button to display the graphic in a smaller format and to attach a hyperlink to the full-size graphic. You can also create graphic hotspots that visitors can click to move to another location. (Maps are a good example of graphics that might use hotspots.)

3. Finally, click an insertion point below the graphic and press Delete to remove the extra space between the graphic and the horizontal line below it. Here are the results:

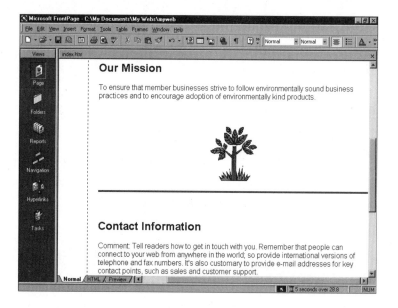

If the graphic you insert has a background with a color different from that of your page, you can make the background color transparent so that the graphic blends in better with the page. To do so, you select the graphic and then click the Set Transparent Color button on the Picture toolbar. When Front-Page warns you that the image will be converted to gif format, click OK. (See the adjacent tip for more information.) Then point to the graphic's background. When the pointer looks like the eraser end of a pencil with an arrow attached, click once to make the background transparent. The background of the page then shows through.

The tree graphic you inserted is embedded in the home page but is not yet saved as part of the home page file. Follow these steps to update the web page with the newly inserted graphic:

1. Click the Save button. FrontPage displays the dialog box shown on the facing page.

Graphic formats

Graphic Interchange Format (GIF) and Joint Photographic Experts Group (JPEG or JPG) graphics are commonly used in Web pages because they can be displayed by most Web browsers. These formats also have the advantage of being compressed to save transmission time and storage space. Other graphic formats you might run across have the filename extensions PICT, BMP, PCX, TIFF, and EPS.

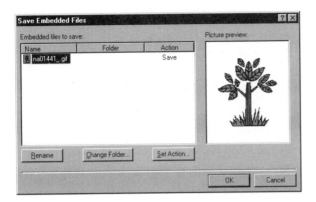

2. Click OK to add the graphic file to the files that comprise the Redmond BEAT Web.

Enhancing Your Web

Before we wrap up this chapter, we want to show you ways of modifying elements such as theme, background, and colors of your web to better suit your needs.

Modifying a Theme

When you applied the Blank theme to the Redmond BEAT web, FrontPage applied the formatting and color scheme assigned to that theme to all of your pages. But sometimes you may want to make changes to the formatting of a preset theme. As an example, let's quickly make some modifications to the Blank theme:

1. With the home page displayed in page view, choose Theme from the Format menu to display a dialog box similar to the one shown earlier on page 328.

2. With the default theme (Blank) selected in the themes list, click the Modify button at the bottom of the dialog box. FrontPage displays a row of buttons below the Sample box.

3. Click the Colors button and then click the Custom tab to display the options shown on the next page.

> **More ways to modify a theme**
>
> When modifying a theme, be sure to check out all of the options available to you in the Themes dialog box. For example, when you click the Colors button, you can select a different color scheme on the Color Schemes tab and modify those colors further on the Color Wheel tab. With the Graphics and Text buttons, you can change such items as the graphics used for certain elements or the text style used for various headings.

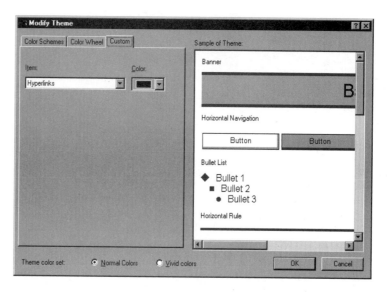

4. Click the arrow to the right of the Item box and then select Heading 1.

5. Now click the arrow to the right of the Color box and select red from the second row.

6. Repeat the previous steps to format all Heading 2 and Heading 3 paragraphs as red. Then click OK.

7. Because you cannot save formatting changes to a preset theme, click the Save As button to display the Save Theme

No theme on a page

In certain instances, you may want to have one or more pages of your web not use the theme you have applied. To remove a theme from a page, display the page, right-click a blank area of the page, and choose Theme from the shortcut menu to display a dialog box similar to the one shown earlier on page 328. With the Selected Page(s) option selected, click (No Theme) in the themes list and then click OK.

Changing the background without using a theme

If you want to change the background of a page without using a theme, first remove the theme from the page (see the adjacent tip). Next right-click a blank area of the page and choose Page Properties from the shortcut menu. On the Background tab, click the Background Picture check box and then click the Browse button to navigate to a specific image file you want to use as your background, or click the arrow to the right of the Background box and select a different background color. If none of the standard color choices meet your needs, click More Colors to display additional options. (On this tab, you can change the colors used for text, hyperlinks, visited hyperlinks, and active hyperlinks.) You can also click the Get Background Information From Another Page option at the bottom of the dialog box and then click the Browse button to navigate to a file which uses the background you want to apply to the current page. To implement your changes, click OK.

dialog box. Type *Redmond BEAT* as the name for the new theme and click OK.

8. Finally, click the All Pages option in the Apply Theme To section and click OK to apply the new theme to all the pages of the web.

9. Choose Exit from the File menu, clicking Yes if FrontPage asks if you want to save any elements of your web.

You have now created your first FrontPage web using a wizard and have learned a bit about making alterations to a web. In the next chapter, you will become even more skilled in web-page creation as you add and change hyperlinks and then prepare your web for storage on a Web server.

15

More About FrontPage

In this chapter, we look at some of the more complex elements you can add to a web. You create various types of hyperlinks and bookmarks. You also work with navigation bars. Then you see how to prepare your web for publication, and how to publish it on a Web server.

Though the sample web you create here is very simple, you'll be able to use hyperlinks and bookmarks to create more complex webs that visitors can navigate with ease.

Web pages created and concepts covered:

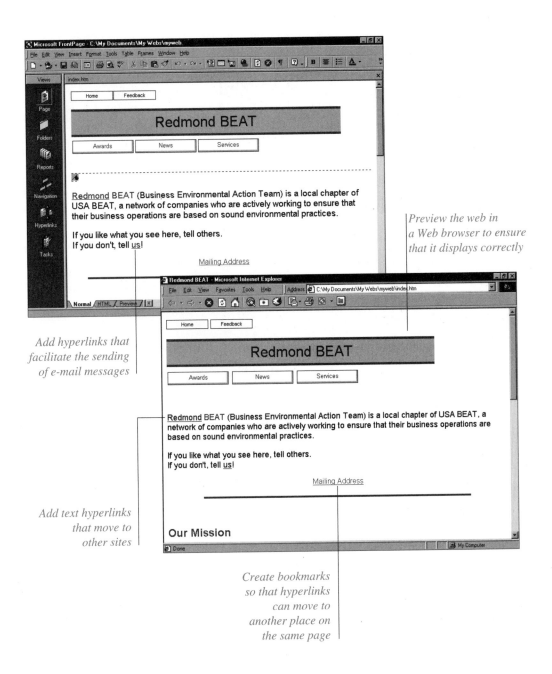

Preview the web in a Web browser to ensure that it displays correctly

Add hyperlinks that facilitate the sending of e-mail messages

Add text hyperlinks that move to other sites

Create bookmarks so that hyperlinks can move to another place on the same page

You have now successfully built your first FrontPage web and should be familiar with the basic techniques for modifying it. In this chapter, you add various types of hyperlinks and bookmarks to the web. Then you prepare it for publication. Finally, we'll discuss how to publish your web on your local computer, on an intranet, or on a Web server hosted by an Internet Service Provider (ISP).

Adding Hyperlinks

Hyperlinks

One of the greatest features of the Web is the capability of quickly traveling to any other Web site in the world with just a click of the mouse. This ease of movement is made possible by *hyperlinks*, which are pointers that store the address (or location) of either another page within the same web on your computer or a Web page on another computer. In Web jargon, this address is called a *uniform resource locator*, or *URL* (see the tip below). The place that a hyperlink points to is called the *target*. Usually a target is another Web page, but it can also be an image, a sound clip, or even a movie snippet.

Targets

When you use a FrontPage wizard to create a web, the wizard automatically adds hyperlinks between the web's pages. However, you will probably want to add or change links as your web evolves. In this section, we show you several types of text hyperlinks and how to add and edit them. Text hyperlinks are represented by a word or phrase on a page, and they are the simplest and most common type of hyperlink.

URLs

Every Web site has a *uniform resource locator (URL)* that identifies the protocol your browser must use and the computer on which the site's files are stored. A typical URL starts with *http* (for HyperText Transfer Protocol) followed by *www* (for World Wide Web), followed by the site's domain name (which is associated with a specific Web server). The domain name might be followed by the directory and filename of a specific page at the site. (With recent versions of most browsers, you have to type the *http* part of a URL only if the site's address doesn't begin with *www*.)

Linking to a New Page

First let's create a hyperlink to a new page in the Redmond BEAT web. Follow these steps:

1. Start FrontPage. Then click the arrow to the right of the Open button on the toolbar and select Open Web from the button's drop-down list.

2. Navigate to the My Documents\My Webs\myweb folder on your hard drive and click Open.

3. Display the folder list, double-click the News page (news.htm) to open it in page view, and then close the folder list.

4. Select the word *Media* in the main heading and click the Hyperlink button on the Standard toolbar to display this dialog box:

The Hyperlink button

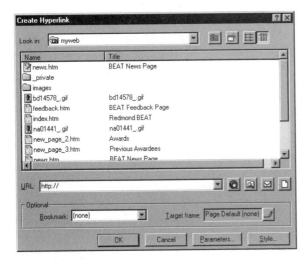

Here you can view a list of all of the folders and pages that make up your web.

5. You want to create a link to a page that doesn't yet exist, so click the Create A Page And Link To The New Page button to the right of the URL box. FrontPage displays this dialog box:

The Create A Page And Link To The New Page button

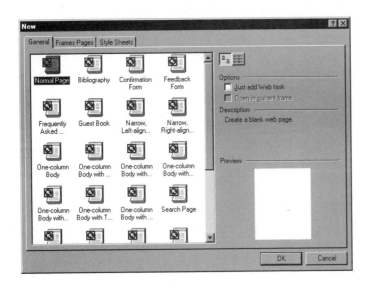

New dialog box options

In the New dialog box, you can create several types of pages from the General tab, including bibliographies, FAQs, guest books, and various types of forms. Click the Frames Pages tab to select a frames page template. (A frames page divides the browser window into separate areas, each containing a different page.) Click the Style Sheets tab to select a design template on which you can base your new page.

6. With the Normal Page icon selected on the General tab, click OK. FrontPage displays a new page like this one:

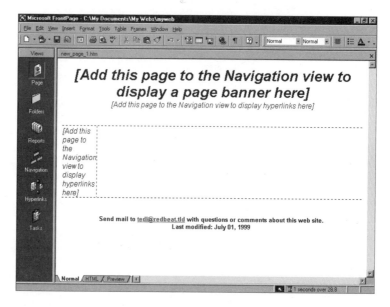

7. At the insertion point, type *Redmond Television Network*.

8. Click the Save button to display the Save As dialog box and click Save to save the new page with the name *redmond_television_network*.

9. Display the News page in page view and notice that the word *Media* is now underlined and formatted with the text hyperlink color used by the Blank theme.

10. Next point to *Media*, hold down the Ctrl key, and notice that the pointer changes to a hand.

11. While still holding the Ctrl key, click the mouse button once to display the Redmond Television Network page.

Recognizing text hyperlinks

Experienced Web users recognize text that is blue and underlined as a hyperlink. They also recognize text that is purple and underlined as a hyperlink that has already been visited. If you are not using a theme, FrontPage assigns these default colors. To change the color scheme of hyperlinks, use the Background tab of the Page Properties dialog box. If you are using a theme, FrontPage may assign different text hyperlink colors which you can change by modifying the theme (see page 344). Recent versions of Web browsers display the target address of a hyperlink when you move your pointer over it, providing yet another way to recognize a hyperlink.

Linking to an Existing Page

On page 356, we'll show you how to link to existing pages in your web by using navigation bars. However, sometimes you will want to create a separate text hyperlink to an existing page. Follow these steps:

1. Display the home page in normal view, click an insertion point at the end of the Our Mission text, and press Enter.

2. Next type *We provide several useful services to accomplish this goal.*

3. Select the word *services* and click the Hyperlink button on the toolbar.

4. In the Create Hyperlink dialog box, select the Services page from the list of files, and then click OK.

Adding E-mail Hyperlinks

One type of text hyperlink commonly used in Web pages is the e-mail address hyperlink. Because you used a FrontPage wizard in Chapter 14, the Redmond BEAT web already has links that allow visitors to send e-mail directly to Ted Lee. E-mail hyperlinks, also referred to as *mailto* hyperlinks, can easily be added to your pages so that your visitors can communicate with you. Follow these steps:

Mailto hyperlinks

1. With the home page displayed in normal view, select the word *us* in the introductory text.

2. Choose Hyperlink from the Insert menu and click the Make A Hyperlink That Sends E-mail button to the right of the URL box to display this dialog box:

The Make A Hyperlink That Sends E-mail button

3. Type *info@redbeat.tld* in the Type An E-mail Address box and click OK. FrontPage adds the address to the URL box in the Create Hyperlink dialog box and adds *mailto:* in front of it. Click OK again to create the hyperlink.

4. If you want, switch to the Preview tab and click the new mailto link. Your Web browser starts and opens a message window with the hyperlink's e-mail address already inserted in the To edit box, ready for you to send a message.

5. If necessary, click the Close button to close the window without sending a message and then close your browser.

Adding Links to Other Web Sites

So far, we have shown you several ways to use hyperlinks to make it easier to move around your web. However, to make your web really useful, you will most likely want to link it to other Web sites. Thankfully, this task is as easy as creating any other type of hyperlink. For this example, you will create a link to The City of Redmond Web site. Bear in mind that the Web is by nature dynamic, so what you see when you connect to this site may be different from what is shown in our screen graphics. Let's get started:

1. Scroll to the bottom of the home page and click an insertion point just below the Webmaster E-mail address at the bottom of the text box.

2. Type *Contact Online Press Inc. about computer training courses* and format the text as bold.

3. Select the words *Online Press Inc.* and click the Hyperlink button on the toolbar.

Adding graphic hyperlinks

When a word or phrase won't do the trick, you can use a graphic image to create a fancier hyperlink. For example, you can use scanned pictures or digital photographs. To create the hyperlink, select the graphic and click the Hyperlink button on the Standard toolbar. In the list of files, select the page you want the hyperlink to jump to or enter an address in the URL box. Then click OK.

4. In the URL edit box of the Create Hyperlink dialog box, type *www.quickcourse.com* and click OK.

That was easy enough because you were given the Quick Course URL. What do you do if you don't know the URL? You can find the Web resources you need for your web without leaving FrontPage. As an example, let's add a link to the Web site maintained by the city of Redmond. Try this:

1. With the home page displayed in normal view, select the word *Redmond* in the first line of the introductory paragraph.

2. Click the Hyperlink button on the toolbar.

The Use Your Web Browser To
Select A Page Or File button

3. Click the Use Your Web Browser To Select A Page Or File button to the right of the URL box.

4. Connect to the Internet if prompted. You then see your Web browser's starting page.

5. Type *www.yahoo.com* in the Address bar to display the site of one of the Web's best-known search services.

6. In the Search box, type *Redmond, WA* and click Search. The results of your search look something like those shown here:

Searching for a Web site

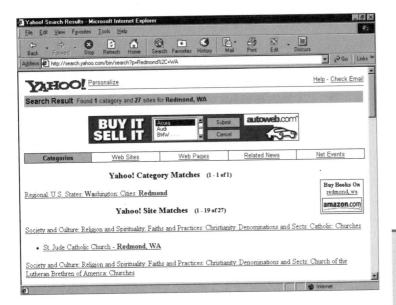

7. Now scroll until you find the *City of Redmond* entry, and then click this hyperlink to jump to the Web site located at *www.ci.redmond.wa.us/*.

8. Click the FrontPage button on the Windows taskbar. The Create Hyperlink dialog box is displayed, with the address for the City of Redmond page entered in the URL box.

9. Click OK and then test your new hyperlink by using the Preview tab.

10. If necessary, disconnect from the Internet when you finish.

Linking to a file on your computer

You can create hyperlinks in your webs to specific files on your computer, such as any Office document. First select the text you want to use as the hyperlink and then click the Hyperlink button on the toolbar. Next click the Make A Hyperlink To A File On Your Computer button to the right of the URL box to display the Select File dialog box. Navigate to the file you want to use and then click OK. When visitors to your site click this hyperlink, their Web browser opens the file in its originating application in a separate window.

Adding Bookmarks

You may think of a bookmark as a long, flat object that marks your place in a printed book. More recently, however, this term has been used by some Web browsers to refer to a Web page that you have marked for a return visit. (Internet Explorer uses the term *favorite* instead of *bookmark*.) In FrontPage, a bookmark (which is also called an *anchor*), has the more traditional meaning.

Clicking a regular hyperlink takes you to the top of a particular page. But suppose you want to jump to a specific location elsewhere on the same page. Then you need to create a hyperlink to a bookmark that you insert in the text expressly for this purpose. For example, you might want to bookmark all the major topics of a long, multi-screen page so that visitors can click hyperlinks to jump directly to specific topics, rather than having to scroll down to find the topic they want.

In this section, you will add two bookmarks to the Redmond BEAT home page and then create hyperlinks to them from elsewhere on the page. Follow these steps:

1. Display the Home page in normal view and then click an insertion point to the left of *Redmond BEAT* in the opening paragraph.

2. Press Enter and then move back up to the newly inserted paragraph.

3. Choose Bookmark from the expanded Insert menu to display the dialog box shown on the facing page.

The DHTML Effects toolbar

You can apply special effects to various elements on your web pages by using the DHTML (Dynamic HyperText Markup Language) Effects toolbar. Display the toolbar, select the element you want to have a special effect, then select an option from the toolbar's On box. (The special effect will be displayed when the chosen event occurs.) Next select options from the Apply and Effect boxes. For example, if you click an insertion point in a particular paragraph and select Mouse Over as the event, Formatting as the effect, and Choose Border... (with a dashed border) as the setting, a dashed border will appear around the paragraph when you point to that paragraph in a Web browser.

4. In the Bookmark dialog box, type *The Top* in the Bookmark Name edit box and then click OK. (If you select text before choosing the Bookmark command, that text appears in the Bookmark Name edit box.) FrontPage inserts a bookmark icon (a flag) where the insertion point is located.

5. Scroll down the page to the phone and address section, click an insertion point at the end of the *Contact Online Press* line, and press Enter to create a new paragraph.

6. Type *Return to Top*, select the text, click the Bold button to toggle it off, and then click the Center button.

7. With the text still selected, click the Hyperlink button.

8. Click the arrow to the right of the Bookmark box in the Optional section, select The Top from the drop-down list, and then click OK.

9. Click an insertion point in the front of the address text and create a bookmark called *Mailing Address*.

10. Scroll to the top of the page and click an insertion point between the introductory text and the horizontal bar.

11. Type *Mailing Address* and center the text. Then create a hyperlink that jumps to the Mailing Address bookmark.

12. Now test the two bookmarks by switching to the Preview tab and clicking each hyperlink in turn to check whether they jump to the correct locations on the page.

13. Switch back to normal view and save your work.

Removing bookmarks

You can remove a bookmark as easily as you can create one. Select the text that has been bookmarked or select the flag icon, right-click it, and choose Bookmark Properties from the shortcut menu to display the Bookmark dialog box. Then with the bookmark name still selected, click the Clear button. FrontPage clears the bookmark, but leaves the text that represented it still on the page. If you inserted a bookmark without first selecting text, the flag icon remains on the page after you clear the bookmark. Simply select the icon again and press Delete.

Working with Navigation Bars

Navigation bars offer yet another way for visitors to move around your site. Because you used a wizard to create the Redmond BEAT web, FrontPage included navigation bars in the *shared border* regions of each page. (See the tip below for more information about shared borders.) After you determin- ed the structure of your web (see page 333), FrontPage added the appropriate hyperlinks to the navigation bars for you. The hyperlink buttons that make up the navigation bars need some cleaning up, but first let's make some adjustments in navigation view:

Shared borders

1. Switch to navigation view by clicking the Navigation icon on the Views bar. Notice that although you added a new page to the Redmond BEAT web, this page is not reflected in the web's navigation structure.

Updating the navigation structure

2. To add the page, display the folder list, select the Redmond_Television_Network page, and drag it below the News box. When FrontPage displays a line indicating that this page is a child page of News, release the mouse button.

3. Close the folder list.

Shared borders

Shared borders are areas that are common to each page of a web. (The Redmond BEAT web has shared borders on the top, bottom, and left sides of the pages.) These areas can include elements such as text, buttons, or graphics. You can change the settings for shared borders on individual pages of a web by first displaying the page you want to change in page view and choosing Shared Borders from the Format menu. Then select or deselect the borders you want to remove or display, as you do on page 358.

4. Double-click the News box to view that page in page view and notice that FrontPage has updated the button in the left shared border.

5. Switch to the Preview tab and click the button to see if it moves you to the correct page.

That takes care of updating the navigation bars for the entire web. However, on some web pages, the layout of the buttons is not logical. Let's fix that now:

1. Display the home page in normal view. Notice that there are no buttons below the Redmond BEAT heading. You want the buttons for the child pages of the Home page to appear here instead of in the left shared border.

2. Select the *Edit the properties* placeholder in the top border, right-click the selection, and then choose Navigation Bar

Properties from the shortcut menu to display the dialog box shown here:

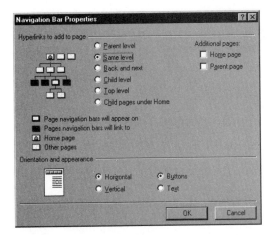

3. Click the Child Pages Under Home option in the Hyperlinks To Add To Page section, make sure the options in the Additional Pages section are deselected, check that the Horizontal and Buttons options are selected in the Orientation And Appearance section, and then click OK.

Now the same navigation buttons appear in both the top and left borders of the home page. But if you delete the buttons on the left side, they will be deleted from all pages because they appear in a shared border. Here's how to remedy the situation:

1. Choose Shared Borders from the Format menu to display the dialog box shown on the next page.

Adding navigation bars to one or all pages

To add a new navigation bar to a page, start by clicking an insertion point where you want the navigation bar to appear. (If the insertion point is in a shared border, the new navigation bar will be added to all pages.) Next choose Navigation Bar from the Insert menu and then select the hyperlinks option you want for the navigation bar in the Hyperlinks To Add To Page section. In the Orientation And Appearance section, select either the Horizontal or Vertical option to determine the orientation of the navigation bar and select either Text or Buttons to determine the appearance. (The Buttons option works only if you have applied a theme to your web.) Then click OK.

Reformatting navigation bars

To change the formatting of a navigation bar when you haven't applied a theme, select the navigation bar and make changes to the font size, type, or color. If you have applied a theme and want to reformat a navigation bar, you can either switch to another theme or modify the theme to your specifications (see page 343).

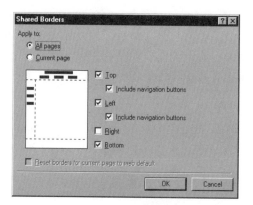

2. Select the Current Page option, click the Left check box to deselect it, and click OK. Here are the results:

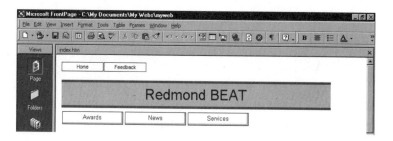

3. Save all of your changes.

Preparing Your Web for Publishing

Changing the default navigation bar name

By default, FrontPage uses the names *Home*, *Up*, *Back*, and *Next* for its standard navigation buttons. If you want to change these names, you can do so by choosing Web Settings from the Tools menu and then displaying the Navigation tab. Type a new name in the appropriate edit box and click OK. To restore the default settings, display the dialog box again and click the Default button.

When you have finished creating a web, you will probably be anxious to publish it on a Web server for all the world (or all your organization) to see. But before you take that big step, you should verify that the information, graphics, and hyperlinks in your pages are correct. Final preparations include checking spelling and grammar (see the tip on the facing page), checking that the hyperlinks work properly, and previewing the pages in a Web browser to make sure everything looks OK on the screen. Once you have completed these tasks, your web will be ready for public viewing.

Checking Hyperlinks

The Redmond BEAT web doesn't contain many hyperlinks, but you should still double-check them to verify that they jump to the correct place. Bear in mind that sites on the Web change constantly, and a hyperlink to another site that is fine today might not be fine tomorrow. To check your hyperlinks, you will explore two more FrontPage views: hyperlinks view and reports view.

Checking in Hyperlinks View

Hyperlinks view gives you an overview of all the hyperlinks in a particular web, much the same as navigation view gives you an overview of the organization of a web's pages. Let's look at the Redmond BEAT web in hyperlinks view now. Follow these steps:

1. With the home page displayed, click the Hyperlinks icon on the Views bar to display your web as shown below. (If necessary, click the Folder List button on the toolbar to close the folder list.)

The Hyperlinks icon

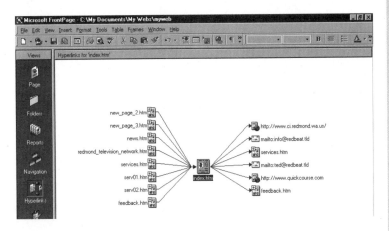

As you can see, FrontPage displays a diagram with the home page (index.htm) in the middle and all the linked pages displayed on either side. The arrows show how each page is connected. Links from the pages on the left are represented by the arrows to the home page. Links from the home page are represented by arrows to the pages on the right.

2. Click the plus sign attached to the news.htm icon on the left side of the window to display the News page's hyperlinks, as shown on the next page.

Checking spelling

Before publishing a web on a Web server, you should thoroughly proofread the text for spelling and grammatical errors. To spell-check one page of your web, display the page in page view and click the Spelling button on the Standard toolbar. The options available for dealing with words identified by the spell checker are the same as those available with the other Office applications. To spell-check multiple pages, switch to navigation view or folders view and click the Spelling button. With the Entire Web option selected, click Start to begin the spell check. After all the pages have been checked, you see a dialog box that lists any potential misspellings FrontPage finds. You can then move to the appropriate page in page view to fix the problem. You can also select an item in the list and click the Add Task button to add a reminder to the tasks list to fix the misspelling.

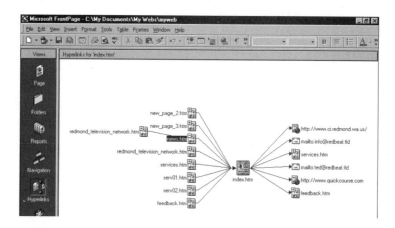

3. Click the minus sign to collapse the News page's hyperlinks.

Checking in Reports View

As you just saw, hyperlinks view is helpful for looking over the layout of your hyperlinks, but it doesn't tell you whether they are all working correctly. You can right-click individual hyperlinks in hyperlinks view and choose Verify Hyperlink from the shortcut menu, but there is a better way. To check whether all the hyperlinks in a web are functional, you can use reports view. Follow these steps:

The Reports icon

1. Click the Reports icon on the Views bar. Your screen looks like the one shown below. (We dragged the Reporting toolbar out of the way so that it doesn't obscure the files list.)

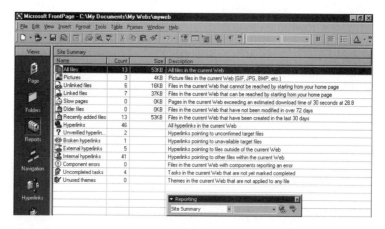

The Verify Hyperlinks button

2. To verify the web's hyperlinks, click the Verify Hyperlinks button on the Reporting toolbar. FrontPage shows this dialog box:

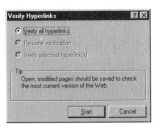

3. With the Verify All Hyperlinks option selected, click Start. If one or more of the hyperlinks is to a site on the Web, you may be prompted to connect to the Internet. FrontPage quickly tests any links that haven't already been verified. When testing is complete, your screen looks like this:

Editing Hyperlinks

If you are fortunate, you will see no Broken symbols in the Status column. However, when problems do occur, you need to know how to edit a hyperlink. For example, we have a broken serv03.htm hyperlink, which can be fixed by following these steps:

1. Right-click the broken serv03.htm hyperlink and choose Edit Hyperlink from the shortcut menu. FrontPage displays this dialog box:

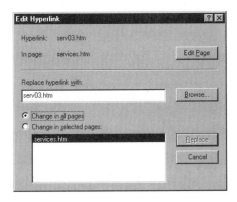

Customizing hyperlinks view

You can customize the way hyperlinks view displays hyperlinks by right-clicking the background and choosing a command from the shortcut menu. If you choose Show Page Titles, FrontPage displays the title of each page instead of the filenames. To display hyperlinks to graphics, choose Hyperlinks To Pictures. To show repeated hyperlinks, such as multiple links on one page that all point to the same file, choose Repeated Hyperlinks. If you want to display bookmark hyperlinks, choose Hyperlinks Inside Page. Finally, to display a different page in the center of the hyperlinks map, right-click the page you want displayed in the middle and choose Move To Center. To reverse any of these settings, right-click to display the shortcut menu and choose the command again to toggle it off.

The Edit Hyperlink dialog box shows the name of the link and where it is located in your web. In the Replace Hyperlink With edit box, you can type the correct address, if you determine that the one you are editing is incorrect. You can also indicate whether to replace the link on all the pages on which it appears, or only on the pages you select from the list at the bottom of the dialog box. You can also click the Edit Page button to move directly to the page in question.

2. Click Edit Page to display the Services page, which as you can see here, includes links to three child pages with the problem link highlighted:

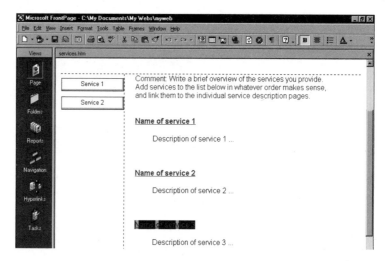

You deleted the third services page back in Chapter 14 (see page 331) but didn't delete the hyperlink on its parent page.

3. With the Name of Service 3 hyperlink selected, press Delete to eliminate the problem. Then select and delete its description placeholder text and save your changes.

Previewing a Web

The final step in preparing your web for publication is to preview it so that you can check for placement of items on the pages, color schemes, legibility of text with a particular background, and so on. With FrontPage, you have two ways to preview your web: on the Preview tab and in a Web browser.

Other available reports types

You can select other report types by clicking the arrow to the right of the Report box on the Reporting toolbar and selecting from the drop-down list. You can create reports that include recently added files, recently changed files, slow pages, pages with component errors, and so on. With some report types, you can change the option in the Report Setting box to fine-tune the report even further.

You have already used page view's Preview tab several times to examine your pages. This method is handy, because it is easily accessible, but the Preview tab doesn't always render your web pages accurately. It is best, and nearly as easy, to preview your pages using your Web browser before exposing them to other people's scrutiny. For this example, you will use Internet Explorer, but if possible, you should check your web in other browsers as well, so that you can detect any design problems that might arise because of browser differences. Follow these steps to preview your web:

1. Display the Redmond BEAT home page in page view and click the Save button.

2. Click the Preview In Browser button on the Standard toolbar. You may be prompted to connect to the Internet. You can click the Work Offline button to remain unconnected, but bear in mind that if you stay offline, you will not be able to test the links to other Web sites. If you want to test these links, go ahead and connect. Regardless of whether you are working offline or online, your screen now looks something like the one shown here:

The Preview In Browser button

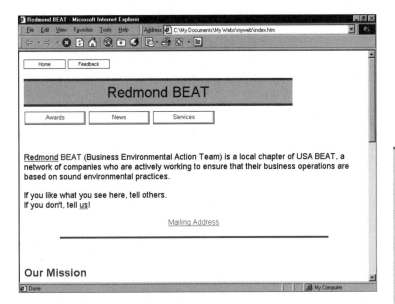

3. Test the various hyperlinks in your web to verify that they move you to the correct location.

Recalculating hyperlinks

You should occasionally recalculate the hyperlinks on your pages so that they are updated and repaired. Choose Recalculate Hyperlinks from the Tools menu and click Yes. When you recalculate hyperlinks, FrontPage also deletes unused themes, updates shared borders and navigation bars, and synchronizes certain data.

4. When you are finished testing, close the browser window and, if necessary, disconnect from the Internet.

Publishing a Web

After investing so much time and energy in creating your web, you will want to be able to share it with other people. You do this by *publishing* your web on a Web server so that other people can view it. To publish your web, you need to know the address of the server you will use to host it. (In some cases, you might actually create the web on the computer that will function as its server.) Once you have this information, you can send the web to that server. In the case of an intranet server, the process is pretty simple, and undoubtedly someone in your organization will be able to guide you. In the case of an Internet server, things are a little more complex, so we'll briefly look at some of the issues here.

Finding a Web Presence Provider

In order for your web to be viewable on the Web, the server that will host it must support FrontPage Extensions. If your Internet Service Provider (ISP) allows you to place a Web site on its server, check that it can support a site created with FrontPage. (FrontPage refers to organizations that host Web sites as *Web Presence Providers*, or *WPP*s.) If it can't, you need to locate a WPP that can. FrontPage can assist you in finding a provider that has the necessary extensions installed on its server so that all FrontPage features will run properly. Let's try locating one right now:

1. With your web open in page view, choose Publish Web from the File menu. FrontPage displays this dialog box:

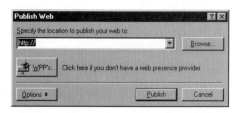

2. Click the WPP's button to begin the procedure for locating a provider.

Browser specifications

If your organization has standardized on a particular browser and you are publishing on an intranet, you can tell FrontPage to use features that will work only with that browser (or a specific version of that browser). Choose Page Options from the Tools menu, click the Compatibility tab, and then make your selections from the Browsers, Browser Versions, and Servers drop-down lists. FrontPage then shows you which of its features you can use in the Technologies section of the dialog box.

3. When prompted, connect to the Internet. FrontPage moves to a page that lists some of the larger WPPs. You can also click a hyperlink to the FrontPage WPP List, which you can browse in several ways, including alphabetically and geographically. You might find your current WPP in one of these lists, or you might locate a new one.

4. After you finish exploring the WPP list and related pages and have the information you need, return to the Publish Web dialog box, click Cancel, and disconnect from the Internet.

You can now contact the WPP and if necessary, establish an account that enables you to publish your own Web site.

Sending the Web to a Server

The next step in publishing your web is to send it to the Web server. The procedure for uploading your web files is simplified by the Microsoft Web Publishing Wizard, but you will still need specific instructions from your Webmaster or WPP. Follow these steps:

1. With your web open in page view, choose Publish Web from the File menu to show the dialog box shown on the facing page.

2. In the Specify The Location edit box, enter the URL of your Web server, click Publish, and if necessary connect to the Internet when prompted.

3. When the Microsoft Web Publishing Wizard asks for a user name and password, enter the name and password given to you by your Webmaster or WPP and click Finish. FrontPage then begins to transfer your web files.

4. If you see a Publishing FrontPage Components dialog box, click Continue to display a dialog box that tracks the progress of the file transfer from your computer to the server.

5. After FrontPage completes the transfer, the only thing left to do is check your site on your intranet or the Web.

That ends this brief introduction to FrontPage. Creating Web pages has never been easier, and as you hone your FrontPage skills, you will see them continually expand and improve.

Deleting a FrontPage web

After practicing with FrontPage, you may end up with a web that you no longer need. You can't delete the web using normal Windows techniques because of all of the associated files that FrontPage created behind the scenes. Deleting a FrontPage web is not difficult, but bear in mind that deleting a Web is a permanent action and cannot be undone. First open the web you want to delete and display the folder list. Next right-click the main folder and choose Delete from the shortcut menu. FrontPage warns you that the deletion is a permanent action and offers two options: you can remove only the FrontPage information, leaving intact any files you have used in your web pages, such as text files or graphics; or you can remove the web in its entirety. Click the option you want and then click OK.

16

More Office Techniques

We discuss Office's language options and then introduce the Office shortcut bar, which provides speedy access to programs and files. Next you recycle documents from one application to another, and finally, you take a look at Office's Web publishing capabilities.

This chapter gives you an overview of the efficiency with which you can use Office to create whatever documents you need to get your job done.

Documents created and concepts covered:

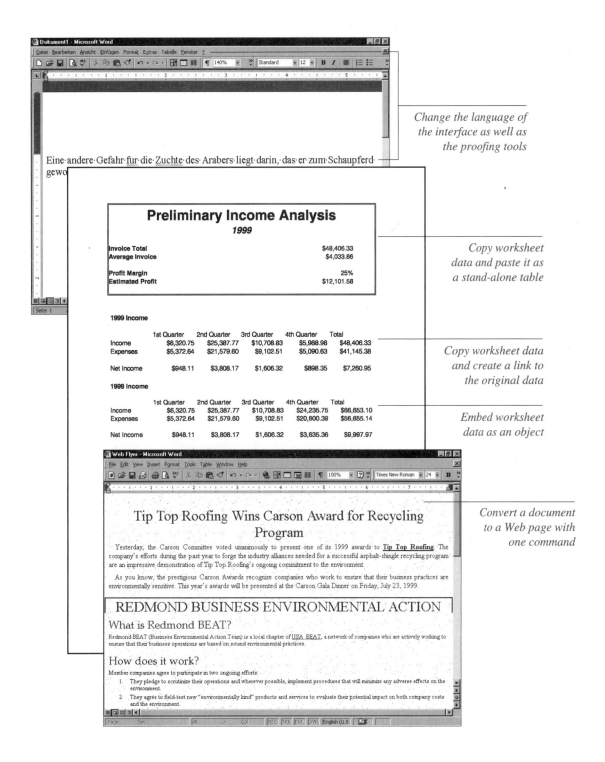

Change the language of the interface as well as the proofing tools

Copy worksheet data and paste it as a stand-alone table

Copy worksheet data and create a link to the original data

Embed worksheet data as an object

Convert a document to a Web page with one command

Y ou've seen that the applications that comprise Microsoft Office 2000 share many features, making it easy
to apply the skills you acquire with one of the applications to the others. In this chapter, we cover some additional
Office techniques that apply to the suite as a whole rather than
to one application in particular.

Using More Than One Language

The Language Pack

Microsoft Office is a best-seller worldwide, but the new language capabilities of Office 2000 make it a premium international product with broad appeal to companies with offices in
other countries. We start by showing those of you who work
in companies that have purchased the Language Pack how to
switch the language you use with your Office applications. (If
this does not apply to you, you can skip this section and rejoin
us on page 371.) Provided that the Office 2000 Language
Pack has been installed on your network, you can change the
language of the screen at any time, without having to reinstall
Office. You can even create your documents in other languages.
(The Language Pack includes support for the languages used
in all countries except India, Vietnam, and Thailand.) To
enable support for multiple languages, follow these steps:

1. Click the Start button and choose Microsoft Office Tools and
   then Microsoft Office Language Settings from the Programs
   submenu to display this dialog box:

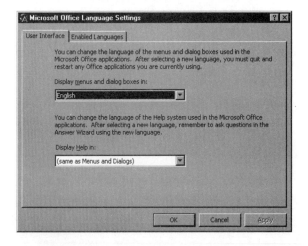

2. Read the information on the User Interface tab and then click the Enabled Languages tab to display these options:

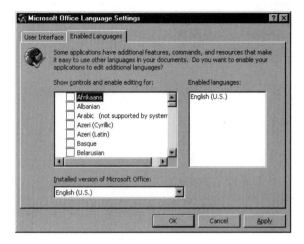

3. Scroll the list of available languages and click the check boxes to the left of French and German. Click the check boxes of any other languages you think you might want to use.

Enabling other languages

4. Click the User Interface tab, change the Display Menus And Dialog Boxes In setting to German, and click OK.

Changing the interface language

5. When a message box appears to tell you that your changes will take effect the next time you start an Office application, click OK.

Now let's start Word so you can see how the program looks with the new settings in place:

1. Begin by choosing New Office Document from the top of the Start menu.

2. If you see a dialog box prompting you to insert the Microsoft Office Language Pack CD-ROM, insert it or indicate another location from which the Language Pack can be accessed, and then click OK. You then see the dialog box shown on the next page.

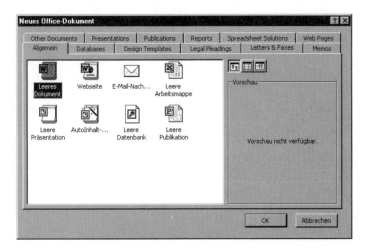

3. Double-click the Leeres Dokument (Blank Document) icon to start Word with a new, blank document open.

Telling Word to detect the language

4. Choose Sprache (Language) and then Sprache Bestimmen (Set Language) from the Extras (Tools) menu. Then in the Sprache dialog box, select the Sprache Automatisch Erkennen (Detect Language Automatically) option and click OK.

5. Type the text shown here (we've magnified the window for readability):

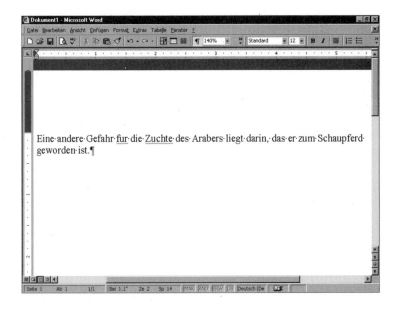

As you can see, the names on the title bar, menu bar, and status bar are now in German. Word recognizes that you are typing in German and indicates on the status bar that it will use the German proofing tools. (You can type in another language when the English user interface is in effect, and provided you have enabled that language, Word will recognize it and respond accordingly.) If automatic spell-checking is turned on, Word spell-checks your text, indicating any misspellings with red, wavy underlines.

Spell-checking other languages

6. Close Word without saving the document, and then set the user interface back to English for the rest of the chapter.

After this brief demonstration, we'll leave you to explore how to put the Office multi-language capabilities to work for you.

Using the Office Shortcut Bar

With the Office applications, you almost always have more than one way to accomplish the same task so that you can work with your computer the way that is most comfortable for you. The Office shortcut bar provides an alternative way of quickly getting started with whatever task you need to perform. Follow these steps to display the Office shortcut bar and take it for a test drive:

1. Click the Start button and choose Programs, Microsoft Office Tools, and then Microsoft Office Shortcut Bar. Insert your installation CD-ROM if prompted. This dialog box appears:

Displaying the Office shortcut bar

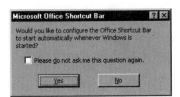

If you click the Yes button, a shortcut to the Microsoft Office Shortcut Bar program will be created in your Startup folder. Windows runs the programs in this folder each time it starts.

2. Click No. Looking like a regular toolbar, the shortcut bar appears and docks itself along an edge of your screen.

3. If necessary, point to a blank area of the shortcut bar and drag it to the top of the screen, where it looks like this:

4. Use ScreenTips to familiarize yourself with the buttons on the bar.

The Office shortcut bar buttons

By default, the Office shortcut bar consists of the following:

- **The Control menu icon.** As with application Control menu icons, you can click this icon to display a menu of useful commands, including the Customize command used to tailor the Office shortcut bar to the way you work.

- **The Office Toolbar button and name.** By default, the shortcut bar displays the Office toolbar, but as you'll see in a minute, it can display other toolbars as well.

- **The New Office Document button.** Click this button to start an Office application with a new, blank document in its window.

- **The Open Office Document button.** Click this button to start one of the Office applications with an existing document in its window.

- **The New Message, New Appointment, New Task, New Contact, New Journal Entry, and New Note buttons.** Click these buttons to start Outlook 2000 with the corresponding task displayed in the workspace.

  Your toolbar may also display an Access, Excel, FrontPage, Outlook, PowerPoint, Publisher, or Word button, depending on which program you last used. You can click this button to start the corresponding application and a new document.

  When the shortcut bar is docked along an edge of the screen, it takes up screen space that might otherwise be available to an open program. You can keep the shortcut bar open but tuck it out of sight, as you'll see as you follow these steps:

1. Point to a blank area of the shortcut bar and drag it to the middle of your screen. It becomes a floating toolbar like this one:

Moving the shortcut bar

(The shape of the floating shortcut bar varies, depending on the number of buttons displayed.)

2. Click the shortcut bar's Minimize button to shrink it to a button on the taskbar.

Minimizing the shortcut bar

3. Click the Microsoft Office Shortcut Bar button on the taskbar to redisplay the floating toolbar, and then double-click its title bar to dock the toolbar at the top of the screen.

Customizing the Office Shortcut Bar

You can customize the Office shortcut bar in several ways, some of which we'll show you here. If you like using the shortcut bar, you can explore other options on your own later.

1. Click the Control menu icon to display the Control menu, and then choose Customize to display this dialog box:

The Control menu icon

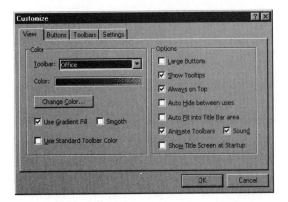

The options on the View tab control the way the Office shortcut bar looks and behaves on the screen. (You can experiment after you understand how the shortcut bar works.)

Displaying and Hiding Toolbars

As we've said, by default the shortcut bar displays the Office toolbar, but you can display other toolbars at any time. Follow these steps:

1. Click the Toolbars tab to display a list of the toolbars that can appear on the shortcut bar:

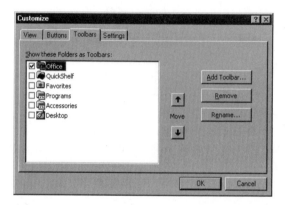

2. Click the Accessories check box and then click OK. The shortcut bar now looks like this:

As you can see, the Office toolbar is hidden below its button on the left side of the shortcut bar, and the buttons on the Accessories toolbar are now displayed.

3. Click the Office button. The Accessories toolbar shrinks under its button at the right end of the shortcut bar, and the buttons on the Office toolbar are once again displayed.

4. Turn off the Accessories toolbar by right-clicking the shortcut bar and deselecting Accessories from the shortcut menu.

Displaying and Hiding Buttons

You can use the Accessories toolbar to start the programs that come with Windows with just the click of a button. However, if you use most of these programs only rarely, it's not worth cluttering up the shortcut bar with an entire toolbar. Instead, you can add buttons for the programs you use most often to the Office toolbar, and you can add folder buttons for direct

---

Creating custom toolbars

To create a custom toolbar to add to the Office shortcut bar, start by choosing Customize from the Control menu. Then, when the Customize dialog box appears, click the Add Toolbar button on the Toolbars tab, select the Create A New, Blank Toolbar option, enter a name for the toolbar, and click OK. Next click the Buttons tab of the Customize dialog box. Be sure the name of the custom toolbar appears in the Toolbar box and click the Add File or Add Folder button to add files and/or folders to the new toolbar. When you're ready, click OK to add your customized toolbar to the Office shortcut bar.

access to the files you use most often. As a demonstration, let's add two buttons to the Office toolbar:

1. Choose Customize from the Control menu and click the Buttons tab to display these options:

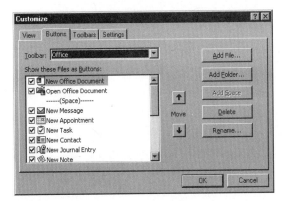

2. Click the Add File button to display the Add File dialog box. Display the contents of the Windows folder and double-click Calc to add a button for the Windows Calculator program to the Show These Files As Buttons list.

3. Next click the Add Folder button to display the Add Folder dialog box. Display the contents of your hard drive, click the My Documents folder, and click Add to add a button for that folder to the Show These Files As Buttons list. Then click OK. As you can see here, the Office toolbar now includes instant access to Calculator and the My Documents folder:

Here's how to hide a button:

1. Choose Customize from the Control menu and then click the Buttons tab.

2. Scroll the Show These Files As Buttons list, deselect the My Documents check box, and click OK. This button no longer appears on the toolbar.

3. Now suppose you decide you won't need the My Documents button again and you want to delete it. Choose Customize from

Hiding vs. removing

A good rule of thumb to remember when you're working with the Office shortcut bar is to hide rather than remove the default toolbars and buttons so that you can easily restore them. To hide toolbars or buttons, simply choose the Customize command from the Control menu, click the Toolbars or Buttons tab of the Customize dialog box, and deselect the toolbars or buttons by clicking their check boxes. (Before you can hide a button, you must use the Toolbar drop-down list on the Buttons tab to select the toolbar on which the button resides.) When you create custom toolbars or add custom buttons to the Office shortcut bar, you might want to use the Remove button on the Toolbars tab or the Delete button on the Buttons tab to remove toolbars and buttons that have become obsolete.

the Control menu, click the Buttons tab, select My Documents, click the Delete button, and click OK. Confirm that you want to remove the button from the Office shortcut bar. (Even though the message in the confirmation dialog box implies that you are deleting the contents of the My Documents folder, you are really only deleting all references to the My Documents button.)

Turning off the Office shortcut bar

4. You can experiment later with setting up the Office shortcut bar to suit the way you work. For now, click the Control menu icon and choose Exit from the drop-down menu to turn off the bar.

Recycling Office Information

Throughout this book, we've emphasized the efficiencies you can achieve by recycling information rather than retyping it wherever you need it. So far, however, we have concentrated on recycling within a single application. In this section, we'll look at various ways you can reuse the information from one application in another application.

Importing and Exporting Information

When you want to use an entire file created in one application in another application, the simplest way is to open the file in the receiving application. As an example, let's open an Excel worksheet in Word:

Opening an Excel worksheet in Word

1. Start Word and click the Open button on the Standard toolbar.

2. In the Open dialog box, change the Files Of Type setting to All Files, navigate to the folder containing the workbook you want to import, and double-click the name of the workbook. (You may have to insert the installation CD-ROM to activate this feature.) This dialog box appears:

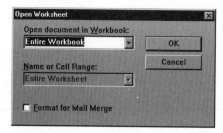

3. Click the arrow to the right of the Open Document In Workbook box, select Invoices 1999 from the drop-down list, and with Entire Worksheet in the Name Or Cell Range box, click OK. Here is the worksheet opened as a document in Word:

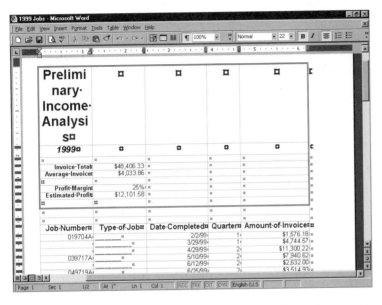

You will obviously have to massage the table into shape with Word formatting techniques, but at least you won't have to type it from scratch.

4. Click the Save button to save the document, and when Word tells you that it will be saved in Word format, click Yes. Then close the document and minimize Word.

Here's another example. Suppose you want to export a table of Access data in a format you can use in Excel. Follow the steps below:

1. Choose Open Office Document from the top of the Start menu and double-click Roofs to start Access with the Roofs database open.

Exporting an Access table in Excel format

2. Display the Jobs table and choose Export from the File menu to display the dialog box shown on the next page.

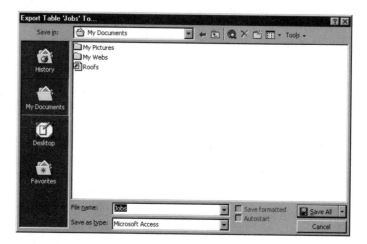

3. Change the Save As Type setting to Microsoft Excel 97-2000 and click Save All to save the entire table in Excel format.

Opening the exported file

4. Choose Open Office Document from the Start menu and double-click Jobs to start Excel with the Jobs workbook open, like this:

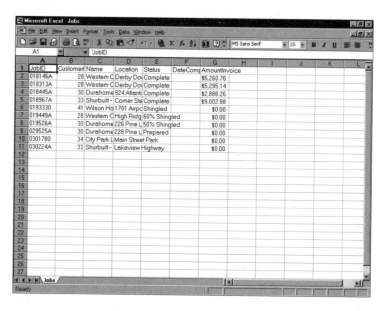

5. Close the Jobs workbook. Then close Access.

You can import and export documents or parts of documents in most applications, but the methods are not always this simple. For example, you import an Access table into Excel using the Microsoft Query program. When you want to work with a file created in another application, start by checking the Open command options, and then look for a Get External Data or Import command. Also, check the source program for an Export command. Along the way, the Office Assistant may offer a tip that will tell you exactly how to proceed, or you can look in the application's Help feature for guidance.

Copying and Pasting Information

The simplest way to recycle part of a document is to copy and paste it via the Windows or Office Clipboard. Try this:

1. In Excel, open the 1999 Jobs workbook, select A1:E9 on the Invoices 1999 sheet, and click the Copy button on the Standard toolbar.

Pasting a worksheet range as a Word table

2. Maximize Word, open a new document, and click the Paste button on the toolbar to insert the copied range of the worksheet as a Word table.

3. Save the document as *Sales Analysis*. Here are the results:

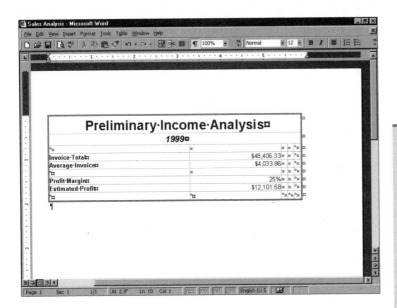

Graphing Word tables

You can use Microsoft Graph to plot graphs of the data in Word tables. Select the data and click the Copy button. Then choose Object from the Insert menu and double-click Microsoft Graph 2000 Chart in the Object Type list to open Graph. Select a cell in the datasheet and click Paste to insert the data you have copied. Graph displays the plotted data in a graph. Click outside the graph to close Graph and view the results.

Linking and Embedding Information

As you have just seen, when you simply paste information from a worksheet into a Word document, the information is translated into a Word table. You could create the information in Word and get the same result, but when the data already exists in another application, you can save yourself a lot of typing by recycling the information instead. However, the power of the Office applications far exceeds this simple kind of copy-and-paste recycling. With Office, you can create documents that are a patchwork of pieces created in the different Office applications. These patchwork documents allow you to maintain information in files that can be manipulated by the application that created them, but also use that information in files created by other applications. For example, if you want to use an Excel worksheet that relies on a SUM function in a Word report, copying and pasting the worksheet would freeze the results of the function. If you later updated the worksheet so that the SUM function produced new results, you would have to copy and paste the worksheet again to update the Word report. With Office, you can recycle the information in a way that ensures the report always reflects the latest results of the worksheet's SUM function. This type of recycling is made possible by *OLE*, which is pronounced *olay*. You don't

OLE →
have to be an OLE expert to recycle information, but understanding a bit about the concept of OLE helps you decide which of a couple of different recycling methods to use. So here is a quick rundown:

Objects →
The O in OLE stands for *object*, and an object is an item or an element of a document. It can be a block of text, a graphic, a table, a graph, and so on. Each object consists of data that determines how the object is displayed and data that determines its content. The application that creates the object is called

Servers and clients →
the *server*, while the application that receives the object is called the *client*. The document in which the object was created is called the *source document*, and the client document in

Source and container documents →
which the object is used is called the *container document*.

Linking and embedding →
To create a patchwork document, you can *link* an object to the container document (the *L* in *OLE*), or you can *embed* the object (the *E*). When you link information stored in a source document to a container document, you need both the source document and the container document in order to be able to show the object. When you embed information, the information

becomes part of the container document, and you no longer need the source document.

So how does all this influence how you go about recycling information? If the object you want to use in a container document is likely to change and you want to be sure that every instance of the object in every container document where the information is used reflects the changes, it is most efficient to create the information in its own source document and then link the object where it's needed. If the information is not going to change, embedding might be the best way to go because embedded information can be edited in the container document without the source document having to be present. Bear in mind, however, that documents that contain embedded objects can get very large.

So that's the scoop on OLE. Now let's see how you might use it. To learn a couple of ways to create container documents, you'll use the Sales Analysis document now on your screen and the Annual worksheet in the 1999 Jobs workbook. Follow these steps to link the Word document and the worksheet:

1. Press Ctrl+End to move to the end of the document and then press Enter to add some space.

Linking a document

2. Maximize Excel, activate the Annual sheet of the 1999 Jobs workbook, select A1:F7, and click the Copy button. If the Clipboard toolbar appears (see the tip on page 21), close it.

3. Maximize Word and choose Paste Special from the Edit menu to display this dialog box:

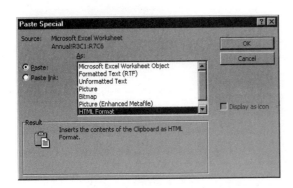

More about linking

By default, when you open a document that contains a link to another file, Word updates the linked information. In addition, it updates the information if the source file changes while the linked document is open. The source file does not have to be open for this updating to happen, but it does have to be available to your computer and be stored exactly where it was when the link was established. Moving or renaming the source file breaks the link. To reestablish it, choose Links from the Edit menu, select the link, click Change Source, double-click the source file, and click OK.

4. Select the Paste Link option, select Microsoft Excel Worksheet Object in the As list, and then click OK. Word pastes a copy of the worksheet selection in the document, linking the copy to the original worksheet.

5. Save the document.

You'll test the worksheet link in a moment. For now, let's embed a copy of the same range so that you can explore yet another technique. This technique will embed the entire active sheet of the selected workbook. To avoid embedding the Annual worksheet's graph as well as the income statement, you'll first move the graph to a different sheet and save the workbook with the Annual sheet active. Follow these steps:

1. Maximize Excel and insert a new sheet in 1999 Jobs by choosing Worksheet from the Insert menu.

2. Next move the graph to the new sheet by clicking the graph to select it, clicking the Cut button, clicking the Sheet1 tab, and then clicking the Paste button. Deselect the graph and rename Sheet1 as *Graph* (see page 108).

3. Move to cell A1 on the Annual sheet and save the workbook.

Now for the embedding operation:

Embedding a document

1. Maximize Word, press Ctrl+End to move to the bottom of the document, and if necessary, press Enter to add some space.

Embedding documents as icons

The Display As Icon option in the Object dialog box allows you to embed an object as an icon. You might use this option, for example, if you want to include supporting information with a document without cluttering it up with information that not everyone wants to read. If you select this option, the object appears as a small graphic, and double-clicking the graphic displays the actual object.

2. Choose Object from the Insert menu and then click the Create From File tab to display these options:

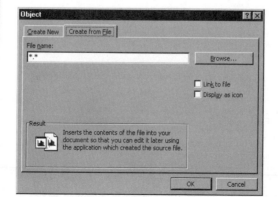

3. Click the Browse button, double-click 1999 Jobs in the Browse dialog box, and click OK to close the Object dialog box.

4. Save the Sales Analysis document.

To see the effects of the different types of objects, let's make a change to the worksheet:

1. Switch back to Excel, move to the Invoices 1999 sheet, and change the amount in cell E24 to *$20,000*.

Changing the source document

2. Move back to the Annual sheet, which because of the links you created back in Chapter 5, has been updated to reflect the changed amount.

3. Save the 1999 Jobs workbook.

4. Switch back to Word, change the zoom setting to 90%, and scroll the Sales Analysis document until you can see the "bottom line" for each worksheet, as shown below. (If you don't see all of the embedded worksheet, see the adjacent tip.)

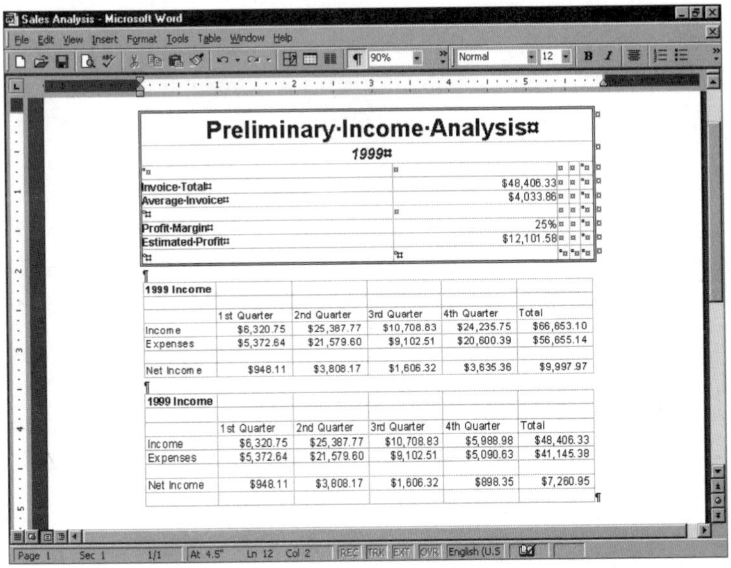

The effects on the container document

Displaying specific cells

When you embed a worksheet in a document, too many or too few cells may be displayed. To control what you see, double-click the embedded worksheet to activate Excel, and then increase or decrease the size of the frame that is surrounding the worksheet to display specific cells. (You can also select the rows or columns you don't want to display and choose Row or Column and then Hide from Excel's Format menu.) Click outside the Excel frame to return to the document. This can be a tricky process, and you may need to play around to get it right.

Word has updated the linked table (the second table) to reflect the invoice change in the source document. To update the first table, you can use regular Word editing techniques. To update the embedded table, you must work through Excel, the application that created the object. Follow the steps on the next page.

Editing an embedded object ──────▶

1. Double-click the embedded table. Excel's menus and tool-bars replace Word's, and the table now appears as a work-sheet with a grid of lettered columns and numbered rows, as shown here:

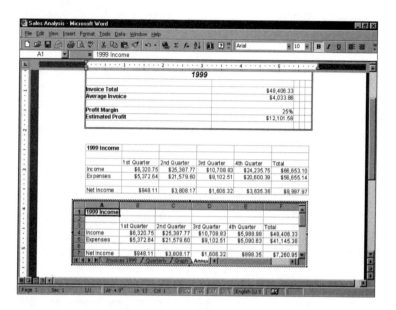

2. Type *24235.75* in cell E4 and click the Enter button on the for-mula bar. The values in the remaining cells in the 4th Quarter and Total columns are automatically updated because the for-mulas in those cells remained intact during the embedding procedure.

3. Click outside the worksheet's frame to return to the document, where the embedded table now matches the linked table.

4. Save and close the document, but leave Word open.

After working through these examples, you should have some idea of the advantages and disadvantages of the various ways of recycling information among Office applications.

Office Web Publishing

If you work for an organization that maintains a Web site for communication with the outside world via the Internet, or that distributes information via an internal Web-like intranet, you may need to convert the documents you create with the Office

Embedding presentations

You can embed a presentation just like any other object. For example, you could send a letter to clients about a new product and embed in the letter a presentation that reinforces your sales pitch. Choose Object from the Insert menu, click the Create From File tab, select the filename of the presentation, and either click OK to insert the first slide of the presentation as a graphic, or select the Display As Icon option and click OK to embed the entire presentation as an icon. In the latter case, clients who have PowerPoint can double-click the icon to view the presentation.

applications to HTML so that they can be viewed as Web pages with a Web browser. With the Office applications, you can simply save a file as an HTML document in the application in which you created it, and let the application take care of all the details. As an example, let's save a Word document as a Web page. First let's preview it, just as you would a document you were about to print:

1. Close all the running applications except Word, and then open the Flyer document you created way back in Chapter 3.

2. Choose Web Page Preview from the File menu to see how your document will look when viewed as a Web page. Microsoft Internet Explorer 5, the Web browser that ships with the Office 2000 suite, starts and your screen now looks like this:

3. Scroll through the document to see how it looks. As you can see, some of Word's formatting won't be implemented when the file is converted to HTML.

4. Choose Source from Internet Explorer's View menu. The coding that controls how your document looks is now displayed in a separate window by Notepad, the text editor that comes with Windows, as shown on the next page.

Previewing Web documents

Online collaboration

If you are using Office 2000 in a networked Windows NT environment and have the MS Office Server Extensions loaded on your server, you can take advantage of Office's online collaboration features. (Check with your network administrator to see if your computer is set up correctly.) With online collaboration, you can hold meetings or discuss a particular document over the Internet or an intranet. For more information, see the Help feature of the application from which you want to collaborate.

5. Scroll the window to get an appreciation for how much work Word will have to do when it converts the document, and then close Notepad.

6. Close Internet Explorer to return to Flyer in Word.

Follow these steps to convert the document:

Converting to HTML

1. Choose Save As Web Page from the File menu to display this dialog box:

Saving on a Web server

To save a file on a web server, click the Web Folders icon in the Save As dialog box to display the locations that are available to you. Select the Web location you want to use and then click Save. To set up the Web locations so that they can be accessed from the Web Folders icon, open Windows Explorer and click Web Folders. Next double-click Add Web Folder to work through a series of dialog boxes that help you specify the URL of the Web location you want to add.

Notice that the Save As Type setting is Web Page and that the page title will be What Is Redmond BEAT, the first heading to which you applied a style in the Flyer document. (Even though you applied character formatting to the two preceding headings, they were not identified as headings as far as Word is concerned.) This page title will appear in the title bar of the Web browser used to view the page.

2. Click the Change Title button to display this dialog box:

Specifying the page title

3. Type *Redmond BEAT* and click OK.

4. Back in the Save As dialog box, change the File Name entry to *Web Flyer* and then click Save to save the Flyer document as an HTML file.

5. When Word warns you that some of the document's formatting can't be converted to HTML, click Continue. Your screen now looks similar to the one shown on page 385, except that if you look closely, you'll see that the Web Flyer document is now displayed in Word in web layout view, instead of in Internet Explorer.

Once you have converted a document to a Web page, you will probably want to apply formatting that is supported by Web browsers to jazz up the page. Your organization may have issued guidelines about what formatting is required to make your Web pages look like others on its Web site, but here's one quick way to add some visual interest, in case you have free reign:

1. Press Ctrl+Home to move to the top of the page and then choose Theme from the Format menu to display a dialog box similar to the one shown earlier on page 328.

Applying a theme

2. Select a theme in the Choose A Theme list and check out the sample shown in the adjacent box. (If a theme is not installed, Word can't display a sample.) Finish by selecting Romanesque and clicking OK. Turn the page to see the result.

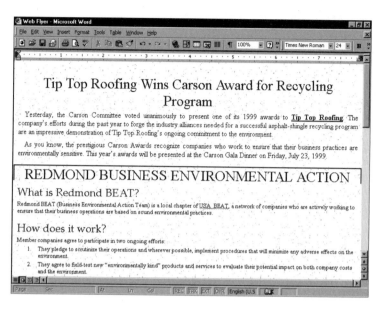

3. Click the Save button to save the HTML file, and then simply close it.

You can now send this file to your Webmaster for posting on a Web site or intranet, or you can choose Save As Web Page from the File menu again and specify the location of your Web server in the Save In box. And what if you later need to make an adjustment to the file? Fortunately, you can always open an HTML file in the application that created it—in this case, Word—and continue work. Called "round-trip" editing, this capability means that you will always be able to use the features of the Office applications to update your documents, instead of having to make changes to a Web page by manipulating its HTML code.

Round-trip editing

The very simple example we have shown you here barely scratches the surface of the Office Web capabilities. Now that you have learned some basic skills, you have the freedom to experiment with the other applications to see some of the possibilities.

Index

A

absolute references 96, 112
Access 2, 170
Access button 372
action queries 208
active
    cell 79, 80, 81, 84
    window 19
Add Holidays button 249
address
    books 222
    cards 231, 234, 235
Address Book button 222
addresses
    in Excel 79
    in Outlook 231
    in Word 231
Align Left button 23, 89, 305
alignment of text/values
    in Excel 80, 81, 82, 89
    in Publisher 291, 305
    in Word 23
Align Right button 23, 89
Align Text Vertically command 291
All Entries button (AutoText
    toolbar) 35
Allow Zero Length property 184
anchors. See bookmarks
And operator 110, 206
Animation Effects button 164
Animation Effects toolbar 164
animation in slides 163, 165
appending records with queries 210
Apply Design button 144
Apply Formatting command 293
appointments
    attaching files to 251
    canceling 251
    conflicting 248, 257
    custom time slots for 244
    editing 249
    finding 252
    private 245
    recurring 245, 247, 250, 251
    reminders 242, 244, 245
    rescheduling 250
    scheduling 243, 244
    setting start/end times 245
arguments 94
    text values as 109
arithmetic 91
    date and time 83
arithmetic operators 91
Arrange All command 19, 142
Arrange command 106

arranging windows 19
Assign Task command 266
attaching files
    to appointments 251
    to messages 224
attachments 226, 229
AutoCalculate area 79, 93
AutoComplete 35, 91
AutoCorrect 6, 36, 37
AutoCorrect command 36, 63
AutoCreate 244
AutoFill 85, 111, 115, 116
AutoFormat As You Type 63
AutoFormat command 89
autoformatting worksheets 89
autolayouts 139, 140, 148, 153
AutoPreview 225
AutoSum button 74, 93, 116
AutoText 33, 34
AutoText button 35
AutoText toolbar 34
AVERAGE function 99
averages in Excel 94, 99
axes 122, 158

B

background
    in FrontPage, transparent 342
    in PowerPoint, adding graphics 152
backups, in Publisher, saving 278
birthdays for contacts 235
Blank Document template 54, 68
Bold button 15, 23, 74, 89, 291
Bookmark command 354
bookmarks 348, 354
BorderArt 316
Border button 75
borders
    in Excel, around cells 98
    in FrontPage, shared 338, 356
    in PowerPoint
        around graphics 151
        around graphs 159
    in Publisher
        around frames 292
        around graphics 315
        around pages 316
    in Word
        around paragraphs 61
        around tables 75
Borders And Shading command 60
Break command 62, 65
breaks
    line 59, 310, 339
    page 65
    section 62

builds, slide 164
Bullet command 139
bulleted lists 339
    in FrontPage 339, 340
    in PowerPoint 133, 134, 135,
        139, 140
    in Publisher 296, 297
    in Word 63, 64
bullet groups in PowerPoint,
    selecting 137
Bullets And Numbering command 64
Bullets button 64, 340
buttons 13
    vs. commands 13
    displaying more/fewer 15
    on Office shortcut bar 372, 374
By Column button 155
By Row button 155
byte number format 180

C

calculation area in Excel, creating 97
calculations in Excel 91
Calendar 234. See also appointments,
    meetings
Calendar icon 242
Calendar Options button 246
Camera Effect button 164
Cancel button 80
canceling
    appointments 251
    meetings 256
Cancel Meeting command 256
capital letters, small 60
Caption property 182
captions for graphics in Publisher 313
categories
    for contacts 232, 237
    creating 236
    for tasks 264
Categorize command (shortcut
    menu) 264
Cell Height And Width command 73
cells
    in Excel 79
        addresses/references 79, 94, 96,
            112, 113
        attaching comments 87
        borders around 98
        clearing 87
        inserting and deleting 88
        naming 95, 101
        preformatting 98
        selecting 80
        shading 98
    in Word tables 73

Cells command 88, 89, 98, 99, 111, 115
Center button 23, 59, 74, 89, 338
centering
in Excel
entries across columns 98
graphs on page 125
text 89
worksheets on page 103
in FrontPage, text 338
in Word
table entries 73, 74
text 23, 59
Change Picture/Recolor Picture
command (shortcut menu) 316
Change Text/Edit Story In Microsoft
Word command (shortcut
menu) 279
character
formats 22, 59
styles 68
characters
nonprinting 32, 54
spacing between 292
Character Spacing command 292
Chart Objects box 120
charts. See graphs
chart sheets 79
Chart Type button 122, 161
Chart Type command 119, 122, 156
Chart Wizard button 118
child pages 330
Choose Web Theme button 328
choosing commands 9, 10, 12
Clear command 87
Clear Contents command (shortcut
menu) 88
clearing cells in Excel 87, 95
Click and type 23
clip art. See graphics
Clipboard 20, 21
Clipboard toolbar 14, 21, 381
Clip Gallery 3, 311, 340, 341
adding graphics to 149
Clip Gallery Tool button 311
Close command 29
closing
documents 29
forms 177
print preview 25
publications 281
workbooks 109
Collapse All button 137
Collapse button 42, 138
collapsing
outlines 42, 114, 137, 138
webs 330

color
of font, changing 338
of frame background,
changing 293
of graphics, changing 152, 316
of objects, changing 318
schemes 281
of text, changing 294
Color button 160
Column/AutoFit Selection
command 90, 99
Column/Hide command 383
columns
in Access 170
adjusting width 176
in Excel 78
adjusting width 90, 99, 116
centering entries across 98
deleting 88
hiding 383
inserting 88, 110
selecting 84, 88
in Graph, adjusting width 157
in Publisher, multiple 294
in Word
adjusting width 73
deleting 74
multiple 62
Columns button 62
Columns command 88
Column Width command 157, 176
Column/Width command 90, 116
combination graphs 124
commands
vs. buttons 13
choosing 9, 10, 12
displaying more on menus 10
toggle 11
comments, attaching to cells 87
conditional formatting 100
configuration differences 4
Connect Frames toolbar 278
Consolidate command 113
consolidating values in Excel 113
contact list 222, 231, 239
contacts
adding to list 232, 236, 238
assigning to categories 232, 237
birthdays/anniversaries 234
deleting 235
editing 234
organizing 235
sorting 237
tracking activities 239
Contacts 231

Contacts icon 231
Control menu 29
Control menu icon 372
controls, in Access 194
Copy button 20, 57, 85, 285, 379
Copy command 85
Copyfit Text command 284
copyfitting text, automatic 284
copying
in Access 190
tables 209
between applications 379
in Excel 85
with AutoFill 85, 111
formatting 99
and linking 115
sheets 107
between workbooks 107
in Publisher, between
publications 285
in Word 20
between documents 57
with drag-and-drop 39
styles to other documents 71
correcting mistakes 6, 81
Create Shortcut Wizard 242
criteria, specifying in queries
204, 206
Crop button 151
cropping graphics 151
currency in Excel 90, 99
Current View button 263
Current View command 257
custom
dictionaries 51
field formats 181
forms 194, 235
graphs 123
lists 115
Office shortcut bar 373
reports 212, 213
styles 69
templates 57
time slots for appointments 244
toolbars 374
Custom Animation command 165
Custom.dic 49, 50
Customize command (Office shortcut
bar Control menu) 373
Customize command (shortcut
menu) 13
Custom Rotate button 319
Custom Shapes button 317
Cut button 20, 39, 97, 141
cutting vs. clearing 87

D

data
  in Access
    access pages 215
    integrity 181, 184
    types 179, 181
    viewing related 201
  in Excel, displaying efficiently 97
  in Graph
    entering 155
    labels 163
    markers 120
databases 2, 170
  vs. spreadsheets 78
database tables 170
  adding
    fields 200
    to queries 207
    to Relationships window 200
  cloning 190
  creating
    from scratch 196
    with Table Wizard 172
  deleting records 178
  editing
    via datasheets 205
    via subdatasheets 202
  entering records 174
  opening 206
  relating 197, 200
  samples 172
  sorting records 187
  structure of
    changing 178, 190, 199
    copying 190, 209
  updating 177
Database toolbar 13
Database Window button 209
Data Labels command 163
datasheets
  in Access 203, 205
  in Graph 154, 155, 161
date
  in Calendar, navigator 243, 244
  in Excel
    arithmetic 83
    formats 83
  in Word, fields 56
Date And Time command 56
dates
  in Access 180
  in Excel 83, 89
Day button 243
decision-making formulas in Excel 109
default text/value alignment in
  Excel 80, 81, 82, 89

Default Value property 183
delegating tasks 265, 266
Delete button 229, 235, 251, 262
Delete/Cells command 74
Delete/Columns command 74
Delete command 88, 178
Deleted Items folder 229, 262
Deleted Items icon 229
Delete Object command 279, 287, 305
Delete Record button 178
Delete Rows command 310, 311
Delete/Rows command 74
Delete Sheet command 109
Delete Slide command 135
Delete Web command 365
deleting
  in Access
    fields 191, 210
    input masks 182
    records 178, 211
  buttons from Office shortcut
    bar 375
  in Excel
    cells 88
    columns 88
    sheets 108
  in FrontPage
    bookmarks 355
    pages 331
    text 336
    webs 365
  in Outlook
    contacts 235
    messages 228
    tasks 262
  in PowerPoint
    bulleted items 135
    slides 135, 138
  in Publisher
    frames 278, 287, 305
    rows from tables 310, 311
    text 278, 285
  in Word
    headings from outlines 41
    rows/columns 74
    styles 69
    tables 74
    text 20, 37
Demote button 43, 134
Demote To Body Text button 43
demoting bulleted items 135
design
  in PowerPoint 138, 144
  in Publisher 279, 282
Design button 200
Design Gallery 303

Design Gallery Object button 303
Design View command 213
desktop publishing 270
DHTML Effects toolbar 354
dialog boxes 11
  help with 27
  moving 186
dictionaries 49, 50
docking toolbars 14
documents
  closing 29
  copying styles to 71
  creating 5, 17, 54, 57
  editing 37
  embedding presentations in 384
  finding 18
  hyphenating 72
  inserting one in another 58
  linking to tasks 258
  opening 18, 57, 58, 377, 378
  organizing 40
  previewing 24, 25, 72
  printing 24, 26, 75
  saving 16, 20, 33, 56, 58, 59
    as templates 57
  spell-checking 49
dollars and cents in Excel 90, 99
drag-and-drop editing
  in Excel, copying/moving entries
    86, 107
  in PowerPoint
    moving slides 143
    organizing with 137
  in Word 39
Draw 317
drawing
  in Access, lines 195
  in Publisher
    lines 292
    shapes 316, 317
  in Word, lines 60
Drawing toolbar 317
Draw Table button 75

E

editing 20
  in Access 202, 205
  embedded objects 384
  in Excel 84
  in FrontPage
    hyperlinks 361
    text 335
  in Outlook
    address cards 234
    appointments 249, 250
    tasks 260

in PowerPoint, slides 141
in Publisher, with Word 279
redoing 21
undoing 21
in Word 37
   drag and drop 39
   during search/replace 44
   smart 40
in WordArt 307
Edit Irregular Wrap button 315
electronic slide shows 166
e-mail 222. *See also* messages
and contact list 238
hyperlinks 351
setting up 220
embedding objects 379, 380, 382
Empty Deleted Items Folder command
   (shortcut menu) 229
Enter button 80, 92
entries
in Access, requiring 183
in Excel
   clearing 95
   completing 80
   copying 85, 86
   editing 84
   linking between sheets 115
   long 81
   moving 86, 97, 107
envelope icon 225, 228
equations. *See* formulas in Excel
error messages 109
events, scheduling 247
Excel 2, 78
Excel button 372
Exchange Server 242, 253, 265
Exclude Row/Col command 156, 161
excluding data from graphs 156, 161
Exit command 29, 345
Expand All button 138
Expand button 42, 138
expanding
menus 10
outlines 42, 114, 138
webs 330
windows 19
Export command 377
exporting files 376
Extend Selection mode 39

F
FAQs 32
fields
in Access 170
   adding to database tables 200
   adding to queries 210

captions 182
date/time 180
default values 183
deleting 191, 210
descriptions 179
foreign key 196
formats 180
hiding/unhiding 186
indexing 183
moving 186
names 196
number 180
primary key 173, 196, 197
properties 179
with queries 202
requiring entry 183
selecting 176, 186
size of 179
text 179
in Outlook 238
in Word 56
File command 58
filename conventions 16
files
attaching
   to appointments 251
   to messages 224
creating 17
finding 18
importing/exporting 376
managing from Office 18
naming 16
previewing 24, 25
printing 24, 26
saving 16, 17, 20, 33, 386
Fill Color button 293, 318
Fill command 111
fill handle 111
Filter By Selection button 185, 217
filtering records 185, 217
Find button 46, 47, 186, 252
Find command 44, 46
finding
in Access, records 185
files 18
in FrontPage
   Internet service
      providers (ISPs) 364
   Web site addresses 352
in Outlook, appointments 252
in Word
   formats 46
   text 44, 47
Flip Horizontal button 320
flipping objects 320

Flip Vertical button 320
floating toolbars 14
Folder List button 331, 334, 359
folder list, displaying/hiding 230,
   334, 359
folders, creating in Outlook 230
Folders icon 330
Font box 22
font, changing 22, 24, 59, 291
   color of 338
   size of 22, 24, 89, 97, 281, 286,
     291, 338
Font Color button 294
Font command 60
Font Size box 22
footers
   in Access reports 193
   in Word 64
foreign keys 196
Format Cells command (shortcut
   menu) 90
Format Legend command (shortcut
   menu) 163
Format Painter button 60, 99, 293
Format Picture button 151
Format property 180
formats
   field 180, 181
   finding/replacing 46
   graphic 149, 342
   painting 60, 293
format, tab-delimited 327
formatting
   in Access, dates/times 180
   in Excel 89, 111, 115
      conditional 100
      copying 99
      dates 89
      dollars and cents 90, 99
      worksheets 89
   in FrontPage, Web pages 338
   in PowerPoint
      displaying/hiding 142
      graphs 159, 162
   in Publisher 291
   "round-trip" 388
   in Word 15, 58, 72
      bold 15, 23
      character 22, 59
      gridlines 75
      headers/footers 66
      italic 15
      paragraph 22, 69, 71
      underlining 15, 23
   in WordArt 306

Formatting toolbar 13
forms in Access 176, 191, 194, 215
formula bar 79
formulas in Excel 91, 92
    copying with AutoFill 111
    decision-making 109
    referencing their cells 94
    using names in 95
Forward button 227
forwarding e-mail messages
        227, 228
frames, in Publisher
    adjusting margins 295, 315
    borders around 292
    changing background color 293
    deleting 278, 287, 305
    moving 287, 288
    shading 293
    sizing 286, 287, 308
    text 277, 289, 290
FrontPage 3, 324
FrontPage Server Extensions 364
function names 94
functions in Excel 94
    in AutoCalculate area 93
    help with 101
    nested 110
    pasting 100

G
Go To Page command 276
Go To Today button 245
grammar checker 7
Graph 3, 117, 153, 154
graphics
    in FrontPage 340
        file formats 342
    in PowerPoint 148
        animating 165
        file formats 149
        searching for 149
    in Publisher 311
        downloading from Microsoft
            Clip Gallery Web page 313
        searching for 313, 315
graphs 153
    in Access 192
    in Excel 117
    in PowerPoint 153
    in Word, creating from
        tables 379
greeked text 302
gridlines, in Word tables 75
grid, query by example (QBE) 204
Group And Outline/Auto Outline
    command 114

Group And Outline/Clear Outline
    command 114
grouping objects 277, 318, 319
Group Objects button 318, 319
groups on Outlook bar 221
guides
    hiding/displaying 289, 320
    layout vs. ruler 289
    pointer, on rulers 286, 287
    ruler 289, 290

H
handles
    fill 111
    move 13
    selection 120, 194
Header And Footer command 65
Header And Footer toolbar 65
header pane 222
headers
    in Access 193
    in Excel 102
    in Word 64
headings
    in Excel
        centering across columns 98
        entering 80
    in Publisher, formatting 291
    in Word
        breaking 59
        in outlines 41, 43
height of rows in Excel, changing 91
help 27
    with keyboard shortcuts 22
Hide Boundaries And Guides
    command 320
Hide Columns command 186
hiding
    columns/rows 383
    folder list 334
    guides 289
    toolbars 12, 15
    Windows taskbar 6
    wizards 274, 280
Highlight Entire Story command 296
highlighting 7
holidays, adding to Calendar 249
home page 330
HTML 215, 324, 337, 385
HTTP 348
Hyperlink button 349, 351, 352, 353
Hyperlink command 351
hyperlinks 324, 334, 348
    creating 349, 351
    editing 361
    e-mail 351

to files 353
graphic 352
recognizing 350
targets 348
testing 350, 358
to Web sites 352
Hyperlinks icon 359
HyperText Markup Language (HTML)
        215, 324, 337, 385
HyperText Transfer
        Protocol (HTTP) 348
hyphenating
    in Publisher 297
    in Word 72

I
icons, embedding objects as 382
IF function 109
importing
    files 376
    graphics 149, 312
    scanned images 314
    Web pages 326
Inbox 222
indenting first line in Word 70
Indents And Lists command 296
Indexed property 183
indexing fields 183
Input Mask property 181
input masks 181
Insert Chart button 161
Insert Clip Art button 148, 149
Insert File button 224, 251
Insert mode 38
Insert Page Number button (Header
    And Footer toolbar) 66
Insert Picture From File button 149
insertion point 6, 21, 23, 80
Insert Table button 73
integer number format 180
Internet
    e-mail, setting up 220
    publishing on 384
Internet Explorer 3, 385
    viewing data access pages
        with 216
Internet service providers
    (ISPs) 220
    finding 364
intranets 324, 384
Italic button 15

J
Journal 263
Justify button 23
justifying text 23

K

kerning 292
keyboard shortcuts 22, 232
keys
    foreign 196
    primary 173, 196, 197

L

labels
    in Access 194
    in Graph
        data 163
        datasheets 154
Language/Hyphenate command 72
Language/Hyphenation command 297
languages, switching 368
Laser Text Effect button 164
layout guides vs. ruler guides 289
left-aligning text 23
legends, graph
    formatting 163
    moving/sizing 158
Like operator 205
line
    breaks 59, 310, 339
    spacing, changing 302
Line/Border Style button 292,
        315, 316
Line button 195
Line Spacing command 302
lines
    in Access, drawing 195
    in Publisher, drawing 292
    in Word
        drawing 60, 75
        of text, selecting 9
Line Weight box 75
linking. See also hyperlinks
    in Access, database tables 197, 200
    vs. embedding 381
    in Excel
        while consolidating 114
        while copying 115
    objects 379, 380
    in Outlook, tasks with
            documents 258
    between worksheets and
            graphs 121
Links command 381
List Properties command (shortcut
    menu) 340
lists
    bulleted 63, 64, 133, 296, 297, 339
    contact. See contact list
    converting to regular text 297
    custom in Excel 115

numbered 63, 71, 297, 339
to-do. See to-do list
logical operators 110, 206
logos 303, 304, 315
long
    integer number format 180
    text/values in Excel 81, 82

M

macro sheets 79
mailing labels, creating 214
mailto hyperlinks 351
margins
    in Excel, setting 124
    in Publisher
        adjusting in frames 295
        adjusting around objects 315
    in Word, setting 25, 72
Mark Complete button 261
marking messages 225
master category list 236
maximizing windows 19
Measurements toolbar 288
measurement units 291
meetings 253, 255, 256
memos 55
menu bar 9
menus 9, 10, 12
Merge And Center button 98
merging presentations 143
messages
    attaching files to 224
    with attached files 225
    and contact list 238
    converting
        to appointments/tasks 244
        to contacts 238
    courtesy copies 223
    creating 222, 224, 238
    deleting 228, 229
    forwarding 227, 228
    marking as read/unread 225
    moving to folders 230
    no original in replies 228
    organizing 228
    outgoing
        not saving in Sent Items
            folder 228
        options 224
    previewing 225
    priority of 224
    reading attachments 226
    responding to 226
    retrieving 225, 228
    saving 229
    selecting 229

sending 222, 223, 224, 227, 228
    to multiple recipients 222
    from Outbox 225, 228
    sensitivity level of 224
    storing in Outbox 223
    urgent 225
Microsoft Access 2, 170
Microsoft Clip Gallery 3, 311, 340, 341
Microsoft Clip Gallery Web page 313
Microsoft Excel 2, 78
Microsoft FrontPage 3, 324
Microsoft Graph 3, 117, 153, 154
Microsoft Internet Explorer 3, 385
Microsoft Map 3
Microsoft NetMeeting 253
Microsoft Office 2000 Language
    Pack 368
Microsoft Organization Chart 3
Microsoft Outlook 3, 220
Microsoft PowerPoint 2, 128
Microsoft Publisher 3, 270
Microsoft's Web site 3, 29
Microsoft Word 2, 32
misspelling alerts 6, 17, 20, 34, 48
mixed references 113
Month button 243
MONTH function 111
More Buttons button 13, 15, 22, 135
mouse pointers in Publisher 285
Move Down button 42, 136
move handle 13
Move Or Copy Sheet command 107
Move Up button 42, 136, 137, 138
moving
    among Outlook components 221
    among pages 275
    among records 177
    among slides 132, 133, 141
    controls/labels 194
    entries in Excel 86, 97, 107
    fields 186
    frames 287, 288
    graphics 150, 313
    graphs 121, 160, 382
    information between
            applications 376
    messages to folders 230
    Office shortcut bar 373
    in publications 275
    records with queries 209
    sheets 107, 108
    slides 143, 144
    in tables 73, 74, 309
    text 20, 39, 141
    toolbars 14

web pages 332
    in workbooks 79
multi-language support 368
multiple columns 62, 294
Multiple Pages button (Print Preview
    toolbar) 67

N

name box 79, 95
Name/Define command 95, 101
Name/Paste command 96
names in Excel 95, 101
naming
    cells 95, 101
    files 16
    ranges 95
    sheets 107, 113, 115
navigation bars 356, 357
Navigation icon 329
Navigation toolbar 330
nested functions in Excel 110
NetMeeting 253
New All Day Event command 248
New Appointment button 372
New button 17, 106
New button (AutoText toolbar) 34
New command 54, 57, 116, 139, 282
New Contact button 232, 236, 372
New Contact button (Office
    shortcut bar) 232
New/Contact command 232
New/Folder command 230
New Journal button 372
New Mail Message button 222, 224
New Message button 372
New Message To Contact button 238
New Note button 372
New Object button 176, 177, 192, 193,
    206, 208, 210, 211, 212
New Office Document button 372
New Office Document
    command 5, 369
New Page button 326, 332
New/Page command 332
New Record button 177
New Recurring Appointment
    command 246
New Recurring Meeting command 255
New Slide button 140
New Task button 258, 259, 372
New Task button (Office
    shortcut bar) 258
New Task Request command 265
Next Find/GoTo button 45, 46
Next Slide button 132, 133
noncontiguous ranges, selecting 118

nonprinting characters 32, 54
Normal style 68
Normal View button 44, 131
Notes 236
Nudge command 313
nudging objects 313
numbered lists 63, 71, 297, 339
number fields in Access 180
Numbering button 64, 71
numbers. *See also* values
    page 67
    as text 82

O

object area of slides 132
Object command 382, 384
Object Frame Properties button 315
objects 380
    embedded 383, 384
    linking/embedding 379, 380, 382
    in Publisher
        adding to Design Gallery 303
        changing color 318
        flipping 320
        grouping/ungrouping 277,
            318, 319
        nudging 313
        rotating 319
        selecting multiple 318
Office Assistant 5, 27, 32
Office Clipboard 21, 381
Office On The Web command 29
Office shortcut bar 232, 371
Office toolbar button 372
OLE 380
one-to-many relationships 198, 200
online
    collaboration 385
    meetings 253
Open button 18, 57, 58, 106, 285,
    348, 376
Open command 142
opening
    data access pages, in Internet
        Explorer 216
    database tables 206
    Database window 209
    documents 18, 57, 58, 377, 378
    in FrontPage
        pages 339
        webs 348
    presentations 142
    publications 271, 285
    reports 214
    workbooks 106
    worksheets in Word 376

Open Office Document button 372
Open Office Document
    command 377, 378
open paragraphs 71
operators
    arithmetic 91
    logical 110, 206, 209
order of calculation, overriding 92
Organization Chart 3
organizing
    contacts 235
    documents 40
    messages 228
    presentations 136, 137, 144
    tasks 257, 263
    webs 329
Or operator 110, 206
Outbox 223
    sending messages from 225, 228
Outbox icon 223
Outline command 41
outlines
    in Excel 114
    in PowerPoint 136
    in Word 40
outline view 40, 43
Outline View button 44, 136
Outlining toolbar 41, 136
Outlook 3, 220
Outlook bar 221
    creating shortcuts on 230
Outlook button 372
Outlook Today 242
overflow area 281
overriding order of calculation 92
Overtype mode 38

P

page
    breaks 65
    controls 275, 301
    layout, changing 25
    numbers 66, 67
Page Numbers command 67
Page Setup button (Header And Footer
    toolbar) 66
pages
    in FrontPage
        adding 332
        deleting 331
        editing 335
        formatting 338
        inserting graphics 340
        moving 332
        opening 339
        parent/child 330

previewing 336
  removing themes 344
  renaming 333
in Publisher
  borders around 316
  moving among 275
  quick 272
Web 385
  adding themes 387
  assigning titles 386
in Word
  previewing multiple 67
  printing specific 26
Page Setup command 25, 72
painting formats 60, 293
paper clip (attached file) icon 225
paragraph
  formats 22
  marks, displaying/hiding 32
  styles 68
Paragraph command 69, 71
paragraphs
  in FrontPage, space before 339
  in Word
    borders around 60, 61
    formatting 69, 71
    inserting in existing text 33
    open (space before) 71
    selecting 9
    shading 61
parent pages 330
Paste button 20, 39, 57, 85, 97, 141,
    285, 379
Paste command 85
Paste Errors table 190
Paste Function button 100
Paste Special command 115, 381, 383
Pattern button 160
Personal Information command 273
personal information sets 271,
    273, 285
PhotoDraw 3
picas 291
Pick Up Formatting command 293
Picture/Clip Art command 148, 341
Picture Frame Tool button 312
Picture/From File command 149
Picture/New Drawing command 317
pictures. See graphics
Picture toolbar 341
placeholders
  in FrontPage 335
  in Publisher 277
Plan A Meeting command 253
planning meetings 253
pointer guides on rulers 286, 287

points 291
PowerPoint 2, 128
PowerPoint button 372
preformatting cells in Excel 98
presentations 2, 128
  adding slides 140
  autolayouts 139, 140, 148, 153
  creating
    with AutoContent Wizard 128
    based on design template 139
  embedding in Word documents 384
  merging 143
  opening 142
  organizing 136, 137, 144
  saving 131
  special effects 163
  switching design templates 144
presentation window 131
Preset Animation box 165
Preview In Browser button 363
previewing
  documents 24, 25, 72
  graphs 124
  messages 225
  pages 212
  Web pages 336, 362, 385
  worksheets 102
preview pane 222
Previous Find/GoTo button 45
Previous Slide button 132, 141
Primary Business personal information
    set 285
Primary Key button 197
primary keys 173, 196, 197
Print button 26, 103, 125, 203, 321
Print command 26
printers, selecting 26
printing 24, 26
  contact list 239
  documents 75
  graphs 124, 125
  publications 321
  query datasheets 203
  schedules 248
  worksheets 103
print preview 24, 25, 67, 72, 102,
    124, 212
Print Preview button 24, 25, 67, 72,
    102, 124
priority
  of messages 224
  of tasks 259, 260, 264
private appointments 245
Promote button 41, 43, 135
promoting bulleted items 135
proofreading 51

properties, field 179
publications
  closing 281
  copying text between 285
  creating
    based on design set 282
    with wizards 271
  design of, changing 279
  graphics, inserting 311
  hyphenating 297
  moving in 275
  opening 271, 285
  printing 321
  quick 272
  saving 275, 278, 283
  symbols, inserting 305
  text in 277
Publisher 3, 270
publishing
  Office documents on Web 384
  webs (FrontPage) 358, 364
Publish Web command 364, 365

Q
queries 202
  action 208
  creating 203, 206, 208, 210
  criteria, specifying 204, 205, 206
  database tables 207
  datasheets, printing 203
  fields
    adding 210
    selecting 202
  records
    appending 210
    deleting 211
    moving 209
    selecting 204
    updating 208
  running 204, 205, 207, 209
  saving 207
  select 202
  type of, changing 208, 210
query by example (QBE) grid 204
Query Type button 208, 210
quick publications 272
quitting Office applications 29

R
range references 84
ranges
  copying into 111
  deselecting 84
  naming 95
  selecting 84, 118
reading messages/attachments 226
Recolor Picture button 152

record selector 174
records in Access 170
  copying 190
  deleting 178
    with queries 211
  entering 174
    in forms 176, 177, 195
    with queries 210
  filtering 185
    via data access pages 217
  finding 185
  grouping in reports 212
  moving
    among 177
    with queries 209
  selecting with queries 204
  sorting 187
    via data access pages 217
  updating with queries 208
Rectangle Tool button 316
Recurrence button 251, 259
Recurrence command 247
recurring
  appointments 245, 247, 250, 251
  meetings 255
  tasks 259
recycling information 376
Redo button 21
references
  absolute 96, 112
  cell 79, 80
  mixed 113
  range 84
  relative 112
  using in other cells 94
referential integrity 196, 198
relationships in Access 197, 200
Relationships button 197, 200
relative references 112
reminders
  appointments 242, 244, 245
  saving 278
  tasks 262
Remove Filter/Sort command 177, 187
Remove From Calendar button 256
Remove Recurrence button 251
renaming web pages 333
repeating Find command 45, 46
Replace command 46, 47
replacing in Word
  formats 46
  text 20, 37, 46
Reply button 226
Reply To All button 227
Reporting toolbar 360
reports 211

Reports icon 360
Required Entry property 183
rescheduling appointments 250
responding
  to meeting requests 256
  to messages 226
  to task requests 267
retrieving messages 225, 228
Return To Task List command 267
Reviewing toolbar 258
right-aligning text 23
right-clicking 13
RIGHT function 109, 110
Rotate Left button 320
Rotate Right button 320
rotating objects 319
"round-trip" formatting 388
Row/Height command 91
Row/Hide command 383
rows
  in Access 170
  in Excel 78
    changing height 91
    hiding 383
    inserting 88, 91
    selecting 84, 88
  in Word 73, 74
Rows command 88, 91
Ruler command 10, 32, 54, 160
ruler guides 289, 290
Ruler Guides/Clear All Ruler Guides
  command 290
rulers
  options 288
  pointer guides on 286, 287
  turning on/off 10, 11, 32, 54, 160
Run button 205
running queries 204, 205, 207, 209

S
Same As Previous button (Header And
  Footer toolbar) 66
Save And Close button 233, 234
Save And New button 233
Save As command 16, 17, 56, 58,
  275, 283
Save As Web Page
  command 33, 386
Save Attachments command 229
Save button 16, 17, 20, 33, 59, 80,
  131, 194, 195, 278
Save command 16, 155
saving
  databases 171
  documents 56, 58, 59
    as templates 57

files 16, 17, 20, 33
  in different folder 16
  on a Web server 386
forms 194, 195
graphs 155
message attachments 229
messages for use in another
  program 229
presentations 131
publications 275, 278, 283
queries 207
reminders 278
webs 335
workbooks 80
worksheets, as templates 116
scanned images, importing 314
schedules, printing 248
scheduling
  appointments 243, 244
  events 247
scientific notation 82
ScreenTips 14, 372
scroll bars 275
Search Browse Object button 47
searching for graphics 149,
  313, 315
sections 62
Select All command 21, 24, 141, 143,
  164, 229
Select Browse Object button 45
Select/Column command 74
Selected Axis Title command 158
Selected Chart Area command 159
Selected Plot Area command 162
selecting
  in Access
    controls 194
    fields 176, 186
    with queries 202, 204
  in Excel
    cells 80
    columns 84, 88
    graphs 121
    noncontiguous ranges
      84, 118
    ranges 84
    rows 84, 88
  in Outlook, messages 229
  in PowerPoint
    all slides 143, 164
    bulleted items 134, 141
    bullet groups 137
    graphics 150
    parts of slides 141
    title area 134
printers 26

in Publisher
   graphics 311
   multiple objects 318
   stories 281
   tables 309
in Word
   lines/paragraphs 9
   sentences 8
   tables 74, 75
   text 7, 21, 24
   words 7, 39
selection
  bar 9
  handles 120, 194
select queries 202
Select/Row command 74
Select/Table command 74, 75
Send And Receive button 225, 228
Send And Receive command 225
Send button 223, 224, 227, 228
sending
  meeting requests 255
  messages 222
    to contacts 238
    courtesy copies 223
    with file attachments 224
    to multiple recipients 222
    from Outbox 225, 228
Send Status Report button 266
Send To Back command 152
sensitivity level of messages 224
sentences, selecting 8
Sent Items folder 228
Sent Items icon 229
servers
  application 380
  Web addresses of 364
Set Transparent Color button 342
Setup button (Print Preview
    toolbar) 124
shading
  in Excel, cells 98
  in Publisher, frames 292, 293
  in Word, paragraphs 61
Shading button (WordArt toolbar) 307
Shadow button (WordArt toolbar) 307
Shape box (WordArt toolbar) 306
shapes, drawing 316, 317
shared borders 338, 356
sheets 79. *See also* worksheets
  chart, creating graphs on 118
  copying 107
  deleting 108
  linking entries between 115
  moving 107, 108

naming 107, 113, 115
types of 79
sheet tabs 79
Shift-clicking 7
shortcut bar, Office 232, 371
shortcut menus 12
shortcuts
  keyboard 22, 232
  Office shortcut bar 232
  on Outlook bar 230
Show All Headings button 43
Show Formatting button 142
Show Heading 1 button 41, 43
Show/Hide ¶ button 32, 54
Show Next button (Header And Footer
    toolbar) 66
Show Table button 200, 207
single number format 180
size of
  fields, specifying 179
  font, changing 22, 24, 89, 97, 281,
    286, 338
  frames, changing 286, 287, 308
  graphics, changing 150, 151,
    313, 341
  graph legends, changing 158
  graphs, changing 120, 160, 163
  logos, changing 304
  thumbnails, changing 143, 144
Size And Position command 288
slide
  autolayouts 139, 148, 153
  shows, electronic 166
Slide command 131
Slide Layout button 153
slides
  adding 140
    graphics 148
    graphs 161
    sound/video 165
  animation 163, 165
  background, adding graphics 152
  builds 164
  deleting 135, 138
  displaying/hiding formatting 142
  editing 141
  layout, changing 153
  moving 143, 144
    among 132, 133, 141
  object area 132
  selecting 164
    all 143
    parts of 141
  title area 134
  transitions 143, 163

Slide Show button 166
Slide Sorter toolbar 164
Slide Sorter View button 142, 164
Slide Transition Effects box 164
Slide View button 131, 148, 165
Snap To Ruler Marks command 289
Sort Ascending button 187, 217
Sort Descending button 187
sorting
  contacts 237
  database tables, via data access
    pages 217
  records 187
  tasks 263
sounds, adding to slides 165
spacing
  between characters 292
  between lines 302
  before paragraphs 339
special effects in PowerPoint 163
spell-checking
  in Excel 85
  in FrontPage 359
  in Word 48
spelling alerts 6, 17, 20, 34, 48
Spelling And Grammar button 49
Spelling button 85, 359
spreadsheets. *See* worksheets
Standard toolbar 13
starting
  Access 171, 190
  Excel 78
  FrontPage 325
  new Office document 369
  Office shortcut bar 371
  Outlook 220, 242
  PowerPoint 128
  Publisher 270
  Word 5, 32, 369
status bar 38, 79, 80, 275
status reports for tasks 266
stories 277, 281
Stretch To Frame button (WordArt
    toolbar) 307
structure of database tables
  changing 178, 190, 199
  copying 190, 209
Style box 68, 70
Style command 69, 71
styles 41, 59, 68
subdatasheets 201, 202
subdocuments 43
subordinate bulleted items in
    PowerPoint 134
SUM function 93, 114

switching languages 368
Symbol command 305
symbols, inserting in publications 305

T

tab-delimited format 327
Tables And Borders button 74
Tables And Borders toolbar 74
tables. *See also* database tables
    in Publisher 308
    in Word 72
tabs, sheet 79
taskbar, displaying/hiding 6, 19
taskpad 243
tasks
    adding to list 244, 258
    assigning to categories 264
    delegating 265, 266
    deleting 262
    due dates, assigning 259, 260
    editing 260
    linking to documents 258
    managing 262
    marking as complete 261
    organizing 257, 263
    ownership of 265, 267
    priority 259, 260, 264
    recurring 259
    reminders 262
    responding to requests 267
    sorting 263
    status reports 266
    tracking 261, 266
Tasks 257
Tasks icon 257, 329
templates
    in Excel 116
    in PowerPoint 132
        design 138, 139, 144
    in Publisher, saving 278
    in Word 54, 57, 68
text
    in Access, fields 179
    in Excel
        as arguments 109
        default alignment 80, 82, 89
        numbers as 82
    in FrontPage
        centering 338
        deleting 336
        editing 335
        hyperlinks 348
    greeked 302
    in PowerPoint
        moving between slides 141
        positioning on slides 140

in Publisher 277
    adding frames for 289
    aligning 291, 305
    changing color of 294
    copyfitting 284
    copying between
        publications 285
    deleting 278, 285
    editing with Word 279
    flowing around graphics 315
    hyphenating 297
    saving as file 278
    selecting 281
in Word
    aligning 23
    bold 15, 23
    centering 23, 59
    copying 20, 39, 57
    deleting 20, 37
    editing 37
    entering 6
    finding 44, 47
    formatting 58, 72
    italic 15
    justifying 23
    moving 20
    in outlines 43
    replacing 37, 46
    selecting 7, 21, 24
    underlined 15, 23
Text Box command 123
Text Frame Properties button 295
Text Frame Tool button 289, 290, 318
Text In Overflow indicator 281,
    284, 286
Theme command (shortcut menu) 344
Themes command 387
themes in FrontPage
    applying to webs 328, 387
    modifying 343
    options 328
    removing 344
Thesaurus 48
3-D pie graphs 122, 161, 162
thumbnails 142
time management 242
times
    in Access 180
    in Excel 83
time slots 243, 244
title
    area of slides 134
    slide 130
titles
    in Graph, adding 157
    in Word, formatting 59

Titles command 157, 158
to-do list 243, 257
    adding tasks 258, 259
    deleting completed tasks 262
toggle commands 11
toolbars 13
    Animation Effects 164
    AutoText 34
    Clipboard 14
    custom 11, 374
    Database 13
    displaying more/fewer buttons 15
    docking 14
    Drawing 317
    floating 14
    Formatting 13
    Header And Footer 65
    Measurements 288
    moving 14
    on Office shortcut bar 374
    Outlining 41, 136
    Slide Sorter 164
    Standard 13
    Tables And Borders 74
    Toolbox 194, 195
    turning on/off 11, 12, 15, 36
    WordArt 306
Toolbars command 11
Toolbars/Customize command 11
Toolbox toolbar 194, 195
totaling
    entries, in Word tables 74
    values, in Excel 93
tracking
    contact activities 239
    tasks 261, 266
transitions in slides 143, 163
transparent graphic background 342
type of
    data, specifying 181
    graph, changing 121, 156, 161
    query, changing 208, 210

U

Underline button 15, 23
underlying
    formulas 92
    values vs. displayed 99
Undo button 21, 122
Undo Delete command 251
undoing editing 21
ungrouping, objects 318, 319
Ungroup Objects button 277, 318
Ungroup Objects command 319
Unhide Columns command 186
units of measurement 291

Universal Resource Locators
    (URLs) 348
updating
    database tables 177
    records with queries 208
urgent messages 225
URLs 348
user interface, changing language
    of 368

V

Validation Rule property 184
values
    in Access 183
    in Excel
        adding to graphs 121
        consolidating 113
        default alignment 81, 82, 89
        displayed vs. underlying 99
        formatting 89, 99, 111, 115
        long 82
        totaling 93
Verify Hyperlinks button 360
videos, adding to slides 165
View button 177, 178, 184, 195, 207
    changing view 177
View Datasheet button 156
views
    in Access
        datasheet 174, 177, 184, 191
        design 178, 190, 200, 207
        form 174, 177, 195
        switching 177, 184, 191, 195
    in FrontPage
        hyperlinks 359
        page 326, 334
        reports 360
        switching 334
        tabs 336
        tasks 328
    in Graph, datasheet 156
    in Outlook
        appointments 252
        address cards 237, 238
        phone list 237
        switching 237, 243, 263
        tasks 264
        task timeline 264
    in PowerPoint
        normal 131
        outline 136
        slide 131, 132, 148, 165
        slide sorter 142, 164
        switching 131, 136, 142
View Show command 166
viruses 226

W

Web
    pages 324, 385. See also webs
        adding themes 387
        assigning titles 386
        formatting 338
        importing 326
        previewing 336, 385
        types of 349
    publishing 384
    servers 324, 364, 386
    sites 324
        addresses of 348
        finding addresses 352
        inserting hyperlinks to 352
        Microsoft 3, 29
Web Page Preview command 385
webs (FrontPage) 324
    applying themes 328
    background, changing 344
    collapsing/expanding 330
    creating 324
        with wizards 326
    deleting 365
        pages 331
    design of 325
    opening 348
    organizing 329
    planning 324
    previewing 362
    publishing 358, 364
    saving 335
    sending to Web servers 365
Week button 243
whole word selection 7
width of columns, adjusting
    in Access 176
    in Excel 90, 99, 116
    in Word 73
wildcards
    in queries 205
    in Word, find/replace 46
windows, manipulating 19
Wizard button 278, 304
wizards 54
    AutoContent 128
    Brochure 300
    Chart 118
    Corporate Presence Web 326
    Create Shortcut 242
    Fax 55
    Flyer 283
    Form 192
    Internet Connection 220
    Microsoft Web Publishing 365
    Outlook 2000 Startup 220

Postcard 271
Report 212
Simple Query 203
Table 172
Web Page 33
Word 2, 32
Word button 372
WordArt 3, 305
WordArt Frame Tool button 306
WordArt toolbar 306
words, selecting 39
    whole 7
word-wrapping 6
workbooks 79, 106
    adding worksheets 80
    closing 109
    creating 106, 116
    inserting sheets in 382
    moving around 79
    opening 106
    saving 80
    viewing more than one 106
workday, adjusting in Calendar 246
working offline 220
Worksheet command 80
worksheets 78
    adding to workbooks 80
    adjusting margins 124
    centering on page 103
    vs. databases 78
    editing 84
    embedding partial 383
    formatting 89
    graphs on 117
    inserting 382
    linking to graphs 121
    opening in Word 376
    outlining 114
    previewing 102
    printing 103
    saving as templates 116
World Wide Web. See Web
Wrap Text To Frame button 315
Wrap Text To Picture button 315

Z

Zoom box 276
Zoom button 212
Zoom command 276
Zoom Control box 143, 144
Zoom In button 277
zooming
    to actual size (100%) 285
    in/out 25, 102, 143, 144,
        212, 276
Zoom Out button 277